THE BEST MINDS
OF MY GENERATION
A Literary History
of the BEATS

Also by Allen Ginsberg

POETRY

Howl and Other Poems

Kaddish and Other Poems

Empty Mirror: Early Poems

Reality Sandwiches

Angkor Wat

Planet News

*Airplane Dreams: Compositions from
  Journals*

The Gates of Wrath: Rhymed Poems

The Fall of America: Poems of These States

Iron Horse

First Blues

Mind Breaths

Plutonian Ode and Other Poems

Collected Poems

White Shroud Poems

Cosmopolitan Greetings: Poems

Death & Fame: Last Poems

Wait Till I'm Dead: Uncollected Poems

PROSE

Indian Journals

The Yage Letters,
  with William Burroughs

Allen Verbatim: Lectures on Poetry,
  Politics, Consciousness
  (Gordon Ball, editor)

Journals: Early Fifties, Early Sixties
  (Gordon Ball, editor)

As Ever: The Collected Correspondence of
  Allen Ginsberg & Neal Cassady
  (Barry Gifford, editor)

Composed on the Tongue
  (Donald Allen, editor)

Straight Hearts' Delight: Love Poems
  and Selected Letters 1947–1980,
  with Peter Orlovsky
  (Winston Leyland, editor)

Howl, Original Draft Facsimile,
  Fully Annotated (Barry Miles, editor)

Journals: Mid-Fifties
  (Gordon Ball, editor)

The Book of Martyrdom and Artifice
  (Bill Morgan, editor)

The Letters of Allen Ginsberg
  (Bill Morgan, editor)

Spontaneous Mind: Selected Interviews
  (David Carter, editor)

Family Business: Selected Letters Between
  a Father and Son
  (Michael Schumacher, editor)

Jack Kerouac and Allen Ginsberg:
  The Letters (Bill Morgan and
  David Stanford, editors)

The Selected Letters of Allen Ginsberg and
  Gary Snyder (Bill Morgan, editor)

Deliberate Prose: Selected Essays
  1952–1995 (Bill Morgan, editor)

The Essential Ginsberg
  (Michael Schumacher, editor)

I Greet You at the Beginning of a Great
  Career: The Selected Correspondence
  of Lawrence Ferlinghetti and
  Allen Ginsberg (Bill Morgan, editor)

THE BEST MINDS OF MY GENERATION

A Literary History of the BEATS

ALLEN GINSBERG

**WITH A FOREWORD BY
ANNE WALDMAN
EDITED BY BILL MORGAN**

Grove Press
New York

Published simultaneously in Canada
Printed in the United States of America

FIRST EDITION

ISBN 978-0-8021-2649-8
eISBN 978-0-8021-8948-6

First Grove Atlantic hardcover edition: April 2017

Library of Congress Cataloging-in-Publication data is available for this title.

Grove Press
an imprint of Grove Atlantic
154 West 14th Street
New York, NY 10011

Distributed by Publishers Group West

groveatlantic.com

17 18 19 20   10 9 8 7 6 5 4 3 2 1

Contents

Foreword

By Anne Waldman

Allen Ginsberg devotedly, and with a loving perseverance, incubated these lectures on his primary literary Beat colleagues during his first teaching job at Naropa Institute, the first Buddhist-inspired university in the west, which was founded in the summer of 1974. It is a remarkable delineation, focused on the writing of his colleagues, their lives, and their intricate relationships.

Our visit to Boulder, Colorado, a small college town on the spine of the Rocky Mountains resulted in a poetics department he and I founded with poet Diane di Prima: The Jack Kerouac School of Disembodied Poetics. And Allen and I worked together twenty-three years during the summer writing sessions until his death in 1997 as I continued on. We landed on this rocky mountain site somewhat spontaneously, yet with the rock-solid twenty-five-hundred-year old foundation of Tibetan Buddhism at the helm. This was something unique in contemporary literary annals. We had no permanent building then, no library, no stationery, scant budget, were *sans* telephone. But we had a curious American aspiration toward a more expansive poetics, as we sat between the kinetic poles of east and west near Denver, a place where Neal Cassady had roamed and hustled and pondered the thoughts of a speedy alchemist. Denver, the place of all possible crossroads. Negative ions dancing on the spine of the continent. And we had a project in mind—an "academy of the future" (apt phrase from a John Ashbery poem), which was spurred by our confidence in poetry and its attendant poetics as a spiritual practice. "Keep the world safe for poetry" became a trenchant motto.

Allen was inspired to create the Poetics Program at Naropa, with its Buddhist ambience, as an extraordinary opportunity to bring his "best minds" together, to gather his people to a safe haven where they could continue the *sacra coversazione* and emotional dynamics and literary work. All that messy imbricated history would find rest and purpose here. Kerouac's ghostly consciousness hovered over the premises. Allen would create a Beat Literary canon while most of his compadres were still alive. Where it all began, who met whom when, under what circumstances. His own unique eye-witnessed version. Gregory Corso quipped instead how it was getting time to set up the Beat retirement home! I was in my twenties when we began Naropa, having helped found the Poetry Project at St. Mark's Church in-the-Bowery, in New York, developing my own sense of Outrider community that straddled all the schools of the New American Poetry. The Beat archive resonated in me, I had grown up with it, and the movement was not over. Everyone was productive. This Colorado iteration wasn't a "second act" for the Beats. Allen wasn't yet fifty. He was writing constantly; he was a motivated teacher.

We were guests at the invitation of the Tibetan Buddhist meditation teacher Chögyam Trungpa, who was gathering students, scholars, artists, and meditation teachers from many traditions. We mused about a lama steeped in an ancient tradition coming to the United States with the odd and charming request: "Take me to your poets!" Whoever arrived in America specifically looking for poets? And subsequently invited poets to start their own program, within an institute that was to be "a hundred-year project at least"? We had no formal training as teachers. We did not hold those kinds of academic credentials and had no English department backing us. We weren't a writing program, but a *reading* and writing program, a live experiment, a "conglomeration of tendencies," and a poetry *sangha* inspired by the contemplative backdrop of impermanence and by "specimens of spiritual breakthroughs." Allen summed up the modus operandi of the Beat Literary movement as "inquisitiveness into the nature of consciousness, with literature as a 'noble means.'" Kerouac most of all seered this profundity. We were all phantoms in space. The transitoriness of existence was the basis of everybody's tenderness. This was the spiritual insight of the Beats as Allen nailed it. And this could also include Burroughs's less holy history, the prophetic clarity of his cut-up apocalyptic futures, the ones we all now seem to be living in. Allen hoped Naropa would be an experiment in visionary tenderness. Allen was also the astute impresario and ingenious PR agent of this worldwide cultural intervention. This unique body of lectures is a testament to his canon building and his imperatives for understanding and propagating the Beat ethos.

We named our pedagogical experiment The Jack Kerouac School of Disembodied Poetics because Kerouac had realized the first Buddhist Noble Truth of Suffering. "Disembodied" because we had none of the accoutrements of a poetics department and we were going to teach ghosts like Shakespeare, Kit Smart, Blake, Whitman, James Joyce and Gertrude Stein. Allen also taught an English poetry and prosody class guiding students through the mazes of the *Norton Anthology*.

It was the Beat course, however, that galvanized Allen's energy and purpose. He often said he would not have joined Naropa were it not for the meditative "hook." These lectures therefore are enhanced by Allen's deepening understand of the Buddhist view (he had taken vows with Trungpa). Not that he hadn't insights of emptiness and read D. T. Suzuki and sought out the Dalai Lama in India but he had found a practice—*shamatha vipassana*—insight meditation, which located a larger existential view. The four noble truths, particularly the strongly emphasized truths of suffering and impermanence, were already haunting him. Allen was one of the most famous poets and celebrities in the world, and yet settling at Naropa grounded him enough to interpret and "transmit" his history and spiritual poetics and that of his closest literary friends. And a practice of compassion and view of the inter-connectedness of all life was understood as a way out of suffering.

I watched Allen prepare for class in his town house apartment in Boulder and later at his rented house on Bluff Street assiduously reading, marking passages. Some of these were already in his marrow. He was always good at memorization. And it had been Kerouac's prose, in particular his bop prosody, that had set his own course. Jack was the master here. It was through Jack's work that he had found his own carriage, his "voice," his power and purpose. Allen always had a sense of his personal debt to Jack. He would read great swaths of Jack's text aloud, often weeping. His metabolism was adhesive to the heaves and rhythms, epiphanies and kinetics of the work he was so entangled in. He highlights particularly luminous phrases. They had pushed his own poetry into being, its quixotic rapture. Wild mind was invoked. "Mind is shapely, Art is shapely." This wild mind work was *shapely*, was elegant, was exquisite, and he emphatically wanted the world to understand this.

In these lectures, the primary focus is on the heart buddies and the generative years and writing in New York: Jack, William, Gregory, with minor appearances by Neal Cassady, John Clellon Holmes, Peter Orlovsky. West Coasters Philip Whalen and Gary Snyder, coming later into Allen's sphere, are absent. There are lectures on Allen's own writing methods as well. The book includes chunks of the core texts interspersed with Allen's personal insider exegesis. His intellectual, psychological scrying. I can't think of any other contemporary writer so generous with his peers.

This is a male/queer book. It touches on erotics, on male camaraderie, crime's karma, heart-to-heart communication, influence, literary pursuit. And pushes to disabuse the world of the juvenile delinquent bad boy reputations. It is a compendium of useful knowledge, a mandala for future study, and an area of scholarship begging wider critical attention. Ginsberg's scrutiny is riveting and obsessive and generous perhaps to a fault to his comrades, but it is a wild ride for the students on the other side of the equation.

Allen's commentary is riddled with "takes" gleaned from Jack, and he invokes the instinctual hipness of Jack himself. The subvocal mind flashes. His teaching here is refreshed, unfiltered. It's straight talk. You hear intimate details throughout, perhaps more than you ever want to know about William Burroughs's preferred sexual posture. But William holds gravitas as the elder, eminence grise, with cool prophetic clarity, a brilliance. Gregory—whose formative years were spent in a prison library, in love with Keats and Shelley—is on the other hand a "dousing wand for poetic beauty."

Editor Bill Morgan has done an admirable, heroic, and exhaustive job of winnowing down and of siphoning many pages from the Naropa classes, the ur-classes, but much more substantively from the Brooklyn College lectures, which is this book's core, covering additional texts and Allen's commentary. This was not a dead Lit 101 class. It evolved, gathered steam. Many friends and former students I know firsthand benefited from the Brooklyn years. This was a rare pedagogical experience and included the often startling legendary narratives.

But what is most interesting and new to me, beyond the spiritual and personal investigation, is Allen's assessment and insistence on the influence of black culture and jazz on the Beats, which is also a "spiritual" thing. This is the imperative I come away with. An understanding that Black America really *is* the salvation of the USA. Proclaiming "jazz a clarion of a new consciousness" is correct and a tribute to Allen's perspicacity. This is what we need to remember. This needs saying again and again, and given recognition more than ever now. That's what makes this book of Allen's talk real, true, and fiercely relevant. And it is a heartening survey from that perspective. I love the lists of what these guys were listening to; not only Brahms's Trio No. 1 and Mahler's Symphony No. 1, but more excitedly, it's "Salt Peanuts" and "Oop Bop Sh'Bam" by Dizzy Gillespie, it's King Pleasure and Charlie Parker, and "The Chase" by Dexter Gordon, and Billie Holiday's "Fine and Mellow" and "I Cover the Waterfront."

Allen is giving credit where credit is more than due, but his analysis constitutes an accurate prophecy. Jack Kerouac had said, "The earth is an Indian thing," as it continues to be, and this too is a cogent axiom as the planet and its denizens suffer the effects of climate change and there's an urgent necessity on the part of many to look to native knowledge and wisdom. As I write this tribal activists are protesting an egregious pipeline at Standing Rock in North Dakota, and Black Lives Matter is changing the frequency toward full civil rights, equality, recognition, reparation. There is so much more work to do. The walls of white supremacy are tumbling down in spite of the recent political debate and outcome, with its bigotry and racism. The Beats were on the progressive side of this.

And where might we position, in our current dystopia, our fragile Anthropocene, the provocative dismembering body of work that constitutes the opus of William Burroughs? And the prescience within this "body" that destabilizes many concomitant and parallel realities, revealing identity and gender to be fluid constructs? I speak of this often, and publicly, to help my own cognitive dissonance within our contemporary society. I would say the "Burroughs effect" defies categories. "The basic disruption of reality" is what he posits. In the last decade and more, we have witnessed a self-fulfilling prophecy mirrored in Burroughs's work, his vivid revelations and resonance and constructs, in his dark investigation of the "limits of control." We have disturbing images of torture from Abu Ghraib, from Bagram, the force feeding at Guantánamo; we see "terrorists" in perpetual "lockdown"; we have the drone wars taking out "suspects"; there are hundreds of thousands of deaths on our hands in the combined horrific Middle East follies. There are the horrors of displacement and forced migrations. We have the "extraordinary renditions," "waterboarding," and the ominous threats of greater suffering, greater divides in the culture, and planet meltdown.

We have myriad "ghosted" bodies—emanating out of the eternal war scenarios, broken lives, and broken neurological pathways. A Bosch-like intensity. Intricacies of surreal body parts: animal with human, experiments of genetic hybrid, sheep and mouse cloning and the like, transplants of all kinds, the torture of the animal, human/metal cyborgian hybrids or advanced robotic weaponry, the drones and reapers. We have the pharmaceutical and porn industries' marketing and control of desire, euphemism and lies of Operation Enduring Freedom, Shock and Awe, the Clean Air Act or "refined interrogation techniques" or "disposition matrix" (kill list), which amplify words as killer viruses. We have the World Wide Web spying on our lives, NSA monitoring cell phones, whistle-blowers in lockdown. We have killer viruses, AIDS, Ebola, Zika. We have an unprecedented situation in our current US governance that defies all civic norms and poses many threats that the Beats were already on to. Burroughs stands alone in his satiric powerful takedowns.

The women are missing here unless as mothers, lovers, wives, sometimes victims, hamstrung by ignorance, societal prejudice, a patriarchal dominance yet to fully crumble. But many were outstanding poets and writers and their story is unfolding with impressive research and investigation. The Beats were culpable bystanders, although I never felt personally excluded by the mid-sixties. There is palpable fluidity in these men. They are essentially softies. The female principle of cultivating atmosphere, of providing nourishment, emotional depth, and ambiguity drives so much of Ginsberg's writing and brotherly love. Love is at the heart of the narrative. Allen often quoted Ezra Pound's "what thou lovest well remains."

Scholarship has been more intellectual in more recent years outside the US of A. One critic sees Kerouac as an "action writer" placed in the milieu with Jackson Pollock and John Cage. Deleuze and Guattari acknowledge Burroughs's "set of potentials," an effect that propagates itself from medium to medium. Beat enclaves—communities of artists (of all genders and ages) around the world who consider themselves part of a spiritual lineage that grasped and held so many other realities and beauties of experimental art and life and alternative politics—are legion. Something propelled these writers into a spotlight of Whitmanic adhesiveness. Being in the right place at the right time. More interested in the fellaheen than the Industrial Military Complex.

Naropa University has gender-free bathrooms now, there's a diversity center in what used to be music archivist and filmmaker Harry Smith's residence, which was later the first Naropa recording studio. Brooklyn College is also changing with the times. We are yet again at another trembling crossroads in American culture.

And for whatever future we have, it will have been informed, in part, by the literary power, aspirations, and influence of the Beats who met in an Outrider, rhizomic community through the nexus of Columbia University. Professor Ginsberg will capture and hold our attention for many semesters yet to come. There is something still radically prescient, deeply personal, and riveting in this luminous textbook.

Editor's Preface

Naw, this isn't a lost generation,
this is a beat generation
—Jack Kerouac

History of the Courses

In the summer of 1977 Allen Ginsberg decided that the time had come to teach a course on the literary history of the Beat Generation. By then he was the codirector of the poetry department at the Naropa Institute in Boulder, Colorado. The college, now known as Naropa University, had been founded in 1974 by the Tibetan lama Chögyam Trungpa Rinpoche, a lineage holder of both the Kagyü and Nyingma Buddhist traditions. As early as 1972 Trungpa had met with Ginsberg, Anne Waldman, Diane di Prima, and John Cage to seek their help in organizing a poetics department for his proposed school and in 1974 the first courses were taught at what Ginsberg and Waldman dubbed The Jack Kerouac School of Disembodied Poetics. Ginsberg would remain on the faculty and devote himself to teaching at Naropa until his death, in 1997, often for little or no pay. He was a born teacher and loved sharing his knowledge with bright, young students.

When Ginsberg began his very first lecture to his class that summer, he explained that they would cover the major work of the writers of the Beat Generation and would focus on the 1940s, '50s, and '60s. Initially his plan was to bring the students up to date on what each poet was doing, concluding with his or her present work. "So the story is not finished but is ongoing, and this Naropa Institute, the Buddhist conjunction with whatever conception or inspiration was involved with the Beat vision, your presence here and my teaching here is a part of that continued humorous story," he said. "In other words, the movie continues and you are now in it," he told his class. He outlined ambitious plans for the following twenty sessions of two hours each, and recited a long list of books he hoped to cover during that period. "So we'll actually have the forties, fifties, sixties, and seventies to cover. It's a little bit more than I'd planned on," he remarked at one point. As the weeks passed, however, it became apparent that Ginsberg would not have time to bring the students up to date, and in fact he'd be lucky if he could cover just the 1940s during the forty-plus hours he had available to lecture. Of course it was difficult for him to stick strictly to even a single decade because works begun in the late forties might not have been completed or published until the early fifties, and Burroughs's earliest work was from the thirties. By the end of the term Allen was still working his way through the mid-1940s.

In 1981 and 1982 he decided to tackle the project again by offering two more courses at Naropa. This time he tried to be more realistic about how much he could cover in a single term. Even so, he still wasn't able to complete the historical survey of the Beat Generation and as time passed there were more and more years to cover. Later, when he was appointed to the faculty of Brooklyn College, he revisited the topic twice, first in 1987 and then for the last time in 1994. By that time nearly twenty years had passed since the original course was conceived. During the intervening years more work by

Beat writers had been published and more scholarship about those writers had accumulated. If Ginsberg hadn't passed away in 1997 he certainly would have tried once more to bring his overview of literary history up to date.

Over the years Ginsberg frequently asked the Beat writers themselves to visit his classes and speak to the students about their own work. This made the classes even more popular and afforded the students the chance not only to read and study the works of the Beats but to meet them and ask questions of them directly. It proved to be a wonderful experience. The students worked with William Burroughs, Gregory Corso, Herbert Huncke, Peter Orlovsky, Michael McClure, Ray Bremser, Carl Solomon, Amiri Baraka (LeRoi Jones), and many others to, as Ginsberg put it, "study at the feet of the masters." With the support of the Wolfe Institute at Brooklyn College, Allen also hosted several reading series that featured appearances by most of the remaining members of the Beat movement.

In the end, Ginsberg taught the "Literary History of the Beat Generation" course five times for a total of nearly a hundred lectures, which covered a staggering amount of material. Many people are surprised to learn that Ginsberg was a demanding teacher who expected his students to be well read and well prepared for each class. He often heaped more reading assignments on them than they could ever hope to complete. He provided students with an anthology of source material and a course bibliography; the latter is included as an appendix to this book.

Ginsberg mentioned several reasons for offering the course. First of all, many students at Naropa had requested that Allen talk about himself and the Beat Generation, the literary movement that Ginsberg had played a key role in creating. No one knew the topic better than he did. Allen acknowledged that, in addition to the students enrolled in his class, he was also speaking to "scholars and future interested people" with the knowledge that his words were being recorded and preserved. He hoped that someday he'd have the time to edit these tapes himself and create a complete documentary history of his own literary generation. And, finally, he was well aware that his knowledge and intelligence were transient, that his memory would fade, and that he would eventually die, leaving his personal interpretation incomplete unless he took steps to document it himself. For those reasons these lectures were always intended to be a permanent, "once and for all" record of what Allen considered to be the high points of Beat literature.

This was typical of Ginsberg who always felt that it was his job to document the era, preserve the literature, and educate the people as to the importance of the movement he had created nearly single-handedly, for without Ginsberg there would be no Beat Generation. Although there were a dozen or more notable writers working independently, they were not thought of as a literary group. It was Allen who helped forge the public's perception of these writers as a unified group, exposing them to wider readerships as the fame and importance of the Beat Generation grew. The biggest problem facing Ginsberg in the organization of his course's curriculum was how to condense the writings of dozens of poets and novelists into reasonably short discussions. And quite frankly that was something he could never do. A single comment about Herbert Huncke would lead to a two-hour discussion of the world around Times Square in the 1940s and might delve into subjects such as drugs, world politics, sex, storytelling, and morality. An introductory remark on Burroughs's earliest writing might expand to include a reading of that work, a discussion of Burroughs's youth and friends, visionary experiences, and the power and meaning of words themselves. Allen's explanation of the importance of that work to Burroughs's development might stretch to several weeks of classroom conversation. As a result some of his lectures break off into tangents and often resemble musings as he formulated his ideas in front of the students. Many times his train of thought breaks from the strict narrative that his syllabus had set forth and his digressions open new doors to the understanding of the Beat writers.

Scope of the Courses

Ginsberg also faced the problem of separating the work of the writers from their biographies. In addition he was faced with trying to distance their writing from the social phenomenon the Beats inadvertently spawned as their work became public. It was an impossible task, because the lives of most of these writers became their work. Allen comments several times in these tapes on this fusion—how Kerouac and Burroughs became one with their work. This was further complicated by the writers themselves who muddied the waters even more by refusing to acknowledge that they were part of any "Beat Generation." Understandably, the writers did not want to be pigeonholed into a group that was frequently characterized in the media as nothing more than a bunch of juvenile delinquents. In Kerouac's opinion the Beat Generation had ceased to exist by the late 1940s, but Allen did his best to extend membership to writers who were barely in their teens during the 1940s.

Just who were the Beat Generation writers in Ginsberg's eyes? In conversation, Allen conveyed a broad idea of who was "Beat." These writers ranged in age from William S. Burroughs, born in 1914, to Anne Waldman, born in 1945, too wide a range of years for a single generation. This is a problem that I as editor had to wrestle with in order to shape his lectures into a tightly knit single volume. Allen believed the original group that coalesced around Kerouac, Burroughs, Lucien Carr, and himself in the neighborhood of New York's Columbia University in the 1940s was the core of the Beat Generation. These figures are the people he covered in depth in his classes and returned to again and again in his lectures. It is not because Ginsberg didn't want to include the members of the San Francisco Renaissance and the Black Mountain writers in his history of the Beat Generation, but it was purely because he ran out of time. In some of his later years he addressed the work of younger writers and included them in readings and bibliographies, but he did not lecture about them to the extent that he tackled Kerouac, Burroughs, and also Corso.

Editorial Process, Selection of Texts

Ginsberg's lack of focus on the younger members of the group made it possible for this editor to place greater emphasis on the original New York Beats and their roles in the conception of the movement. Allen began each of his five courses with extensive lectures on Kerouac, Burroughs, and Corso, then as time permitted he might or might not get to Gary Snyder, Robert Creeley, Ray Bremser, Philip Whalen, Philip Lamantia, Michael McClure, Diane di Prima, Lawrence Ferlinghetti, John Clellon Holmes, and the others. There was a good deal of repetition and overlap in his discussions on the work of the first three writers and I have collated his comments to make the lectures from the five course offerings as seamless as possible. Although time-consuming, this was easier than it might sound, because Allen's opinions changed little over the nearly twenty years during which he taught the course. Ginsberg always considered Kerouac to be the greatest writer, Burroughs to be the greatest intellect, and Corso to be the most naturally gifted poet. He often returned to the same lines in their texts to point out an interesting or remarkable passage and his admiration for certain key works never seemed to waver.

Ginsberg's method of teaching was simple enough. He organized his lectures by author, more or less chronologically. He taught his students through a series of examples. He selected what he considered to be the most interesting and important texts and commented on why he thought each was essential, distinct, or remarkable. Through that process he presented a picture of each writer's style in a way that a narrative alone could not. He followed that same system throughout the five courses. We are grateful to be allowed to reprint so many of those texts by his fellow writers here, thus avoiding a great number of cross-references to outside resources. In some cases the texts were too long or their importance was not great enough to Ginsberg's discussion to warrant several pages of reprinted material. In those few truncated entries the symbol [. . .] has been inserted to indicate that a portion of the original has been deleted. Otherwise texts are as Allen read them in class.

This is the twelfth book I have edited for the Ginsberg Trust since Allen's death and my twenty-eighth book on the subject of the Beat Generation. Most of my editorial projects with the Beats have required little or no introduction because their works stand on their own merits and I have always tried to keep myself out of the story whenever possible. In this case, however, there were many more editorial decisions that I needed to make and so it seems important to outline my method.

To begin with, Ginsberg made tape recordings of every lecture he gave. The quality of the tapes vary from day to day, but Allen was obsessive-compulsive in this way and he tried to do his best to document every word. The Naropa tapes from 1977, 1981, and 1982 have been digitized and are available online. In addition, several original cassette tapes exist in the Ginsberg Archive at Stanford University. Many of the Brooklyn College tapes for the 1987 and 1994 classes can also be found at Stanford. I was also lucky enough to be able to transcribe tapes recorded by the Brooklyn College reference librarian William Gargan, who as a serious student of the Beat Generation attended all of Ginsberg's classes and made his own set of tapes. His recordings were essential in many cases where the "official" tape was either missing or inaudible.

After gathering all the tapes I slowly transcribed every Ginsberg word and utterance. In the end those transcripts totaled nearly 400,000 words, nearly 2,000 pages of text. As someone who is as anal retentive as Allen was (in fact on more than one occasion he mentioned that I shared that trait with him), I would have loved to have published the complete transcript, unedited and unabridged. That would not have been as useful as it seems, however, due to the frequency of repetition. Considerable editing had to be done to pare this compendium down to the size you hold in your hands.

The lectures were then arranged by subject, chronologically. This was the way that Allen approached most of the subjects, but some rearrangement was necessary. The focus remains on the individual writers. For example, because he talked about *On the Road* five separate times, these statements had to be collated and repetitive statements had to be eliminated. This involved reading each sentence carefully and selecting the best, clearest, and most enlightening description of a given work.

Allen repeatedly mentions that Corso "tailored" his poems, and I must admit that this work is also the result of tailoring. Due to the nature of classroom lectures, unnecessary spoken words and asides have been omitted without the use of ellipses, because nearly every paragraph would contain a few of these and the work would become unwieldy and distracting. Student questions and remarks have also been deleted. All words not spoken by Ginsberg during his discussions have been placed within brackets [ ]. These additions were made as sparingly as possible where needed to clarify particular comments.

Because the transcripts were taken from spoken lectures, sentence breaks and punctuation are my own, not necessarily Allen's. Occasionally he stopped mid-sentence, thought of a better way to phrase something, and then began anew. These awkward breaks have been mended without distorting the substance of a thought. Ginsberg also had a few habits that would be distracting if all were reproduced. A majority of the sentences in his lectures begin with the word "so." Allen used it in much the same way that some speakers use the word "um," as a pause or a bridge to another topic. "So let's see where we were," for example. He also used more than his share of the words "actually" and "like" and these have been thinned out without further note. The scholar who wants to hear all these imperfections will be able to find the complete lectures on websites or on cassette tapes, as mentioned earlier.

This book is designed to give Ginsberg's perspective and history of the Beat Generation, and therefore I have not included the comments of either the students or the various poets who visited his classroom. I believe that given the space restrictions of a single volume it is not critical to this history to give Corso's interpretation or opinion about a particular poem. It is Ginsberg's opinion that we're presenting, even when Corso's might be of equal interest.

I took it upon myself to adjust certain basic facts that were stated incorrectly. In no instance did I change Ginsberg's opinions or ideas about anything, but in some cases his memory was faulty, e.g., Joan

Burroughs died in 1951, not 1950, as Allen stated in one lecture, and the title of the Burroughs's book Allen discussed or noted at one point was *The Exterminator,* not *Exterminator!,* which was a different book with a very similar title. I have kept these corrections to a minimum but the changes were generally not noted.

Finally, the usual scholarly footnotes and bibliography have been added, which is in keeping with the way Allen would have prepared the book for publication himself, but these notes are my own.

The purpose of this book is to present Allen Ginsberg's version of history. Perhaps this will lead to further interest and study of a group that remains among the most influential literary movements of the twentieth century.

THE BEST MINDS OF MY GENERATION

OF MY GENERATION

A Literary History
of the BEATS

A Definition of the Beat Generation

[edited transcript of a lecture by Allen Ginsberg]

To begin with, the phrase "Beat Generation" rose out of a specific conversation with Jack Kerouac and John Clellon Holmes in 1950–51 when discussing the nature of generations, recollecting the glamour of the "lost generation." Kerouac discouraged the notion of a coherent "generation" and said, "Ah, this is nothing but a beat generation!" They discussed whether it was a "found" generation, which Kerouac sometimes referred to, or "angelic" generation, or various other epithets. But Kerouac waved away the question and said "beat generation!" not meaning to name the generation but to un-name it.

John Clellon Holmes then wrote an article in late 1952 in the *New York Times* magazine section with the headline title of the article, "This Is the Beat Generation."[1] And that caught on. Then Kerouac published anonymously a fragment of *On the Road* in *New World Writing*, a paperback anthology of the 1950s, called "Jazz of the Beat Generation,"[2] and that caught on as a catchphrase, so that's the history of the term.

Secondly, Herbert Huncke, author of *The Evening Sun Turned Crimson*,[3] who was a friend of Kerouac, Burroughs, and others of that literary circle from the 1940s, introduced them to what was then known as "hip language." In that context, word "beat" is a carnival "subterranean," subcultural, term, a term much used in Times Square in the 1940s. "Man, I'm beat . . ." meaning without money and without a place to stay. Could also mean "in the winter cold, shoes full of blood walking on the snowbank docks waiting for a door in the East River to open up to a room full of steam heat . . ." Or, as in a conversation, "Would you like to go to the Bronx Zoo?" "Nah, man, I'm too *beat*, I was up all night." So the original street usage meant exhausted, at the bottom of the world, looking up or out, sleepless, wide-eyed, perceptive, rejected by society, on your own, streetwise. Or, as it is now termed, *fini* in French, finished, undone, completed, in the dark night of the soul or the cloud of unknowing. "Open," as in Whitmanic sense of "openness," equivalent to humility, and so it was interpreted into various circles to mean both emptied out, exhausted, and at the same time wide open—perceptive and receptive to a vision.

Then a third meaning of the term, as later modified by Kerouac, considering the abuse of the term in the media—the term being interpreted as being beaten completely, without the aspect of humble or humility, or "beat" as the beat of drums and "the beat goes on," which are all mistakes of interpretation or etymology. Kerouac, in various lectures, interviews, and essays, tried to indicate the correct sense of the word by pointing out the root—*be-at*—as in beatitude, or beatific. In his essay "Origins of the Beat Generation"[4] Kerouac defined it so. This is an early definition in the popular culture, though a late definition in the subculture: he clarified his intention, which was "beat" as beatific, as in "dark night of the soul," or "cloud of unknowing," the necessary beatness of darkness that proceeds opening up to light, egolessness, giving room for religious illumination.

The fourth meaning that accumulated was "Beat Generation literary movement." That was a group of friends who had worked together on poetry, prose, cultural conscience from the mid-forties until the term became popular nationally in the late fifties. The group consisting of Kerouac; William Burroughs, author of *Naked Lunch* and other books; Herbert Huncke; John Clellon Holmes, author of *Go, The Horn,* and other books, including memoirs, and other cultural essays; Allen Ginsberg, myself, member of the American Institute of Arts and Letters since 1976; then Philip Lamantia met in 1948; Gregory Corso met in 1950; and Peter Orlovsky encountered in 1954; and several other personages not as well known as writers were in this circle, particularly Neal Cassady and Carl Solomon. Neal Cassady was writing at the time, [but] his works weren't published until posthumously.

In the mid-1950s this smaller group, through natural affinities or modes of thought or literary style or planetary perspective, was augmented in friendship and literary endeavor by a number of writers in San Francisco, including Michael McClure, Gary Snyder, Philip Whalen, Philip Lamantia, and a number of other lesser-known poets such as Jack Micheline, Ray Bremser, or the better-known black poet LeRoi Jones—all of whom accepted the term at one time or another, humorously or seriously, but sympathetically, and were included in a survey of Beat general manners, morals, and literature by *Life* magazine in a lead article in the late 1950s by one Paul O'Neil,[5] and by the journalist Alfred Aronowitz in a large series on the Beat Generation in the *New York Post.*[6]

Part of that literary circle, Kerouac, Whalen, Snyder, and, additionally, poet Lew Welch, Peter Orlovsky, Ginsberg, and others, were interested in meditation and Buddhism. Relationship between Buddhism and the Beat Generation can be found in a scholarly survey of the development of Buddhism in America, *How the Swans Came to the Lake,* by Rick Fields.

The fifth meaning of the phrase "Beat Generation" is the influence on the literary and artistic activities of poets, filmmakers, painters, and novelists who were working in concert in anthologies, publishing houses, independent filmmaking, and other media. The effect of the aforementioned groups—in film and still photography Robert Frank and Alfred Leslie; in music David Amram; in painting Larry Rivers; in poetry and publishing Don Allen, Barney Rosset, and Lawrence Ferlinghetti—extended to fellow artists; the bohemian culture, which was already a long tradition; to the youth movement of that day, which was also growing; and [to] the mass culture and middle-class culture of the late 1950s and early 1960s. These effects can be characterized in the following terms:

- general liberation: Sexual "Revolution" or "Liberation," Gay Liberation, Black Liberation, Women's Liberation too;
- liberation of the word from censorship;
- decriminalization of some of the laws against marijuana and other drugs;
- the evolution of rhythm and blues into rock and roll, and rock and roll into high art form, as evidenced by the Beatles, Bob Dylan, and other popular musicians who were influenced in the 1960s by the writings of Beat Generation poets and writers;
- the spread of ecological consciousness, emphasized by Gary Snyder;
- opposition to the military-industrial machine civilization, as emphasized in the works of Burroughs, Huncke, Ginsberg, and Kerouac;
- attention to what Kerouac called, after Spengler, "Second Religiousness" developing within an advanced civilization;

- respect for land and indigenous peoples as proclaimed by Kerouac in his slogan from *On the Road,* "The earth is an Indian thing."

The essence of the phrase "Beat Generation" can also be found in *On the Road* in another celebrated phrase, "Everything belongs to me because I am poor."[7]

CHAPTER 1

Course Overview

One thing I'll try to do is talk sequentially in such a way that it will make sense for scholars as well as for ourselves and record what I'm doing because I'm getting senile and I don't remember very much anymore. I can't remember who fucked who, when, or who wrote what anymore, and this may be one of the last times I'll actually be able to remember that and get it straight. My own tendency would be just to talk and talk and talk, assuming that you'll understand what I'm talking about, but I found that sometimes the references that I make are my own private references that people don't understand.

[I'll try] to summarize what I can remember of the literary aspect, or intellectual, or spiritual, as well as gossip, history of early meetings with William Burroughs and Jack Kerouac, Herbert Huncke and Carl Solomon and Gregory Corso, among other people.[8]

First, I want to run down the 1940s. What I'll cover is a reading list, music of the forties, specific albums by Charlie Parker, King Pleasure, Thelonious Monk, Dexter Gordon, bebop of that time that influenced Kerouac's rhythmic style. Musical phrasings that he imitated directly to get sentences and the prose for *On the Road*. I'll talk about Symphony Sid who was the disc jockey who played all the great early bop classics from midnight till morn. That will bring up the idea of the relation between speech and music, as in "Salt Peanuts, Salt Peanuts," which is [from] a Dizzy Gillespie classic. The music for that was literally lifted from speech phrasings, "salt peanuts, salt peanuts," and Kerouac took it back from *da-ta-da* to his own prose.

In other words, black musicians were imitating speech cadences and Kerouac was imitating the black musicians' breath cadences on their horns and brought it back to speech. It always was speech rhythms or cadences as far as the ear that Kerouac was developing. All passed through black music. I'll cover music as an influence to Kerouac and then a discussion of *The Town and the City*.

The notion of fellaheen, which Kerouac got out of [Oswald] Spengler, *fellaheen,* a word that Kerouac uses a lot in *On the Road*. Spengler uses it to talk about the people who are not in the big city media scene, but are just dolts running around in their own cow pastures, living their own eternal lives throughout history. The people out in the provinces whose life is the same everywhere, oppressed, unnoticed, compared to the city people who are subject to constant hallucinations and empire transitoriness. Similar to Yeats's idea, "turning and turning in the widening gyre, the falcon cannot hear the falconer, things fall apart, the center cannot hold, mere anarchy is loosed on the world."[9] The center cannot hold, nobody knows what's going on anymore. Everything is so complicated.

A discussion of the minor but interesting writer called Herbert Huncke, whose book *The Evening Sun Turned Crimson* was originally written around that time. Huncke was a fellow that first turned Burroughs on to junk. Burroughs's idea of the forties was "What if truth broke out? What if everybody started talking frankly."

[I will discuss] Times Square mid-1940s sociology and Dr. Alfred Kinsey who was hanging around and writing his book on human male sexuality in which we are all (Kerouac and Burroughs and Huncke and others) subjects. We entered into history that way first, before we started writing. A discussion of Benzedrine, which was the early speed, and its effect on the Times Square denizens of the forties. I'll read a little bit out of *Lonesome Traveler* and *Doctor Sax* and talk about Kerouac's idea of phantoms, human beings as phantoms in vast space. I'll tell about my meeting with Kerouac and use the book *Vanity of Duluoz,* the vanity of Kerouac, as a retrospective autobiography by Kerouac, to cover that period of the forties. If you're ever interested in checking back through the forties, Kerouac's *Vanity of Duluoz* does that.

We'll talk about the mutual recognition of the transitoriness of existence, which is the basis of everybody's tenderness. The realization that we were all sitting in a classroom like a bunch of meek-boned ghosts and we're not going to be here very long. And so therefore there was a certain glimpse of the flowerness of the moment, as a basis of our literary understanding. I'll talk about a poet named Mark Van Doren, who was a professor at Columbia and who was friends with Kerouac. Raymond Weaver, who first read Kerouac's writings as a professor at Columbia. Weaver, a mystic who had discovered Herman Melville's manuscript of *Billy Budd* in a trunk, was Kerouac's first major literary connection. Raymond Weaver had taught in Japan and was the one professor at Columbia who had some sense of meditation and Zen and semantics and paradox, the first Gnostic professor we'd met. I'll give an account of the circle of friends of 1945 around Columbia.

We'll cover my meeting with Gregory Corso in the 1950s and what was being read by everybody at the time. What Burroughs had recommended to us for reading, which was Spengler's *Decline of the West,* Korzybski's *Science and Sanity* to keep our language straight, Kafka's *Castle* and *Trial,* Rimbaud's *Season in Hell* and

Illuminations, Jean Cocteau's *Opium,* Blake's *Songs of Innocence and Experience,* William Butler Yeats's *A Vision,* Raymond Chandler and John O'Hara detective stories. That was what we were all reading among ourselves.

I'll cover some of Kerouac's *Mexico City Blues.* Describe Burroughs's lifestyle, sitting around in a black, somewhat soup-stained vest, in a furnished room over Riordan's Bar in New York, experimenting with drugs and [meeting] with local crooks on Times Square just to see what that sociology and mentality was like. I will talk a little bit about sitting down with William Burroughs, myself, and Kerouac, spending an hour a day for about a year with Burroughs psychoanalyzing me and doing the same with Kerouac. This at a time when Burroughs was being psychoanalyzed by a Dr. [Paul] Federn who had been analyzed by Freud. He was also working with a doctor, Lewis Wolberg, on hypnoanalysis.

I'll also talk about my early writing and Kerouac's early writing around Columbia, and about Dostoyevsky, whom we all were reading, particularly *The Idiot* and *The Possessed.* I recommend for any basic course on the Beat Generation to familiarize yourself with *The Idiot,* Prince Myshkin. He was Dostoyevsky's idea of the most beautiful human being he could imagine, the creation of a saint in literature. So the later writings of Dostoyevsky were everybody's preoccupation, because they were full of totally heartfelt human beings confronting each other. I'll talk about meeting Neal Cassady in 1946 and his influence on everybody, his energy, coming up from Denver.

We encountered William Carlos Williams in 1948, adding some touch of influence and information from the twenties, from the great lineage of American poetry practice of Ezra Pound and the Imagists and Objectivists. Gregory Corso's early poetry. First contacts with Zen Buddhism. Kerouac's early ideas on spontaneous prose.

What I'll propose to do is read from the texts, read my favorite fragments or things that were important to us as a group at the time. Big sentences that knocked everybody out, that turned everybody on. Jack would write something and he'd send me a letter saying, "I just wrote this yesterday, what do you think of that?" Or I would send him a poem, or we'd get a letter from Burroughs with some amazing statement and I would copy it and send it to Kerouac. I'll try and read those gists, which were historical epiphanies for us.

CHAPTER 2

Kerouac's "Origins of the Beat Generation"

I'll begin with Jack Kerouac's "Origins of the Beat Generation." I'm skipping somewhat ten years, but as with my own little prefatory material and Kerouac's essay, this is a general survey of the term "Beat" and its use and the ethos of what was called the Beat Generation. The most authoritative word obviously would be Kerouac's. After *On the Road* was published in 1957 he was very famous and sought after. Much misunderstood for his sensitivity and taken to be somewhat of a juvenile delinquent. He was more of a recluse and so he stayed home, but there was one occasion where he was invited out to Hunter College to give a lecture. Kerouac invited me to go along with him and when we arrived we found that the occasion was a debate of the Beat Generation with Kerouac set up to be attacked by James Wechsler, a liberal pundit, editor of the *New York Post*, Ashley Montagu, an anthropologist, and John Wain, a novelist from England [and a member] of a group called the "Angry Young Men." The Angry Young Men didn't have quite the genius that the Beat Generation would compose and didn't have a spiritual agenda. It was more like a social protest group, not directly involved with the nature of consciousness.

John Wain was more or less a conservative and thought of Kerouac as some boorish American and said so. Ashley Montagu dithered a bit but was basically sympathetic, speaking of it in terms of rebellion of the young against their parents, or the difficulty of living in speeded-up, mechanized society, the breakup of the family, etc. James Wechsler interpreted it as some sort of radical rebellion, but he felt that it was too passive and it didn't involve itself in action. He actually got up on stage and shook his fist at Kerouac and said, "You gotta fight for peace." Kerouac started laughing and picked up James Wechsler's hat and put it on his head and walked around in a circle on stage instead of arguing with him. Wechsler got insulted and thought this was some kind of rude response instead of a rational tempered response to his proposition. Wechsler didn't know about Zen masters and Zen answers. Jack just did it intuitively.

Kerouac was also told that he wasn't allowed to read the speech he had prepared, but Jack got up and read it, which was a document of considerable worth. It remains a beautiful classic prose essay, very surprising because what was expected was some kind of statement of rebellion against prevailing mores. Instead Kerouac wrote an enthusiastic prose poem, lyrically praising the things that he liked. I just want to point out some key passages which have stuck in my head all these years.

[The Beat Generation] goes back to the 1880s when my grandfather Jean-Baptiste Kerouac used to go out on the porch in big thunderstorms and swing his kerosene lamp at the lightning and yell "Go ahead, go, if you're more powerful than I am strike me and put the light out!" while the mother and the children cowered in the kitchen. And the light never went out.[10]

I mean if you wanta talk of Beat as "beat down" the people who erased the crucifix . . .

Oh, Kerouac had his photo taken for *Mademoiselle* or the *New York Times* magazine and when it was printed they erased the crucifix that had been put around his neck by Gregory Corso.

As a matter of fact, who's *really* beat around here, I mean if you wanta talk of Beat as "beat down" the people who erased the crucifix are really the "beat down" ones and not the *New York Times,* myself, and Gregory Corso the poet. I am not ashamed to wear the crucifix of my Lord. It is because I am Beat, that is, I believe in beatitude and that God so loved the world that he gave his only begotten son to it. I am sure no priest would've condemned me for wearing the crucifix outside my shirt everywhere *no matter where* I went, even to have my picture taken by *Mademoiselle.* So you people don't believe in God? So you're all big smart know-it-all Marxists and Freudians, hey? Why don't you come back in a million years and tell me all about it, angels?

Recently Ben Hecht said to me on TV, "Why are you afraid to speak out your mind, what's wrong with this country, what is everybody afraid of?" Was he talking to me? All he wanted me to do was speak out my mind *against* people, he sneeringly brought up Dulles, Eisenhower, the Pope, all kinds of people like that and habitually he would sneer at with Drew Pearson, *against* the world he wanted, this is his idea of freedom, he calls it freedom. Who knows, my God, but that the universe is not one vast sea of compassion actually, the veritable holy honey, beneath all this show of personality and cruelty.[11]

No, I want to speak *for* things, for the crucifix I speak out, for the Star of Israel I speak out, for the divinest man who ever lived who was a German (Bach) I speak out, for sweet Mohammed I speak out, for Buddha I speak out, for Lao-tse and Chuang-tse I speak out, for D. T. Suzuki I speak out.

Suzuki in 1948 was giving lectures on Zen at Columbia and John Cage and a lot of artists and scholars [attended].

. . . why should I attack what I love out of life. This is Beat. Live your lives out? Naw, *love* your lives out. When they come and stone you at least you won't have a glass house, just your glassy flesh.[12]

He was defining it as glee. Any of you who know Thomas Wolfe's prose might remember that there's a passage in which Wolfe speaks of a kind of joy or glee or enthusiasm or overflowing of feelings that sometimes occurs that makes him want to cry a high squealy note of pleasure. I think Kerouac picked up on that. He's defining the Beat Generation in terms of images from American comic strips or personal experience.

. . . the maniacal laugh of certain neighborhood madboys, the furious humor of whole gangs playing basketball till long after dark in the park, it goes back to those crazy days before World War II when teenagers drank beer on Friday nights at Lake ballrooms and worked off their hangovers playing baseball on Saturday afternoon followed by a dive in the brook—and our fathers wore straw hats like W. C. Fields. It goes back to the completely senseless babble of the Three Stooges, the ravings of the Marx Brothers (the tenderness of Angel Harpo at harp, too).[13]

[It goes back] to train whistles of steam engines out above moony pines. To Maw and Paw in the Model A clanking on to get a job in California selling used cars making a whole lotta money. To the glee of America, the honesty of America, the honesty of oldtime grafters in straw hats as well as the honesty of oldtime waiters in line at the Brooklyn Bridge in *Winterset,* the funny spitelessness of old big-fisted America like Big Boy Williams saying "Hoo? Hee? Huh?" in a movie about Mack Trucks and sliding door lunchcarts. To Clark Gable, his certain smile, his confident leer. Like my grandfather this America was invested with wild self-believing individuality and this had begun to disappear around the end of World War II with so many great guys dead (I can think of half a dozen from my own boyhood groups) when suddenly it began to emerge again, the hipsters began to appear gliding around saying, "Crazy, man."[14]

He was putting that kind of hot hipster talk, enthusiasm, in line with old-fashioned American individualistic Whitmanic enthusiasm, rather than beat or hip as it was interpreted by some journalists as retiring, cool, pathological, silent, slightly paranoid, pot-smoking paranoid. Then his version of the word "Beat."

Anyway, the hipsters, whose music was bop, they looked like criminals but they kept talking about the same things I liked {he's talking about people that he met around Times Square and around Greenwich Village in the mid- and late 1940s}, long outlines of personal experience and vision {this is actually what this history is about, "long outlines of personal experience and vision"}, night-long confessions full of hope that had become illicit and repressed by the war, stirrings, rumblings of a new soul (that same old human soul). And so Huncke appeared to us and said "I'm beat" with radiant light shining out of his despairing eyes, a word perhaps brought from some midwest carnival or junk cafeteria. It was a new language, actually spade (Negro) jargon but you soon learned it, like "hung-up" couldn't be a more economical term to mean so many things. Some of these hipsters were raving mad and talked continually. It was jazzy. Symphony Sid's all-night modern jazz and bop show was always on. By 1948 it began to take shape. That was a wild vibrating year when a group of us would walk down the street and yell hello and even stop and talk to anybody that gave us a friendly look. The hipsters had eyes. That was the year I saw Montgomery Clift, unshaven, wearing a sloppy jacket, slouching down Madison Avenue with a companion.[15]

By 1948 the hipsters, or beatsters, were divided into cool and hot.

This is actually quite funny and it relates to a pamphlet published by Norman Mailer called *The White Negro,* which defined the hipster as a white person who was in the position of alienation or outsiderness in relation to society or having undergone a sea change internally so that he's ultimately black in the sense that he's out of the majority culture and in another psychological world. The psychological world that Mailer defines was that of psychopathology basically. Someone who didn't want to show emotion. His is a kind of hyper-intellectualized version, very different from Kerouac. Kerouac was making a very clear distinction.

By 1948 the hipsters, or beatsters, were divided into cool and hot. Much of the misunderstanding about hipsters and the Beat Generation in general today derives from the fact that there are two distinct styles of hipsterism: the "cool" today is your bearded laconic sage, or schlerm {he just made up a word} before a hardly touched beer in a beatnik dive, whose speech is low and unfriendly, whose girls say nothing and wear black: the "hot" today is the crazy talkative shining eyed (often innocent and openhearted) nut who runs from bar to bar, pad to pad looking for everybody, shouting, restless, lushy, trying to "make it" with the subterranean beatniks who ignore him. Most Beat Generation artists belong to the hot school, naturally since that hard gemlike flame needs a little heat.[16]

Walter Pater, an English essayist of exquisite manners and mind, referred to some artwork or some poem as "burning with a hard gemlike flame"[17] and that became a standard buzz phrase for aesthetic judgments in small talk and novels, almost corny. Kerouac is citing this corny little phrase in a kind of traditional-sounding way assuming that the audience is literate enough to know who Walter Pater is and what the "hard gemlike flame" is. It was a subtle literary reference in the midst of this "hot" essay. Jack says this ethos or this sense of life is still

. . . the same, except that it has begun to grow into a national generation and the name "Beat" has stuck (though all hipsters hate the word).

The word "beat" originally meant poor, down and out, deadbeat, on the bum, sad, sleeping in subways. Now that the word is belonging officially it is being made to stretch to include people who do not sleep in subways but have a certain new gesture, or attitude, which I can only describe as a new *more*. {*More*, meaning social custom, social style, social ethos, norm.} "Beat Generation" has simply become the slogan or label for a revolution in manners in America. {That's pretty sharp for 1959.} Marlon Brando was not really the first to portray it on the screen. Dane Clark {this is an old movie star} with his pinched Dostoyevskyan face and Brooklyn accent, and of course {John} Garfield, were first. The private eyes {Raymond Chandler and John O'Hara the early detective fiction of the 1930s and 1940s} were Beat. In *M,* Peter Lorre started a whole revival, I mean the slouchy street walk.[18]

That's really true today. You see those guys wearing baggy pants, descendants of the parachute pants, wearing an odd weird Franken-stein haircut. It all comes out of Peter Lorre. It's a continuation of the same style as the murderer in the German movie *M* of the 1930s.

... my hero was Goethe and I believed in art and hoped some day to write the third part of *Faust,* which I have done in *Doctor Sax.* Then in 1952 an article was published in the *New York Times* Sunday magazine saying, the headline, "This Is a Beat Generation" (in quotes like that) and in the article it said that I had come up with the term first "when the face was harder to recognize," the face of the generation.[19]

But when the publishers finally took a dare and published *On the Road* in 1957 it burst open, it mushroomed, everybody began yell-ing about a Beat Generation. I was being interviewed everywhere I went for "what I meant" by such a thing. People began to call themselves beatniks, beats, jazzniks, bopniks, bugniks, and finally I was called the "avatar" of all this. {See, he got pissed off.}

Yet it was as a Catholic, it was not at the insistence of any of these "niks" and certainly not with their approval either, that I went one afternoon to the church of my childhood (one of them), St. Jeanne d'Arc in Lowell, Mass., and suddenly with tears in my eyes and had a vision of what I must have really meant with "Beat" anyhow when I heard the holy silence in the church—I was the only one in there, it was five p.m., dogs were barking outside, children yelling, the fall leaves, the candles were flickering alone just for me—the vision of the word Beat as being to mean beatific. . . . There's the priest preaching on Sunday morning, all of a sudden through a side door of the church comes a group of Beat Generation characters in strapped raincoats like the I.R.A. {Irish Republican Army} coming in silently to "dig" the religion . . . I knew it then.

But this was 1954, so then what horror I felt in 1957 and later 1958 naturally to suddenly see "Beat" being taken up by every-body, press and TV and Hollywood borscht circuit to include the "juvenile delinquency" shot {shot meaning take} and the horrors of a mad teeming billyclub New York and L.A. and they began to call *that* Beat, *that* beatific. . . . Bunch of fools marching against the San Francisco Giants protesting baseball, as if (now) in my name and I, my childhood ambition to be a big league baseball star hitter like Ted Williams so that when Bobby Thomson hit that home run in 1951 I trembled with joy and couldn't get over it for days and wrote poems about how it is possible for the human spirit to win after all![20]

He concludes with a statement on violence, because the main shot was that Beat groups were cruel psychopathic knife-wielding juvenile delinquent literary murderers, which is the take which con-tinues. It was the proclamation of Norman Podhoretz in 1958 in

Partisan Review as a literary critic attacking the Beat Generation group, particularly Kerouac, as "Know-Nothing Bohemians."[21]

And my father too, Leo, had never lifted a hand to punish me, or to punish the little pets in our house, and this teaching was delivered to me by the men in my house and I have never had anything to do with violence, hatred, cruelty, and all that horrible nonsense which, nevertheless, because God is gracious beyond all human imagining, he will forgive in the long end . . . that million years I'm asking about you, America.

And so now they have beatnik routines on TV {this is very witty}, starting with satires about girls in black and fellows in jeans with snapknives and sweatshirts and swastikas tattooed under their armpits {this all came true with the punk generation} it will come to respectable MCs {master of ceremonies} of spectaculars coming out nattily attired in Brooks Brothers jean-type tailoring and sweater-type pull-ons, in other words, it's a simple change in fashion and manners, just a history crust—like from the Age of Reason, from old Voltaire in a chair to romantic Chatterton in the moonlight—from Teddy Roosevelt to Scott Fitzgerald. . . . So there's nothing to get excited about. Beat comes out, actually, of old American whoopee and it will only change a few dresses and pants and make chairs useless in the living room and pretty soon we'll have Beat secretaries of state and there will be instituted new tinsels, in fact new reasons for malice and new reasons for virtue and new reasons for forgiveness.

But yet, but yet, woe, woe unto those who think that the Beat Generation means crime, delinquency, immorality, amorality . . . woe to those who attack it on the grounds that they simply don't understand history and the yearnings of human souls . . . woe unto those who don't realize that America must, will, is changing now, for the better I say. Woe to those who believe in the atom bomb, who believe in hating mothers and fathers, who deny the most important of the Ten Commandments, woe unto those (though) who don't believe in the unbelievable sweetness of sex love, woe unto those who are the standard bearers of death {That's a little quote from Marxist rhetoric}, woe unto those who believe in conflict and horror and violence {and here he's talking directly about Norman Podhoretz and Norman Mailer, they thrive in that atmosphere of cruelty, it's their natural element} and fill our books and screens and living rooms with all that crap, woe in fact unto those who make evil movies about the Beat Generation where innocent housewives are raped by beatniks! Woe unto those who are the real dreary sinners that even God finds room to forgive.[22]

He's always got this little edge of letting go of his anger or letting go of his resentment. "Woe unto those who spit on the Beat Generation, the wind will blow it back." Pretty good and quite prophetic. The Beat Generation is primarily a spiritual movement and so what I have put together are specimens of spiritual breakthroughs, or epiphanous experience, or illuminated experience, or alterations of consciousness, or psychedelic insight, articulated by people who were there from the beginning, part of the original group.

CHAPTER 3

Reading List

The reading list I made up is mostly centered on the forties and fifties. The most interesting literary material begins in the forties. A lot of the most famous like *On the Road* and a lot of Kerouac's great matters are done from the early fifties on. Actually the Beat Generation as it was known as a social phenomenon didn't start until about 1958 or 1959 and so there's all that literature when it surfaces and becomes public. Then there's the continued work of Kerouac and Burroughs, flowering in the sixties. My own work comes toward some kind of climax with "Kaddish" in the early sixties. Whatever transformation socially took place in the sixties, [as well as the] development of Cassady's work and transformation of that is in the sixties, or seventies, perhaps. A lot of Gregory Corso's major work comes through in the mid-sixties also. Then there's a whole period of re-consideration and re-creation and re-flowering in the seventies. What we're involved in is something that is a consideration of a group of writers whose work continues on into the present.

There is what may seem like a random list of writers from Shakespeare through André Gide as well. These were all people that Burroughs or Kerouac or myself or others read as part of the ethos of the forties and fifties and were determining influences on Beat writing, like Dostoyevsky's novel *The Idiot,* Rimbaud's *Season in Hell,* Wolfe's American novels, Kafka's *Trial,* so what I'm giving you in a sense is a reading list of the stuff we read in the forties, mostly [books] handed to Kerouac and myself by Burroughs, plus a list of Beat writers of the present time.

CHAPTER 4

Visions

What we started with in the forties was a preoccupation with the literary inquisitiveness as to the nature of consciousness. There were key phrases like "supreme reality," or a "new vision," or in Burroughs's more laconic terminology, the last phrases of *Junkie*, "a final fix." There were visions, actual visions, like Gary Snyder's satori experience in 1948 in Portland, Oregon, or my own 1948 auditory hallucination of Blake's voice. Kerouac in his *Scripture of the Golden Eternity* mentions falling backwards in a breath-faint and seeing with his eyes closed some golden ash left over from existence. Burroughs in the preface to *Junkie* talks about an early adolescent experience of seeing little men walking around on a plateau on the moon or something. Cassady was constantly talking about simultaneity of consciousness [whereby] our ordinary minds generally had six simultaneous levels of reference going on at the same time. Peter Orlovsky had had some solitary, tearful vision of his own when the trees bowed down and talked to him around 1955. Gregory Corso reported from Greece in 1960 some taste of skinless light—a pretty good phrase—that indicated some gap that put the word "skinless" next to the word "light." The word "light" is always used in mystical experience, "skinless light" I never heard before, so that sounded authentic.

Everybody involved [in the Beat Generation] literarily had had some form of break in the ordinary nature of consciousness and experience or taste of a larger consciousness or satori of some sort. There always was, as the central preoccupation, concern with the very nature of consciousness and with what you could call visions or visionary experience. In the forties sometimes referred to by Yeats's term "unity of being." But how did we get cut off from natural mind? And was natural mind some kind of original Indian visionary state of consciousness?

We saw literature as a noble means of investigation of our own minds and our own natures and our own emotions. The poem, as Gregory puts it, is a probe, a probe into whatever—death, hair, army, mom, clowns, a probe into reality or unreality. And through the fifties, there had been among ourselves a use of teaching aids, supplementary aids and sacraments relating to change of consciousness. There was a lot of grass from the forties on, and from 1952 peyote, yagé, mescaline, and acid, all before 1960.

The word "rebellion" didn't come up until politically involved people came on the scene and began interpreting it in terms of Marxian and non-Marxian modes. I think it was Lawrence Lipton, in his book *The Holy Barbarians*,[23] who used the word "rebellion" and made a Marxian interpretation of what was going on, which completely missed the point. The notion of rebellion didn't come in at all. It wasn't a political or a social rebellion. There were social and political concomitants, or correlative applications, but the main thing was, what is the nature of hearing, smelling, tasting, seeing, thinking mind? What are the different modes of consciousness or modalities? What can you get out of a half-sleep or dream state in terms of writing or articulation? Kerouac kept books of dreams and I have enormous records of dreams going back to the forties, which are made into poems often.

We were interested in areas of consciousness, psychoanalytic anthropology, Spengler. You might say a rebellion against social form, a dissatisfaction with the stereotypes, thought forms, and modes of thinking that we learned in grammar school or something. Burroughs's constant preoccupation was: what was the consciousness of a psychopath? To find that out Burroughs tried to do second-story jobs or go down with robbers into the subway and roll drunks. I think he even prepared to hold up a store once, to find out what it felt like to be a psychopath, which he defined as someone without any kind of conscience at all. Somewhat like Raskolnikov with his murder in *Crime and Punishment*. Raskolnikov murders in order to see what it feels like to contact reality in some ultimate way.

In fact John Clellon Holmes wrote a long article, "This Is the Beat Generation,"[24] in which he brought up that Raskolnikov element of violence. That offended Kerouac, because Kerouac thought that the probe was much more interesting and impersonal and intimate and gentle and it didn't have to be involved with all that psychopathic nonsense, except in a very highly stylized, elegant, aristocratic way, perhaps like what Burroughs was investigating. But Burroughs is a special character, so that was all right. Because anything Bill did was intelligent and if he tried to hold up somebody in the subway it was sure that he'd fail and make a fool of himself anyway. It would turn into some sort of W. C. Fieldsian comedy, and he certainly wouldn't hurt anybody. He might want to, but he wouldn't be able to. He was too much of a Faustian coward.

The motif of Beat Generation is basically misunderstood, a misinterpreted area. There's this superimposition of the idea of a social rebellion, which was the communist interpretation through Lawrence Lipton. This was kind of single level and rationalistic. That's the *Time* magazine view, that it could be interpreted as the psychopathy of millions of middle-class kids trying to kick their parents in the teeth, rebelling against wearing shoes, wanting to have dirty hair and bedbugs. Holmes interpreted it in a sociological, psychological way, not a Marxian way, as Raskolnik rebellion, *acte gratuit,* as Raskolnikov's murder of the old lady is a gratuitous act, an unreasonable, accidental act, a chance act, an act that you do because it just doesn't make any sense so it interrupts the normal common sense of life and confronts you with the blood of reality unto murder as in Dostoyevsky.

My view was that that was very unsophisticated, that Raskolnikov was very stupid, very unhip. The *acte gratuit* seemed to be very square, because it was relying on a set of ideas, because he thought he didn't contact reality and he thought theoretically he could contact by murder. It sounded like a totally square notion, unmellow, relying completely on some kind of upside-down school teacher logic. Burroughs had a certain interest in that from the point of view of chance, but I don't think Burroughs ever got all the way into Raskolnik experiment for the sake of some moral contact with ultimate reality. We were subtle enough to realize that that was heavy-handed, obnoxious pushiness. Kerouac and Burroughs and I also had a sense of good manners, I mean, you just don't go up to someone and murder them because you want to contact reality. It's ridiculous, thinking you're going to contact reality that way. Maybe you shouldn't contact reality, if that's the way you got to go.

We had all had some vision of supreme reality, a break in the nature of ordinary consciousness, which revealed a vaster consciousness than any *acte gratuit.* The universe is bigger than mind, bigger than idea, bigger than category, bigger than our conceptions. We all appreciated that early. And so I always felt very timid about imposing my ideology on the universe. Nobody thought that ideas meant anything, quite rightly I think. Ideas were just formulations. To attempt to encounter or confront the vastness of all the shadows on every leaf on one single tree with some sentence of ideas is immeasurably stupid. The element of aggression, of ideological insistency, was considered unhip and by unhip I mean lacking in awareness.

Our basic search for some kind of original mind, or heart-mind, was not in that sense rebellion at all, although in the search for a larger heart or larger mind, naturally some social conventions would be broken. The whole problem was to come to some original relationship with mind and with compassion and with sympathy, to come to a direct awareness rather than doing it because it said so here in a book or in society. Half of the rules of society are war rules anyway, uncompassionate. Even the good ones like "do unto others" very often are applied abusively, so social convention was no guideline for how to guide yourself out of your heart sympathies.

There was a notion that if we could arrive at some condition of total sensory openness, eye, ear, taste, smell, touch, mind, if all senses were alert and open, then there would be a simultaneity of noticing of detail, some kind of scheme or web that would approximate visionary coherence. So we had some primitive notions like that, of total illumination. And we also had some experiences of it with a little peyote, a lot of grass, the experience of the daydream, and the dream labyrinth of opiates, which is a classical experience in Baudelaire and De Quincey and other writers going back probably to Asiatic philosophers.

I want to emphasize *that* as the iron theme that runs through the forties, fifties, sixties, and seventies. The same theme was being pursued by various different tactics, methods, and explorations of different areas. By 1958 we had all concluded that drugs, peyote, psychedelics were interesting and were useful aids, but they weren't supreme reality. They were maybe catalysts. Acid, grass might be a catalyst to some sort of a reminder of an eternal mind, but not a satisfactory conclusion to the search. [Mainly because] you have to keep taking drugs all the time. Certainly for people who are sitting around in a state of inertia, or in a state of stereotyped moralistic mentality, it's a good thing to drop acid. That's why during the sixties I was interested in acid as a way of getting everybody in America a little bit hip, for opening up mind. At least you get a sense of that relative nature.

CHAPTER 5

Jazz, Bebop, and Music

There's some music I'd like to recommend also. Listen to Brahms's Trio No. 1 and Brahms's Sextet, Mahler's Symphony No. 1 with the "Frère Jacques" theme, some forties music, Thelonious Monk's "Round About Midnight," one little tune and any of the early forties Thelonious Monk, some of the forties Dizzy Gillespie, like "Salt Peanuts," "Opp Bop Sh'Bam." They have those little funny bebop rhythm prosodies in them. "The Chase" by Dexter Gordon, and Wardell Gray. Lester Young of that era, "Lester Leaps In." Billie Holiday's "Don't Explain," "Fine and Mellow," "I Cover the Waterfront," and "Yesterdays." If you get a chance at hearing some bass work by Slam Stewart and some of the mouthings, the bebop mouthings with words, by King Pleasure. And whatever early Lennie Tristano records you can find. Also a favorite inspirational tune that turned Cassady on to some ecstatic American mind, Charlie Barnet's "Cherokee," which is the thirties and then in the forties, The Honeydrippers and I think it was Louis Jordan's version of "Open the Door, Richard." And anything you find of Charlie Parker's from the forties is fine.

I've mentioned these people because these were specific totemistic pieces of music that either Kerouac, Cassady, Burroughs, or myself had inside our heads, 1943 to 1947. If you look at the liner notes on the albums or look it up in books, you can go on from there. King Pleasure was interesting because he was one of the few people who took Charlie Parker music and simply took syllables and by following each note he made actual sentences, poetic sentences. It promised to develop into a whole genre, but I don't think it ever did, [maybe] because the bop itself got more and more complicated and was harder to speak, to sing as sentences.

In a sense, Seymour Wyse, a friend of Jack Kerouac's who taught Kerouac jazz, said that he thought that bop killed itself or jazz killed itself with bop. That was his vision then, because bop had gotten so complex that it had gotten out of the range of simple blues melody. It seemed at that time that King Pleasure was mouthing at the limit as Charlie Parker was making bird note–flighted melodic lines. King Pleasure seemed to be able to follow that and hear it, and syllable by syllable make poems out of it.

CHAPTER 6

Music, Kerouac, Wyse, and Newman

We're actually starting in 1938 or 1939 [when] Jack Kerouac's best friend at Horace Mann High School was an English jazz fanatic, Seymour Wyse. In the late 1930s they went to Harlem to hear Thelonious Monk and Dizzy Gillespie and Charlie Parker playing at Minton's. When I first came on to that scene about 1944, Kerouac introduced me to Wyse. Seymour was working down in the Village in the Chelsea Record Shop with Jerry Newman, a completely unknown personage of that time. Newman himself was central to the development of a lot of literary articulations later on. He and Wyse taught Kerouac about early bop and jazz, took him up to the clubs. Newman had a record company called Esoteric Records, which recorded Monk and Parker and Gillespie and Charlie Christian. He turned Kerouac on to uptown bop in an intimate way since Jerry knew the musicians well, and recorded them. They weren't just Horace Mann kids going up and hanging around on the outside, they were involved with the musicians, often drinking and talking with them.

Newman also contributed to Burroughs's literary development. Burroughs credits Jerry Newman with the inspiration for his sense of routines and cut-ups. Newman had a fantastic collection of weird tapes, like the famous one that Burroughs picked up on, the drunken newscaster. A BBC newscaster was drunk and was reading the news, making a lot of slips, like "Princess Margaret spent a pleasant weekend inside her parents at Balmoral Castle." That was the one sentence I remember which turned Burroughs on to the idea of what might happen if you said in public what you said in private. What if the private and unconscious broke through into the public and people wrote as they thought? What if truth broke out in the media, or even in the novel? So the drunken newscaster was one of Burroughs's earliest turn-ons in his whole literary method. Doctor Benway comes out of that.

Kerouac's early education in New York was with Seymour Wyse and Jerry Newman. When I first met Kerouac we used to go down to talk to Seymour and he would play us whatever was around, newly issued records of Charlie Parker or Lester Young. We had access to a lot of music, actually a whole record store back in 1944. To the extent that Kerouac's biography is involved with music and bop and to the extent that Kerouac's prose is a reflection of his study of Charlie Parker's rhythms and breath, to the extent that Kerouac's prose style is derived from that, Seymour Wyse would be the big influence. Wyse and Kerouac used to riff together, verbally, and sing along with a lot of the records that Wyse played in the store.

All that experience of the exhalation of breath spirit in bop music was, according to Kerouac, the determinant influence on his prose and poetry style, particularly in pieces like "Brakeman on the Railroad," the first manuscript of *On the Road,* a lot of the long passages of *Visions of Cody,* and long passages of *Old Angel Midnight.* That was all determined by about 1943 or 1944, that is, his ear was determined by then. It wasn't yet reflected in his writing. In *The Town and the City* he didn't really use the long breath, variable noted line, that was later described as a bird flight, like Charlie Parker, until he started his spontaneous writing style with *On the Road*. There were evidences of it before in the later chapters about Times Square in *The Town and the City*. You get some echo of bebop consciousness and bebop paranoia and amphetamine and Benzedrine use in the city part of [that book].

"Lester Leaps In" by Lester Young was the theme song of Symphony Sid, who was the all-night bebop radio disc jockey of the early forties. He had a funny professional bebop hippie tone of voice that enters into Kerouac's prose. Kerouac [made] a recording in which he imitates Symphony Sid's tone of voice as a professional announcer, announcing his latest novel or his latest vision.

Dizzy Gillespie's "Salt Peanuts" and "Opp Bop Sh'Bam" are important because that particular rhythm "salt peanuts, salt peanuts" runs through Kerouac's prose. When I use the phrase "spontaneous bop prosody," I'm thinking of "salt peanuts, salt peanuts," or some squiggle of rhythm in Kerouac's head that follows that odd accenting, the irregular accenting, the noniambic accenting of Gillespie.

By then the drum and the bass, the rhythm instruments, had become solo instruments, so that instead of a metronomic rhythmic base, stereotyped and automatic as were iambic pentameter or even symmetrical count of stress, instead there was a new variable accenting, a new variable measure, a new variable beat. A new variable rhythm section rather than the traditional rhythm section in old-time Dixieland or jazz.

It was precisely at that time that William Carlos Williams was introducing the notion of the variable measure of speech in poetics while saxophonists such as Lester Young and Charlie Parker and trumpeters such as Dizzy Gillespie and later Miles Davis were doing the same thing in jazz. The saxophone echoed the breath of speech and it was as if it was speaking in accents of conversation or excited rhapsodic talk. There was an element introduced into music of the actual voice as spoken through the saxophone or trumpet that echoed the oddities of rhythm of black speech. This was important to Kerouac because it influenced his prose line.

It seemed to culminate in the sixties and seventies with Ornette Coleman, who extended the speech to include "Aee aee," a completely open-throated mantric expression of black voice, or Don Cherry, who is blowing human voice through his trumpet. In other words, speech went into the saxophone rhythms and phrasings and long breath was manifested, a funny long sentence breath ending "moop" was manifested through the saxophone breath. That's audible in Lester Young and Charlie Parker and somewhat in Gillespie's horn. Kerouac then drew from those accents, phrasings, rhythms, and patterns of breath for his prose.

Now William Carlos Williams wasn't listening to this, he was listening to common pattern Rutherford speech, ordinary talk. People saying, "I've eaten the plums which you left in the icebox and which you were probably saving for breakfast, forgive me, they were delicious, so sweet and so cold." But the musicians were talking to each other on the street, so jazz is more like urban street talk with very stylized gestures and accents. They were getting it from and feeding it into the music. This was Kerouac's conscious theory beginning in the 1940s and he applied it in some passages of *The Town and the City* and consciously applied it later in *Mexico City Blues*. This was the basis of his style and these are key to all of his writings thenceforth, just little classic three-minute songs that went in and out of everybody's ears including his.

The musicians were imitating the humor of actual speech phrasing and transferring it right into the music and taking inspiration for the musical phrasing and rhythm from human speech. They refreshed the whole mainstream of American jazz with the rhythms of actual talk just as the mainstream of American poetry, through William Carlos Williams, was being refreshed, rhythmically, through the hearing and imitation of actual spoken speech. It was all going on simultaneously. There was nothing more American than jazz, and in American poetry nothing more American than Williams.

There's such a close parallel between the music and the poetics that I think you can hear it. At the time it was consciously commented on by the musicians themselves. This seems to lead up to someone vocalizing bebop lines, someone going around the other end and taking the bebop lines and putting them syllable by syllable to poetry. Which is what Mr. King Pleasure did.

These records were almost instantaneously played and caught public attention, first by the cognoscenti of jazz, but pretty soon [everyone was saying] "ooo-bop sha-bam" and "google mop" was appearing in *Dick Tracy*. It introduced a whole new element of relaxed hip speech. Charlie Parker is probably the closest to Kerouac's deep soul and sound, in the sense that he took this kind of variable rhythmic base, exhalation, breath inspiration into highly imaginative flights of rhythm. They rainbow-arced over the chorus in a birdlike flight, including anything the mind could think of that would be harmonically correct, or harmonically pretty or weird, like "oonk," which he included in the saxophone sentence. At Kerouac's best, he wanted his rhythm to be a long flighty sentence sounding like Parker's "Ornithology" or [Gillespie's] "Night in Tunisia." Probably that very moment was for Kerouac the acme of bop and the acme of that kind of phrasing and statement. It was reflected in Kerouac's "239th" and "241st Choruses" of *Mexico City Blues,* written eight or ten years later after he first heard it on Symphony Sid.

239th Chorus

Charley Parker Looked like Buddha,
Charley Parker, who recently died
Laughing at a juggler on the TV
after weeks of strain and sickness,
was called the Perfect Musician.
And his expression on his face
Was as calm, beautiful, and profound
As the image of the Buddha
Represented in the East, the lidded eyes,
The expression that says "All is Well"
—This was what Charley Parker
Said when he played, All is Well.
You had the feeling of early-in-the-morning
Like a hermit's joy, or like
                    the perfect cry
Of some wild gang at a jam session
"Wail, Wop"—Charley burst
His lungs to reach the speed
Of what the speedsters wanted
And what they wanted
Was his Eternal Slowdown.
A great musician and a great
                    creator of forms
That ultimately find expression
In mores and what have you.

That was Kerouac's later comment on those two particular solos,
particularly the toot that wailed off onto little bird flight in "Night
in Tunisia."

Next, Kerouac the philosopher, whose slow, dumb, brilliant philosophy, the meditator, was influenced by Thelonious Monk in "Round About Midnight." The quality in that is the thoughtful simplicity, single notes, just cutting corners, abstracting the melody to its essential blueness and just playing those blue notes. There's a kind of philosophic calm as distinct from Parker's hyperexcited flight. It's as if the key notes were extracted from the curve of the flight and just "plonk plonk plonk plonk bonk" put in place in right rhythmic order, just a little bit off or on, just a little bit hesitant in or after the exact bar time. In Monk's thoughtful composition of "Mysterioso" there is a kind of mysterious quality of laconic intervention in the chords. He just makes a comment here and there at the crucial moment of tune transition.

So far we have the instrumental, now language. The blues always were a great poetry. The great poetess of blues Billie Holiday was also a famous lover of Lester Young. Both of them were junkies, so they reflected the whole junkie-hip consciousness, the world-weary disillusionment, and at the same time a kind of homosexual sentimentality nostalgia of beautiful lesbians of yore, or bisexual sentimentality of beautiful lesbians of yore. Unfulfilled Eros, which I think historically signals that ripeness of desire which preceded the sexual revolution. It was the direct and frank emotional expression of so much feeling and so much tenderness denied, body touch unmade, that led finally to some kind of breakthrough where people finally said, "Well, why not?" On all levels, heterosexual revolution and homosexual revolution and bisexual revolution and lesbian revolution. There's a peculiar quality of mournfulness and nostalgia and desire mixed in that, which affected everybody in the 1940s.

The one who was the most affected by it was Herbert Huncke, who was an instructor to both Burroughs and Kerouac for their hip voyages and explorations of Times Square. His favorite records of Billie Holiday were "Lover Man," "Don't Explain," and "I Cover the Waterfront." The last one interesting because symbolically that low-down trip to the waterfront, the docks in New York, that she describes, the blues of the docks, the blues under the bridges, was directly associated in Kerouac's mind with Hart Crane and Kerouac's own associations as a seaman. His early novel was *The Sea Is My Brother,* never published,[25] so Billie Holiday's "I Cover the Waterfront" was a major icon of the Beat litterateur's mid-forties.

Holiday's "Don't Explain" is the acme of junkie forgiveness and tolerance. You just beat me for my junk and you stole my stash, hush now don't explain. I don't need any explanations, just love me some more and don't leave me. It's that junkie masochism, but it's the crowning statement of early junkie forgiveness and tolerance of any trespass against the body and soul. There's an element of the beat-down-dog persecuted junkie in police state morality there, which is probably one of the original Beat themes and perceptions. The law's been changed since, but it was one of the causes of "Beatness" that produced a psychology of looking at society from the grave up, or from the ground up, looking from the underside, beyond society's conceptions of good and evil, which in those days in matters of human emotion, sexuality, and poetry, censorship, and drugs were medieval compared to what common judgment and opinion offers now as standard understanding.

You couldn't read *Lady Chatterley's Lover* and you couldn't read Henry Miller in those days. Things like that were banned, illegal. You couldn't smoke any grass without being thought a dope fiend, literally, that was the language, fiend. A variety of citizen called fiends had been invented by one of the bureaucracies of the government and Billie Holiday was one of the people that were officially classified as fiends. A producer of all this intelligence and beauty and music and melancholy and sprightliness of language, and she was officially classified as a fiend. There was a revolutionary insight into the hallucinatory nature of official government classifications and terminology. It came from the experience of junkies, sick in love with their own fidelities, nostalgias, comradeships, and arts, under circumstances that by hindsight seem as cruel as Jean Valjean being pursued by his demonic policeman, Inspector Javert, in *Les Misérables*. I mean that's an old classic of a hurt right and wrong. In the 1940s and 1950s that hurt was not recognizable except by those who are down under the heel of the law.

Last of all was King Pleasure who isn't a great like these other artists, but he's one that brought a lot of things to the poetic table [when] he started writing words for the beautiful solos that the musicians were making. His "Moody's Blues" is a verbal vocalization of a saxophone solo by James Moody, which King Pleasure set words to and sang. So what he's singing are words of a saxophone solo that he'd heard.

There were other things similar like Slam Stewart, a bassist, who hummed sweatingly along with his bowed bass, so that you would have syllables coming from his mouth at the same time as very complicated bass figurations. The point I am making is that the musician was expressing some kind of language, talk, and then it was re-expressed from his instrument back into talk. You see how close it is to somebody actually talking with the same kind of rhythms as speech. It's actual American speech that was being vocalized by the saxophones and then retranslated into black English.

There was a slightly apocalyptic element at the time in all this breakthrough of new sound, new music, new rhythms, or as the great Socratic statement goes, "When the mode of the music changes, the walls of the city shake." That did introduce a new way of hearing, a new body rhythm. And they continued that tradition of scat singing swift-syllabled echoing of instrumental solos. You can see already a real conscious correlation of the new music in America with poetics or prose.

> Oh the pots and pans the racket of their fear, the kitchen of the sea, the Neptunes down here, the herds of sea cows wanta milk us, the sea poem I aint finished with, the fear of the Scottish laird rowing out with a nape of another fox' neck in the leeward shirsh of S H A O W yon Irish Sea! The sea of her lip! The brattle of her Boney! The crack of Noah's Ark timbers built by Mosaic Schwarts in the unconditional night of Universal death.[26]

CHAPTER 7

Times Square and the 1940s

For Kerouac's accounts of New York City in the forties, you'd have to check out the sections on New York and Times Square in *The Town and the City*. That's among the best writing in that book. He's hit his stride in that. What he was trying to do was write a big bildungsroman, like Thomas Mann's *Buddenbrooks,* a family novel that dealt with generations and social history. His big inspiration was Thomas Wolfe, as far as American prose, so it was a Wolfean-style novel. He was reading a lot of Thomas Mann, and he had read a lot of Sherwood Anderson and a lot of Hemingway, and mainly Wolfe, some Thoreau. During the time he was writing, he first picked up, through Burroughs, on the prose by Louis-Ferdinand Céline and probably around the mid-forties through Burroughs some Proust, Gide, and Céline. Anderson he'd read himself, Thomas Wolfe he picked up himself.

In *The Town and the City* Kerouac splits up his own nature, and his family, into a number of brothers and sisters, describing the history of the family in small-town Galloway, pretty accurate to his own experience in Lowell.

The Town and the City begins with a study of family life in the small town, moves to the city where the family breaks up, then winds up fragmented in Brooklyn. The hero, Peter Martin, ends up walking around Times Square with strange interesting characters, or people that he'd met up at Columbia or people that he'd met in Horace Mann.[27] Kerouac's mind was already ripened and matured by 1947, his worldview had been determined. His loneliness had been established, his awareness of death had come on him because he'd sat with his father and watched his father die, which is probably the central love experience of his life, the central drama. And so *The Town and the City* is about that death of his father. His father died embittered and angry, apparently.

Originally it was a Gnostic search. Then, when Kerouac's father died, I think Jack realized the basic mortal transitoriness. Mutable sorrow of existence. And so he got interested in becoming the recording angel of the dream scene, and began recording his dreams, literally, as well as the dream of life itself. He was the recording angel of the dream of life, knowing that it was nothing but a dream. By means of swimming in the seas of prose, he would arrive at a satisfactory vision of life for the benefit of other people. In *Visions of Cody* he has a note as to why he's writing. "I'm writing this book because we're all going to die" is how it begins. He's got the line, "In the middle of the dream my heart broke open, or my heart opened inwardly to the lord." It's a form of prayer, actually, for Kerouac it was prayer. Supplication to the lord and a prayer. It was spiritual but it was much more romantic and devotional and ended up Catholic devotional. Then for the period of 1953 to 1955 when he was undergoing Buddhist inspiration it was to wake people up from the dream of nightmare existence.

Jack didn't have to pick anything to write about, he was in the midst of a life that was interesting enough and all he had to do was look around and write about his life, he didn't have to invent a literature. We were writing at that time in the direction of what later in poetry came to be called confessional or in prose new journalism, or a novel based on autobiography. We just looked around and took reality as the subject of the novel. There were precursors who had already realized that fiction in a sense was already dead. Or the kind of fiction that people used to practice, making up a big, huge fictional novel. Kerouac did it and did a very brilliant job with *The Town and the City,* but then he plunged directly into writing about the people he loved in his next book.

It's all recorded in *The Town and the City.* Kerouac is out on his own in New York wandering Times Square with postwar apocalyptic-minded characters. Mystic heads, dope fiends, sex freaks, new nature hippies. A central figure [that he meets] there is Herbert Huncke. Burroughs talks about him in his book *Junkie* as Herman, so you can cross-reference them.

When we get to Burroughs we'll cover his view of Times Square in the forties. It will intersect with Kerouac's *The Town and the City.* It was a time when Kerouac and Burroughs and myself were hanging around in the company of Herbert Huncke, who was a hustler, denizen, and part-time junkie. Huncke was also an employee of Doctor Alfred Kinsey, who was hanging around Times Square taking statistical material on the sex life of the vagabond population. Huncke was one of his agents scouting, getting people to interview. And among the people that were interviewed for the original Kinsey Report were Herbert Huncke, William Burroughs, Jack Kerouac, and myself. It was a funny historical coincidence.

Huncke is quite an interesting writer and he influenced Burroughs and Kerouac. He was a figure in Kerouac's writing mind, Burroughs's and John Clellon Holmes's as well. Encouraged by all of us, he wrote quite a few stories which are authentically good, they're like Sherwood Anderson or something, American primitive, but so direct and in such perfect spoken language that, for me, they've always been classics, but not well known.

I would say that Times Square was the central hangout for Burroughs, Kerouac, and myself from about 1945 to 1948. It was probably the most formative period of early Spenglerian mind, where that language of zap, hip, square, beat was provided over the Bickford's cafeteria tables[28] by Huncke. I would say Herbert Huncke is the basic originator of the notion of Beat Generation or notion of the ethos of Beat and of the conceptions of Beat and square, what they meant in our mouths were more or less what they meant in his mouth, because we heard it from him. I never heard the word "hip" until I heard him talking. So actually, Huncke, a man of no fortune, is a minor but seminal figure both in vocabulary and in attitudes. In fact I would say he probably is the person from whom that whole stylization and vocabulary, later known as hip including the very word "Beat," emerged.

Huncke spent the 1930s in Chicago, came to New York, and was there about five years when Burroughs moved down to an apartment over Riordan's Bar on Eighth Avenue. His purpose was to explore Eighth Avenue, the gambler's and honky-tonk bars around Madison Square Garden nearby, the old men's bars, the hustler's bars, the junkie and teahead and narc agent's bars, social meeting places around Times Square. All the hustlers from 42nd Street, the car thieves, second-story men, burglars who were trying to unload hot goods, people trying to sell grass, junkies coming in and out to score, undercover narcs trying to keep track on everybody, young kids who couldn't make it with the rodeo, black chauffeurs who smoked grass and listened to Charlie Parker and read Kahlil Gibran stopped there, Columbia students like myself or Kerouac or a few other people, old schmekers like Bill Garver who made his living and supported his junk habit by stealing overcoats from Horn & Hardart[29]—all used to come into the Angler Bar.[30] Kerouac describes them in *The Town and the City*.

At that time, Times Square was built for amphetamine heads and hustlers because there was a Horn & Hardart and a Bickford's which had tables where hustlers and junkies could sit with a cup of coffee all night talking. They were pretty much unbothered under the marquee of the Apollo Theatre,[31] which was showing Jean Gabin in *Le Quai des Brumes* (*Port of Shadows*), or Peter Lorre in *M,* or *Children of Paradise, The Blood of the Poet*. The great Jean Gabin series influenced Kerouac enormously, hairy-wristed masculine Gabin who was a man's man, but with tenderness and sensitivity, so it had appealed to Kerouac's nature, as distinct from overly macho American with no delicacy.

All the Times Square hustlers were looking at those movies. The lumpen criminals were going to see *Metropolis* and *M*, and then able to stay up all night and dunk coffee with shiny blackened dirty fingers. There's a little scene in Burroughs's *Naked Lunch* which takes place in Bickford's in which the young hustler is dunking his pound cake, and a description of "black and shiny fingers." He's just had a meet with a john who took him to a hotel room and got him in bed and turned into some green slimy clammy creature exuding cum all over him, and the hustler says, "Well, I guess you can get used to anything, I got a date with him tomorrow."

I would say that those days were the diamond point of our youthful opening up and probably the most determining experience. The aspect of eternality that was most noticeable was the sky, the openness of the sky above the cornices of the buildings. For the first time in my consciousness, I noticed the red apocalyptic glow in the sky caused by the neon lights. It gave a kind of garish, Technicolor intensity to the very heavens we were walking under. It made it seem like some biblical scene, the last of days or pre-apocalyptic moments when there was a buildup of electrical emphasis under the stars.

At that time almost everybody was eating Benzedrine inhalers. You could get Benzedrine by opening up an inhaler and then swallowing it with a cup of coffee. The effect was very fast and lasted for eight hours or so, very strong. Kerouac was using Benzedrine when he wrote some of the later passages of *The Town and the City*. Around 1945 I started using amphetamine, too, for writing. Amphetamine was introduced onto the scene by a friend of Herbert Huncke, Vicki [Russell]. [She] was a girl who hustled around Times Square, a statuesque, very intelligent girl, partly dyke, partly hustler. Vickie turned both Burroughs and Kerouac on to the Benzedrine inhalers and then Kerouac reported back to me and I found it useful for writing for a while. I'd take it and write for a whole weekend, until the writing turned to gibberish toward Sunday night.

There are pictures of all those people in *The Town and the City* and there are also some visions of Times Square and that red light above. There was a Pokerino place, which had an undersea, subterranean, greenish blue light, open all night. People would go in there and play the pinball machines with an amphetamine intensity, getting deeper and deeper into the fluorescent consciousness around them. There's a picture of that in *The Town and the City* and that would intersect with some of *Junkie,* some of *On the Road,* and some of *Visions of Cody*. In *Lonesome Traveler,* Kerouac also describes Times Square in a section called "New York Scenes."

My friends and I in New York city have our own special way of having fun without having to spend much money and most important of all without having to be importuned by formalistic bores,

such as, say, a swell evening at the mayor's ball.—We dont have
to shake hands and we dont have to make appointments and we
feel all right.—We sorta wander around like children.—We walk
into parties and tell everybody what we've been doing and people
think we're showing off.—They say: "Oh look at the beatniks!"[32]

Esquire asked Kerouac to write about entertainment in New York,
but it was too difficult and too boring. Then Jack said, "Wouldn't it
be fun if we just wrote about hanging around on the streets and going
to Times Square, because the articles usually are about going to the
Pavillion[33] for supper or the Playboy Club, or something elegant?"
So we decided we would write about an authentic evening on Times
Square.

> Take, for example, this typical evening you can have: —
> Emerging from the Seventh Avenue subway on 42nd Street, you
> pass the john, which is the beatest john in New York—

This *Esquire* article is to open with a big description of the subway john as one of the major sights of New York, which it was if
you wanted to get in touch with what was going on under the skin.

you never can tell if it's open or not, usually there's a big chain in
front of it saying it's out of order, or else it's got some white-haired
decaying monster slinking outside, a john which all seven million people in New York City have at one time passed, and taken
strange notice of—past the new charcoal-fried-hamburger stand,
Bible booths, operatic jukeboxes, and a seedy underground used-
magazine store next to a peanut-brittle store smelling of subway
arcades—here and there a used copy of that old bard Plotinus

sneaked in with the remainders of collections of German high-school textbooks—where they sell long ratty-looking hotdogs (no, actually they're quite beautiful, particularly if you havent got 15 cents and are looking for someone in Bickford's Cafeteria who can lay some smash on you) (lend you some change).—

Coming up that stairway, people stand there for hours and hours drooling in the rain, with soaking wet umbrellas—lots of boys in dungarees scared to go into the Army standing half-way up the stairway on the iron steps waiting for God Who knows what, certainly among them some romantic heroes just in from Oklahoma with ambitions to end up yearning in the arms of some unpredictable sexy young blonde in a penthouse on the Empire State Building—some of them probably stand there dreaming of owning the Empire State Building by virtue of a magic spell which they've dreamed up by a creek in the backwoods of a ratty old house on the outskirts of Texarkana.— Ashamed of being seen going into the dirty movie (what's its name?) across the street from the New York *Times*—The lion and the tiger passing, as Tom Wolfe used to say about certain types passing that corner.—

Leaning against that cigar store with a lot of telephone booths on the corner of 42nd and Seventh where you make beautiful telephone calls looking out into the street and it gets real cozy in there when it's raining outside and you like to prolong the conversation, who do you find? Basketball teams? Basketball coaches? All those guys from the rollerskating rink go there? Cats from the Bronx again, looking for some action, really looking for romance? Strange duos of girls coming out of dirty movies? Did you ever see them? Or bemused drunken businessmen with their hats tipped awry on their graying heads staring catatonically upward at the signs

floating by on the Times Building, huge sentences about Khrushchev reeling by, the populations of Asia enumerated in flashing
lightbulbs, always five hundred periods after each sentence.—
Suddenly a psychopathically worried policeman appears on the
corner and tells everybody to go away.—This is the center of the
greatest city the world has ever known and this is what beatniks
do here.—"Standing on the street corner waiting for no one is
Power," sayeth poet Gregory Corso.

Instead of going to night clubs—if you're in a position to make
the nightclub scene (most beatniks rattle empty pockets passing
Birdland)—[34]

He's using "beatniks" here consciously because I think the *Esquire*
editors said, "Well, now, give us a beatnik New York," because there
was a good deal of media publicity about beatniks of such garish
nature that Jack thought that it would be charming to write an essay
on beatniks' appreciation of the shades of subway paint.

The word "beatnik" was coined by Herb Caen, a gossip colum-
nist in the *San Francisco Chronicle*, at the time of Sputnik, because
the Beat poets were supposed to be so far out of this world, like the
Sputnik. Immediately a whole race of beatniks arose. Somewhat of
a Frankenstein image, beatniks, the idea of Big Daddy and kill your
mother in the bathtub, unwashed hair, bearded, crab lice, angry at
the government and angry at their parents, living in filth, not making their beds, stealing, ax murderers, that whole genre up unto the
elegant horror of Mansonism. The beatnik wave bugged Kerouac
because people would come up to him and say that they could drive
faster than Neal Cassady and get him in their car and try to kill him.
There's a generation of people who thought that "beatnik" meant
angry at the world rather than weeping at the world.

This was written in 1960 and described wandering around New York in the late 1950s with some flashbacks to the 1940s. It has all grown old now. At this point, Kerouac's just writing with a certain sardonic nostalgia, almost making fun of it. His original impression of Times Square was of a big room, which is a concept we shared. "It was some kind of appreciation of space itself that was our earliest intimation of Dharma Kia." The world hanging in space, the skyscrapers hanging in space. The key was the vision of the enormous roof of sky above the cornices of the buildings. If you became conscious of standing in that great room and looked about you, you'd see this handiwork of intelligence in every direction. And you'd realize you were not standing in New York City but you were standing in the middle of the universe, the vast open sky. It's that awareness of himself in space that characterizes Kerouac's work, mine somewhat, and the whole Beat period of the forties. It was the first discovery of a crack in consciousness, that we were made of the same suchness, that we were ghosts.

The climax of *On the Road* for me is when they're coming back from Mexico, and there's this sudden vision of the Shrouded Stranger on the road, saying "Ooo." It is the key and most visionary moment in *On the Road*, because it's a poetic apparition in the midst of all that romantic naturalism. All of a sudden there's a little Faustian figure, Doctor Sax walking on the road. It's the hint of time and death and egolessness and woe, the first noble truth [of Buddhism]. The phantom says, "Go moan for man," the truth of suffering. We knew that something great was happening and all I could say was "wow." "Wow" finally becomes the mantra for the whole book. There's this early hint in *On the Road* of mind which is already Buddhist-oriented. Appreciating the phantom nature of beings, of ourselves, an awareness of the mortal, "Go moan for man."

CHAPTER 8

Carr, Ginsberg, and Kerouac at Columbia

I was living in the Union Theological Seminary at 122nd Street and Broadway in the second half of my freshman year at Columbia. I had been housed at the seminary with a few roommates because the college [dorms] were filled with V-12 sailors.[35] I was in my room after having been there several weeks and heard Brahms's Trio No. 1, which I never heard before, coming from a room across the hall. It's a classical Brahms piece with a kind of romantic haunting melody. So I went out to find the source of the music, knocked, and the door was opened by the most angelic-looking kid I ever saw, blond hair, pale, "Hollow of cheek as though it drank the wind and took a mess of shadows for its meat."[36] He was Lucien Carr, a St. Louis friend of Burroughs, and he had become a close friend of Kerouac. Lucien had been kicked out of a lot of private schools and finally landed at Columbia [where he] hung around the West End bar. He drank a lot of beer and knew a funny girl named Edie [Parker], who was living with Kerouac at the time in an apartment near the Columbia campus. Edie introduced Lucien to Kerouac who had just come back from a trip in the Merchant Marine where he'd been up past Greenland and saw submarines and watched ships torpedoed. He had written his first novel, called *The Sea Is My Brother,* a mystical, heady-prose work. He had been reading a lot of Thomas Mann and Thomas Wolfe and so it had heavy Germanic symbolic prose. There wasn't much naturalistic plot, but a lot of prose poetry about the surface of the ocean, the stars at night, the bow of the ship lifting and falling, the romance of being a sailor, hidden mysterious angels under the waves, and great whales moaning in the north. Or at least something like that, something Gnostic and pretty.

Lucien had already met Jack and told me to go see him. I went up to the apartment one day and knocked on his door. I should explain I can't remember very clearly and specifically a lot of actual situations. I also found that things that Kerouac wrote about are not quite reliable either. He was a novelist, he invented little details, or condensed seasons, so that his account isn't quite accurate either, and in many instances I'm so recollective of his account that I think it's what actually happened when it's just his version of a story. I can't propose what I'm saying as authentic fact, but only as my recollections, [and] they have to be checked against other people's versions.

I went to see Jack at Lucien's suggestion, because I had a crush on Lucien and would go anywhere he suggested I go. He said there was this great, dark-haired, romantic seaman, who looked like Jack London, who wrote books about the sea, which sounded sensitive and great. So I went to see him with some trepidation because I had heard he was a big tough football player and I was a sensitive fairy from New Jersey with all sorts of romantic notions and a very soft vulnerable heart. I was capable of falling in love with anybody at a glance, but I hadn't told anybody that I was queer. I hadn't said anything about my love life to anybody because I was afraid I'd be rejected, afraid I'd be put down, just too timid, afraid of being ashamed. It seemed so delicate and personal and eccentric that if I did tell people what my love was like it might be like turning over a stone and seeing the worms underneath. Or if I did expose myself it might turn out that the reason for my being in love with men was something so shameful and horrible that it would be even worse than being in love with men.

Naturally I couldn't say what was on my mind at all. I might be swooning with delight inside but at the same time sitting there with a stiff back trying to maintain a conversation about politics and [act] smart. I walked into Kerouac's apartment where he was sitting eating his breakfast and said I was a friend of Lucien's. I don't remember what the conversation was, but he said something straightforward, like "Do you want a drink?" And I said, "No, no, discretion is the better part of valor," which is some little tagline I heard when I was twelve and when I didn't know what to say that's what I'd say.

Kerouac was a very mellow, shrewd, observant, tolerant person, so there was mutual curiosity. He saw my shallowness and I saw some of his gruffness. I was in love with Lucien [and] I also fell in love with Kerouac. I found that I could be in love with a lot of people at the same time, partly because it was never consummated, I didn't sleep with anybody, and I didn't even tell 'em. My romantic feeling for Lucien was so great and strong at the time that I thought it was some Goethean *Sorrows of Werther,* or final drama of life. I felt that same nostalgia for Kerouac. I mean they were very beautiful people, Kerouac was physically very beautiful as you can see from early photos, but psychologically, mentally, spiritually, and heartwise he was extraordinarily sensitive, very intelligent, very shrewd, and very compassionate. Compassionate toward the awkward kid.

Actually *Vanity of Duluoz* is Kerouac's last long book, but it [tells the story of] that period. It's one period that Jack never wrote about, partly out of respect for Lucien. He didn't want to invade Lucien's life with a biographical novel and it was only after decades and decades that everybody mellowed, matured, and calmed down. It is much different than what he would have written ten or twenty years earlier. Earlier [it] would have been a huge, romantic Dostoyevskean novel, *Vanity of Duluoz,* in which everybody's beauty was a vanity, everybody's tolerance was egotism. It's a late disillusioned version and a very precious one for that reason, because it's a view of youth seen from the advantage of illness and age and total realism, no longer clinging to the images and archetypes and loves of youth. Rather than being disadvantaged, that's really an advantage, because you can see from the other side of the grave then.

[Kerouac and I] walked to the Union Theological Seminary together. I was flattered that he would walk with me, was interested. On the way we got into a long conversation about the nature of phantoms and ghosts and our own melancholy about the ghost presence. I told him a story about when I was twelve or so, in Paterson, walking home at night from the movies. I would pass by the hedges of the church across the street from my house and my heart would ache thinking how mysterious the universe was, how lonely I was in it.

It was the first time that I ever went back and began appreciating the archetypal romance of child mind thought. Truly the first time I began talking from my own mind instead of saying "discretion is the better part of valor." So here I was actually talking out of my native mind, out of experience that was my own rather than of something I had read in a book, or thought I was supposed to say. It was nice, and he let me and was interested and curious. And he said, "Gee, I had thoughts like that all the time when I was in Lowell." He went on to say that he used to stand in the backyards at night when everybody was eating supper and realized that everybody was a ghost eating ghost food. Or that he was a ghost watching the living people.

At the Union Theological Seminary I pointed out that that was the door that I'd met Lucien at, and the music was Brahms's Trio. We had some kind of mutual understanding about it, that here was where I'd encountered some kind of beauty. As I turned from the dormitory suite, I bowed to it and made a gesture of farewell, saying "good-bye door."

We had a long excited conversation about other people who had that same awareness and [wondered if] everybody was like that. Of course everybody's like that, that's what everybody's heart is to the extent that they're conscious and sensitive. Everybody has the same soul, everybody is the same, really. So that was the basis of our understanding. It was a question of the melancholy that we felt, a sadness or pain at being lonesome and dying in the universe. Aware already of the suffering of it, aware of the transitoriness of it, the ghostly, phantom-like nature of it. New York City standing in eternity and then gone.

The teachers at that time around Columbia were Lionel Trilling, Mark Van Doren, Meyer Schapiro, and best of all Raymond Weaver. Trilling was a learned, elegant literary critic, who in a sense tried to revive the humanistic solidity and good manners of mid-nineteenth-century England. Trilling loved Lucien [Carr], and liked Kerouac and liked me a great deal, we were in his class. He was completely baffled by us. He probably thought I was crazy, because I was going downtown and hanging around with Huncke and Burroughs on Times Square. He liked me, but he worried that I was getting into some awful terrible problem with myself. Which I did. I wound up getting busted and going to jail and he had to help get me out.

Trilling didn't want to hear about Burroughs. It was probably my fault, I gave him such a romantically exaggerated version of hanging around Times Square, smoking marijuana with the hustlers and thieves, and Bill Burroughs as a Harvard graduate who's got the long needle in his arm like Dr. Mabuse.[37] So that probably scared Trilling off.

The other teachers around were Mark Van Doren, who wrote rhymed verse, much like Robert Frost, actually a good poet and a very good man. Later when I freaked out and got busted and was talking about having visionary experiences with [William] Blake and seeing light, Van Doren was able to understand and said, "Ah, well, can you describe the light?" He'd had some experience of his own and didn't freak out, but was curious and inquisitive about the nature of my experience. Whether hallucinatory or real, at least he was open to listen.

Van Doren's office mate at Columbia was a very rare character, hardly known to anybody nowadays, Raymond Weaver, author of the first biography of Herman Melville, *Herman Melville: Mariner and Mystic*. He discovered the manuscript of *Billy Budd* in a trunk. Weaver was a real scholar and had intelligence enough to pick up on Melville before Melville was known. To read *Pierre, or, The Ambiguities*, and the *Confidence-Man*, and all of Melville's great novels, and then search out manuscripts, like a good scholar should. Weaver was probably, in the terms of academic professorhood, the super professor of all professors in America. Kerouac took his early novel *The Sea Is My Brother* to Weaver who read it very sympathetically. Weaver had been in Japan and had used a Zen style [of] questioning in his class as part of his teaching technique, so Jack came away from Weaver with a list of books to read. That was the first introduction of mystical, Gnostic, zap-mind, Zen-style literature that we encountered.

There were a couple fairies on the faculty that were interesting, but mostly the tone was anti-Whitmanic. Whitman wasn't seriously taught. Much more attention then was being paid to John Crowe

Ransom and Allen Tate, and what are now known as academic poets. There was a definite put-down, a snob put-down, of Whitman. In the 1940s, William Carlos Williams was considered some kind of big provincial jerk, raw and crude. Nobody understood Ezra Pound's quantitative prosody and nobody understood what Williams was doing with his measure of American speech. He had the reputation within the avant-garde with Duchamp and the surrealists, but not within the academy. They were still stuck with "The Waste Land" and early Ezra Pound, probably as universities are now stuck with myself and [Charles] Olson.

I'm describing the fourth floor of Columbia College [which was the English Department], because the literary breakthrough that took place with Burroughs, myself, and Kerouac had to do with the literary old-fashionedness or conservatism of the English Department there. We were picking up on Genet, Céline, Shakespeare, Thomas Wyatt, Marvell, Milton, and Blake. I was having visions of Blake. We were reading Christopher Smart, Gregory [Corso] was reading Shelley and Keats, Edgar Allan Poe, Emily Dickinson (a crank in her room with funny squiggles), Melville's *Billy Budd,* and Melville as poet. None of the English majors ever heard of Melville as a poet. Thomas Wolfe, whom Thomas Mann thought was the greatest prose writer in America because of the symphonic power of his prose sentences, influenced Kerouac. At Columbia, Wolfe was considered to be some kind of loudmouth, just as many academics now consider Kerouac some kind of a nature boy dope. Rimbaud who Lucien was reading was introduced to the scene. Dostoyevsky who I had read and Kerouac had read, particularly his image of Prince Myshkin in *The Idiot,* [was important].

CHAPTER 9

Kerouac, Columbia, and *Vanity of Duluoz*

Kerouac's *Vanity of Duluoz* covers an early period but [was] written by late hindsight. Now as you know Kerouac was supposed to have become an old drunken stumblebum in the years before his death, incapable of any kind of artwork, totally disillusioned and screwed up. This book, with some of his finest prose and most curious hindsights, was written within a year of his death. This is one of his major novels and a departure from the romantic tradition.

Here's his hindsight on his youth, this is a little before the bebop era and then on into the forties, so I'll just run through the book picking out highlights. I'm bringing it up to point out that he did not decline as an artist and his late work is a necessary addition to the early romances. If you're going to have Kerouac, you also have to get the disillusioned Kerouac, because he's a wise man too, though a bitter one. His book is [subtitled] "An Adventurous Education."

The moral of what I'm saying is, as when I said "Adventurous Education," let a kid learn his own way, see what happens. You cant lead a horse to water. Just as I'm writing exactly what I remember according to the way that I want to remember in order, and not pile the reader with too much extraneous junk, so, let a kid pick out exactly what he wants to do in order not to grow up into a big bore rattling off the zoological or botanical or whatever names of butterflies, or telling Professor Flipplehead the entire history of the Thuringian Flagellants in Middle German on past midnight by the blackboard.

In these cases, the mind knows what it's doing better than the guile, because the mind flows, the guile dams up, that is, the mind strides but the guile limps. And that's no guileless statement, however, and that's no Harvard lie, as MIT will measure soon with computers and docks of Martian data.[38]

That's funny, almost W. C. Fields, very easy, flippant, sardonic, cynical, but delicately detailed improvisation, that "MIT will measure soon with computers and docks of Martian data." Looking back on his youth and seeing his vanity, seeing his own karmic hollowness and his own faults, which very few writers have dared, much less dared near their deathbed.

This [book was written] as if spoken to his wife, somewhat parallel to Herman Melville's poems to his wife in the character of an old sailor smoking his tobacco talking to his wife. If you know Herman Melville's poetry, that's one of Melville's favorite roles, the old seaman back from the sea, many years later talking about his early companion Ned Bunn, "Ah Ned what years and years ago in the South Seas" in their island paradises, but now recalling for his wife.

The classic authors were all people that Kerouac or Burroughs or myself or others took from. That's why I spoke of Melville, meaning Melville's poetry there, Melville's *Billy Budd,* Melville's "Bartleby, the Scrivener," Melville's mad Ahab, Melville's biblical prose, all these are reference points in Kerouac. *Pierre, or, The Ambiguities* especially because of the conscious weird prettiness of the Shakespearean prose of it.

In this education, flow versus guile, Kerouac was actually talking about his literary method and also his method of honesty, a personal honesty in writing. He's often been called anti-Semitic and there's a little element of that in him. You get a good clear honest version of it here, [although] not quite anti-Semitism. This is pure Kerouac as I knew him in his relation to Jews.

> Anyway sometimes at lunch, [Jonathan Miller, my high school friend,] seeing my awful peanut butter sandwiches, he'd offer me some of his chicken sandwiches beautifully prepared by his maid, and the football team would guffaw. I was not popular with the other members of the football team because they thought I was hanging around with the nonathletic Jewish kids and snubbing the athletes, for sandwiches, favors, dinners, two-dollar term papers, and they were right I guess. But I was fascinated by Jewish kids because I'd never met any in my life, especially these well-bred, rather fawncy dressers, tho they all had the ugliest faces I ever saw and awful pimples. I had pimples too, tho.[39]

It's a very funny book, it's very honest in that way. "I had pimples too, tho." He's trying to register what he really thought and be somewhat naked about it, as distinct from his earlier books where everything is romanticized. He doesn't have second thoughts, like "I had pimples too, tho." There's another little passage about the Jews.

> What annoyed me was the way the football team, that is, the other ringers from New Jersey, looked down on me for playing around

with the Jewish kids. It wasnt that they were anti-Semitic, they were just disdainful I think of the fact these Jewish kids had money and ate good lunches, or came to school some of em in limousines, or maybe, just as in Lowell, they considered them too vainglorious to think about seriously.[40]

I think that was his basic attitude, which is that he was a goy Canuck and not used to Jews. They were strange to him and interesting and weird and pimply and slimy and faggoty, like me, and sort of threatening. At the same time romantic, because he was in love with me too, and Lucien Carr was part Jewish, [so] it was a very complicated matter for him.

Now I begin to feel bad about football and war. And showing off. But after the game (HM 27, Garden City 0) my father is beaming and all delighted as we shower. "Come on Jacky me boy, we're going out and hit the town tonight." So we go down to Jack Delaney's steak restaurant on Sheridan Square, myself little knowing how much time I was destined to spend around that square, in Greenwich Village, in darker years, but tenderer years, to come.

Ah, it's Good Friday night and I'm going to write what I want.[41]

By showing off he means his entire career, he's finally come to feel that that's just showing off, which is quite a disillusioning comedown, it's just simple when he says it. Then a separate sentence. "Ah, it's Good Friday night and I'm going to write what I want." Very few writers have that open accomplishment and clarity. He's at the summit of his career, he's already written enough to make him immortal, and now he's playful with his disillusionment.

By the time he wrote this, he had married Stella Sampatacus, the sister of his early best friend, Sebastian Sampas, who died in World War II. Kerouac was in love with him, as Sampas was in love with Kerouac. In those days I don't think it ever got beyond just saying that they loved each other in a poetic way. This will give you some late statement of Kerouac's particular kind of idealism in relation to Sebastian Sampas.

Anyway, wifey, that's how I finally started to talk to your brother, Sabbas, who said he was the Prince of Crete, which he probably was once, but only recently of Spartan or Maniatti, descent.

Big curly-haired guy, thought he was a poet, and was, and as we got to be friendly began to instruct me in the arts of being interested (as they say in Mexico, *interesa*) in literature and the arts of kindness. I put him in this chapter (say I archly) about Columbia, because he really belongs to that period which followed the adolescence of the prep school and introduces the serious business.

Among my souvenirs, by God, is the friendship of Sabbas Savakis.

And I'll tell you why in plain English poesy: he'd sing me "Begin the Beguine" in a big voice whether we were crossing the bridge, sitting in saloons or just on my doorstep or his own father's doorstep in the Lower Highlands. He'd yell Byron at me: "So we'll go no more-a-roving / So late into the night . . ." It's not because he died in the war, on the beachhead at Anzio wounded, died in an Algiers North Africa hospital of gangrene, or probably broken heart, because a lot of other guys died in World War II including some I've already mentioned in this book (Kazarakis, Gold, Hampshire, others I dont even know what happened), but because the memorabilia of my knit just knits a knight in my night's mind. *That's* plain English poesy? Because, okay, he was a great kid, knightlike, i.e., noble, a poet, goodlooking, crazy, sweet, sad, everything a man should want as a friend.[42]

Mixed with that idealistic sweetness is constantly the bathos of samsaric pain, particularly in relation to his father, who he sat with while his father died of cancer in the 1940s.

In fact that was the summer, too, when Pa unexpectedly joined me and the boys on the 2½-mile walk on a particularly hot evening and he too, whipping off his clothes, yipped and ran in his shorts to the edge of the brook and jumped in feet first. But he weighed 250 pounds and the weather'd been dry all August and he landed standing in 3 feet of water and almost broke his ankle. It really almost broke my heart, to see him so happy in his yipping leap and end up toppling over in that little fetid pint of water.[43]

There's a real samsaric leap there, which is continuous through Kerouac, the constant disillusion and tragedy. And there's a compassion and clarity there too that you find very rarely expressed anywhere in writing.

In *Vanity of Duluoz* there is a visionary description by Kerouac of something that involves some sense of gap, that even at the moment of greatest pleasure or fulfillment, there's a certain empty center of which one becomes conscious and leads one to think that the world was too full of suffering for anybody to take time out enough to realize the basic difficulty and dissatisfaction of existence. The advantage of the human world is that you can stop and think. So here's Kerouac stopping and thinking.

One night my cousin Blanche came to the house and sat in the kitchen talking to Ma among the packing boxes. I sat on the porch outside and leaned way back with feet on rail and gazed at the stars for the first time in my life. A clear August night, the stars, the Milky Way, the whole works clear. I stared and stared till they stared back at me. Where the hell was I and what was all this?

I went into the parlor and sat down in my father's old deep easy chair and fell into the wildest daydream of my life. This is important and this is the key to the story, wifey dear:

As Ma and Cousin talked in the kitchen, I daydreamed that I was now going to go back to Columbia for my sophomore year, with home in New Haven, maybe near Yale campus, with soft light in room and rain on the sill, mist on the pane, and go all the way in football and studies. I was going to be such a sensational runner that we'd win every game, against Dartmouth, Yale, Princeton, Harvard, Georgia U, Michigan U, Cornell, the bloody lot, and wind up in the Rose Bowl. In the Rose Bowl, worse even than Cliff Montgomery, I was going to run wild. Uncle Lu Libble for the first time in his life would throw his arms around me and weep. Even his wife would do so. The boys on the team would raise me up in Rose Bowl's Pasadena Stadium and march me to the showers singing. On returning to Columbia campus in January, having passed chemistry with an A, I would then idly turn my attention to winter indoor track and decide on the mile and run it in under 4 flat (that was fast in those days). So fast, indeed, that I'd be in the big meets at Madison Square garden and beat the current great milers in final fantastic sprints bringing my time down to 3:50 flat. By this time everybody in the world is crying Duluoz! Duluoz! But, unsatisfied, I idly go out in the spring for the Columbia baseball team and bat homeruns clear over the Harlem River, one or two a game, including fast breaks from the bag to steal from first to second, from second to third, and finally, in the climactic game, from third to home, zip, slide, dust, boom. Now the New York Yankees are after me. They want me to be their next Joe DiMaggio. I idly turn that down because I want Columbia to go to the Rose Bowl again in 1943. (Hah!) But then I also, in mad midnight musings over a Faustian skull, after drawing circles in the earth, talking to God in the tower of the Gothic high steeple of Riverside Church, meeting Jesus on the Brooklyn Bridge, getting Sabby a part on Broadway as Hamlet (playing King Lear myself across the street) I become the greatest writer that ever lived and write a book so golden and so purchased with magic that everybody smacks their brows on Madison Avenue. Even Professor Claire is chasing after me on his crutches on the Columbia campus. Mike Hennessey, his father's hand in hand, comes screaming up the dorm steps to find me. All the kids of HM are singing in the field. Bravo, bravo, author, they're yelling for me in the theater where I've also presented my newest idle work, a play rivaling Eugene O'Neill and Maxwell Anderson and making Strindberg spin. Finally, a delegation of cigar-chewing guys come and get me and want to know if I want to train for the world's heavyweight boxing championship fight with Joe Louis. Okay, I train idly in the Catskills, come down on a June night, face big tall Joe as the referee gives us instructions, and then when the bell rings I rush out real fast and just pepper him real fast and so hard that he actually goes back bouncing over the ropes and into the third row and lays there knocked out.

I'm the world's heavyweight boxing champion, the greatest writer, the world's champ miler, Rose Bowl and (pro-bound with New York Giants football non pareil) now offered every job on every paper in New York, and what else? Tennis anyone?

I woke up from this daydream suddenly realizing that all I had to do was go back on the porch and look at the stars again, which I did, and still they just stared at me blankly.

In other words I suddenly realized that all my ambitions, no matter how they came out, and of course as you can see from the preceding narrative, they just came out fairly ordinary, it wouldnt matter anyway in the intervening space between human breathings and the "sigh of the happy stars," so to speak, to quote Thoreau again.

[. . .]

When I looked up from that crazy reverie, at the stars, heard my mother and cousin still yakking in the kitchen about tea leaves, heard in fact my father yelling across the street in the bowling alley, I realized either I was crazy or the world was crazy; and I picked on the world.

And of course I was right.[44]

I guess everybody's had that daydream, or one form of it or other. He's given very honestly, archetypically his own. But having carried his archetypal fantasy to the extreme and been mindful of it, and even playful with it, he came to a strange conclusion having played out the possibility to the very end, coming to the emptiness at the end of game. That informs almost all of his writing and all of his life from there on, the emptiness at the end. Or *Mexico City Blues*, "217th Chorus":

Rack my hand with labor of nada
Run 100 yard dash
in Ole Ensanada
S what'll have to do,
this gin & tonics

Perss o monnix
twab
twab
twabble
all day

Even the writing finally is "rack my hand with labor of nada," nada, nothing. Nice vowels. That was one of my favorite lines in Kerouac. This is an exposition of all the daydream and all the considerations and third thoughts that lead to that empty disillusionment.

The rhetoric here is the rhetoric of Louis-Ferdinand Céline's prose. His are basic attitudinal reference books as well as prose reference books for all of Kerouac's prose and all of Burroughs's prose. Doctor Louis Ferdinand Auguste Destouches, who wrote under the pseudonym of Louis-Ferdinand Céline, who had somewhat of a paranoiac attitude, just as Kerouac had a little elegant touch of in his doting old age.

There's a small vision of all the boys in school. He just ran away from the football team. "Okay, be back at eight." The coach tells him, "Be back at eight."

And I went out and took the subway down to Brooklyn with all my gear, whipped out a few dollars from the suitcase, said goodbye to Uncle Nick saying I was going back to Baker Field, walked down the hot September streets of Brooklyn hearing Franklyn Delano Roosevelt's speech about "I hate war" coming out of every barbership in Brooklyn, took the subway to the Eighth Avenue Greyhound bus station, and bought a ticket to the South.

I wanted to see the Southland and start my career as an American careener.[45]

And that's how he got started on the road.

> This was the most important decision of my life so far. What I
> was doing was telling everybody to go jump in the big fat ocean
> of their own folly. I was also telling myself to go jump in the big
> fat ocean of my own folly. What a bath!
> It was delightful. I was washed clean.[46]

Then having gotten out into America, there is a section where he
becomes disillusioned on his first trip. He's learned from Wolfe that
America [can] be seen as a poem and instantly was disillusioned with
that. Which on a larger scale is reflected in Gregory Corso's *Elegiac
Feelings American*. That was Corso's book written after Kerouac's
death. Like Shelley writing an ode called "Adonaïs" on Keats, Corso
has an elegy on Kerouac's death. Corso's is in the grand tradition of
great poets' elegies for other late lamented dear poets. The point that
Corso makes is that if the singer is a singer of the nation, and the
nation decays, then what happens to the singer?

> It was November, it was cold, it was woodsmoke, it was swift waters
> in the wink of silver glare with its rose headband out yander where
> Eve Star (some call it Venus, some call it Lucifer) stoppered up her
> drooling propensities and tried to contain itself in one delimited
> throb of boiling light.[47]

A year before his death, Kerouac is still capable of these little
cadenzas about the star. It's really pretty, I stopped and reread it.
The "boiling light" is pretty, it's just pure invention there. It's his
whole attitude toward writing over decades and millions of pages.

It comes to that "delimited throb of boiling light," easily tossed off the fountain pen.

> Ah poetic. I keep saying "ah poetic" because I didn't intend this to be a poetic paean of a book, in 1967 as I'm writing this what possible feeling can be left in me for an "America" that has become such a potboiler of broken convictions, messes of rioting and fighting in streets, hoodlumism, cynical administration of cities and states, suits and neckties the only feasible subject, grandeur all gone into the mosaic mesh of Television (Mosaic indeed, with a capital *M*), where people screw their eyes at all those dots and pick out hallucinated images of their own contortion and are fed ACHTUNG! ATTENTION! ATENCIÓN! instead of Ah dreamy real wet lips beneath an old apple tree? Or that picture in *Time* Magazine a year ago showing a thousand cars parked in a redwood forest in California, all alongside similar tents with awnings and primus stoves, everybody dressed alike looking around everywhere at everybody with those curious new eyes of the second part of this century, only occasionally looking up at the trees and if so probably thinking "O how nice that redwood would look as my lawn furniture!" Well, enough . . . for now.
>
> Main thing is, coming home, "Farewell Song Sweet from My Trees" of the previous August was washed away in November joys.[48]

Then Kerouac comes back home, having quit the team, having goofed up, and having run away to the South. This is interesting because I remember trips like this where all of a sudden he'd disappear, cut out and go on an adventure, and I'd say, "Oh god, he's irresponsible, undisciplined."

When I read his books I always realize that he was enormously broodingly vaster of mind and heart than myself and that my irritation was jejune, egoistic, self-defensive, and contributed to his death and disillusionment. I always feel guilty. Occasionally I'll also realize he was full of shit and totally vain. It wasn't wisdom at all, it was some kind of paranoiac vanity. That's why he drank himself to death. I mean the whole book is saying it, the *Vanity of Duluoz*.

> At midnight, in bright moonlight, I walked Moody Street over crunching snow and felt something awful that had not been in Lowell before. For one thing I was the "failure back in town," for another I had lost the glamour of New York City and the Columbia campus and the tweeded outlook of sophomores, had lost glittering Manhattan, was back trudging among the brick walls of the mills.[49]

Since he cut out of Columbia, he'd broken that pattern of Fitzgeraldean novelistic nostalgia. Now he was into some kind of awful grid of having to face the solitude of being a writer, and not just sliding along on the fantasy of youthtime romance with money making it all right. "The glamour of the tweeded look of sophomores." He has some suggestions for writers here, since he's describing a time when his writing method begins getting codified, clarified.

> That's how writers begin, by imitating the masters (without suffering like said masters), till they larn their own style, and by the time they larn their own style there's no more fun in it, because you cant imitate any other master's suffering but your own.[50]

Kerouac is saying it's all right to begin by imitating the masters, but when you get your own style, you'll have your own suffering to write about and there's no more fun in it. He begins to examine his own early writings, his own diaries of age eighteen or nineteen, when he went out on the military sea transport.

All eyes peeled for the periscope. Wonderful evening spent before with the (not Navy, excuse me) Army gun crew near the big gun, playing popular records on the phonograph, the Army fellas seem much more sincere than the hardened cynical dockrats. Here's a few notes from my own personal log . . .

Here he is at the age of forty-six, saying here's a few notes from my own personal log of my Salingeresque days of 1938.

"There are a few acceptable men here and there, like Don Gary, the new scullion, a sensible and friendly fellow. He has a wife in Scotland, joined the Merchant Marine to get back to Scotland, in fact. I met one of the passengers, or construction workers, an Arnold Gershon, an earnest youth from Brooklyn. And another fellow who works in the butcher shop. Outside of these, my acquaintances have so far been fruitless, almost foolish. I am trying hard to be sincere but the crew prefers, I suppose, embittered cursing and bawdry foolishness. Well, at least, being misunderstood is being like the hero in the movies." (Can you imagine such crap written in a scullion's diary?)

That was his 1967 comment on that. Then it gets interesting, because he's mixing his old early diary writing with little phrases to hop it up a little bit to make it funnier, or parody, or just being playful, quoting himself at eighteen and playfully adding on some new cadenza.

"Sunday July 26: A beautiful day! Clear and windy, with a choppy sea that looks like a marine painting . . . long flecked billows of blue water, with the wake of our ship like a bright green road . . . Nova Scotia to larboard. We have now passed through the Cabot Straits." (Who's Cabot? A Breton?) (Pronounced Ca-boh.) "Up we go, to northern seas. Ah there you'll find that shrouded Arctic." (That wash of pronounced sea-talk, that parturient snowmad ice mountain plain, that bloody Genghis Khan plain of seaweed talk broken only by uprisings of foam.)

That's a little parenthesis he threw in on top of his old journal. His pure appreciation of vowels and the babble of the mind, the playfulness of it, and the easiness of the writing of this. With the implication that it all comes to nothing in the end. The uprisings of foam.

Yessir, boy, the earth is an Indian thing but the waves are Chinese. Know what that means? Ask the guys who drew those old scrolls, or ask the old Fishermen of Cathay, and what Indian ever dared to sail to Europe or Hawaii from the salmon-tumbling streams of North America? When I say Indian, I mean Ogallag.[51]

There's that alcoholic mouthing playfulness. "The earth is an Indian thing" is a favorite line originally from *On the Road* somewhere. Fellaheen comes out of Spengler, from the volumes that Burroughs handed him when we went to visit Burroughs in 1944. Kerouac was identifying himself more and more with fellaheen and the earth as an Indian thing.

I didn't know what he meant at first, I got mad when I heard him say that. I was always getting mad at his works of genius. I thought he meant, "white people are not supposed to be here, only the Indians have the earth, that the earth is owned by the Indians." Later, I learned that it meant that the Indians know their own geography, they know all the plants and the medicines, like saying that the earth is a gardener's thing. I took it as political at first, some anti-Semitic comment.

The next chapter is just pure messing around, he must have got drunk then. His method of writing is useful to know. This book is divided into something like thirteen books altogether, then each book within it is divided into anywhere between five and thirteen little chapters, chapterettes. Each chapterette is one session of writing, wherever the writing leads. That's how the book is composed. One day he'll write maybe a paragraph, and that's a chapter. The next day he'll get interested and idly write three pages, so that's a whole other chapterette. Then when he's piled up enough of these little chapterettes to account for a season or an idea that he meant to cover in his mind's eye chronologically, he'll move on.

But my hands werent sea-netted and chapped by rope and wire, as later the next year as deckhand, at present time I was a scullion. I'd vaguely heard of Shakespeare yelling about that, he who washes pots and scours out giant pans, with greasy aprons, hair hanging in face like idiot, face splashed by dishwater, scouring not with a "scourer" as you understand it but with a goddamned Slave chain, grouped in fist as chain, scratch, scroutch, and the whole galley heaving slowly.

Oh the pots and pans the racket of their fear, the kitchen of the sea, the Neptunes down here, the herds of sea cows wanta milk us, the sea poem I aint finished with, the fear of the Scottish laird rowing out with a nape of another fox' neck in the leeward shirsh of S H A O W yon Irish Sea! The sea of her lip! The brattle of her

Boney! The crack of Noah's Ark timbers built by Mosaic Schwarts
in the unconditional night of Universal death.
    Short chapter.[52]

It was just a little piece of writing which didn't lead anywhere or
it led to a little lyric, but nowhere in terms of the narrative, but he
didn't eliminate it or make it into anything. Just a short chapter. In
this book there's a lot of little comments on the writing, like "proceed
to book V." The writing is so easy, almost negligent. Remember that
phrase he used when he tossed off a play, "my newest idle work." This
writing is very idle, he's just talking to his wife so he doesn't have to
be a great litterateur, he can just idly make whatever little nonsensical ditties he wants to.

It must have been psychologically difficult until he finally sat
down, [and then] it was like falling off a log. All he had to do was
remember a few details, occasionally pulling out his old journals,
writing it down, and then making funny little comments, like "O
gee." Loose and relaxed, honest. He didn't care, he no longer was
maintaining his mythology. In fact he even mentions in his book
that among mythologizers he's an expert.

If you're interesting in writing writing, pure writing, there's that
delightful playfulness, negligence, the word "idle" that he used comes
through very clearly. I mean not everybody can be that idle and care-
less. He's like an accomplished master painting with a few strokes.
He'd done it so much that he knows how to turn a phrase just to
turn a phrase, just when there's nothing to talk about. Where did
he get that? You may notice it in "the sea of her lip, the brattle of
her boney, the shallow of the un-Irish sea," there's a little element of
Joyce's *Finnegans Wake* and *Ulysses,* which were also great archetypes
for him.

CHAPTER 10

Lucien Carr's Influence on Kerouac

Lucien Carr was so central to everybody's mythology that it's hard to give a course on [the] literary history of the Beat Generation without adducing his tongue as part of the literary background. The great documentation of that is a text by Kerouac called "Old Lucien Midnight" later retitled "Old Angel Midnight." It was Kerouac's Lucienesque gibberish, a Joycean *Finnegans Wake* style, an unconscious language based mainly on Lucien's language. Jack seemed to hear Shakespeare through Lucien Carr's speech. Lucien also had a pure tongue, a beautiful tongue, and we all considered him the great Shakespearean tongue among us. In the end Lucien decided that he didn't want to cast any shadow, unlike us egotists.[53]

There's a real interesting chorus in *Mexico City Blues,* which maybe is a summary of all that. It's a mixture of Shakespeare, Lucien Carr, and W. C. Fields.

217th Chorus

Sooladat smarty pines came prappin down
My line of least regard last Prapopooty

And whattaya think Old Father Time
made him? a western sponeet
Without no false on bonnet,
Trap in the cock adus time of the Nigh,
Slight the leak of recompense being
hermasodized
By finey wild traphoods in all
their estapular
glories
Gleaming their shinging-rising spears
against the High Thap All Thup —
So I aim my gazoota always
to the God, remembering the origin
Of all beasts and cod, Bostonian
By nature, with no minda my own,
Could write about railroads, quietus
These blues, hurt my hand more,
Rack my hand with labor of nada
—Run 100 yard dash
in Ole Ensanada—
S what'll have to do,
this gin & tonics
Perss o monnix
twab
twab
twabble
all day

I don't know if that makes sense to you? I've heard it so often
that it's clear as a bell. Old soldier smartypants, "Sooladat smarty

pines," came parading, farting down. "My line of least regard last Prapopooty," last Friday. Soldier smartypants, egotistical smarty-pants came parading himself down my line of least regard, my line of fire, my line of indifference last Friday. And what do you think time made out of him? He's just imitating a Shakespeare sonnet and writing anything that comes in his mind. It's attitudinal partly, but also there are hints in puns.

This is specifically Lucien Carr's speech that he's parodying. I chose this because it is a sample of the prose of *Old Angel Midnight*. It's good, it's funny, it's just drunken talk, with all the sounds of talk, so you don't have to worry about what it means. It has all sorts of suggestions in the syllables and in the associations and the puns. It is Sunday afternoon with all the sounds of the universe coming in the window of the ear. That's from the beginning page of "Old Angel Midnight" and as I said it was Lucien's sound that Jack was interested in.

It's just funny playfulness. It's Kerouac doing anything he wants. You don't have to fit into anybody's rules, you don't even have to make sense, you don't have to make a story, as long as you are grounded. It's a demonstration of the emptiness of mind, the emptiness of art.

CHAPTER 11

Kerouac and
Vanity of Duluoz, Part 2

Kerouac had gone crazy in the navy. The war is on and he's in a navy psycho ward. He's decided that the world is crazy and he doesn't want to have anything to do with it. He just wants to be a novelist, but he doesn't want to have any truck with the world or responsibility. His father visits him and then Sebastian Sampas, his old youthtime, Shelleyan, poetic, idealistic fellow friend.

> Then in comes Sabby in a U.S. Army uniform, sad, idealistic, crewcutted now, but dream-minded, try to talk to me, "I have remembered, Jack, I have kept faith," but the nutty manic depressive from West Virginny shoves him in a corner and grabs him by the private's sleeves and yells "Wabash Cannonball" and poor Sabby's eyes are misting and looking at me saying, "I came here to talk to you, I only have twenty minutes, what a house of suffering, what now?"
>
> I say "Come in the toilet." West Virginia follows us yelling, it was one of his good days. I said "Sabby dont worry, the kid's okay, everybody's okay . . . Besides," I added, "there's nothing for me or you to say . . . Except, I s'pose, that time when Bartlett Junior

High School was burning down and my train was taking me back to New York prep school and you ran alongside, remember? in the snowstorm singing "I'll See You Again' . . . huh?"

And that was the last time I saw Sabby. He was fatally wounded on Anzio beachhead after that.[54]

That's his belated farewell to the person he felt closest to as a poet, who died young. That's Kerouac's legend of the lost, pure, innocent poet. I think there was a great love that they shared.

Jack mentions that the book comes to a pivotal point and changes while he's writing it. He's aware of it while writing [and treats it like] a quality of empty playfulness in this particular novel. It's odd that he knows what he's doing, or maybe he decided that once he had written something that was it. In this passage he has a little conversation about football with his teammates.

I said "After I make my break, and may not sink anything and you miss some dumb choice, I'll slice that first ball into the corner with a little scythe, as soft as your Devil."

"And therefore you're the Devil."

"No, I'm his wind. And I'm gone as much from his influence, as this ungraspable handshake."

This is where the book, the story, pivots.

This is known by Massachusetts Yankees as "deep form."

Funny halfbacks dont have to sell Pepsi-Cola.[55]

He's seeing himself as a funny halfback, but he can go and be a novelist instead of being like the rest of the halfbacks, getting fat and old, selling Pepsi-Cola. Book X pivots in the sense that the first half was his Horace Mann High School days and then he goes on into

New York with Burroughs and Carr, Huncke, myself. He just decided then and there, "Well I better get on with it, get into the story" and so he informs the reader. There's a little bit about his Catholicism here and his notions of God, which I thought were pretty good because he was summarizing thoughts, philosophical thoughts. Emptily making a few conclusions, negligently,

> Because when I saw the face of my beloved dead cat Timmy in the Heavens, and heard him mew like he used to do in a little voice, it surprised me to realize he wasnt even born when World War II was on, and therefore at this moment, how can he even be dead? If he wasnt born, how can he be dead? So just an apparition in molecular form for awhile, to haunt our souls with similarities to God's perfection, in Timmy's case the perfection was when he'd sit like a lion on the kitchen table, paws straight out, head erect and full-jowled, and God's imperfection when he was dying and his back was a skeletal run of ribs and spinal joints and his fur falling off and his eyes looking at me: "I may have loved you, I may love you now, but it's too late . . ." Pascal says it better than I do when he says: "WHAT SHALL WE GATHER FROM ALL OUR DARKNESS, IF NOT A CONVICTION OF OUR UNWORTHINESS?" And he adds, to show you right path:
> "There are perfections in Nature which demonstrate that She is the image of God"—Timmy sittin like a lion, Big Slim in his prime, Pop in his prime, me in my careless 1943 youth, you, all— "and imperfections"—our decay and going-down, all of us—"to assure us that She is no more than His image." {That nature is no more than the image of God. Then Kerouac's comment:} I believe that.

"God is Dead" made everybody sick to their stomachs because they all know what I just said, and Pascal said, and Paschal means Resurrection.[56]

And Pascal, the philosopher, said, and "paschal," paschal lamb, means resurrection. He makes a little Catholic statement there, just from an aesthetic point of view. "'God is Dead' made everybody sick to their stomachs" was his final comment on that as an intellectual thesis.

When we first got together, I think supreme reality was the ideal that we were chasing after as the "new vision." Kerouac and I both used that phrase, "new vision," coming probably from Lucien Carr who was carrying around Yeats's *A Vision* and coming from the paragraph in Rimbaud's *Season in Hell* which goes, "When shall we go beyond the shores and mountains, to hail the birth of fresh toil; fresh wisdom, the rout of tyrants and demons, the end of superstition, to adore—as newcomers—Christmas on earth!" It is a little visionary moment in Rimbaud that is so poignant and sweet and sad, because he failed to make it, but we decided that we were going to make it so we wanted Christmas on earth. It was my obsession, but Kerouac used the phrase also, "supreme reality," as being what we were chasing after.

I thought, for instance, I heard a big fistfight and wrestling rough-and-tumble on the steel deck right over my pillow one morning, fifty guys fighting, with clubs and sledgehammers, but it was "Pueee puee pueee" the scream of the "All hands on deck" attack warning, and I realized I was listening to depth charges going off in a submarine attack. I just turned over and went back to sleep. Not because we had 500-pound bombs and couldnt do anything about anything anyhow, but because I was just naturally sleepy and I had figured out in the Navy nuthouse: "I could get killed walking across the street, if Supreme Reality's arranged it, so why not go to sea?" And besides, ding-blast it, I WAS just simply sleepy all the time. They called me "Sleepy Dulouse." Like Beetle Bailey, you might say . . . ZZZZZ.[57]

The chapter ends with those "Z Z Z Z Z" snoring sounds. "I could get killed walking across the street, if Supreme Reality's arranged it, so why not go to sea?" His sleepiness was a characteristic thing. It was just like cutting out of a scene which got too complicated. When he met a situation which seemed to be irresolvable, he simply dropped it and went south.

CHAPTER 12

Meeting Burroughs and Ginsberg's Suspension from Columbia

We had [each] met Burroughs individually before. Lucien Carr had brought me down to Greenwich Village where a friend of his, Dave Kammerer, lived, but he wasn't home. Burroughs lived around the corner and we went there, so that was my first meeting with him. Lucien had gone out the night before, gotten drunk, and some bloody fight had erupted. He wound up on the floor fighting with some gay guy or girl and had bitten a piece of his/her ear off, which I thought was pretty shocking and amazing. I never heard of anything like that in Paterson, New Jersey. I had just arrived at Columbia and I didn't know people went around getting drunk, biting people's ears off.

Burroughs was seated on a low couch near the fireplace and I was seated on an upturned log end which served as a coffee table. Lucien was telling this story and Burroughs said, "In the words of the immortal bard, 'tis too starved an argument for my sword,'" meaning the argument is foolish and stupid so why get into a fight about it? That was Burroughs's laconic judiciousness instantly displayed. That one quotation made me appreciate the wit of Shakespeare, the accuracy of the phrasing "a starved argument."

The other thing I remember that Burroughs said, the first literary recollection of his nature and conversation, was that there was a lesbian girl who lived upstairs from his apartment. Bill said he liked her because she was "straightforward, manly, and reliable." For me, that was the determining phrase of all that later became gay liberation in my brain. It was just the ordinariness of that, judging individuals by character.

When we all went to see Burroughs, it was for that laconic, mellowed-out, cooled-out experience. Later when we were living in Joan Burroughs's apartment, both Jack and I spent an hour a day free associating with Burroughs acting as psychiatrist. It was a regular formal psychoanalysis with Burroughs as our listener. Mine came to a conclusion when I finally burst out and said "nobody loves me." When I finally came out with it, I wept. Burroughs sat there, sort of impersonally, friendly, listening, accommodating, and welcoming. It was a breakthrough for me, a realization of my actual feelings.

About a year later I was living in Hartley Hall at Columbia and had just written a long poem called "The Last Voyage" derived from reading Baudelaire's "Voyage" and Rimbaud's "Drunken Boat / Bateau livre." The Baudelaire ended with a favorite quote of all of ours: "O death old Captain, raise the anchors it's time let's go, plunge to the bottom of the gulf, heaven or hell, what does it matter? At the bottom of the unknown to find the new." It related to our new vision, supreme reality.

Kerouac came uptown from seeing Burroughs and I read him my big poem "The Last Voyage." He had just had a conversation with Burroughs in which Burroughs had said, "Well, Jack, you know, the trouble with you is, you are tied to your mother's apron strings and it's going to get narrower and narrower and sooner or later you're going to be right in there, not able to move away from your mother, that's your fate, your destiny." Kerouac was chilled by that. It was an accurate insight on Burroughs's part, because Jack was hung up on his mother. I didn't realize it, but he was internalizing a great deal of his mother's ideas. It was a prophetic night and by the time we got all this talking done it was late. Kerouac didn't want to go back to Long Island, so he stayed over with me and slept in my bed. I was a little scared because Jack didn't know I was gay or [that I] was interested in him. I thought he'd probably get very angry and I didn't want to bring it up, too difficult.

Kerouac had been banned from the campus as an "unwholesome influence on students," according to the college. Earlier on the day Kerouac had come to see me, I had noticed that the windows were dirty. We had a blue-uniformed scrub lady that I thought was a little anti-Semitic. She hadn't cleaned the windows in my room, so I had decorated them by finger painting [in the dirt], "Butler has no balls" (Nicholas Murray Butler was the president of the school at the time) and "Fuck the Jews," thinking she'd wipe it off and clean the windows. It was jejune college humor. But she didn't wipe it off, she reported it to the dean, and as Kerouac and I were sleeping off the poetic night like innocent lambs the door opened and in walked the dean. Kerouac opened one eye, saw the situation instantly, jumped out of bed, and ran into my roommate's room. He got in the empty bed and pulled the covers over his head and went back to sleep. What reminded me of that was this thing about "and besides dang blast it, I was just sleepy all the time," when he pulled the covers over his head during the depth-charge bombing. Then the dean left and I got dressed, ready to face some kind of music. Kerouac got up and went home, back to his mother. He wasn't sticking around with me in this crisis, so I went into the dean's office alone.

I had already read Céline's *Journey to the End of the Night,* Burroughs had given [that to] me. The hero, Ferdinand Bardamu, and his friend Robinson are in a café, drinking, getting a little bit drunk. The time is the beginning of World War I. All of a sudden they see a big happy parade of drunkards coming down the street with bands and fifes and flags and ladies and everybody's happy and arm in arm they get up and join the parade. They wander off to the edge of town, still drunk, where a gate shuts behind them and they find that they're in the army. In chapter two, they're in the field of battle and Bardamu looks around and there are all these people crying for their mommies with shells whistling overhead with insane captains issuing contradictory orders to march forward into the teeth of battle. Céline has a sentence about, "I suddenly realized that everybody around me was completely insane, and if I wanted to survive the situation, I had better take steps to disassociate myself completely with their mad schemes, or to evade completely, or make myself invisible." It was a very funny sentence. I think it's one of the great moments of Western literature, when the hero wakes up in the middle of the battle and realizes that everybody around him is crazy and figures he better get out of there.

I would say that is hipness, that attitude of waking up in the midst of society and finding that everybody was crazy. It was all a mad scheme that was going to destroy everybody and nobody was going [to] get out alive. With that attitude in mind I walked into the dean's office. He faced me across his desk and said, "Mr. Ginsberg, I hope you realize the enormity of what you've done." I flashed on that scene in Céline where he's surrounded by dangerous madmen in every direction. And realized, you know, you're getting into a very dangerous situation, of getting fucked up forever for this. And I said, "Oh, I do sir, I do. If you can only tell me what I can do to make this up." Cringing and snibbling and terrified and agreeing with him to get out of the situation.

Afterward I went to see Trilling. I remember Trilling was very funny. He didn't know what the whole thing was about really and at the same time he knew me and he knew Kerouac and he realized that there was something stupid about it. He said, "Well I've talked to the dean but there doesn't seem to be anything I can do, he's made up his mind." It was finally decided that I had to withdraw from Columbia and not return until I had become more matured. I had to get a letter from a psychiatrist saying that I had worked for about a year out in the world and was now mature enough to be a member of the academic community.

The thing that rung in my ears was "Mr. Ginsberg, I hope you realize the enormity of what you have done," because actually I hadn't done anything. I was afraid to do anything. I wanted to do something [with Kerouac]. I lay there longing all night, thinking and dreaming, but I didn't do nothing.

But back to Kerouac. There was a pretty phrase that I always liked here. He's on the ship:

> . . . and I'm wondering, "Joseph Conrad wasn't wrong, there are old scadogs who've been to everywhere from Bombay to British Columbia smoking their pipes on poops of old sea vessels, practically born at sea they are, and die at sea, and dont even look up . . . Even have cats down below for the rats, and sometimes a dog . . . What tobacco they smoke? What they do, where they go when they put on their glad rags in Macao, to do what?"[58]

I thought that phrase "glad rags in Macao" was a pretty sound. I think that's the essence of Kerouac, playful, stylish actually. His is an odd ear. The music is made there. I want to finish with one paragraph.

> And it was that last morning before we got ready to sail to Brooklyn that I devised the idea of "The Duluoz Legend," it was a gray rainy morning and I sat in the purser's office over his typewriter, he was having his last drunk I guess, and I saw it: a lifetime of writing about what I'd seen with my own eyes, told in my own words, according to the style I decided on at whether twenty-one years old or thirty or forty or whatever later age, and put it all together as a contemporary history record for future times to see what really happened and what people really thought.[59]

"To see what really happened and what people really thought." That's exactly what Kerouac did. A simple idea, what people really thought, and that is the conception of his literary career. It was a big surprise to me that you could do that.

CHAPTER 13

Kerouac and
The Town and the City

The Town and the City is extraordinary as a first novel and it really is Kerouac prose, in and out, beginning to end. There are touches of great violins of Kerouac sound, melancholy violins of time passing. Some of the panoramic consciousness you'll get in *On the Road* and *Visions of Cody,* awareness of October's red sun setting at the end of the football field while the heroes are tackling each other in the dusk and the high school teacher is banging his fist on his desk in despair at growing old, simultaneously. There's that same melancholy space-time consciousness. When I first read the opening paragraph of *The Town and the City* I thought it was a great monument and I cried and wrote a sonnet.

> The town is Galloway. The Merrimac River, broad and placid, flows down to it from the New Hampshire hills, broken at the falls to make a frothy havoc on the rocks. {That's immediately Kerouac, "a frothy havoc on the rocks."} Foaming on over ancient stone towards a place where the river suddenly swings about in a wide and peaceful basin, moving on now around the flank of the town, on to places known as Lawrence and Haverhill, through a wooded

valley, and on to the sea at Plum Island, where the river enters an infinity of waters and is gone. Somewhere far north of Galloway, in headwaters close to Canada, the river is continually fed and made to brim out of endless sources and unfathomable springs.[60]

From the very beginning he's already got his mouth full of vowels. He's enjoying that, though in this case they're a little more romantic, more out of Thomas Wolfe's unfathomable and vaguer vowels. From Wolfe he got these long symphonic prose sentences, and also the personal quality, the glee or joy of person that he put into all of his novels.

There's a passage in Wolfe, where Wolfe describes a sense of joy and glee and ecstasy that sometimes overwhelms him and makes him squeal. It was Kerouac's favorite reference point within the universe of Wolfe, the fact that great big huge Thomas Wolfe would come up with this completely personal, intestinal squiggle of joy. It's that little personal cry that Kerouac got out of Wolfe, as well as the large-scale canvas, many characters, endless book, like river flowing over rocks, broadening out.

When he was writing *The Town and the City,* he divided himself up into three people. He wrote about his family, but in an imaginary way. His actual family was his brother, Gerard, who died as a child, his sister, Nin, and himself. In this book he broke the fictional Martin family up into a number of brothers and sisters. The brothers all represented different aspects of himself. He was very conscious of that. The three that count are actually Kerouac's portrait of his own nature and his division of himself.

The eldest son is Joe, at this time around seventeen years old. This is the kind of thing he does: he borrows a buddy's old car—a

'31 Auburn—and in company with a wild young wrangler like himself drives up to Vermont to see his girl. That night, after the stamping furors of roadside polkas with their girl friends, Joe runs the car off a curve and into a tree and they are all scattered around the wreck with minor injuries. Joe lies flat on his back in the middle of the highway, thinking: "Wow! Maybe it'll be better if I make out I'm almost dead—otherwise I'll get in trouble with the cops and catch holy hell from the old man."

They take Joe and the others to the hospital, where he lies in a "coma" for two days, saying nothing, peeking furtively around, listening. The doctors believe he has suffered serious internal injuries. Once in a while the local police come around to make inquiries. Joe's buddy from Galloway, who has only suffered a minor laceration, is soon up out of bed, flirting with the nurses, helping with the dishes in the hospital kitchen, wondering what next to do. He comes to Joe's bedside twenty times a day.

"Hey, Joe, when are you gonna get better, pal?" he moans. "What the *matter* with you? Oh, why did this have to happen!"

Finally Joe whispers, "Shut up, for krissakes," and closes his eyes again gravely, almost piously, with mad propriety and purpose, as the other boy gapes in amazement.

That night Joe's father comes driving over the mountains in the night to fetch his wild and crazy son. In the middle of the night Joe leaps out of bed and dresses and runs out of the hospital gleefully, and a moment later he is driving them all back to Galloway at seventy miles per hours.[61]

I think that Kerouac was reading *The Brothers Karamazov* at the time, and so he divided himself up somewhat similarly into Dostoyevsky characters. Joe would be the equivalent of Dmitri, a solid, all-American (or all-Russian) man. He was the macho male involved with motorcycles, car wrecks, having girls, driving one hundred miles north for dates, and pool halls. What develops ultimately into his adoration for Neal Cassady or Dean Moriarity. That's one element which Kerouac sees in himself, the average straight all-American guy.

The next of the Brothers Karamazov was Ivan the intellectual, the mentalist, somewhat like Burroughs. This is a composite of Kerouac himself, the side that is sickly, city intellectual, with little elements taken from Burroughs's character and behavior and physiognomy.

> His brother, Francis Martin, is always moping and sulking. Francis is tall and skinny, and the first day he goes to High School he walks along the corridors staring at everyone in a sullen and sour manner, as though to ask: "Who are all these fools?" Only fifteen years old at the time, Francis has a habit of keeping to himself, reading or just staring out the window of his bedroom. His family "can't figure him out." Francis is the twin brother of the late and beloved little Julian, and like Julian his health is not up to par with the rest of the Martins. But his mother loves him and understands him.
>
> "You can't expect too much from Francis," she always says, "he's not well and probably never will be. He's a strange boy, you've just got to understand him."
>
> Francis surprises them all by exhibiting a facile brilliance in his schoolwork, amassing one of the highest records in the history of the school—but his mother understands that too. He is a dour, gloomy, thinlipped youngster, with a slight stoop in his posture, cold blue eyes, and an air of inviolable dignity and tact.

I think he got that "cold blue eyes, and an air of inviolable dignity and tact" from Burroughs.

In a large family like the Martins, when one member keeps aloof from the others, he is always regarded with suspicion but at the same time curiously respected. Francis Martin, a recipient of this respect, is thus made early aware of the power of secretiveness.

That is pretty smart writing for a kid of twenty-seven. The book was probably begun about the time we were all living together in an apartment with Burroughs, Joan Burroughs, and Hal Chase. Kerouac was coming in and out of town, like Francis coming into town, hanging around with me and Burroughs. And Joe Martin, the all-American, was hanging around with Hal Chase, going down to the bar, getting drunk, and chasing girls.

"You can't rush Francis," says the mother. "He's his own boss and he'll do what he likes when the time comes. If he keeps so much to himself it's because he has a lot on his mind."

"If you ask me," says Rosey, "he's just got something wrong up here." And she twirls her big finger around her ear. "You mark my word."

"No," says Mrs. Martin, "you just don't understand him."[62]

This division of Kerouac into three is not my idea, this is what he was saying at the time. He'd say, "I'm writing this book *The Town and the City*, and I got it all worked out, I got all different parts of myself in it." He was very conscious of doing it and telling us he was doing it. He said, "Francis is a part of me that's like Burroughs," and then he would read the passage about Francis. The third [brother] is the sensitive Kerouac. Neither the decadent nor the all-American Joe, but the Christian saint or Buddhist bodhisattva.

Thirteen-year-old Peter Martin is shocked when he sees his sister Ruth dancing so closely to another boy at the high school dance—after the annual minstrel show in the school auditorium. Looking over the entire dance floor, rose-hued and misty and lovely, he decides that life is more exciting than he supposed it was allowed. {Completely Kerouac there.} It is 1935, the orchestra is playing Larry Clinton's "Study in Red" and everyone begins to sense the thrilling new music that is about to develop without limit. There are rumors of Benny Goodman in the air, of Fletcher Henderson and of new great orchestras rising. In the crowded ballroom, the lights, the music, the dancing figures, the echoes all fill the boy with strange new feelings and mysterious sorrow.

"Mysterious sorrow," I guess that's the first noble truth of Kerouac. It's the glimpse of little puppets of eternity, clawing each other in their vanity, with great clouds brewing overhead in an empty sky.

By the window Peter gazes out on the brooding Spring darkness, burning with the vision of the close-embracing dancers, stirred by the tidings of the music and filled with an infinite longing to grow up and go to high school himself, where he too can dance embraced with shapely girls, sing in the minstrel show, and perhaps to be a football hero too.

"See that fellow with the crew-cut?" Ruth points out for him. "The chunky one over there, dancing with that pretty blonde? That's Bobby Stedman."

To Peter, Bobby Stedman is a name emblazoned on hallowed sports pages, a weaving misty figure in the newsreel shots of the Galloway-Lawton game on Thanksgiving Day, a hero of heroes. Something dark and proud and remote surrounds his name, his figure, his atmosphere. As he dances there, Peter cannot believe his eyes—can this be Bobby Stedman *himself*? Isn't he the greatest, speediest, hardest-running, weavingest halfback in the state? Haven't they printed his name in big black letters, isn't there a slow pompous music to his name and to the proud dark world surrounding him?

That's a romantic description of a football hero.

Then Peter realizes that Ruth is dancing with Lou White, himself. Lou White, another remote and heroic name, a figure on rainswept or snowlashed fields, a face in the newspapers glowering in exertion over the taut center position.[63]

[There is] something very intelligent about that. He's already got his archetypal thought forms picked out, his imagery of brooding spring darkness, of mysterious sorrow. Some words are a little vague, but there is an amazing amount of particular detail in all of this. The almost Genet-like rhetorical lushness, the slow pompous music to his "heroic name." It's somewhat ironic too, a funny humor in his rhetoric.

And when again he sees him on the day of the big Thanksgiving game, far down on the field hunched over the ball, Peter can't believe that this remote god has come to his house to see his sister and laugh at jokes. The crowds roar, the Autumn wind whips among the flags around the stadium, Lou White far away snaps back the ball on the striped field, makes sensational tackles that evoke roars, trots about and is cheered thunderously off the field as he leaves his last game for the school. The bands play the alma mater song, broken in the wind.

"I'm going to be playing in this game in two years," says Peter
to his father.

"Oh, you will, hey?"

"Yes."

"Don't you think you're a little too small for that? Those boys
out there are built like trucks."

"I'll get bigger," says Peter, "and strong too."

His father laughs, and from that moment Peter Martin is finally
goaded on by all the fantastic and fabulous triumphs that he sees
possible in the world.[64]

The third brother is sensitive, but also like the one with celestial
ambition, celestial football ambition, or celestial poetry ambition.
There are also a couple of other little kids described, he's broken the
family up into a few more archetypal infants. He's already setting
the style and nature of his brooding, already beginning to try and
describe the conscious subjectivity of his characters by projecting the
awareness that he already has developed and which he sees in me and
Burroughs and other people. The element that I was referring to as
panoramic consciousness or time consciousness, like my conversation
in the dorm about saying "Good-bye door, good-bye step number
one," the awareness of time passing in its own space.

If on some soft odorous April night the twelve-year-old Elizabeth Martin is seen strolling mournfully beneath the dripping wet
trees, pouting and fierce and lonely, with her hands plunged deep
in the pockets of her little tan raincoat as she considers the hor-
rid legend of life, and broods as she returns slowly to her family's
house—be sure that the darkness and terror of twelve-years-old
will come to womanly days of ripe warm sunshine.

Or if that boy there, the one with the resolute little face, who wets his lips briefly before replying to a question, who strides along with determination and absorption towards his objective, who tinkers solemnly in the cellar or garage with a gadget or old motor, says very little and looks at everyone with a level blue-eyed stare of absolute reasonableness, if that boy, nine-year-old Charley Martin, is examined carefully as he goes about the undertakings of his self-assured and earnest young existence, dark wings appear above him as if to shade a strange light in his thoughtful eyes.

And finally, if on some snowy dusk, with the sun's sloping light on the flank of a hill, with the sun flaming back from factory windows, you see a little child of six, a boy called Mickey Martin, standing motionless in the middle of the road with his sled behind him, stunned by the sudden discovery that he does not know who he is, where he came from, what he is doing here, remember that all children are first shocked out of the womb of a mother's world before they can know that loneliness is their heritage and their only means of rediscovering men and women.

This is the Martin family, the elders and the young ones, even the little ones, the flitting ghost-ends of a brood who will grow and come to attain size and seasons and huge presence like the others, and burn savagely across days and nights of living, and give brooding rare articulation to the poor things of life, and the rich, dark things too.[65]

That's pretty good for a young man. I can't write like this, it's too big, too much detail. It was criticized for being too brooding and vast, as *On the Road* was. Naturally that dross slowly disappears. His awareness of the details of life and the enormous attention to detail remains.

Like one sentence, "Young Peter Martin hears the long echoing hoot of the Montreal train broken and interrupted by some vast shifting in the March air." That's very odd, that "vast shifting in the March air," because there is a funny sensitivity to the outer panoramic consciousness of the universe I was talking about. "Panoramic consciousness" is a phrase taken from Buddhist meditation terminology. It describes the transitional point between quieting the mind and extending the mind out into awareness of panoramic space around. One of the things that always struck me when I first came across the Buddhist notion of panoramic consciousness was how early and how greatly Kerouac displayed that awareness of vast space.

> Young Peter Martin hears the long echoing hoot of the Montreal train broken and interrupted by some vast shifting in the March air, he hears voices coming suddenly on the breeze from across the river, barkings, calls, hammerings, which cease almost as soon as they come. He sits at the window awake with expectation, the eaves drip, something echoes like far thunder. He looks up at broken clouds fleeing across the ragged heavens, whipping over his roof, over the swaying trees, disappearing in hordes, advancing in armies. There's a smell of gummy birch, rank and teeming smells like mud that's dark and moist, of dark unlimbering branches of last Autumn's matted floor dissolving in a fragrant mash, of whole advancing waves of air, misty March air.[66]

It's lyrical and it's new, because it's oddly appropriate even though the language is very loudmouthed romantic, not softmouthed romantic. It's amazingly well balanced for being youthful springtime recollections of childhood. It's detailed and hard and precise, for the purposes of making a long powerful sentence with vowels that end it.

The Idiot and *The Brothers Karamazov* were our favorite books then, because those books dealt with heroes who were constantly rushing up to each other and looking in each other's eyes and asking about each other's souls and getting into big conspiracies or crimes or emotional climaxes together. That served as a model for our own behavior toward each other. We associated Alyosha from *The Brothers Karamazov* somewhat with Kerouac, or somewhat with me, or somewhat with Lucien, composites. Dostoyevsky's description of his mystical experience of auras before his epileptic fits was very intriguing to us. Little glimpses of visions, because we were talking about visions all the time.

Kerouac was always talking about visions. He was having them every other day. By vision he meant a perception [whereby for example he] suddenly sees his family moving around him, or he comes into the city and sees all of us cramped in our apartment conspiring, so he has a vision of us as a bunch of Dostoyevskean creeps conspiring. His visions were sort of like in Dostoyevsky.

I was involved with supreme reality and Kerouac was involved with his raw youth fantasy about becoming the greatest writer since Shakespeare, or Thomas Wolfe, one or the other. In fact when we went to visit Burroughs, it occurred to us that we were raw youths going to visit Versilov.[67] We couldn't figure out why Bill didn't declare himself an artist, why he insisted that he was just an exterminator or a remittance man. Why didn't he have the romantic notion of being an artist like we did?

Continuing on the same theme in *Vanity of Duluoz,* Kerouac's first glimpse of Burroughs.

Someday, in fact, I'll write a book about Will just by himself, so ever onward the Faustian soul, so especially about Wilson Holmes

Hubbard I dont have to wait till he dies to complete his story, he above all's best left marching on with that aggressive swing of his arms thru the Medinas of the world . . . well, a long story, wait.

But in this case he's come to see me about Claude, but saying it's about the Merchant Marine. "But what was your last job?" I ask.

"Bartender in Newark."

"Before that?"

"Exterminator in Chicago. Of bedbugs, that is."

"Just came to see ya," he says, "to find out about how to get papers, to ship out." But when I had heard about "Will Hubbard" I had pictured a stocky dark-haired person of peculiar intensity because of the reports about him, the peculiar directedness of his actions, but here he had come walking into my pad tall and bespectacled and thin in a seersucker suit as tho he's just returned from a compound in Equatorial Africa where he'd sat at dusk with a martini discussing the peculiarities . . . Tall, 6 foot 1, strange, inscrutable because ordinary-looking (scrutable), like a shy bank clerk with a patrician thinlipped cold bluelipped face, blue eyes saying nothing behind steel rims and glass, sandy hair, a little wispy, a little of the wistful German Nazi youth as his soft hair fluffles in the breeze— So unobtrusive as he sat on the hassock in the middle of Johnnie's livingroom and asking me dull questions about how to get sea papers . . . Now there's my first secret intuitive vision about Will . . .

That's the way that Kerouac uses the word "vision," it was very common that use of rhetoric and that attitude. It always baffled me because Jack was always having visions and I never had any real visions and I didn't know what he meant by visions, except maybe some big take on things.

Now there's my first secret intuitive vision about Will, that he had come to see me not because I was a principal character now in the general drama of that summer but because I was a seaman and thus a seaman type to whom one asked about shipping out as a preliminary means of digging the character of said seaman type. He didn't come to me expecting a jungle of organic depths, or a jumble of souls, which b'God on every level level I was as you can see, dear wifey and dear reader, he pictured a merchant seaman who would belong in the merchant seaman category and show blue eyes beyond that and a few choice involuntary remarks, and execute a few original acts and go away into endless space, a flat, planed "merchant seaman"— And being queer, as he was, but didnt admit in those days, and never bothered me, he expected a little more on the same general level of shallowness. Thus, on that fateful afternoon in July of 1944 in New York City, as he sat on the hassock questioning me about sea papers (Franz smiling behind him), and as I, fresh from that shower, sat in the easy chair in just my pants, answering, began a relationship which, if he thought it was to remain a flat plane of an "interesting blue-eyed dark-haired goodlooking seaman who knows Claude," wasnt destined to remain so (a point of pride with me in that I've worked harder at this legend business than they have)— Okay, joke . . . Tho, on that afternoon, he had no reason to surmise anything otherwise than shoptalk from your aunt to mine, "Yes, you've got to go now and get your Coast Guard pass first, down near the Battery . . ."[68]

It's funny self-intelligence there, a little bit out of Dostoyevsky. The characters are very conscious of their relation to each other, as on a stage. Not the self-consciousness of guilty skulking, fearful, but more a humorous, playful self-consciousness. In 1967, all I wrote was a nice poem on acid, "Wales Visitation," an exorcism of the Pentagon, and a couple little squiggles of poetry, but Kerouac wrote this whole thing. It's amazing, year after year, book after book, all comprising what he called the Legend of Duluoz. "I've worked harder at this legend business than they have," he said.

CHAPTER 14

Kerouac and
Visions of Cody, Part 1

Visions of Cody was finished in the early 1950s. It was one of the books I brought [with me] to San Francisco when I left New York in 1953, because I couldn't find a publisher in New York. My first reaction to it was of horror, dismay, disgust, and anger, because it didn't seem like a novel. It took me about a year to get used to it, but the publishers could never get used to it. There's a long Thomas Wolfean, Proustian, introductory section about Denver and Cody in Denver, the panoramic consciousness of the football field. That was submitted as a sample of a novel, at the time called *On the Road*, to A. A. Wyn Company with Carl Solomon as editor. On the basis of which they gave Kerouac an advance to write a novel.

Visions of Cody, really visions of Cassady, is a collection of illuminative moments or perceptions. The structure of the book was the great moments placed in whatever chronological order they fell into. It was to be intense epiphanies. Since we were reading James Joyce's *Stephen Hero* and *Portrait of the Artist as a Young Man*, there was a notion of epiphany, a moment of clear perception.

I had the idea that Kerouac was influenced by Neal reading Proust aloud. In 1947 when Cassady was in town we had a copy of Scott

Moncrieff's translation of Proust and Neal would read that aloud when we were high on grass. He read Proust very beautifully and he enjoyed the long organic sentences that were inclusive of many varieties of thought forms and associations that rose during the composition of the sentence. In other words, as in Milton, Proust used long sentences to include everything in his mind. I remember Neal reading aloud while we were all high on tea one long sentence in Proust, which was a description of Baron de Charlus, which began with a description of his curly Jewish French European oily ringlets, black hair, and ending with some glimmering image of the Hanging Gardens of Babylon, all in one sentence. At the time Neal was talking about how our consciousness went down six levels at once, our conversation and awareness. It was the first idea I ever heard about a thought being that spacious and that complicated and that infoliated, not just being simple declarative statements. Neal seemed to be enjoying that particular meditation, which grew out of his specialty, which was driving. While paying attention to the road and the car and the mechanics of the car and the sound of the car, Neal simultaneously smoked grass, listened to "Open the Door, Richard" or some rhythm and blues number coming out of the radio, kept time with one hand to the dashboard, maybe even trying to get his thumb up the cunt of whatever girl he had sitting next to him, while trying to keep up some metaphysical conversation with me, or with Kerouac, about Edgar Cayce, or Buddhism, or prose, pointing out the interrelatedness of all the different elements going on at once, pointing out there's a kind of ecstatic swing to the whole process of thought and car motion and physical activity. That influenced Kerouac, that kind of prose, meaning simultaneity of mind.

Kerouac thought he would try and do it in Thomas Wolfean prose, or Proustian prose, or logical syntactical prose, and so that chapter in *Visions of Cody* which ends with a description of a tackle in the red October sun on the football field was given to Carl Solomon as a sample of the novel for which he got a contract. I forgot what he submitted to Carl, it was either this or *On the Road* itself. He turned in the great mass of *On the Road* as a single continuous sentence on a scroll. He went off to San Francisco or maybe Mexico, finished the book, including all of the typing of tapes that were made of him and Neal, plus all the other visions of Neal he had, and then turned it in. That freaked me out because it wasn't anything like a novel that I had expected and I was acting as his agent. I was stupidly in the role of an agent and expected him to turn out what he promised to turn out, a normal symphonic syntax sentence, and I got freaked out and wrote him abusive letters, saying, "How dare you pull this on us!" I was running around to crazy Carl Solomon trying to peddle Jack's book and Jack sends in a book even crazier than Carl Solomon. My reaction was shameful. Later I got into it and it seemed to be the greatest work that he did.

Nobody would publish *Visions of Cody* except a hundred-page excerpt, which was put out by James Laughlin at New Directions as a limited edition [in 1959]. The book was not published for twenty years, though it should have been published in sequence after *On the Road,* to show Kerouac's natural development. That would have blown people's minds because it would have shown the depth of his art and the controversial complicated nature of it. Maybe all the critics would have been shocked like I was for a year. Instead his publishers asked him to write a nice easy book for people, to explain who all these characters were, and what his ideas were about the Beat Generation. So he sat down and wrote *The Dharma Bums* in simple, short sentence style as a commercial offering. He'd already accomplished this huge work of experimental prose, so it was time for him to write something short and sweet and simple. In the opening of *Vanity of Duluoz*, he says,

> All right, Wifey, maybe I'm a big pain in the you-know-what but after I've given you a recitation of the troubles I had to go through to make good in America between 1935 and more or less now, 1967, and although I also know everybody in the world's had his own troubles, you'll understand that my particular form of anguish came from being too sensitive to all the lunkheads I had to deal with just so I could get to be a high school football star, a college student pouring coffee and washing dishes and scrimmaging till dark and reading Homer's *Iliad* in three days all at the same time, and God help me, a W R I T E R whose very "success," far from being a happy triumph as of old, was the sign of doom Himself. (Insofar as nobody loves my dashes anyway, I'll use regular punctuation for the new illiterate generation.)[69]

That's his first paragraph, he's pissed off. It was easy for him because he'd written so much anyway, it doesn't make any difference to him. Behind most of Kerouac's later work is the legend of the forties, which he did not even get to write on account of the hypersensitivity of Lucien Carr. At Lucien's insistence, Kerouac never wrote about him until many years later. Here's his first notion of Burroughs.

> The fascination of Hubbard at first was based on the fact that he was a key member of this here new "New Orleans School" and thus this was nothing more than this handful of rich sharp spirits from that town led by Claude, their falling star Lucifer angel boy demon genius, and Franz the champeen cynical hero, and Will as observer weighted with more irony than the lot of em, and

others like Will's caustic harming buddy Kyles Elgins who with him at Harvard had "collaborated on an ode" to 'orror which showed the *Titanic* sinking and the ship's captain (Franz) shooting a woman in a kimono to put on her said kimono and get on a life boat with the women and children and when heroic spray-ey men shout "Madame will you take this fourteen-year-old boy on your lap?" (Claude) Captain Franz smirks "Why of course" and meanwhile Kyles' paranoid uncle who lisps is hacking away at the gunwales with a Peruvian machete as reaching hands rise from the waters "Ya buntha bathadts!" and a Negro orchestra is playing the *Star-Spangled Banner* on the sinking ship . . . a story they wrote together at Harvard, which, when I first saw it, gave me to realize that this here New Orleans clique was the most evil and intelligent buncha bastards and shits in America but had to admire in my admiring youth. Their style was dry, new to me, mine had been the misty-nebulous New England Idealist style tho (as I say) my saving grace in their eyes (Will's, Claude's especially) was the materialistic Canuck taciturn cold skepticism all the picked-up Idealism in the world of books couldnt hide . . . "Duluoz is a shit posing as an angel."[70]

Actually it's a view of himself. Cynical, cold, and underneath it all observant, rather than the mask of the misty-nebulous New England idealist style. Further visions of Burroughs, 1945 or 1946.

"Well why don't you wear a merchant seaman uniform man like you said you wore in London for your visit there, and get a lot of soft entry into things, it's wartime, isn't it, and here you go around in T-shirt and chino pints, or paints, or pants, and nobody knows you're a serviceman proud, should we say?" and I answered: "'Tsa

finkish thing to do" which he remembered and apparently took
to be a great proud statement coming straight from the saloon's
mouth, as he, a timid (at the time) middleclass kid with rich parents had always yearned to get away from his family's dull "subur-
ban" life (in Chicago) into the real rich America of saloons and
George Raft and Runyon characters, virile, sad, factual America
of his dreams, tho he took my statement as an opportunity to say,
in reply:

"It's a finkish world."

Harbinger of the day when we'd become fast friends and he'd
hand me the full two-volume edition of Spengler's *Decline of the
West* and say "EEE di fy your mind, my boy, with the grand actuality of Fact." When he would become my great teacher in the
night. But in those early days, and at this about our third meeting,
hearing me say, "'Tsa finkish thing to do" (which for me was just
an ordinary statement at the time based on the way seamen and
my wife and I looked proudly and defiantly on the world of un-
like-us "finks," a disgusting thing in itself granted, but that's what
it was), hearing me say that, Will apparently marveled secretly,
whether he remembers it now or not, and with timid and tender
curiosity on top of that, his pale eyes behind the spectacles looking
mildly startled. I think it was about then he rather vaguely began
to admire me, either for virile independent thinking, or "rough
trade" (whatever they think), or charm, or maybe broody melancholy philosophic Celtic unexpected depth, or simple ragged
shiny frankness, or hank of hair, or reluctance in the revelation
of interesting despair, but he remembered it well (we discussed it
years later in Africa) and it was years later that I marveled over that,
wishing we would turn time back and I could amaze him again
with such unconscious simplicity, as our forefathers gradually

unfolded and he began to realize I was really one, one, of Briton blood, and especially, after all, one kind of a funny imbecilic saint. With what maternal care he brooded over my way of saying it, looking away, down, frowning, "'Tsa finkish thing to do," in that now (to me) "New Orleans way of Claude's," snively, learned, pronouncing the consonants with force and the vowels with that slight "eu" or "eow" also you hear spoken in that curious dialect they speak in Washington D.C. (I am trying to describe completely indescribable materials) but you say "deu" or "deuo" and you say "f" as tho it was being spat from your lazy lips. So Will sits by me on the bench in that irrecoverable night with mild amazement going "hm hm hm" and "It's a finkish world" and he's instructing me seriously, looking with blank and blink interested eyes for the first time into mine. And only because he knew little about me then, amazed, as "familiarity breeds contempt" and bread on the waters there's a lotta fish after it.

Where is he tonight? Where am I? Where are you?[71]

That's a nice little piece of meditation. I think he gets hung up on Burroughs's character, the next chapter begins, "O Will Hubbard in the night!"

O Will Hubbard in the night! A great writer today he is, he is a shadow hovering over western literature, and no great writer ever lived without that soft and tender curiosity, verging on maternal care, about what others think and say, no great writer ever packed off from this scene on earth without amazement like the amazement he felt because I was myself.

Tall strange "Old Bull" in his gray seersucker suit sitting around with us on a hot summernight in old lost New York of 1944, the grit in the sidewalk shining the same sad way in 'tween lights as I would see it years later when I would travel across oceans to see him just and just that same sad hopeless grit and my mouth like grit and myself trying to explain it to him: "Will, why get excited about anything, the grit is the same everywhere?"

"The grit is the same everywhere? What on EARTH are you talkin about, Jack, really you're awfully funny, hm h mf hmf?" holding his belly to laugh. "Whoever heard of such a thing?"

"I mean I saw the grit where we sat years ago, to me it's a symbol of your life."

"My LIFE? My dear fellow my life is perfectly free of grit, dearie. Let us relegate this subject to the I-Dont-Wanta-Hear-About-It Department. And order another drink . . . *Really.*"

"It blows in dreary winds outside the bars where you believe and believingly bend your head with the gray light to explain something to someone . . . it blows in the endless dusts of atomic space."

"My G A W D, I'm not going to buy you another drink if you get L I T E R A R Y!"

XIV

At this time I'm writing about he was a bartender down on Sixth Avenue (Avenue of the Americas, yet.) (Okay). How my head used to marvel in those days, tug at my heartstrings, break almost . . .[72]

That's amazing, someone talking about himself like that, recollecting years before. I suppose that's universal. It's Kerouac's vision of Burroughs, by hindsight. Now, his vision of me is by hindsight pretty interesting.

I was sitting in Johnnie's apartment one day when the door opened and in walks this spindly Jewish kid with horn-rimmed glasses and tremendous ears sticking out, seventeen years old, burning black eyes, a strangely deep mature voice, looks at me, says "Discretion is the better part of valor."

"Aw where's my food!" I yelled at Johnnie, because that's precisely all I had on my mind at the moment he walked in. Turns out it took years for Irwin to get over a certain fear of the "brooding football artist yelling for his supper in big daddy chair" or some such. I didn't like him anyway. One look at him, a few days of knowing him to avouch my private claim, and I came to the conclusion he was a lecher who wanted everybody in the world to take a bath in the same huge bathtub which would give him a chance to feel legs under the dirty water. This is precisely the image I had of him on first meeting. Johnnie also felt he was repugnant in this sense. Claude liked him, always has, and was amused, entertained, they wrote poems together, manifestoes of the "New Vision," rushed around with books, had bull sessions in Claude's Dalton Hall room where he hardly ever slept, took Johnnie and Cecily out to ballets and stuff downtown when I was out in Long Island visiting my folks.[73]

That's his first version of me and his view of Lucien Carr again. Claude (Carr) in this novel has an older friend [Franz Mueller (Kammerer)], a friend of Hubbard (Burroughs), who has been following him around, trying to make him for a decade, since he was a kid.

Wherever Claude went, Mueller followed. Claude's mother even tried to have the man arrested. At the time, Hubbard, Franz' closest friend, remonstrated again and again with him to go off someplace and find another boy more amenable, go to sea, go to South America, live in the jungle, go marry Cindy Lou in Virginia (Mueller came from aristocrats somewhere). No. It was the romantic and fatal attachment: I could understand it myself because for the first time in my life I found myself stopping in the street and thinking: "Wonder where Claude is now? What's he doing right now?" and going off to find him. I mean, like that feeling you get during a love affair. It was a very nostalgic *Season in Hell.* There was the nostalgia of Johnnie and me in love, Claude and Cecily in love, Franz in love with Claude, Hubbard hovering like a shadow, Garden in love with Claude and Hubbard and me and Cecily and Johnnie and Franz, the war, the second front (which occurred just before this time), the poetry, the soft city evenings, the cries of Rimbaud!, "New Vision!," the great Götterdämmerung, the love song "You Always Hurt the One You Love," the smell of beers and smoke in the West End Bar, the evenings we spent on the grass by the Hudson River on Riverside Drive at 116th Street watching the rose west, watching the freighters slide by.[74]

That's Kerouac's nostalgia for that time and it's the heart of a lot of his writing. It occurred to me early that the people he wrote beautifully about were Burroughs [and] Herbert Huncke. In *On the Road* he wrote really well about Burroughs and Cassady at great length. Later on Gary Snyder, full-length portraits. I remember at the time thinking that his books were like paintings where the central character of the portrait got complete treatment, full flesh and blood, lots of subtlety and color in cheek and eyelid and the subsidiary characters were just sketched in very negligently around them, including myself or Philip Whalen or Kenneth Rexroth. We're almost cartoon sketches, sometimes very unflattering, but his heart went out to certain people that he wrote heroically about.

If you read Cassady's letters, you'll see just how much Cassady admired and loved Kerouac. I was in love with him and saw him as the heroic Faustian writer. The guy who could sit home and pore [over] hundreds of pages full of idyllic sentences in solitude egolessly. I felt like some little squiggly shit writing out a little lyric. And Neal, since he worshipped poetry, was always amazed at Jack's total solidity and extensiveness, his real power of concentration and creation. The only reason anybody was beautiful was because they had seen it through his eyes and expressed it poetically.

Everybody got their own idea of their own beauty out of him. I got my idea that I was beautiful out of his tolerance and acceptance. When you hear yourself echoed in somebody else's indulgent, tender, sympathetic consciousness, you begin to appreciate yourself. We saw him as hero and it was a surprise later to find critics speaking of Kerouac as a weakling that was always following other people around.

You've got to realize that he is the conceiver. I was very much aware of that and the reader should be aware of that. All this wouldn't exist if it weren't for Kerouac. We would be just a bunch of amphetamine-head, faggot, jailbird professors. That kind of phrasing comes from his mind. Kerouac was the energy source.

Burroughs was a source of enormous information and intelligence, also impersonality and cool and balance and good judgment and good sense and good manner and culture and aristocracy and faggotry, not faggotry so much as the high culture of homosexuality. Kerouac had that shining honesty, the simple ragged shiny frankness.

That's one thing that Burroughs didn't have, simple ragged shiny frankness. He had a kind of little boy, Gainsborough Blue Boy delicacy and melancholy and fragility and vulnerability. He was very vulnerable and sweet and sad, like a little boy. He was unexpectedly sensitive, but Kerouac was more of the outgoing football hero with a golden heart. This is all exaggeration obviously, but I think the energy, the enthusiasm came from Kerouac, even the enthusiasm for writing. Burroughs ascribes Kerouac's enthusiasm and encouragement as the greatest single force in making him write, finally.

Burroughs's permissiveness was in exploring the sinister otherworld outside of America. Kerouac was great at America, but as soon as he got across the border, it became an evil other world. Europeans, European fairies, hiding and waiting. Burroughs explored drugs, explored Times Square, and that [is what] intrigued me and Jack, Burroughs's exploration of evil, dark things.

Kerouac and I were both idealistic, looking for a new vision. "High on the peak top bats down in the valley of the lamb" is a little ditty Kerouac wrote. Burroughs was high on the peak top with the bats and he wanted to be down in the valley with the lamb. We saw Burroughs as a sinister agent of facts, but he saw himself not as sinister but as an exterminator. He had studied medicine, so he was more impersonal, more cold-blooded, reptilian. As Robert Bly says of Burroughs, "reptilian consciousness." We reported that back to Burroughs and Burroughs said, "What's he got against reptiles?" Kerouac and I saw Burroughs as very shy, tender, and sweet, with good manners. Quiet with a sense of humor cutting through.

Kerouac was more writer than person. His subject was always America and the promise of America. America as a poem. When America failed to be that idealistic poem of Thomas Wolfe, Jack found it more difficult to lyricize or make rhapsody about America.

It probably took him a long time to say, "I better write a minor book to my wifey, instead of a major Beethovean trilogy about the triumph of soul in America." That must have been hard, but he did it. He was already disillusioned by looking at things through the coffin. He'd already seen through his own vanity, his own egocentric nature and the desire for self-aggrandizement.

CHAPTER 15

Kerouac, Cassady, and *Visions of Cody,* Part 2

In *Visions of Cody,* Kerouac and Cassady were both exploring their first impressions of the universe. I think that was the basis of the rapport they had. What was their earliest vision of the nature of the cosmos as it appeared to the mind of a child or adolescent?

> . . . nobody made a move to notice or even gave much of a crap and Cody would have immediately felt drowned again, except suddenly for the saving memory of a hunch he used to have in boyhood which was whenever he turned his back on the people who were involved with him and even others who happened to be standing nearby, perfect strangers sometimes, they immediately gathered with the speed of light at the nape of his neck to discuss him voicelessly, dancing, pointing, until, jerking his head around for a quick look or just slowly to check, it turned out they'd always twanged back in place with all-to-be-expected fiendish perfect hypocrisy and in exactly the same bland position as before.[75]

There's another vision of driving along and Cody telling Kerouac that his childhood fantasy [had been of] having a knife miles long that came out of the edge of the car. As the car went along it would cut down all the trees and houses and people. Kerouac had a facility for zeroing in on archetypal takes on people and situations. That comes from an aesthetic appreciation of the grandeur and silliness and curious eccentric individuality that kids have in adolescence.

> Around the poolhalls of Denver during World War II a strange looking boy began to be noticeable to the characters who frequented the places afternoon and night and even to the casual visitors who dropped in for a game of snookers after supper when all the tables were busy in an atmosphere of smoke and great excitement and a continual parade passed in the alley from the backdoor of one poolroom on Glenarm Street to the backdoor of another—a boy called Cody Pomeray, the son of a Larimer Street wino. Where he came from nobody knew or at first cared. Old heroes of other generations had darkened the walls of the poolhalls long before Cody got there; memorable eccentrics, great poolsharks, even killers, jazz musicians, traveling salesmen, anonymous frozen bums who came in on winter nights to sit an hour by the heat never to be seen again, among whom (and not to be remembered by anyone because there was no one there to keep a love check on the majority of the boys as they swarmed among themselves year by year with only casual but sometimes haunted recognition of faces, unless strictly local characters from around the corner) was Cody Pomeray, Sr. who in his hobo life that was usually spent stumbling around other parts of town had somehow stumbled in here and sat in the same old bench which was later to be occupied by his son in desperate meditations on life.[76]

That's the opening fanfare, it zeroes in on the notion of character and heroes, and the act of keeping a love check on our heroes. What's he doing this year? Where's he now? or Who's she with? When I first read that sentence I was astounded by it. It was like some great European movie director panning in from a giant overview to one detail, one character, one face. There's a kind of noble drama pronounced in that sentence. I remember I said what a great idea, to keep a love check on all the characters like Dostoyevsky. But in whose mind is this a drama, or who's keeping tabs, what kind of person is it that keeps tabs? Kerouac was keeping a love check on his generation. Then there's a very strange paragraph.

> Have you ever seen anyone like Cody Pomeray?—say on a street-corner on a winter night in Chicago, or better, Fargo, any mighty cold town, a young guy with a bony face that looks like it's been pressed against iron bars to get that dogged rocky look of suffering, perseverance, finally when you look closest, happy prim self-belief, with Western sideburns and big blue flirtatious eyes of an old maid and fluttering lashes, the small and muscular kind of fellow wearing usually a leather jacket and if it's a suit it's with a vest so he can prop his thick busy thumbs in place and smile the smile of his grandfathers . . .

That's an odd idea, because he's taking this juvenile delinquent and making him a Civil War soldier. It is actually what Kerouac had in mind at that time. He was thinking of writing a novel about the Civil War. He had seen all those photos of guys in camps in the Civil War, handsome-looking fellows that you see described by Whitman, and Kerouac realized that they were no different than us. They were living people with the same spermy intelligence that everybody's got, and the same adventures. So he decided he would put Lucien Carr and Burroughs in that scene. You know, Burroughs as some morphine-addicted Southern general, an aristocratic general from a magnolia-treed mansion. He would put in Cassady as a heroic, happy-go-lucky cavalry man with horses and charging and stealing guns and running around getting drunk with the Indians.

> . . . who walks as fast as he can go on the balls of his feet, talking excitedly and gesticulating; poor pitiful kid actually just out of reform school with no money, no mother, and if you saw him dead on the sidewalk with a cop standing over him you'd walk on in a hurry, in silence.[77]

That's such a pretty piece of prose poetry and also full insight, raw insight in the sense that it brings you back home to some sense of the self which is real. I liked this particular passage because it displays that quality of panoramic awareness very clearly.

And then in that vast space, the loneliness. There's a phrase of Kerouac's, "the bleak inhuman loneliness of human nature." I think the loneliness is just inevitable, like the vastness of space. Kerouac wasn't the only American prose writer who liked the word "lone" and used it a lot. The biggest loner, the one who used "lone" most beautifully before him, was Herman Melville. In Melville's poetry, you'll see that same lone soul associating itself with American loneliness. The central image of that for Kerouac was everybody looking for "the center of Saturday night in America," as he put it. Even with all the excitements of Saturday, going out and getting drunk and trying to make out and get laid, we're all going to finally be a lonely crock of shit. For Kerouac, the physical center of the loneliness is in the back alley, under a redbrick building, under a neon sign, with nobody looking at him. Kerouac centered his image of American loneliness on that redbrick wall, which is where everybody wound up, unsatisfied. All the young, wild, lonely seekers wound up vomiting against that wall after the bar closed. That was his vision.

Cody sat there, stunned with personal excitement as whole groups of them shouted across the smoke to other fellows in a tremendous general anticipation of the rapidly approaching almost unbearably important Saturday night in just a few hours, right after supper when there would be long preparations before the mirror and then a sharped-up city-wide invasion of the bars (which already at this moment had begun to roar from old afternoon drinkers who'd swallowed their bar egos long ago), thousands of young men of Denver hurrying from their homes and arrogant clack and tie-adjustments towards the brilliant center in an invasion haunted by sorrow because no guy whether he was a big drinker, big fighter or big cocksman could ever find the center of Saturday night in America, though the undone collar and the dumb stance on empty streetcorners on Sunday dawn was easy to find and in fact fifteen-year-old Cody would have best told them about it; the premonition of this oncoming night together with the dense excitement of everything around the tables in the shadowy hall nevertheless failing to hide certain hints of heartbreaking loss that filtered in with chinks of daylight from the street (October in the poolhall) and penetrated all their souls with the stricken memory not only of wild windblowing coalsmoke and leaves across town, and football games somewhere, but of their wives and women right now, with feminine purposes, with that ravenous womany glee trotting around town buying boxes of soap, Jell-o, floorwax, Dutch Cleanser and all that kind and placing these on the bottom of their wagons, then working up to apples at the fruitstand, containers of milk, toilet paper, half crushable items like that, finally chops, steak, bacon pyramiding to eggs, cigarettes, the grocery slip all mixed up with new toys, new socks and housedresses and lightbulbs, eagering after every future need while their men-louts slammed around with balls and racks and sticks in the dimness of their own vice.[78]

[That's a] nice, long sentence. That business of jumping from pool hall to supermarket and getting all the detail into it comes from Neal Cassady's reading aloud of Proust where there's such a compound of disparate elements put together within one sentence.

Then the ultimate image at the end of Saturday night is the red neon light on a redbrick wall in a back alley of Denver where nothing is happening. People are just vomiting drunk and it's the end of the road, that is to say, all the excitement winds up in a giant disillusioned redbrick wall. The idea of people getting together for a big Saturday night is something that recurs all through his books. This redbrick wall is one of the "unspeakable visions of the individual."

. . . or maybe filling the windowed eyes of a hotel with their sheens, the glitter and yet the hidden beyondish gloom of this drove Cody in his secretest mind as it has myself and most others to further penetrations into the interior streets, the canyons, the ways, so much like the direction music takes in the mind or even the undiscoverable flow of dream images that make dreaming a tragic mystery; and so seeking rushing all dreams into the heart of it, always the redbrick wall behind red neons, waiting.[79]

. . . that was namelessly related in his poor tortured consciousness to the part of the redbrick wall he had always seen from the smooth old waitingroom bench of the Country Jail when his father had been arrested for drunkenness on Larimer Street probably with five or six others taken en masse from a warehouse ramp . . .[80]

Then a page later:

. . . see Cody Pomeray trying to hurry into the heart of the great Denver evening that to him will find its obvious focus in the pool-hall where sometimes the hour is so roaring that with the Tremont parlor backdoor open you can see a solid block of poolhall through the two joints like looking down an endless mirror all cuesticks, smoke, green; hustling to stab the heart of the night or be stabbed but always missing because it is not in the poolhall, or downtown further where the redbrick walls lead further, glowing from blackracked neons into unspeakable secret glittering centers where everything must be happening or at least give modified indication of where to go for it, show down what . . .

. . . listening, I'd say, not to the Hit Parade but the Saturday night dance parade remote bandbroadcasts most networks have (while the woman of the house is ironing the fresh fragrant wash), in your bathrobe and slippers, preferably Chinese style, with the funnies. But Saturday night is to be best found in the redbrick wall behind the neons, it's now infinitely bleaker than ever, like the iron fire escapes at the blind wallsides of those great fat movie auditoriums that squat like frogs in businesslike real estate are so much bleaker on Saturday nights, they cast more hopeless shadows.[81]

Then there's an interesting passage of Cody's direct approach, making friends with the pool shark and reproducing his language, the excitement of his talk, trying to cover all psychological angles at one time. It was the climax of Kerouac's early vision and it was the scene around which *Visions of Cody* was built, like an instant snapshot in eternity. Maybe it is Kerouac's greatest moment of writing.

Kerouac brings many elements of the book together, it's the entire gang out together Saturday night at dusk. Tom Watson having introduced Cody to his poolhall gang, middle-class kids, and then this lower-class kid joins them and shows off. He turns out to be smarter and more interesting and more athletically energetic than all of them. It's a characteristic Kerouac theme, kids playing football in an empty lot, simultaneously paired with the panoramic vision of the entire heaven at sunset. Then he introduces an old man lamenting the passage of life. He realizes that he's on the way down into death and he's already lost his youth and his sex and nobody loves him. It ends with the camera zooming in on Cody's face, making a football tackle.

Suddenly out on East Colfax Boulevard bound for Fort Collins Cody saw a football game going on among kids in a field, stopped the car, said "Watch" ran out leaping madly among kids (with noble seriousness there wearing those tragic lumps like the muscles of improvised strongmen in comedies), got the ball, told one blond-haired boy with helmet tucked underarm to run like hell, clear to the goalpost, which the kid did but Cody said "Further, further," and the kid halfway doubting to get the ball that far edged on back and now he was seventy yards and Cody unleashed a tremendous soaring wobbling pass that dropped beyond the kid's most radical estimate, the pass being so high and powerful the boy completely lost it in eyrieal spaces of heaven and dusk and circled foolishly but screaming with glee—when this happened everyone was amazed except Johnson, who rushed out of the car in his sharp blue suit, leaped around frantically in a mixup of kids, got the ball (at one point fell flat because of his new shiny-bottom shoes that had only a half hour's poolroom dust on 'em) and commanded the same uncomplaining noble boy to run across the field and enragedly unfurled a long pass but Cody appeared out of nowhere in the mad lowering dusk and intercepted it with sudden frantic action of a wildfaced maniac jumping into a roomful of old ladies; spun, heaving a prodigious sky pass back over Johnson's head that Johnson sneered at as he raced back, he'd never been outdone by anybody ("Hey whee!" they yelled in the car); such a tremendous pass it was bound to be carried by the wind, fall in the road out on East Colfax, yet Johnson ran out there dodging traffic as mad red clouds fired the horizon of the mountains, to the west, and somewhere across the field littler tiny children were burning meaningless fires and screaming and playing football with socks, some just meaninglessly tackling one another all over in a great riot of October joy. [. . .] Ah but well, Earl Johnson wanted to throw a pass to Cody and Cody challenged him and said, "Run with the ball and let's see if I tackle you before you reach that Studebaker where the man's standing"; and Johnson laughed because he had been (absolutely) the outstanding runner everywhere (schools, camps, picnics), at fifteen could do the hundred in 10:9, track star speed; so took off not quite realizing what he'd done here giving Cody these psychological opportunities and looking back at him with taunts "Well come on, come on, what's the matter?" And so that Cody furiously, as if running for his life, not only caught up with him but even when Johnson increased his speed in wholehearted realizing race caught up with him easily, in his sheer excitement, with his tremendous unprecedented raw athletic power he could run the hundred in almost ten flat (actually and no lie), and a sad, remote tackle took place in the field, for a moment everybody saw

Cody flyingtackling horizontally in the dark air with his neck bulled on to prove, his head down almost the way a dead man bows his head self-satisfied and life-accomplished but also as if he was chuckling up his coat sleeve at Johnson about-to-be-smeared, both arms outstretched, in a tackling clamp that as he hung suspended in that instantaneous fix of the eye were outstretched with a particular kind of unspeakable viciousness that's always so surprising when you see it leaping out of the decent suits of men in sudden sidewalk fights, the cosmopolitan horror of it, like movie magnates fighting, this savagery explosively leaping now out of Cody's new suit with the same rage of shoulderpads and puffy arms, yet arms that also were outstretched with an unspeakable mute prophesied and profound humility like that of a head-down Christ shot out of a cannon on a cross for nothing, agonized. Crash, Johnson was tackled; Justin G. Mannerly called out "Why didn't you try that in the road I have a shovel in the car" nobody noticing, even as he drove off; and Cody, like Johnson with his knees all bruised and pants torn, had established his first great position of leadership in Tom Watson's famous gang.

Long ago in the red sun . . .[82]

That long sentence ending with that instantaneous fix of the eye, after all the panorama and the red sun. That was his first long sentence writing and his great breakthrough. At the time he was influenced by Cassady's writing and by Proust. All the characters doing some separate thing, but in this instantaneous fix of the eye, all of them related for one epiphanous moment. All of it happening in the red sun in the field by the high school. He started out to write a big formal novel as a continuation of *The Town and the City,* but it led into the realization that everything was going on in his mind at once. Maybe he felt that the whole syntax was too constricting, so he thought what would happen if he just did a whole novel as a single sentence? At first, I think he turned aside from that as being too formalistic and began *On the Road*.

It is Kerouac's opening serenade, or opening cadenza, the first writing he did into the whole theme of *On the Road*. When I first read that I just wept, it seemed so orchestral and so many different elements gathered together within one sentence and such a long breath, and such melodiousness, as if wit, moment to moment, the intelligence of the noticings, that it seemed uncanny, at the same time the philosophy amazing, the panoramic glimpse of time and space, grieving, woeful, and deep.

There's a logical progression of his discovery of the nature of mind with an exposition and explanation to the world. It began with the idea of *Visions of Cody*, epiphanous moments, illuminated moments, or striking poignant moments. Then he extended it out through himself, accepting himself and beginning to dig how amazing his own private fantasy was with *Doctor Sax* and how amazing his private fantasy love history was with a girl, *Maggie Cassidy*. Finally the ultimate personal private vision would be the dredging up of his early traumatic sorrow at the death of his older brother, Gerard, in the late twenties, *Visions of Gerard*, which is maybe the most poignant and lyrical of all of Kerouac's books. I think it's also a point of turnover from a Catholic viewpoint to a totally Buddhist one.

Visions of Cody is the most serious text we'll run into. It's the most creative text, and the most seminal text. It's the one where Kerouac actually undergoes a transfiguration and becomes his art, he ceases to be a guy writing at his art and becomes interchangeable with the art. In a sense he gets crucified by his art or becomes one with his writing. His writing and his personality become identical and he becomes a superprofessional in the sense that he's a saint of writing. That writing is not merely something in which he explores his own character or turns out pretty works, but where every word he writes is part of a larger chronicle rather than individual pieces. It happens in the course of the writing of *Visions of Cody* and for that reason it's an amazing document. Everything after that for the rest of his life is a playing out of a single visionary moment that is registered in *Visions of Cody.*

Burroughs went through a similar experience a few years later. If this was Kerouac's decisive moment where the writing and his personality became identical, Burroughs's moment came around 1953. It is documented in his letters to me in which he enclosed chapters of *Naked Lunch.* Where Burroughs the writer of routines and Burroughs the man become identical, where there's no difference any longer.

The next step for Kerouac, having completed *On the Road,* was a discovery that he made while hanging around in New York with Ed White. White was an architect and carried a sketch pad, so he suggested to Jack that he try taking his notepad outdoors [and] sketch verbally. The first part of *Visions of Cody* consisted in a series of amazing sketches which are a standard workbook for anybody who's writing.

The whole idea is to sketch like a painter, to make drawings of details. He became very interested in those sketches. They were just like poems or something, the sound of a car door at midnight, a little thing on masturbation, streets of New York, long section describing the dust on a coat hanger in the elevated, or his fantastic description of the food in Hector's cafeteria in New York. Almost an apocalypse of food. The other influence was Rimbaud's prose poems, he intended his sketches to be like little Rimbaud prose poems from *Illuminations.*

If you take William Carlos Williams's "No ideas but in things" and carry it out to include the unconscious and relativistic mind, not just the simple middle-class doctor commonsense mind, but also uncommonsense mind and irrational mind, you'll get to what Kerouac was doing. Sort of post-nuclear writing, post-nuclear objectivism, strictly in sketches of life. That led into his interest in writing simultaneously with the life that was going on. The next step was writing about himself going on the road, while he was actually going on the road.

At the end of part two [of *Visions of Cody*] he sketches himself trying to get out of his house, abandon his world, abandon his mother, and go out to California again to meet Cody. That is followed by a whole series of sketches of him missing his ship, then sitting in a bar having missed his ship, until finally he gets out there by bus. In other words, he's sketching his life while he's living it. He's developed his practice of writing like piano playing, where he can play anything he hears, where he can write anything he can think.

By then the writing has become part of the living and the artist merges with the guy who's living. Where he's simultaneously trying to get a ship and writing about getting a ship. There's some discrepancy between his fantasies about getting a ship and what actually happens, so the drama of the writing is his rueful disillusionment as he goes along with his own fantasies about getting a ship. Finally the entire matter merges with the fact that he's sitting there talking to Cassady on a tape recorder, so there's no longer any question of even writing, it's actual conversation. The novel becomes life and the life becomes a novel with these two guys sitting talking on a tape recorder. They taped it and Kerouac later transcribed it from the tape.

Then the next step structurally was to do something even more amazing. He took the same idea of the tape recorder, except that he made the tape recording in his head much more flowery and fantastically, an imitation of a tape made in heaven. The imitation of the tape is Kerouac taking off from the original, which was not entirely satisfactory as singing Shakespearean prose, although it was absolutely satisfactory as a reproduction of brilliant conversation and mental high discontinuous conversation. But it still wasn't Shakespearean enough for Jack, so he makes an imitation of the tape, in heaven, as it were. The two characters talking in heaven in Joycean, babble language. The rest of the book is like a settlement with what's actually going on with the wives, the children, the jobs, the families, the relations between the men and women, what really is going on.

The book ends with a sketch of the railroad tracks, where Cody works, a blade of grass waves in the sunny Frisco afternoon. The end of the book is a little adieu to the hero, which is one of his best poems, I think. It climaxes into a style of prose that combines the fantasy language of the tape with realistic sketching, with the end of a novel, with all the classical aesthetic charms of the conclusion and farewell and adieu and coda.

> Goodbye Cody—your lips in your moments of self-possessed thought and new found responsible goodness are as silent, make as least a noise and mystify with sense in nature, like the light of an automobile reflecting from the shiny silverpaint of a sidewalk tank this very instant, as silent and all this, as a bird crossing the dawn in search of the mountain cross and the sea beyond the city at the end of the land.
>
> Adios, you who watched the sun go down, at the rail, by my side smiling—
>
> Adios, King.[83]

At the end Cody's got to go about his life and Jack's got to go back to his own life and back to his mother. So the last line is "Adios, king. Adios kind king light of mind."

The next thing that he did was to apply the method of sketching to a fantasy he had since he was a kid. It was a fantasy which I had also had, so we shared that particular image, the vision of the shrouded stranger of the night or Doctor Sax. Kerouac's book *Doctor Sax* opens with a sketch of "the wrinkly tar of the sidewalk, also the iron pickets of textile institute or the doorway where Lousy and you and G.J.'s always sittin, and don't stop to think of the words when you do stop, just stop to think of the picture better and let your mind off yourself and its work." That's where that phrase comes from. "Don't stop to think of the words, stop to see the picture better when you do stop."

By this time, you have to realize that he's written *On the Road, Visions of Cody, Doctor Sax,* and "October in the Railroad Earth," all within a period of two years. He's just exploding at writing at this point. He's writing every day, an enormous amount. Everything he's writing is pure gold because of the actuality of his mind at the moment. That's why I keep saying that this book is a crucial one for understanding modern writing to the extent that modern writing is catalyzed by Kerouac.

Then he applied this method of total recall to recollection of his high school romance days with a girl named Mary Carney in a book called *Springtime Mary,* published as *Maggie Cassidy.* Within a year he went back to the method of writing about life while he was living it and wrote *The Subterraneans.* He had an affair with a black girl and he wrote the book as the affair was ending. When he brought it in to show the girl it ended their relationship. She saw what he was thinking through his eyes, which was totally different than what she thought was going on.

Simultaneously he began using the same method to describe his own dreams, to explore the world of dream. He employed total recall and exhaustively recorded every last association going on in his mind. His *Book of Dreams* came from that, as well as the short novel *Pic,* which doesn't appear till posthumous days. That led into his *San Francisco Blues,* the beginning of his writing of little poems. Then *Some of the Dharma,* all by 1954. A tremendous amount of matter.

CHAPTER 16

Kerouac in Old Age

Kerouac in his older age was considered to be politically very reactionary. There was a funny kind of change between young and old in his attitudes, because at one time when he was a sailor he was a member of the communist party. There's a funny line about "I can go hitchhiking down that road and on into the remaining years of my life knowing that outside of a couple fights in bars started by drunks I'll have not a hair of my head harmed by totalitarian cruelty." That's his optimistic vision. There was some old radical left-wing or anarchist tradition in San Francisco, in the society he moved around in. He had been a communist and then he got into some fight with a stevedore and decided the communists were a bunch of bores.

It was an interesting little switch. I always thought that one of the reasons that Jack did come on so holier than thou, or Americanist, later was that he realized he had so much dynamite in his heart, and in his art as well, that it did catalyze great cultural change. He didn't know what he was dealing with in terms of the government and so there was a little edge that maybe he better not do anything too far out politically or get involved, [he should] avoid the authorities. He didn't join in like me and the rest of the Jewish communist intellectuals. He thought that we were devising new reasons for spitefulness, that was his phrase, "new reasons for spitefulness." I think that was true. All along Kerouac objected to the element of aggression, anger, spitefulness, resentment, un-Americanism in the younger generation that grew up. I felt very upset by that, because I thought he meant me, and he did. By hindsight I think it was a pure sharp mind, intelligent, redneck in style, but an intelligent comment.

What was Kerouac's final political conclusion about this? This might put his cultural political take out front. He's in the hospital with phlebitis caused by taking too much Benzedrine.

In fact I began to bethink myself in that hospital. I began to understand that the city intellectuals of the world were divorced from the folkbody blood of the land and were just rootless fools, tho permissible fools, who really didnt know how to go on living. I began to get a new vision of my own of a truer darkness which just overshadowed all this overlaid mental garbage of "existentialism" and "hipsterism" and "bourgeois decadence" and whatever names you want to give it.

In the purity of my hospital bed, weeks on end, I, staring at the dim ceiling while the poor men snored, saw that life is a brute creation, beautiful and cruel, that when you see a springtime bud covered with rain dew, how can you believe it's beautiful when you know the moisture is just there to encourage the bud to flower out just so's it can fall off sere dead dry in the fall? All the contemporary LSD acid heads (of 1967) see the cruel beauty of the brute creation just by closing their eyes: I've seen it too since: a maniacal Mandala circle all mosaic and dense with millions of cruel things and beautiful scenes goin on, like say, swiftly on one side I saw one night a choirmaster of some sort in "Heaven" slowly going "Ooo" with his mouth in awe at the beauty of what they were singing, but right next to him is a pig being fed to an alligator by cruel attendants on a pier and people walking by unconcerned. Just an example. Or that horrible Mother Kali of ancient India and its wisdom aeons with all her arms bejeweled, legs and belly too, gyrating insanely to eat back thru the only part of her that's not jeweled, her yoni, or yin, everything she's given birth to. Ha ha ha ha she's laughing as she dances on the dead she gave birth to. Mother Nature giving you birth and eating you back.

And I say wars and social catastrophes arise . . . not from "society," which after all has good intentions or it wouldnt be called "society" would it?[84]

So you see the [period] of invention and discovery that he was going through. And the eagerness to communicate, which is what this was all about. He was trying to communicate to America the unspeakable visions of the individual. The sketching thing is crucial to the whole school of poetics, because here we have the theory, or here we have the long prose preceding the theory, then we have the theory, and the examples are in the opening pages of *Visions of Cody*.

Basically the theme that [held] all these sketches together was Kerouac wandering around the Bowery in New York and comparing the landscape there with the Larimer Street bum landscape of Denver. He was interpreting New York through Neal's eyes, setting the scene for his observations of the bum, the hobo, the lost father, the deprived childhood, the kind of street experience of the lost, woeful, hopeless rejects of the land. It's what makes anybody who survives it a genius of sympathies.

There is a description of a diner that is quite good. It's the first formal sketch that he's placed in [*Visions of Cody*].

> This is an old diner like the ones Cody and his father ate in, long ago, with that oldfashioned railroad car ceiling and sliding doors— the board where bread is cut is worn down fine as if with bread dust and a plane; the icebox ("Say I got some nice homefries tonight Cody!") is a huge brownwood thing with oldfashioned pull-out handles, windows, tile walls, full of lovely pans of eggs, butter pats, piles of bacon— old lunchcarts always have a dish of sliced raw onions ready to go on hamburgs.[85]

It's just simple, straightforward American pop-eye observations. Kerouac's sketching is leisurely, like when Cézanne goes out with his sketch pad and sits on the road at Mont Sainte-Victoire. He notices everything necessary and he puts it down and finds little archetypal planes and surfaces and curves of the mountain. Here Kerouac is doing the same thing. He connects it emotionally, nostalgically, with Cassady and so it gives him some kind of an undercurrent of love or affection or empathy to connect with.

You have to have some kind of noble vision of the world when you're looking at it in order to get any kind of nobility into the sketching. Nobody can supply you with that noble vision of the world. They can supply you with the suggestion of how to articulate it, but nobody can tell you that this is eternity if you don't know that already. If you don't know that you're in eternity and that what you're writing about is your awareness of the presence of eternity, then there's no way of teaching that.

The final comment on the last pages [of *Vanity of Duluoz*] would be his final, high literary comment on existence.

Forget it, wifey. Go to sleep. Tomorrow's another day.
Hic calix!
Look that up in Latin, it means "Here's the chalice," and be sure
there's wine in it.[86]

That's the last line, and then he drank himself to death. So that's
1967 or 1968. In the mind of the book reviewer for the *New York
Times,* Anatole Broyard, Kerouac was a punch-drunk has-been by
then. In the mind of William Buckley he was just a drunk. In his own
mind, it had all been for nothing, all ashes, all ashes. He thought that
he was the best writer in English since Shakespeare. If you ask me
I'd say he was writing angel books in his illness. I think everybody
who was interested in that kind of literature realized he had done
something immense and permanent.

CHAPTER 17

Burroughs's First Writings and "Twilight's Last Gleamings"

To begin with, [William] Burroughs didn't see himself as a writer. He wrote only one thing when he was at Harvard [in the 1930s] with a friend and classmate named Kells Elvins. It is a sketch called "Twilight's Last Gleamings" and it was Burroughs's vision of America. In this routine or charade or skit, or whatever you call it, lie the seeds of almost all his later work and it's one of his funniest pieces.

The sinking of the *Titanic,* or the ship of state, is a theme that runs throughout Burroughs. How will the passengers, us Americans, react when our ship of state [goes] down? This is a jaundiced or disillusioned view of American character and it's certainly the opposite of wrapping yourself in the flag patriotically. The original was written in 1938, Burroughs's first piece of writing and his only piece of writing up until the time he met Kerouac and myself. He didn't quite see himself as a writer, he saw himself as a man of action. He was more interested in learning how to roll drunks on the subway and hanging around Eighth Avenue with junkies and petty thieves. He was like Jean Genet, interested in that same area of morals or manners. He had a theory that a psychopathic person without a conscience might be an interesting mentality, so he was hanging around with them. He was so pissed off with American moralism that he was checking out the opposite, so this has a kind of cynicism of that nature.

I think it was because Burroughs was too dry-souled and needed a lover and a little companionship and a little bit of encouragement. He wasn't dedicated as a writer, he was dedicated to something else, he was dedicated totally and sacramentally in a sense to exploring his consciousness, in going to the end of his mind. He was going into the pit, the pit of hell or heaven, to see what was at the end.

The outline for the sketch is that a black jazz band is playing "East St. Louis Toodle-Oo" or something and the millionaires are dancing and the sailors are all drinking in the hold and all of a sudden the ship begins to sink, the *Titanic* sinks. The band is ordered to play "My Country Tis of Thee" while the ship of state is sinking. The captain puts on women's clothes and jumps into the lifeboat saying "women and children first." There is an old man based on Kells Elvins's father who had a paretic sarcophagi, a lisp, and couldn't talk straight. He was an uninhibited psychopath who was always jumping in his car and driving up the country roads of Texas leaving a trail of dead chickens behind him saying "bastards, thuns of bithes, they're trying to take all my money."

So he [the captain] jumps in the lifeboat with a machete and while other people are trying to get into the lifeboat, he's chopping off fingers, saying, "Bastards, pithyathed thuns of a bidth, it's my lifeboat." These are characters that will be developed in Dr. Benway and others later on, psychopaths who are out for themselves and yet have a realistic view of human nature. Burroughs's view is comedy, but at the same time he's a cynic, somewhere between W. C. Fields and the Marx Brothers and Louis-Ferdinand Céline and Dracula.

Twilight's Last Gleamings

PLEASE IMAGINE AN EXPLOSION ON A SHIP.

A paretic named Perkins sat askew on his broken wheelchair. He arranged his lips.

"You pithyathed thon of a bidth!" he shouted.

Barbara Canon, a second-class passenger, lay naked in the first-class bridal suite with Stewart Lindy Adams. Lindy got out of bed and walked over to a window and looked out.

"Put on your clothes, Honey," he said, "there's been an accident."

A first-class passenger named Mrs. Norton was thrown out of bed by the explosion. She lay there shrieking until her maid came and helped her up.

"Bring me my wig and my kimono," she told the maid. "I'm going to see the Captain."

Dr. Benway, ship-doctor, drunkenly added two inches to a four-inch incision with one stroke of his scalpel.

"There was a little scar, Doctor," said the nurse, who was peering over his shoulder. "Perhaps the appendix is already out."

"The appendix *out!*" the doctor shouted. "*I'm* taking the appendix out! What do you think I'm doing here?"

"Perhaps the appendix is on the left side," said the nurse. "That happens sometimes, you know."

"Can't you be quiet?" said the doctor. "I'm coming to that!" He threw back his elbows in a movement of exasperation. "Stop breathing down my neck!" he yelled. He thrust a red fist at her. "And get me another scalpel. This one has no edge to it."

He lifted the abdominal wall and searched along the incision. "I know where an appendix is. I studied appendectomy in 1904 at Harvard."

That's Burroughs making fun of himself, because he went to medical school in Vienna.

The floor tilted from the force of the explosion. The doctor reeled back and hit the wall.

"Sew her up!" he said, peeling off his gloves. "I can't be expected to work under such conditions!"

At a table in the bar sat Christopher Hitch, a rich liberal; Colonel Merrick, retired; Billy Hines of Newport; and Joe Bane, writer.

"In all my experience as a traveler," the Colonel was saying, "I have never encountered such service."

Billy Hines twisted his glass, watching the ice cubes. "Frightful service," he said, his face contorted by a suppressed yawn.

"Do you think the Captain controls this ship?" said the Colonel, fixing Christopher Hitch with a bloodshot blue eye.

"Unions!" shouted the Colonel. "Unions control this ship!"

Hitch gave out with a laugh that was supposed to be placating but ended up oily.

"Things aren't so bad, really," he said, patting at the Colonel's arm. He didn't land the pat because the Colonel drew his arm out of reach. "Things will adjust themselves."

Joe Bane looked up from his drink of straight rye.

"It's like I say, Colonel," he said. "A man—"

The table left the floor and the glasses crashed. Billy Hines remained seated, looking blankly at the spot where his glass had been. Christopher Hitch rose uncertainly. Joe Bane jumped up and ran away.

"By God!" said the Colonel. "I'm not surprised!"

Also at a table in the bar sat Philip Bradshinkel, investment banker, his wife Joan Bradshinkel, Branch Morton, a St. Louis politician, and Morton's wife, Mary Morton.

The explosion knocked their table over.

Joan raised her eyebrows in an expression of sour annoyance. She looked at her husband and sighed.

"I'm sorry this happened, dear," said her husband. "Whatever it is, I mean."

Mary Morton said, "Well I declare!"

Branch Morton stood up, pushing back his chair with a large red hand.

"Wait here," he said. "I'll find out."

Mrs. Norton pushed through a crowd on C Deck. She rang the elevator bell and waited. She rang again and waited. After five minutes she walked up to A Deck.

The Negro orchestra, high on marijuana, remained seated after the explosion.

Branch Morton walked over to the orchestra leader.

"Play the Star Spangled Banner," he ordered.

The orchestra leader looked at him.

"What you say?" he asked.

"You black baboon, play the Star Spangled Banner on your horn!"

"Contract don't say nothing 'bout no Star Spangled Banner," said a thin Negro in spectacles.

"This old boat am swinging on down!" someone in the orchestra yelled, and the orchestra jumped down off the platform, and scattered among the passengers.

Branch Morton walked over to a juke box in a corner of the saloon. He saw the Star Spangled Banner by Fats Waller. He put in a handful of quarters. The machine clicked and buzzed and began to play.

"OH SAY CAN YOU? YES YES"

Joe Bane fell against the door of his stateroom and plunged in. He threw himself on the bed and drew his knees up to his chin. He began to sob.

His wife sat on the bed and talked to him in a gentle hypnotic voice.

"You can't stay here, Joey. This bed is going underwater. You can't stay here."

Gradually the sobbing stopped and Bane sat up. She helped him put on a life belt.

"Come along," she said.

"Yes, Honey Face," he said, and followed her out the door.

"AND THE HOME OF THE BRAVE"

Mrs. Norton found the door to the Captain's cabin ajar. She pushed it open and stepped in, knocking on the open door. A tall, thin, red-haired man with horn-rim glasses was sitting at a desk littered with maps. He glanced up without speaking.

"Oh Captain, is the ship sinking? Someone set off a bomb they said. I'm Mrs. Norton, you know. Mr. Norton, ship business. Oh the ship *is* sinking! I know, or you'd say something. Captain, you will take care of us? My maid and me?" She put out a hand to touch the Captain's arm. The ship listed suddenly, throwing her heavily against the desk. Her wig slipped.

The Captain stood up. He snatched the wig off her head and put it on.

"Give me that kimono!" he ordered.

Mrs. Norton screamed. She started for the door. The Captain took three long springy strides and blocked her way. Mrs. Norton rushed for a window screaming. The Captain took a revolver from his side pocket. He aimed at her bald pate outlined in the window and fired.

"You God-damned old fool," he said. "Give me that kimono!"

Philip Bradshinkel walked up to a sailor with his affable smile.

"Room for the ladies on this one?" he asked, indicating a lifeboat.

The sailor looked at him sourly.

"No!" said the sailor. He turned away and went on working on the launching davit.

"Now wait a minute," said Bradshinkel. "You can't mean that. Women and children first, you know."

"Nobody goes on this lifeboat but the crew," said the sailor.

"Oh, I understand," said Bradshinkel, pulling out a wad of bills.

The sailor snatched the money.

"I thought so," said Bradshinkel. He took his wife by the arm and started to help her into the lifeboat.

"Get that old meat outa here!" screamed the sailor.

"But you made a bargain! You took my money!"

"Oh for Chrissakes," said the sailor. "I just took your dough so it wouldn't get wet!"

"But my wife is a woman!"

Suddenly the sailor became very gentle.

"All my life," he said, "all my life I been a sucker for a classy dame. I seen 'em in the Sunday papers lying on the beach. Soft messy tits. They just lie there and smile dirty. Jesus they heat my pants!"

Bradshinkel nudged his wife. "Smile at him." He winked at the sailor. "What do you say?"

"Naw," said the sailor, "I ain't got time to lay her now."

"Later," said Bradshinkel.

"Later's no good. Besides she's special built for you. She can't give me no kids and she drinks alla time. Like I say, I just seen her in the Sunday papers and wanted her like a dog wants rotten meat."

"Let me talk to this man," said Branch Morton. He worked his fingers over the fleshy shoulder of his wife and pulled her under his armpit.

"This little woman is a mother," he said. The sailor blew his nose on the deck. Morton grabbed the sailor by the bicep.

"In Clayton, Missouri, seven kids whisper her name through their thumbs before they go to sleep."

The sailor pulled his arm free. Morton dropped both hands to his side, palms facing forward.

"As man to man," he was pleading. "As man to man."

Two Negro musicians, their eyes gleaming, came up behind the two wives. One took Mrs. Morton by the arm, the other took Mrs. Bradshinkel.

"Can us have dis dance witchu?"

"THAT OUR FLAG WAS STILL THERE"

Captain Kramer, wearing Mrs. Norton's kimono and wig, his face heavily smeared with cold cream, and carrying a small suitcase, walked down to C Deck, the kimono billowing out behind him. He opened the side door to the Purser's office with a pass key. A thin-shouldered man in a Purser's uniform was stuffing currency and jewels into a suitcase in front of an open safe.

The Captain's revolver swung free of his brassiere and he fired twice.

"SO GALLANTLY STREAMING"

Finch, the radio operator, washed down bicarbonate of soda and belched into his hand. He put the glass down and went on tapping out S.O.S.

"S.O.S. . . . S.S. America . . . S.O.S. . . . off Jersey coast . . . S.O.S. son of a bitching set . . . S.O.S. . . . might smell us . . . S.O.S. . . . son of a bitching crew . . . S.O.S. . . . *Comrade* Finch . . . comrade in a pig's ass . . . S.O.S. . . . God-damned Captain's a brown artist . . . S.O.S. . . . S.S. America . . . S.O.S. . . . S.S. Crapbox . . ."

Lifting his kimono with his left hand, the Captain stepped in behind the radio operator. He fired one shot into the back of Finch's head. He shoved the small body aside and smashed the radio with a chair.

"O'ER THE RAMPARTS WE WATCH"

Dr. Benway, carrying his satchel, pushed through the passengers crowded around Lifeboat No. 1.

"Are you all alright?" he shouted, seating himself among the women. "I'm the Doctor."

"BY THE ROCKET'S RED GLARE"

When the Captain reached Lifeboat No. 1 there were two seats left. Some of the passengers were blocking each other as they tried to force their way in, others were pushing forward a wife, a mother, or a child. The Captain shoved them all out of his way, leapt into the boat and sat down. A boy pushed through the crowd in the Captain's wake.

"Please," he said. "I'm only thirteen."

"Yes yes," said the Captain, "you can sit by me."

The boat started jerkily toward the water, lowered by four male passengers. A woman handed her baby to the Captain.

"Take care of my baby, for God's sake!"

Joe Bane landed in the boat and slithered noisily under a thwart. Dr. Benway cast off the ropes. The doctor and the boy started to row. The Captain looked back at the ship.

"OH SAY CAN YOU SEE"

A third-year divinity student named Titman heard Perkins in his stateroom yelling for his attendant. He opened the door and looked in.

"What do you want, thicken thit?" said Perkins.

"I want to help you," said Titman.

"Thtick it up with thwitht it!" said Perkins.

"Easy does it," said Titman, walking over towards the broken wheelchair. "Everything is going to be Okey-dokey."

"Thneaked off!" Perkins put a hand on one hip and jerked the elbow forward in a grotesque indication of dancing.

"Danthing with floothies!"

"We'll find him," said Titman, lifting Perkins out of the wheelchair. He carried the withered body in his arms like a child.

As Titman walked out of the stateroom, Perkins snatched up a butcher knife used by his attendant to make sandwiches.

"Danthing with floothies!"

"BY THE DAWN'S EARLY LIGHT"

A crowd of passengers was fighting around Lifeboat No. 7. It was the last boat that could be launched. They were using bottles, broken deck chairs, and fire axes. Titman, carrying Perkins in his arms, made his way through the fighting unnoticed. He placed Perkins in a seat at the stern.

"There you are," said Titman. "All set."

Perkins said nothing. He sat there, chin drawn back, eyes shining, the butcher knife clutched rigidly in one hand.

A hysterical crowd from second class began pushing from behind. A big-faced shoe clerk with long yellow teeth grabbed Mrs. Bane and shoved her forward.

"Ladies first!" he yelled. A wedge of men formed behind him and pushed. A shot sounded and Mrs. Bane fell forward, hitting the lifeboat. The wedge broke, rolling and scrambling.

A man in ROTC uniform with a 45 automatic in his hand stood by the lifeboat. He covered the sailor at the launching davit.

"Let this thing down!" he ordered.

As the lifeboat slid down towards the water, a cry went up from the passengers on deck. Some of them jumped into the water, others were pushed by the people behind.

"Let 'er go, God-damn it, let 'er go!" yelled Perkins.

"Throw him out!"

A hand rose out of the water and closed on the side of the boat. Springlike, Perkins brought the knife down. The fingers fell into the boat and the bloody stump of hand slipped back into the water.

The man with the gun was standing in the stern.

"Get going!" he ordered. The sailors pulled hard on the oars.

Perkins worked feverishly, chopping on all sides. "Bathtardth, thonthabitheth!" The swimmers screamed and fell away from the boat.

"That a boy."

"Don't let 'em swamp us."

"Atta boy, Comrade."

"Bathtardth, thonthabitheth! Bathtardth, thonthabitheth!"

"OH SAY DO DAT STAR SPANGLED BANNER YET WAVE"

The Evening News

Miss Canon showed your reporter her souvenirs of the disaster: a life belt autographed by the crew, and a severed human finger.

"I don't know," said Miss Canon. "I feel sorta bad about this old finger."

"O'ER THE LAND OF THE FREE"[87]

That was actually Burroughs's first literary production. Kerouac was always a bit abashed, as I was, by Burroughs, but we all recognized his intelligence. Jack said, "He's the most intelligent man in America," because nobody else was cutting through the bullshit the way Burroughs was at that time. I was going to Columbia, nobody talked like that, nobody was so direct and intelligent and cynical, and at the same time funny, well informed, and precise in the description of manners. The nearest thing I know in literature was Louis-Ferdinand Céline's *Journey to the End of the Night*.

It was Kerouac's beatific lyricism that turned Burroughs on to writing, because Burroughs couldn't resist Kerouac's enthusiasm finally. Kerouac was all enthusiasm, lyricism, innocence, fantastic ear, and great heart. And in spite of all his cynicism Burroughs was much affected by that, even though he occasionally thought that Kerouac was naive. Nonetheless, it turned him on to writing as a sacred vocation.

I think Burroughs hates women, or at least did at the time. You can tell that he's making fun of the American male [who is] dominated by the woman, which is pretty much upper-middle-class St. Louis aristocracy. The only people he gives credence to as having some sense are the blacks in the orchestra. They know where they are. I think he also likes the captain and Dr. Benway. He likes Dr. Benway because Benway is so outrageous, he represents that psychopathic element in Burroughs that won't stop at anything. And [he likes] the captain who knows exactly what he's doing. He puts on a woman's kimono and shoots the purser and takes all the jewels and money and knocks out the radio operator so nobody will report it. It sounded like Jonathan Swift's *A Modest Proposal*.

CHAPTER 18

Burroughs, Kerouac, and
And the Hippos Were Boiled in Their Tanks

In 1946 Burroughs had a room above Riordan's Bar near Columbus Circle. He moved [there] in order to explore all the bars up and down Eighth Avenue and Kerouac and I used to visit him and just sit around and talk. Burroughs was checking out all the different bars looking for characters. At the time he was reading John O'Hara, the hard-boiled detective short story writer. O'Hara was put down by the elegant writers of his day as being too commercial, because his first books were great successes, but he was quite interesting. So he, Dashiell Hammett, Raymond Chandler, and others wrote what was called hard-boiled fiction, mostly detective and stylistically quite interesting. They were post-Hemingway in that they didn't go off into a lot of vaporous, gassy, flowery yak, but stuck to "no ideas but in things" as a basic slogan or method. High-precision detail with very good descriptions of people.

Burroughs and Kerouac were reading Chandler and O'Hara for style and they decided to write a collaborative novel, which they called *And the Hippos Were Boiled in Their Tanks*. The title came from a news broadcast that Burroughs remembered. It was a description of a fire in the St. Louis Zoo, saying that the fire broke out and the caretakers got the snakes out of the snake house and rescued the lions, but there was a disaster among the emus and the cat houses and there was a great deal of trouble with the anteater, "and the hippos were boiled in their tanks!" So they used that as a title for the novel and each of them wrote a chapter. It was straightforward and it preceded Burroughs's *Junkie* and Kerouac's *On the Road.*

Around that time Burroughs ran into Huncke in a bar [on Eighth Avenue] at 43rd Street called the Angle. Burroughs gives an account in *Junkie* of the transaction where he tried to sell Huncke some morphine syrettes. That was the beginning of Burroughs's junk habit. I was hanging around and tried out some of those syrettes at the same time. I might have turned out to be a junkie except that I observed Burroughs. I took a lot of junk over the years thereafter, but always irregularly and made sure I simply didn't take it twice in the same week, always irregularly, like ten days in between. I'm not a habit type anyway, I'm a workaholic.

Burroughs didn't see himself as a writer then. "Twilight's Last Gleamings" was the only thing he ever wrote until he met Kerouac. Then the two of them wrote *And the Hippos Were Boiled in Their Tanks.* It was based on Lucien Carr's murder of David Kammerer.[88] Burroughs became interested in Kerouac because he thought Kerouac was a real writer, somebody who actually went home and wrote. Jack didn't just talk about it, he spent hours every day writing and lived only in terms of writing. He saw everything as a writer.

Burroughs saw himself more as an investigator of souls and cities, a person of curiosity, or a picaresque adventurer. He was interested in information and facts, not so much interested in literature. The crucial time came when he killed his wife and was plunged into such despair that writing itself seemed to be the only activity, the only path open for him.[89] It was not so much as redemption, but as a communicative activity which linked him with me and other people, with the rest of humanity, with friends. Burroughs was always cynical about writing in the sense that he always thought it was a romantic thing to do, until he found a function for it that was practical. Either as a conduit, like letters, epistolary writing, communication, or as an investigation of fact after the [discovery of] cut-up, as an investigation of the nature of consciousness, or an investigation into the nature of "the Word" itself, or even consciousness itself, which had become dominated by word and image. The writing and cut-up writing later was a cutting up of consciousness, a way of investigating consciousness, rubbing out the word.

Kerouac was similar, in that his investigation into his prose was also spiritual, it was a spiritual tool for him. Gregory Corso later used the word "probe," poetry as a probe into death, future, police, marriage, hair, bomb, all the conceptions possible gathered from both the conscious and the unconscious. Kerouac's view underwent various changes in the early forties. When he was a young romantic kid of twenty, writing was a kind of Faustian alchemy in his book *The Sea Is My Brother*. When he was reading Rimbaud, the great writer was a seer, who arrived at visions through the long wizened derangement of the senses. Kerouac knew the great line in Rimbaud which is the key to it all: "And springtime brought me the idiot's frightful laughter."[90] That was the payment for deranging his senses.

Burroughs took the Chandler-O'Hara, hard-boiled American fiction and turned it into a total satire of the American character, as in the ship that was sinking and everybody's out for themselves. He revealed the bones of human behavior, exposing what people were really like.

Burroughs is an old faggot, so he's got this protective coloration of a tough exterior, implacable fact. His routines get outrageous, becoming surrealist in fact, and he goes beyond the bounds of propriety. This phase of Burroughs's writing grew out of charades that he played with Kerouac and myself and others. In these we would all assume roles. Kerouac played a young American bumpkin in Paris, innocent in a straw hat. I played a well-groomed Hungarian refugee bringing with me my fake family art collection to sell. And Burroughs played a Lotte Lenya character, a phony lesbian baroness, who would go out and entice young Americans. I was this phony Hungarian of uncertain morals who was a con man and Burroughs was the shill preying upon Kerouac. At one time Bill got up in drag and acted it out, but he would get so carried away that he'd fall down on the floor laughing sometimes, because it was so funny. He would take it to slightly psychopathic, or psychotic, lengths. He would get beyond the bounds of what Jack or I thought was reasonable and would get into boundless, genius strangeness.

That strangeness was partly an outcome of a very interesting psychoanalysis he was going through. He had been psychoanalyzed by Dr. Federn, who was one of Freud's direct pupils, one of the elders in the American Freudian community. Then Burroughs went to Dr. Lewis Wolberg, who was a specialist in hypnotherapy, and under hypnosis Burroughs began to reveal many layers of character. Right underneath the surface of this dignified St. Louis aristocratic Harvard gent was a very prim English governess. She was always taking tea in the afternoon and would have nothing to do with any obscenity, except ultimately she was completely obscene and rapacious. Underneath that were several layers. I think he had six or seven going down, but one of the layers going down was Old Luke, an old white-trash Mississippi anti-Semitic, anti-nigger guy sitting on his back porch near a river, talking about how "I just sit there all day long and fish come floating down the river and pass by . . . and there ain't nothing happening round here except another fish come floatin by, catfish passes by. Did you ever gut a catfish?" Some sort of psychotic Southern sheriff type.

Then underneath that was a Chinaman, on the banks of the Yangtze, living in mud, half human and half mud and half primordial, maybe a junkie even with his opium pipe. He's living on the banks of the Yangtze with nothing to do with any civilization or anything, dumb almost mute, but with a kind of imperturbable Chinese, empty-eyed tolerance of everything. In *Naked Lunch* he evolves into the Chinaman who has the last line in the book, which is the Chinese laundryman, "No glot, c'lom Fliday." Meaning like no answer. There's no god, no answer, no glot, I can't satisfy you. This Chinaman was not vocal, hardly talking, impassive, with a bland impassive gaze. Way down in a basic level of observation more or less from the bottom of the barrel. The ultimate beat character, I guess. The bottom of the economic and social ladder and the bottom of the human ladder of the world. Reduced to the ultimate essential, just coping with the Yangtze, and the mud.

Burroughs had these characters within him, along with several others. I think one of the reasons for that is because Burroughs is a homosexual who has one peculiar erotic situation. I thought it was rare, but he insisted it was not at all, but his favorite way of cumming is when he is screwed by a man. There are a lot of homosexuals who like that, but there are very few who cum from being screwed. However, Burroughs is a very dignified, Harvard man, and this is not exactly a situation where he is in control of his sexual life. He found this, as the Bible says, "inconvenient." When he was younger, he found it demeaning, pretty much against the dignified outer mien that he had, to have to be prone and be screwed in order to have an orgasm.

In the forties he was experimenting with different levels of his own consciousness. There was a prim governess somewhere in his hypnoanalysis, who would cum sighing and fluttering her fan. He found a schizophrenic split between his exterior laconism and dignity and his interior squishiness, or vulnerability. It was an enormous disparate and could be seen as an enormous split in his nature. At that point he got a little bit sick and tired of being the victim, the guy who had to be fucked in order to cum, so there's a whole rehearsal of all these obsessions in *Naked Lunch*. The blue movie section in *Naked Lunch* is really a symbolic playing out of this same objection. He has the image of a guy cumming involuntarily as he was being hung. He sees his situation as similar to the guy being victimized or possessed unto death by being hung. In the blue movie, he makes a kind of cut-up of his own sexual obsession by repeating it over and over in different combinations, Johnny, Mark, and Mary; and then Mary and Johnny hang Mark; and Mary and Mark hang Johnny; and then Mark and Johnny hang Mary; and over and over until he gets bored. That was one method of cut-up, the beginning of cut-up and one motive of cut-up, to cut out all apparent thoughts, feelings, and sensory impressions, including the ultimate sexual conditioning. Burroughs was basically trying to cut out of the body. Thus, his title *The Exterminator,* [a] kind of nihilism.

A lot of Burroughs's writing has to do with a dignified exterior and a completely terrorized, victimized, hung-up, cowardly, schizo-phrenic interior; the dignity on the exterior and supposed degrada-tion of the interior, of the inside life. It's a real situation for him psychologically. Here's this very intelligent, dignified, aristocratic guy with a good education, who was smart enough to acknowl-edge it and to deal with it imaginatively with a sense of humor. To a certain extent it is the key to a lot of Burroughs, the key to his understanding of America. It's another form of addiction also, in a sense an addiction to sex. Writing is a way of exorcising obsessions. It's an old tradition. In Burroughs's case it is therapeutic, by replaying it over and over and over again in different forms it is washed clean of obsessive emotion.

CHAPTER 19

Burroughs, Joan Burroughs, and *Junkie*

In 1951, through inadvertency, Burroughs killed his wife in a William Tell shooting in Mexico City. She had put a gin glass on the top of her skull and drunkenly insisted that he shoot it off and he missed. I had been with her for the month previous and she had been in a suicidal state, so when I heard of the accident I figured that she had, in a sense, killed herself and used him as a means. It was after that that he began writing. Most of the book *Junkie* is his writings that were sent to me in the form of letters from Mexico. It was first published in 1953 and I was the coeditor and agent for those texts.

In the preface to *Junkie,* Burroughs has a couple passages. "I've learned a great deal from using junk. I have seen life measured out in eye droppers and morphine solution."[91] Here he is paraphrasing T. S. Eliot. Both Eliot and Burroughs are from St. Louis and they have a similar tone of voice, [that of] the St. Louis aristocracy. Ultimately they are very similar in [their] method of composition. The later cut-up prose of Burroughs is actually an extension into a larger scale of the panoramic prose novel of *The Waste Land,* which is also collage or cut-up. *The Waste Land* and Burroughs could be almost interchanged. Take a hundred lines of Burroughs's *Cobblestone*

Gardens or some later work and integrate them into *The Waste Land,* stylistically they're very similar.

For all of his breakthrough genius, Eliot didn't produce more than four or five pages of such high-class collage. [It was as if] that were the limit or that he didn't want to. In the preface to *Junkie* is another interesting phrase: "They knew that basically no one can help anyone else."[92] There's no key, no secret that someone else has, that Burroughs can give you. That's pretty implacable.

> He looked like George Raft, but was taller. Norton was trying to improve his English and achieve a smooth, affable manner. Affability, however, did not come natural to him.[93]

This is a very funny way of saying he was really mean. A super understatement, like in Hemingway or hard-boiled detective fiction. Some phrasing emerges here which will recur over and over again in Burroughs's later work, like the more famous *Naked Lunch.*

> Jack [. . .] was not one of those lost sheep looking for a shepherd with a diamond ring and a gun in the shoulder holster and the hard, confident voice with overtones of connections, fixes, setups that would make a stickup sound easy and sure of success.[94]

"A confident voice with overtones of connections, fixes, setups" comes back over and over again as the voice of the CIA agent or the voice of the supreme mafioso in later books by Burroughs.

> The man sat up straighter and swung his legs off the couch. His jaw fell slackly, giving his face a vacant look. The skin of his face was smooth and brown. The cheekbones were high and he looked

Oriental. His ears stuck out at right angles from his asymmetrical skull. The eyes were brown and they had a peculiar brilliance, as though points of light were shining behind them. The light in the room glinted on the points of light in his eyes like an opal.[95]

It's kind of like a light that throws itself directly into your consciousness, some insect consciousness. There is an impersonality, some insect-like or reptilian impersonality to the description. The effects of the description are to make the person's face look like [a chimu] urn, or a Mayan urn, or an empty-eyed statue. I guess it's the vacant look he wanted to capture.

Junkie begins in New York City in the mid-forties, before Burroughs met Joan and before he became addicted. [The following is] Burroughs's description of his first meeting with Herbert Huncke.

In many tenement apartments the front door opens directly into the kitchen. This was such an apartment and we were in the kitchen.

After Joey went out I noticed another man who was standing there looking at me. Waves of hostility and suspicion flowed out from his large brown eyes like some sort of television broadcast. The effect was almost like a physical impact. The man was small and very thin, his neck loose in the collar of his shirt. His complexion faded from brown to a mottled yellow, and pancake make-up had been heavily applied in an attempt to conceal a skin eruption. His mouth was drawn down at the corners in a grimace of petulant annoyance.

"Who's this?" he said. His name, I learned later, was Herman.

"Friend of mine. He's got some morphine he wants to get rid of."

Herman shrugged and turned out his hands. "I don't think I want to bother, really."

"Okay," Jack said, "we'll sell it to someone else. Come on, Bill."[96]

So that is Burroughs's first notice of Huncke.

A few nights after meeting with Roy and Herman, I used one of the syrettes, which was my first experience with junk. A syrette is like a toothpaste tube with a needle on the end. You push a pin down through the needle; the pin punctures the seal; and the syrette is ready to shoot.[97]

These were syrettes of morphine which were left over from World War II and were being sold by army or navy characters loose on Times Square. In those days much less surveillance and much looser scene.

Morphine hits the backs of the legs first, then the back of the neck, a spreading wave of relaxation slackening the muscles away from the bones so that you seem to float without outlines like lying in warm salt water. As this relaxing wave spread through my tissues, I experienced a strong feeling of fear. I had the feeling that some horrible image was just beyond the field of vision, moving, as I turned my head, so that I never quite saw it. I felt nauseous; I lay down and closed my eyes. A series of pictures passed, like watching a movie: A huge, neon-lighted cocktail bar that got larger and larger until streets, traffic, and street repairs were included in it; a waitress carrying a skull on a tray; stars in the clear sky. The physical impact of the fear of death; the shutting off of breath: the stopping of blood.[98]

Just in that one sentence you get a whole key to all of Burroughs's later development as a writer. It's an amazing description of a day-dream or half-dream, hypnogenetic state, with an image that simply gets larger and larger until you fall completely into a dream state. It is a perfect reproduction of the state of picture consciousness during a virgin opiate experience. What's also interesting here is the montage effect, which is characteristic of later Burroughs. The seeds of his montage, cut-up effects are already present in these earliest writings, which are just realistic, naturalistic noticings of phenomena in his own mind and optical experience. Something amazingly intelligent about writing it down, being able to write your dream down that quick, sharp and fast, basically because he's interested in states of consciousness, as well as external description.

I'm going to go through *Junkie* and give highlights like this. I realize that they are keys to the development of his later writing and the images persist throughout his later writing. They were first intro-duced in the earlier text "Twilight's Last Gleamings," about the sink-ing of the *Titanic,* the sinking of Western civilization. Some images come from that, but the whole gamut of Burroughs's vocabulary of hallucinatory images comes from *Junkie.* Once you know the roots you can see the recombinations and permutations of these images and the humor of that in his later work. He met Huncke again in the Angler Bar, which here is called the Angle Bar.

I began dropping into the Angle Bar every night and saw quite a bit of Herman. I managed to overcome his original bad impres-sion of me, and soon I was buying his drinks and meals, and he was hitting me up for "smash" (change) at regular intervals. Her-man did not have a habit at this time. In fact, he seldom got a habit unless someone else paid for it. But he was always high on something—weed, benzedrine, or knocked out of his mind on "goof balls." He showed up at the Angle every night with a big slob called Whitey. There were four Whities in the Angle set, which made for confusion. This Whitey combined the sensitivity of a neurotic with a psychopath's readiness for violence. He was convinced that nobody liked him, a fact that seemed to cause him a great deal of worry.[99]

It was Burroughs's take on not wanting to be liked himself, he wasn't worried if nobody liked him. Burroughs said that when he was young he felt totally out of it, felt like a pariah. This will lead on to the talking asshole in *Naked Lunch* who complains that nobody loves [him].

Burroughs's first impression of teaheads is pretty funny. I thought this particular passage was funny at the time and so did Kerouac. Burroughs's adventures trying to be a marijuana pusher, trying to make his living selling grass. And this was his cynical comment on the romantic idea of going out and being a criminal heroic peddler of weed.

> Herman contacted other teaheads. They all gave us static.
> In practice, pushing weed is a headache. To begin with, weed is bulky. You need a full suitcase to realize any money. If the cops start kicking your door in, it's like being with a bale of alfalfa.

When I got this in the letter I just laughed, it was so obviously true and funny. His idea, the humor of being trapped with a bale of alfalfa, something that you couldn't dispose of.

> Teaheads are not like junkies. A junkie hands you the money, takes his junk and cuts. But teaheads don't do things that way. They

expect the peddler to light them up and sit around talking for half an hour to sell two dollars' worth of weed, if you come right to the point, they say you are a "bring down." In fact, a peddler should not come right out and say he is a peddler. No, he just scores for a few good "cats" and "chicks" because he is viperish. Everyone knows that he himself is the connection, but it is bad form to say so. God knows why. To me, teaheads are unfathomable.

There are a lot of trade secrets in the tea business, and teaheads guard these supposed secrets with imbecilic slyness. For example, tea must be cured, or it is green and rasps the throat. But ask a teahead how to cure weed and he will give you a sly, stupid look and come-on with some double-talk. Perhaps weed does affect the brain with constant use, or maybe teaheads are naturally silly.[100]

I had a romantic notion of smoking grass at that time, but Burroughs was really cynical and really intelligent. He sees right through everything immediately with no illusions. I had this inoculation of disillusionment through Burroughs way back in 1950, but there was still the romanticism of the 1960s that we all had to go through. Everybody got goofy with the teahead sweatshirts and a romanticization of the whole tea ethos.

The doctors of that era—1945–48—had an historical recollection that opiates weren't always illegal and there wasn't always this nationalistic paranoid hysteria about junk and junkies. Around the World War II era junkies were [thought of as] sick people who went to doctors or went to the pharmacy and bought their heroin or opium on an open market. The number of junkies in America was somewhat limited, nothing like they have now, because the cash nexus has entered into the peddling of junk. It is that cash nexus that causes the spread of junk more than the charm of junk itself, oddly enough. In other words, junkies have to go out and score and because the market is so unstable they can't go to a job. [For example], their pusher at eleven in the morning is late so you gotta meet him at two. It's an unstable life and therefore you got to make your living by peddling junk to other people. Therefore, every junkie wants to have clients so that he can score for them and take his junk off the top, that's how the cash nexus enters into the spread of junk addiction.

This is Burroughs's description of "writing croakers," doctors that used to write morphine scripts in the 1940s.

There are several varieties of writing croakers. Some will write only if they are convinced that you are an addict, others if they are convinced that you are not. Most addicts put down a story worn smooth by years of use. Some claim gallstones or kidney stones. This is the story most generally used, and I have seen croakers get up and open the door as soon as I mentioned gallstones. I got better results with facial neuralgia after I had looked up the symptoms and committed them to memory. Roy had an operation scar on his stomach that he used to support his gallstone routine.

There was one oldtime doctor who lived in a Victorian brownstone house in the West Seventies. With him it was simply necessary to present a gentlemanly front. If you could get into his inner office you had it made, but he would write only three prescriptions. Another doctor was always drunk and it was a matter of catching him at the right time. Often he wrote the prescription wrong and you had to take it back for correction. Then, like as not, he would say the prescription was a forgery and tear it up. Still another doctor was senile, and you had to help him write the script. He would forget what he was doing, put down the pen and go into a long reminiscence about the high class of patients he used to have.

Especially, he liked to talk about a man named General Gore who once said to him, "Doctor, I've been to the Mayo Clinic and you know more than the whole clinic put together." There was no stopping him and the exasperated addict was forced to listen patiently. Often the doctor's wife would rush in at the last minute and tear up the prescription, or refuse to verify it when the drugstore called.

Generally speaking, old doctors are more apt to write than the young ones. Refugee doctors were a good field for a while, but the addicts burned them down. Often a doctor will blow his top at the mention of narcotics and threaten to call the law.

Doctors are so exclusively nurtured on exaggerated ideas of their position that, generally speaking, a factual approach is the worst possible.

That's a great sentence.

Even though they do not believe your story, nonetheless they want to hear one. It is like some Oriental face-saving ritual. One man plays the high-minded doctor who wouldn't write an unethical script for a thousand dollars, the other does his best to act like a legitimate patient. If you say, "Look, Doc, I want an M.S. [morphine sulfate] script and I'm willing to pay double price for it," the croaker blows his top and throws you out of the office. You need a good bedside manner with doctors or you will get nowhere.[101]

Kerouac and I used to read these pages and say, "Burroughs is just so intelligent!" I didn't know anybody around Columbia who was simply that factual, that intelligent, and I still haven't met anybody that's funnier than Burroughs. Not cynical, just observant, and no bullshit, with a very good, generous sense of humor.

An early image that emerges in Burroughs over and over that comes through all of his writing began in the 1940s and is in this one paragraph. He's describing kicking his habit.

> Almost worse than the sickness is the depression that goes with it. One afternoon, I closed my eyes and saw New York in ruins. Huge centipedes and scorpions crawled in and out of empty bars and cafeterias and drugstores on Forty-second Street. Weeds were growing up through cracks and holes in the pavement. There was no one in sight.[102]

That's a great prophecy. It's a very powerful image and recurs in Burroughs's work. It comes from Burroughs and his wife visiting the Museum of Natural History in New York and reading Mayan codices like the Madrid Codex. Bill thought the Mayan codices [outlined] a system used by the priests to control the Mayan population. Burroughs was preoccupied with those because they were an undeciphered language, they were primarily visual, they seemed to hold the key to a lot of mysterious history. He had the notion [that] the Mayan empire abandoned some of their cities, leaving them intact. Just as if the people suddenly disappeared. Burroughs's theory was that the Mayan priests had a secret language of their own and controlled the emotions and thoughts of the populace much as television controls the emotions and thoughts of the populace today. That specific emotions for specific days were outlined in the calendars and so it was like a psychological calendar of a manic depressive cycle or emotional cycle that the entire culture would go through at the same time with the priests controlling the calendars and the cycle of feeling. So the hieroglyphic language was a key to their control of your emotions.

One of the most fascinating of the images in the codex, which goes throughout all of Burroughs's prose, is an image of a man looking forward with a very intense expression. There is a small creature, like a monkey, on the back of his neck. In succeeding pictures in this hieroglyphic comic strip, the man's expression becomes increasingly empty and vapid and robotic. The creature on the back of his neck grows bigger and bigger and begins to assume deeper and deeper proportions of intensity and clarity and intelligence and power and cruelty, until at the end the actual face of the man is withered and shrunken and empty and there's this somewhat inhuman crustacean-eyed monster sitting on top of his head who's taken over. Like a junk habit, or Burroughs's own erotic perversity, or a control system, or television that has taken over.

In the case of the talking asshole, a guy develops a ventriloquist act where he makes his asshole talk, but after a while he can't stop his asshole from talking and it interrupts all the time, takes over, and finally the man gets into a fight with the asshole and the asshole [says] in the end it is you who will shut up. Finally the man does shut up, some kind of strange skin, strange membrane starts growing across his mouth and his face becomes depopulated and vacant. That's the passage that says there was no more life in his eyes than in the eyes of a crab at the end of the stalk.

This figures in with Burroughs's idea of possession or the idea of cancer, a cell taking over and replicating itself endlessly at the expense of the host. The notion of entopathetic symbiosis, this symbiotic relationship which is antipathetic. The host is destroyed by cancer, parasitism, notions of bureaucracy slowly draining the energy out of the society or out of the individual. Notions of the drug habit, the habit being a virus with a symbiotic relation to the host. Even sexuality, the human virus. On the simplest level it means sexual obsession, junk addiction, perhaps homosexual obsession, cancer, and police bureaucracy taking over the host.

These are partly parables of maturation, seen as victimage, seen with fear. It's also partly a metaphor for thought control, but the controllers are also control addicts, whether it's the CIA or Hitler or television or the Mafia or the White House or the Mayan priests or the narcotics bureau. They are the other side of the using addicts. Physically addicted in the sense that their livelihoods depend on the addicts, their entire system of physical economy depends on having a job controlling addicts and then moralizing about controlling addicts. They love addicts in that sense, [they are] parasites on the addicts, another virus intelligence that feeds on addiction.

Finally junk itself as a virus, oddly enough. The junk virus, extending later on to the sex virus, sex as another addiction. Extended finally by Burroughs to language as an addiction, language itself as a control mechanism. The very word itself, "in the beginning was the word," say the theists, trying to assert ultimate control over nature and human consciousness. Burroughs's final revolution was "rub out the word." Trace back along the word vine to find the source of control. Who started the whole maya, the illusion, and to what extent does language dictate to our sense of what we see, hear, smell.

I saw that Burroughs's honor among thieves was a lot more honorable than the mores and ethos of the people I was working with at the Associated Press. His estimate of human character was a lot more perceptive and generous than anything I heard in the center of mass communications of America.

About "An Informer":

> The worst of the lot was Gene Doolie, a scrawny little Irishman with a manner between fag and pimp. Gene was informer to the

bone. He probably pulled out dirty lists of people—his hands were always dirty—and read them off to the law. You could see him bustling into Black and Tan headquarters during the Irish Trouble; in a dirty gray toga, turning in Christians; giving information to the Gestapo; the GPU, sitting in a cafeteria talking to a narcotics agent. Always the same thin, ratty face, shabby, out-of-date clothes, whiny, penetrating voice.

The most unbearable thing about Gene was his voice. It went all through you. This voice was my first knowledge of his existence.[103]

Dig the historical trip that Burroughs is on and the historical perception he has about a fink, a rat, an informer. "In a dirty gray toga, turning in Christians." Burroughs's specialty at Harvard was classical history. He had read almost every major work of history that there was on the Roman Empire, so his take on the American Empire is seen through the eyes of someone who has had a lot of exposure to the traditions of nineteenth-century scholarship looking at the decline of Rome. His interest in Spengler comes from that point of view as does his description of these characters. "In a dirty gray toga, turning in Christians." I don't know anybody who's ever projected himself empathetically back to early Christian times and tried to visualize who the finks were who would turn in Christians.

"Giving information to the Gestapo; the GPU, sitting in a cafeteria talking to a narcotics agent." This is great. All the imagination is focused on sitting in a cafeteria talking to a narcotics agent. Someone with a "thin ratty face, shabby out-of-date clothes, whiny, penetrating voice," someone who would inform on you, someone who'd turn you over to the law. There's a great sense of honor through this book. Even when people were being dishonorable, at least they know it.

We're living in an era of informers in America. It's simply contrary to basic human nature. One of the interesting things about *Junkie* is his take on informers and it extends throughout the rest of his books and later career.

The most striking sentence in this book for me was when he was talking about taxi drivers in New Orleans.

> But a complex pattern of tensions, like the electrical mazes devised by psychologists to unhinge the nervous systems of white rats and guinea pigs, keeps the unhappy pleasure-seekers in a condition of unconsummated alertness. For one thing, New Orleans is inordinately noisy. The drivers orient themselves largely by the use of their horns, like bats. The residents are surly. The transient population is conglomerate and unrelated, so that you never know what sort of behavior to expect from anybody.[104]

That completely knocked me out. What an uncanny image, "the drivers orient themselves largely by use of their horns, like bats. The residents are surly." It's that one thought which is a gem. That's Burroughs the aristocrat, "You never know what sort of behavior to expect." The St. Louis aristocrat comes through here as part of the tone. It's one of the funnier elements.

This also blew Kerouac's mind when he saw that, it was such a perceptive sentence. It was the point where his prose was like poetry, something like Saint-John Perse's *Anabasis,* translated by T. S. Eliot, which had been an influence on Burroughs. Perse wrote prose poetry in the style of Rimbaud's *Illuminations,* which has this kind of alert factual imagery that becomes poetry merely by factualness, or perhaps because the perceiver is so smart that he puts these unrelated facts together. It's true in New Orleans, drivers use horns a lot, it is also true that bats orient themselves by little squeaks of radar, but for him to put that together took an anthropologist or a medical student, both of which were Burroughs's specialties.

What has he got to say about fags? As a homosexual, what is his relation to the whole sexual world? Here's a take on a New Orleans gay bar, known in those days as a fag bar. This is a self-put-down, trying to avoid guilt by association.

> In the French Quarter there are several queer bars so full every night the fags spill out on to the sidewalk. A room full of fags gives me the horrors. They jerk around like puppets on invisible strings, galvanized into hideous activity that is the negation of everything living and spontaneous. The live human being has moved out of these bodies long ago. But something moved in when the original tenant moved out. Fags are ventriloquists' dummies who have moved in and taken over the ventriloquist. The dummy sits in a queer bar nursing his beer, and uncontrollably yapping out of a rigid doll face.[105]

He's now in Mexico City looking for junk, looking for a connection. This is a preliminary sketch for another piece of prose, which Burroughs published after *Junkie*, his first piece of real high prose, like prose poetry, called "Interzone."

> One day I was walking down San Juan de Letran and passed a cafeteria that had colored tile set in the stucco around the entrance, and the floor was covered with the same tile. The cafeteria was unmistakably Near Eastern. As I walked by, someone came out of the cafeteria. He was a type you see only on the fringes of a junk neighborhood.

As the geologist looking for oil is guided by certain outcroppings of rock, so certain signs indicate the near presence of junk. Junk is often found adjacent to ambiguous or transitional districts: East Fourteenth near Third in New York; Poydras and St. Charles in New Orleans; San Juan de Letran in Mexico City. Stores selling artificial limbs, wig-makers, dental mechanics, loft manufacturers of perfumes, pomades, novelties, essential oils. A point where dubious business enterprise touches Skid Row.

There is a type person occasionally seen in these neighborhoods who has connections with junk, though he is neither a user nor a seller. But when you see him the dowser wand twitches. Junk is close. His place of origin is the Near East, probably Egypt. He has a large straight nose. His lips are thin and purple-blue (like the lips of a penis).

That's an accurate description, it's amazing. Nobody would think of actually writing that down except Burroughs. "His lips are thin and purple-blue (like the lips of a penis)."

The skin is tight and smooth over his face. He is basically obscene beyond any possible vile act or practice. He has the mark of a certain trade or occupation that no longer exists. If junk were gone from the earth, there might still be junkies standing around in junk neighborhoods feeling the lack, vague and persistent, a pale ghost of junk sickness.

So this man walks around in the places where he once exercised his obsolete and unthinkable trade. But he is unperturbed. His eyes are black with an insect's unseeing calm. He looks as if he nourished himself on honey and Levantine syrups that he sucks up through a proboscis.

What is his lost trade? Definitely of a servant class and something to do with the dead, though he is not an embalmer. Perhaps he stores something in his body—a substance to prolong life—of which he is periodically milked by his masters. He is as specialized as an insect, for the performance of some inconceivably vile function.[106]

A very beautiful purple passage for a hard-boiled book of facts like *Junkie*. Pretty good. The book is a retrospective history of Burroughs's five years as an addict and how he got into it, plus a little childhood recollection. Toward the end of the book there's some curious writing that's prophetic of later *Naked Lunch* writing.

One morning in April, I woke up a little sick. I lay there looking at shadows on the white plaster ceiling. I remembered a long time ago when I lay in bed beside my mother watching lights from the street move across the ceiling and down the walls. I felt the sharp nostalgia of train whistles, piano music down a city street, burning leaves.[107]

I always liked that paragraph, "train whistles, piano music down a city street, burning leaves." This is the essence of Burroughs, condensed down to little sharp nostalgic perfume. It's also the essence of T. S. Eliot's poetry.

I went into the bathroom to take a shot. I was a long time hitting a vein. The needle clogged twice. Blood ran down my arm. The junk spread through my body, an injection of death. The dream was gone. I looked down at the blood that ran from elbow to wrist.

I felt a sudden pity for the violated veins and tissue. Tenderly I wiped the blood off my arm.

"I'm going to quit," I said aloud.[108]

When I jumped bail and left the states the heat on junk already looked like something new and special. Initial symptoms of nationwide hysteria were clear. Louisiana passed a law making it a crime to be a drug addict. Since no place or time is specified and the term "addict" is not clearly defined, no proof is necessary or even relevant under a law so formulated. No proof, and consequently, no trial. This is police-state legislation penalizing a state of being. Other states were emulating Louisiana. I saw my chance of escaping conviction dwindle daily as the anti-junk feeling mounted to a paranoid obsession, like anti-Semitism under the Nazis. So I decided to jump bail and live permanently outside the United States.

Safe in Mexico, I watched the anti-junk campaign. I read about child addicts and senators demanding the death penalty for dope peddlers. It didn't sound right to me. Who wants kids for customers? They never have enough money and they always spill under questioning. Parents find out the kid is on junk and go to the law. I figured that either Stateside peddlers have gone simple-minded or the whole child-addict setup is a routine to stir up anti-junk sentiment and pass some new laws.

Refugee hipsters trickled down into Mexico. "Six months for needle marks under the vag-addict law in California." "Eight years for a dropper in Washington." "Two to ten for selling in New York." A group of young hipsters dropped by my place every day to smoke weed.[109]

I was interested in this because it was 1950 or so, and this is Burroughs's take on the beginnings of a whole new generation of hippies that were slowly beginning to coagulate in the United States.

> I remembered the way Marvin used to pass out every time he took a shot. I could see him lying on the bed in some cheap hotel, the dropper full of blood hanging to his vein like a glass leech, his face turned blue around the lips.[110]

This is precise writing. I could never understand how Burroughs got so smart in that way. "The face turning blue around the lips." Who would know that except somebody who had some real intelligent medical experience? Also, "the dropper full of blood hanging to his vein like a glass leech." I can see him lying on the bed, so it's a visual image that he has, a visual impression.

Detective prose is reflected all through the prose of *Junkie*. In those days it was not considered a classic as it is today, it was considered some kind of confessional work. They thought it might sell copies if they put a horrible cover on it of a wild-looking addict slashing at the arm of a young pretty girl with big tits. Then on the other side is a companion volume, *Confessions of a Narc*, just so the publisher wouldn't get into trouble, they were literally afraid of censorship. They even put in a little footnote saying, "Reputable professors or doctors do not agree with the statements of the author." You would never do that in a book now.

CHAPTER 20

Burroughs and Korzybski

In 1945 I got into a long, long discussion with Lucien Carr about "What is art?" My idea was that art had to be social, because I was sort of a young communist. Lucien said that art was for art's sake, that art was self-ultimate. For weeks at Columbia we argued about the proposition, "If somebody carved a walking stick, was it art? And if you carved it and it was put on the moon and nobody ever saw it, would that be art? Or does art need someone to see it to be art?" We spent weeks arguing this over, consulting Kerouac, and finally we took it to Burroughs, and he said, "This is the most stupid argument I ever heard in my life. It doesn't make any sense at all. Art is a three letter word, [it is] whatever you define it as. If you want to define that as art, then you define it as art. If you don't want to use that word for that situation, then you don't. But to argue whether the thing is art, or isn't art, is obviously a confusion in terms."

It shows how people get tangled up in language and think that problems are real which are just verbal constructions. People think they are unable to untangle them, because they have gotten confused and think that the words have a real reference.

Burroughs was always smart like that. He had studied with Alfred Korzybski, the author of *Science and Sanity,* which is a basic text, a foundation of the study of semantics. Bill gave me a copy of the book and it all boiled down to the fact that you mustn't confuse the word with the thing it refers to and get tangled up, because if you do then you can get into all sorts of [trouble]. Korzybski founded the theory of general semantics, which is the simple Zen thing of the word not being the same as the thing it represents. This [pointing to a wooden table] is not a table, table is T-A-B-L-E, a five-letter word. The word "table" is not identical with this [pointing again to the table]. Most questions like, "Is homosexuality natural?" are like that. What do you mean by the word "natural" and what do you mean by the word "homosexuality"? To begin with, the Moral Majority people, when they use the word "natural," mean something entirely different from biologists. Most arguments turn out to be purely semantic confusion. That was the smartest thing about Burroughs.

If you're liberated from language, you no longer confuse language, words, with the things they represent. Then words become independent objects floating in your brain and you can combine them in amazing unreasonable combinations, like Gregory [Corso] does in making discords. Forget about the world and just mess around with words, that gives a certain amount of freedom. Since most of our thinking process is in words, our thinking about reality is built into the way we've been taught words. Our vision of the universe is pretty much what the words in our head say it's supposed to be like. Two and two's four, good is good, bad is bad, a stove is a stove, a stove is not on the roof. What happens to consciousness if you cut loose from words, if you begin to loosen up the words or the arrangement of words as they have been arranged in your consciousness?

CHAPTER 21

Burroughs and the Visual

The reason I brought that out was that I had a conversation with Burroughs about how he thought. He said the reason he was so much into the Korzybski idea was that he himself thought primarily in pictures rather than in words. Now, I think primarily in words, "subconscious gossip," as the Buddhists call it. Many writers write from that gossip. Burroughs instead writes from pictures. Things like "I could see him lying on the bed in some cheap hotel, the dropper full of blood, hanging to his vein like a glass leech, his face turning blue around the lips." His thinking process is primarily visualization rather than verbalization, so his writing is cinematic. He's always been having pictorial flashes, or a cinematic montage in his head, rather than ideas. Rather than composition of ideas or beautiful sounds as in Kerouac, Burroughs's mentality is picture mind.

William Carlos Williams said that what he'd like to do was to squeeze pictures down into little lines. Poetry to him was taking a picture and squeezing it into short lines. At the moment of writing Kerouac said, "Don't stop to think of the right words, stop to see the picture better." Don't stop to think of the words, because then you just get tangled up in words. Stop to see the picture better, the words will rise accurately and spontaneously to relate to the picture. This is a useful thing for writers if you're writing about something palpable, something that you can actually see. It serves as a corrective to bring you back to some dimension of reality that exists visually, rather than tones, attitudes, abstractions, or generalizations. The tendency toward generalization and nonpictorial generalization is the curse of writing. The discipline of coming back to precise sensory evidence and data, whether picture, sound, smell, taste, or touch, is the right direction. Toward tangibility is the right direction. Burroughs is one hundred percent tangible, visually tangible.

In 1961, Bill was at his typewriter in Tangier, gazing into space with his hands poised over the keys, and I said, "What are you thinking about, Bill?" And he said, "Hands pulling in nets from the sea." It was mystifying, because Bill had always contended from the forties on that, although most people thought in words, he himself thought in pictures. He said there are different modes of thinking. Some of Burroughs's green Venusians think in vibration tones or colors, for example.

When he said "hands pulling in nets from the sea," I thought this was some high metaphysical thing about God pulling in the nets of souls from the eternal ocean. I was curious and said, "What does that mean?" And he said, "Oh, every morning the fishermen come down to the beach before dawn and pull in their nets." He was just remembering hands pulling in nets from the sea.

It sounded like something out Kahlil Gibran or Beethoven, it sounded more cosmic than it was, though the actuality's just as cosmic as anything else you can imagine. Burroughs thinks in pictures. Gregory Corso was thinking, let us say, in discords. Gregory's imagination strays, verbally, into opposites and discords. Kerouac broke up the solidity of phenomena by the constant realization that everything was phantom and so everything became transparent to him. Rigid language no longer dominated.

CHAPTER 22

Burroughs and *The Yage Letters*

In the early fifties, Kerouac and I thought that Burroughs's prose letters were brilliant and should be published. We all got together to read them over and edit them. I had my first acquaintance with South American politics through these letters.

Jan. 30, 1953, Hotel Niza, Pasto
Dear Al,

    I took a bus to Cali because the autoferro was booked solid for days. Several times the cops shook down the bus and everybody on it. I had a gun in my luggage stashed under the medicines but they only searched my person at these stops. Obviously anyone carrying guns would bypass the stops or pack his guns where these sloppy laws wouldn't search. All they accomplish with the present system is to annoy the citizens. I never met anyone in Colombia who has a good word for the Policia Nacional.

    The Policia Nacional is the Palace Guard of the Conservative Party (the army contains a good percentage of Liberals and is not fully trusted). This (the P.N.) is the most unanimously hideous body of young men I ever laid eyes on, my dear. They look like the end result of atomic radiation. There are thousands of these strange loutish young men in Colombia and I only saw one I would consider eligible and he looked ill at ease in his office.

    If there is anything to say for the Conservatives I didn't hear it. They are an unpopular minority of ugly-looking shits.[111]

This is a private insight, which doesn't get into the newspapers, that the cops or the local government are an unpopular minority of ugly-looking shits. My whole view of Latin America was completely straightened out in that one sentence, instead of big arguments over who was liberal versus conservative and socialist versus dictators.

    At one custom stop I met a nacional law who had fought in Korea. He pulled open his shirt to show me the scars on his unappetizing person.

    "I like you guys," he said.

    I never feel flattered by this promiscuous liking for Americans. It is insulting to individual dignity, and no good ever comes from these American lovers.[112]

These are just nice photographs and snapshots and glimpses and vignettes and travel accounts, picaresque amusements, disillusioned to begin with.

February 28, 1953
Dear Allen:

    On my way back to Bogota with nothing accomplished. I have been conned by medicine men (the most inveterate drunk, liar and loafer in the village is invariably the medicine man).[113]

He completely disillusioned me overnight about South American witch doctors.

May 24

> *Ho hum dept.* Rolled again. My glasses and a pocket knife. Losing all my fucking valuables in the service.
>
> This is a nation of kleptomaniacs. In all my experience as a homosexual I have never been the victim of such idiotic pilferings of articles no conceivable use to anyone else. Glasses and traveller's checks yet.
>
> Trouble is I share with the late Father Flanagan—he of Boy's Town—the deep conviction that there is no such thing as a bad boy.[114]

Then a footnote. "Enclose a routine I dreamed up. The idea did come to me in a dream from which I woke up laughing," Burroughs wrote. He thought it was funny and when I read it I thought that it was funny too. This first routine he sent was "Roosevelt After Inauguration." I was a liberal in those days and still am a commie pinko of some sort, but when I got this, it was just outrageous and obviously funny. It was like Alfred Jarry's *Docteur Faustroll* or *Ubu Roi*. It has some element of the school joke, but on the other hand it's amazingly prophetic in terms of what actually goes on in politics.

Another precursor of *Naked Lunch* and his later development is found in a letter from July 10, 1953. It was a letter that Robert Creeley thought was absolutely amazing and that Philip Whalen thought indicated that Burroughs was some extraordinary poet like Rimbaud or Saint-Jean Perse. It's an account of an experience with yagé, an hallucinogenic vine.

Dear Allen,

Last night I took last of Yage mixture I brought back from Pucallpa. No use transporting to U.S. It doesn't keep more than a few days. This morning, still high. This is what occurred to me. Yage is space time travel. The room seems to shake and vibrate with motion. The blood and substance of many races, Negro, Polynesian, Mountain Mongol, Desert Nomad, Polyglot Near East, Indian—new races as yet unconceived and unborn, combinations not yet realized passes through your body. Migrations, incredible journeys through deserts and jungles and mountains (stasis and death in closed mountain valleys where plants sprout out of the Rock and vast crustaceans hatch inside and break the shell of the body), across the Pacific in an outrigger canoe to Easter Island. The Composite City where all human potentials are spread out in a vast silent market.

Minarets, palms, mountains, jungle. A sluggish river jumping with vicious fish, vast weed-grown parks where boys lie in the grass or play cryptic games. Not a locked door in the City. Anyone comes in your room any time. The Chief of Police is Chinese who picks his teeth and listens to denunciations presented by a lunatic. Every now and then the Chinese takes the toothpick out of his mouth and looks at the end of it. Hipsters with smooth copper-colored faces lounge in doorways twisting shrunk heads on gold chains, their faces blank with an insect's unseeing calm.

Behind them, through the open door, tables and booths, and bars and rooms and kitchens and baths, copulating couples on rows of brass beds, criss-cross of a thousand hammocks, junkies tying up, opium smokers, hashish smokers, people eating, talking, bathing, shitting back into a haze of smoke and steam.

Gaming tables where the games are played for incredible stakes. From time to time a player leaps up with a despairing inhuman cry having lost his youth to an old man or become Latah to his opponent. But there are higher stakes than youth or Latah. Games where only two players in the world know what the stakes are.[115]

That's somewhat of an echo of his relationship with me. "Games where only two players in the world know what the stakes are."

Whenever you get blackout drunk you wake up with one of these diseased faceless citizens in your bed who has spent all night exhausting his ingenuity trying to infect you. But no one knows how the diseases are transmitted or indeed if they are contagious. These diseased beggars live in a maze of burrows under the City and pop out anywhere often pushing up through the floor of a crowded cafe.

Followers of obsolete unthinkable trades doodling in etruscan, addicts of drugs not yet synthesized, pushers of souped-up Harmine, junk reduced to pure habit offering precarious vegetable serenity, liquids to induce Latah, cut antibiotics, Tithonian longevity serum . . .

Tithonus was granted immortality by the gods, but not eternal youth, so he was reduced to a mound of dust in a bottle with a consciousness still talking, "I want to die." Tithonian longevity serum. Latah is a schizophrenic condition, where you break out screaming or cursing, or you do something that someone else does. If someone moves their hand, you move your hand in the same way.

> Tithonian longevity serum; black marketeers of World War III, pitchmen selling remedies for radiation sickness, investigators of infractions denounced by bland paranoid chess players, servers of fragmentary warrants charging unspeakable mutilations of the spirit taken down in hebephrenic shorthand, bureaucrats of spectral departments, officials of unconstituted police states; a lesbian dwarf who has perfected operation Begagut, the lung erection that strangles a sleeping enemy; sellers of orgone tanks and relaxing machines, brokers of exquisite dreams and memories tested on the sensitized cells of junk sickness and bartered for the raw materials of the will; doctors skilled in treatment of diseases dormant in the black dust of ruined cities, gathering virulence in the white blood of eyeless worms feeling slowly to the surface and the human hosts, maladies of the ocean floor and the stratosphere, maladies of the laboratory and atomic war, excisors of telepathic sensitivity, osteopaths of the spirit.
>
> A place where the unknown past and the emergent future meet in a vibrating soundless hum. Larval entities waiting for a live one.[116]

A live one is the mark, the john, the host to the virus. That's an amazing piece of prose, I always thought. You have almost all of *Naked Lunch* and all of his subsequent writing in this one brilliant section called "Interzone." It's amazing, the phrasing in it is brilliant, "their faces blank with an insect's unseeing calm."

By 1953 Burroughs had already developed the first embryonic routines that were later to become the passages of "Interzone," all about a future city of totally degenerated civilizations. Many forms of civilization were mixed up, somewhat like Tangier, crossroads not just east and west, but crossroads of future and past. "Interzone" was first conceived on East 7th Street as Burroughs looked out of the window of my apartment. He had seen a lady reach out of her window and start pulling in the laundry across backyard courtyards on lines going from building to building. He began to imagine a futuristic city which would [consist of] catwalks and boardwalks and fire escapes, a great labyrinth where people would all live in different alleyways, hallways, bathrooms, broom closets, a city so old that it had been rebuilt layer upon layer and one building was built upon another building. That developed into the notion of a city which was like the sound of a vibrating soundless hum, and many larval entities waiting for a live one, unborn.

There is an inspiration for this, a precursor, which is *Anabase* [i.e., *Anabasis,* in English] of Saint-John Perse. This is where Burroughs got the method. If you are familiar with Rimbaud you will recognize some of that and then Rimbaud's follower in the twentieth century, Saint-John Perse, who wrote a book called *Anabasis* translated by T. S. Eliot. It is prose poetry and you may get some sense of Burroughs's theme from it. Burroughs's whole method comes straight from Rimbaud and Saint-John Perse in *Anabasis.*

As you may remember one of the Transcendentalists in the nineteenth century, Bronson Alcott, brought back all sorts of oriental texts as well as hermetic writings, which are comparable to Buddhist texts. Whitman cites from the selection. The Transcendentalists took their name from the study of Indian religion, Hindu, Muslim, transmigration of all things. You had that same extensive expansiveness and vastness as a motif in Walt Whitman. Then, amazingly, all through T. S. Eliot's *The Waste Land* are references to Krishna, to

Arjuna, to basic Buddhist notions. At the end of the poem we hear Sanskrit chanting eighty years after the Transcendentalists, which was oriental mind changed into Yankee letters. Remember the end of *The Waste Land* is "Give, sympathise, control."

The Waste Land is not much different than Burroughs. Burroughs's method of cut-up and T. S. Eliot's method [of] collage are practically the same. They both have that montage or collage method that Burroughs calls cut-ups and Eliot got from Apollinaire, which I've described as a jump-cut montage, swift moving from one perception to another or one picture to another. I think that the thing that Burroughs and Eliot have most in common is "music down a windy street," in other words, spare, nostalgic, pungent images that will haunt you with an echo of time past.

Burroughs learned lots from Eliot's translation of Saint-John Perse's *Anabasis*. I remember that that was one of the books that Burroughs gave me and Kerouac back in 1944 when we first met. If you take a combination of Saint-John Perse and *The Waste Land* you'll have much of the nostalgic aftertaste of Burroughs.

CHAPTER 23

Burroughs and *Queer*

Queer was written right after *Junkie,* but there was no way it could be published, in fact it wasn't published for thirty years. In the preface Burroughs talks about how he came to be a writer. It's actually quite a revelation.

So I had written *Junky,* and the motivation for that was comparatively simple: to put down in the most accurate and simple terms my experiences as an addict. I was hoping for publication, money, recognition. Kerouac had published *The Town and the City* at the time I was writing *Junky.* I remember writing in a letter to him, when his book was published, that his money and fame were now assured. As you can see, I knew nothing about the writing business at the time.

My motivations to write *Queer* were more complex, and are not clear to me at the present time. Why should I wish to chronicle so carefully these extremely painful and unpleasant and lacerating memories? While it was I who wrote *Junky,* I feel that I was being written in *Queer.* I was also taking pains to ensure further writing, so as to set the record straight: writing as inoculation. As soon as something is written, it loses the power of surprise, just as a virus loses its advantage when a weakened virus has created alerted antibodies. So I achieved some immunity from further perilous ventures along these lines by writing my experience down.

At the beginning of the *Queer* manuscript fragment, having returned from the insulation of junk to the land of the living like a frantic inept Lazarus, Lee seems determined to score, in the sexual sense of the word. There's something curiously systematic and unsexual about his quest for a suitable sex object, crossing one prospect after another off a list which seems compiled with ultimate failure in mind. On some very deep level he does not want to succeed {this is Burroughs writing about himself}, but will go to any length to avoid the realization that he is not really looking for sex contact.

But Allerton was definitely *some* sort of contact. And what was the contact that Lee was looking for? Seen from here, a very confused concept that had nothing to do with Allerton as a character. While the addict is indifferent to the impression he creates in others, during withdrawal he may feel the compulsive need for an audience, and this is clearly what Lee seeks in Allerton: an audience, the acknowledgement of his performance, which is of course a mask, to cover a shocking disintegration. So he invents a frantic attention-getting format which he calls the Routine: shocking, funny, riveting.[117]

Lee does not know that he is already committed to writing, since it is the only way he has of making an indelible record, whether Allerton is inclined to observe or not. Lee [Burroughs] is being inexorably pressed through the world of fiction. He's already made the choice between his life and his work.[118]

There's an odd [moment] in Kerouac and Burroughs and van Gogh and Artaud and Ezra Pound and probably my own writing, and certainly in Kerouac and James Joyce above all, where the identity of the private person merges with his identity as a writer. The person becomes committed to being a writer and that's what he is in the universe, a scribe, or someone whose action in the world is writing, or art, or painting. Someone whose life and whose writing have merged as one thing. There's a specific point in Burroughs's life where his writing and his life suddenly merge, as there was in Kerouac probably around the time he decided to abandon all revision and just write down what was going on in his mind. Where he became completely a writer in the sense of his life became a life of writing. And in a sense the writer Kerouac replaces the person Jack Kerouac, who used to be just a guy who wrote.

In a sense, what's happening with Burroughs and with Kerouac, the person has become a shaman, the body of the life has turned prophetic, and the message is coming through that body. The person has dedicated himself to being open to the message with more than just his reason, but with his whole body and his imagination and his dreams. His unconscious life and his everyday life are merged. With Burroughs writing becomes a probe into consciousness, or a probe into depth.

Burroughs's preface to *Queer* is something written recently about a book written thirty years ago.

> When I started to write this companion text to *Queer,* I was paralyzed with a heavy reluctance, a writer's block like a straitjacket: "I glance at the manuscript of *Queer* and feel I simply can't read it. My past was a poisoned river from which one was fortunate to escape, and by which one feels immediately threatened, years after the events recorded.—Painful to an extent I find it difficult to read, let alone to write about. Every word and gesture sets the

teeth on edge." The reason for this reluctance becomes clearer as I force myself to look: the book is motivated and formed by an event which is never mentioned, in fact is carefully avoided: the accidental shooting death of my wife, Joan, in September 1951.

I get exactly the same feeling to an almost unbearable degree as I read the manuscript of *Queer.* The event towards which Lee feels himself inexorably driven is the death of his wife by his own hand, the knowledge of possession, a dead hand waiting to slip over his like a glove. So a smog of menace and evil rises from the pages, an evil that Lee, knowing and yet not knowing, tries to escape with frantic flights of fantasy: his routines, which set one's teeth on edge because of the ugly menace just behind or to one side of them, a presence palpable as a haze.

Brion Gysin said to me in Paris: "For ugly spirit shot Joan because . . ." A bit of mediumistic message that was not completed—or was it? It doesn't need to be completed, if you read it: "ugly spirit shot Joan *to be cause,*" that is, to maintain a hateful parasitic occupation. My concept of possession is closer to the medieval model than to modern psychological explanations, with their dogmatic insistence that such manifestations must come from within and never, never, never from without. (As if there were some clear-cut difference between inner and outer.) I mean a definite possessing entity.[119]

This is also the parable of hanging, orgasm, possession that appears in Burroughs's work. A sense of being taken over and invaded and that's why we have all the images of virus and of addiction, addiction as virus, addiction as a possession, in his books.

CHAPTER 24

Burroughs and *Naked Lunch*

Naked Lunch was a series of sketches, or fantasies, or routines, that we originally did for our own amusements. They were imaginative leaps and just pure fun. [Burroughs] was in Tangier, taking eukodol, an artificial junk, when he was at the height of producing *Naked Lunch*. It was [written as] a series of discontinuous sketches. In 1957 Kerouac went to Tangier to help Bill put the whole book together from a big black spring-board binder full of letters and sketches. The problem was, how to separate the letters from the sketches and how to order the routines? How to take Dr. Benway and introduce him and then bring Benway back twice as funny with even more monstrous routines? Appearing over and over, there was a lot of repetition. [Burroughs] would write one routine and then a month later he'd make an improvement on it and so on. It was a vast accumulation of material, a thousand pages at least.

Kerouac was just about to publish *On the Road* and had some money so he went to join Bill in Tangier and then Peter Orlovsky and I went to join him. Kerouac went ahead of us to type up the whole manuscript and find an order to it. Kerouac started typing it, then I arrived and I continued typing, and then a guy named Alan Ansen, who had been secretary to W. H. Auden in Auden's most fertile period writing *The Age of Anxiety*, he came. Ansen was a great admirer of Burroughs's work early on. We all typed routines and put the manuscript together as best we could, but we couldn't solve the problem of continuity.

I thought it should be chronological, to show the development of his mind. But that didn't work and besides he was still adding material. There was a lot of overlapping since he developed the routines and added details over time. It was too hard to take all those versions of the same routine and try to edit them into one single section.

I left to tour Europe in late 1957 and Burroughs went to Paris where we brought some of it to Maurice Girodias of Olympia Press. Then we got a letter from the *Chicago Review* at the University of Chicago asking for material from me and from Burroughs and from Kerouac and from Corso and from Orlovsky. We put together a rough sequence of things from *Naked Lunch*, including the talking asshole [section], and sent about eighty pages of that to the *Chicago Review*. It was accepted by the editors and printed, but then seized by the university administration [before distribution]. When news of the scandal in Chicago reached Paris, Girodias decided that he wanted to publish *Naked Lunch* immediately. However, all Burroughs had were these various routines and he still didn't know how to organize it into a rational continuity, in other words, into a novel.

At the time Burroughs was working on the manuscript with the painter Brion Gysin, who was living in the same hotel. It was Gysin who suggested to Burroughs that he could solve his problem by seeing the novel not as a linear, chronological progression but as a painter sees a painting, seeing the whole thing at one time as a collage, where all the elements are juxtaposed. They just passed it through the typewriter in whatever order it came and sent them over chapter by chapter to Girodias. Brion looked at it and said, "Well, you know

Bill, if you read it this way, it looks as good as any other way." That's how it got put together.

The juxtaposition of these elements was sufficiently illuminating to turn the reader on and the sharp images, routines, comedies, disparate materials that make up *Naked Lunch* need only be put together in some artistic order, sections didn't need to be connected. The "Interzone" section doesn't have to be connected with the Dr. Benway [section] by any kind of a logical order, as if you were taking the reader from New York to Timbuktu and then from Timbuktu to Venus and then from Venus to Tangier, or as Burroughs said, "I'm not American Express." The novelist is not American Express, he doesn't need to provide the reader with a ticket from one place to another, he just presents the places and the reader can juxtapose these places.

CHAPTER 25

Burroughs and the Cut-Up Method

Around 1960, much had been stirring with Burroughs in Europe relating to his idea of cut-ups. The first published evidence of it was a pamphlet put out in Paris, a collaboration between him, Brion Gysin, Gregory Corso, [Sinclair Beiles,] and myself called *Minutes to Go*. I was in South America at the time, but I thought that this cut-up thing was a little bit too frivolous and mechanical. It was inorganic and I figured that in order to get to unity of being or supreme reality or total consciousness it had to be organic.

I was not able to detach the words from the things. Actually it was a challenge to cut up "Howl," which I would have been smart to do way back then. But I felt that the cut-up lacked sufficient reverence for literature, it was too heartless. When Corso objected to the cut-up and said, "My poetry is a natural cut-up," I thought ah-ha, the poet's got it over these rationalistic cut-uppers. I figured there was an element of impersonal heartless Raskolnik intellect at work.

I think "Interzone" is the essence of Burroughs, it's his acme [of] writing. It's a natural cut-up, a cut-up of time, space, various civilizations, and different biological life-forms. "Interzone" is his primary vision in a way and that's developed throughout the rest of his books. Burroughs's notion of cut-up was a spiritual notion in the sense that it was a consequence of his previous searches for enlargement of consciousness and attempts to get away from language. He wanted to get outside of the prison of language and also wanted to get beyond the senses, beyond all thoughts, feelings, and apparent sensory impressions. That was his phrase. He wanted to cut out of reality as we are conditioned to understand reality, out beyond the senses to a place open, blue, like the skies, silent, outside of the body where there are no forms. That was the spiritual or mental ambition behind the cut-up principle. It was the presupposition that all of our sensory impressions were conditioned by language and by the thought forms we grew up with. He began suspecting paranoically (or non-paranoically) that these apparent sensory impressions were programmed into our bodies.

His first attempt was to trace back along the word lines to find out how the words had first appeared and been inserted into our consciousness. He assumed that all of reality, sight, sound, smell, taste, touch, was some sort of hallucination or maya and that behind maya was some kind of empty, unthreatening, open space and that the actual existence of the body and the senses was some kind of plot. He had various theories as to who the senders were. In *Naked Lunch* there's a great political division between the factualists, like Burroughs himself, investigating the senses, the facts; the divisionists, who want to replicate themselves and have dummy images of themselves everywhere so that if they're traveling in foreign countries they'll always have some friends; and the liquifactionists, who want to liquidate everybody who isn't like them, who want to liquidate all opposition.

Burroughs suspected that the entire fabric of reality as we know it is completely conditioned and he began suspecting that the conditioners, the people who were behind the conditioning, were running the entire universe. It is somewhat like an engineer running a sound studio with lots of tape machines and film. It was a question of exploring along word lines and picture lines, in other words, tracing the words that you use and are implanted in your brain, tracing them back to where you first heard those words or where those words and images were coined, to find [the source of] the image bank and who's in control of it. He thought that maybe all senses, all visual impressions, are superimposed on us.

This was very serious as a political proposition. I remember once arriving in Tangier and having to undergo Burroughs's interrogation as to who I was representing. He could detect certain parts of my father or certain parts of Columbia University in intonations of my voice and words and attitudes. It was interesting, but it was a little difficult to see old friend Bill looking at me as if I were a robot sent out to check him out. He assumed that everybody was an agent at that point, not necessarily from the government, but actually an agent for a giant trust of insects from another galaxy. Women were suspect as being some evil Kali mother figures and at one point Burroughs thought maybe you ought to exterminate all the women, just get rid of them all, let them drop off like an unwanted appendage and evolve a male that could give birth. It was just a theory, but typical Burroughs. Kerouac used to appreciate that quality of Burroughs as sort of Faustian experiment, willing to experiment and explore ideas to the extreme, like get rid of all women and see what'll happen.

Minutes to Go and *The Exterminator* were notions that Burroughs developed a few years later into *Nova Express*. Nova is an exploding sun. Burroughs theorized that the purpose of all the hallucinations being laid out was that the planet was being prepared for a takeover by a virus-like form which didn't need people. So the virus had entered the human body as language. Language itself was the virus or the vector for the virus. It was mind-blowing.

Burroughs's thinking is parallel to the Buddhists', except that Burroughs has this trust of giant feminine insects from another galaxy. He's trying to put the blame somewhere in the external universe for this fix that we're all in, whereas the Buddhist view is that we created the whole thing ourselves. They both require strenuous alertness and attention and examination minute to minute, thought by thought, image by image of the entire fabric of appearance and phenomenon. Whether you're a Buddhist or an atheist or a Burroughsian, you still can't get away from examining the entire fabric of reality.

Minutes to Go meant that there are only minutes to go before the atomic explosion that would create nova conditions on this planet. It would be a disturbance on this planet that would extend to the sun if the manipulators had their way. There would be an actual nova in our solar system. At that time there was a great deal of anxiety about the bomb exploding, which was reflected in Burroughs's consciousness (exaggerated and hypersensitized perhaps).

In *Minutes to Go* or *The Exterminator* you'll see the first experiments with the raw material of cut-up. Here is the first notion of tracing along the word lines. If you want to find out where these ideas got implanted on earth or into you, you trace back along the lines of the words, historically, to find out who the ultimate authors of these words were.

Tracing along the word lines, he began examining notions of God and language. In Genesis, remember, "In the beginning was the word." Burroughs wondered who said that? Who laid that trip down? He took a Gnostic interpretation of that opening sentence, "In the beginning was the word," and his conclusion was "rub out the word." If you examine Gnostic versions of the Bible and the word and the Garden of Eden you'll find parallel notions to Burroughs's exterminating angel idea. In the beginning of *The Exterminator* you'll find that these are among the first and earliest explanations of cut-ups.

The Human Being are strung lines of word associates that control "thoughts feelings, and *apparent* sensory impressions." Quotes from Encephalographic Research Chicago Written in TIME. See Page 156 Naked Lunch Burroughs. See and hear what They expect to see and hear because The Word Lines keep Thee In Slots..

Cut the Word Lines with scissors or switch blade as preferred The Word Lines keep you in Time . . . Cut the in lines . . . Make out lines to Space. Take a page of your own writing of you write or a letter or a newspaper article or a page or less or more of any writer living and or dead . . . Cut into sections. Down the middle. And cross the sides . . . Rearrange the sections..Write the result message . . .

Who wrote the original words is still there in any rearrangement of his or her or whatever words . . . Can recognise Rimbaud cut up as Rimbaud . . . A Mellville cut up as Mell ville . . . Shakespeare moves with Shakespeare words . . . So forth anybody can be Rimbaud if he will cut up Rimbaud's words and learn Rimbaud language talk think Rimbaud . . . And supply reasonably appropriate meat. All dead poets and writers can be reincarnate in different hosts.

Cut up . . . Raise standard of writer production to a point of total and permanent competition of all minds living and dead Out Space. Concurrent

No one can conceal what is saying cut up . . . You can cut The Truth out of any written or spoken words . . .[120]

That means that if you take a speech by Nixon in which he's manipulating your mind and you cut up the speech and rearrange it, as Burroughs suggests, you find out what he is actually saying. Just take his words and cut it up and paste down the middle, or cut it in quarters and rearrange it in a different order. In the original the words are given to you in an accepted, socially ordered, sequential, logical order, as you might expect from a reasonable man talking to reasonable people. He can sneak in a lot of hypnosis, like "I am not a thief." But if you take that sentence, and cut it up with "Bebe Rebosa is my friend," it becomes "I am not Bebe Rebosa a thief my friend." So if you cut up the sentence, you don't know if he is saying I am a thief or I am not a thief.

In other words, most writing, most political writing and journalistic writing, is manipulative in the sense that it is trying to convince you of something, some kind of bullshit, some hot air. If you want to make the manipulative phrasing of it stand out like a sore thumb, just cut it up and rearrange it. The manipulative inconsistencies jump out in 3-D.

Around 1960 I did that. My little cut-up experiment was, during the Bay of Pigs crisis, to cut up Khrushchev's speech and Kennedy's speech and mix them together and see what the resultant declaration was. The sentence I arrived at was, "The purpose of these maneuvers is offensive weapons." As simple as that. Both of their minds put together, in other words, their words mixed together, combined to show what was in the language.

Orwell's essay on language "Politics and the English Language" is a great essay, which Burroughs cited often for this very purpose. Orwell points out the style of phrasing that is manipulative bureaucratese. The more manipulative and bureaucratese it is, the more abstract and Latinate it is, the fewer pictures and sensory references there are in it.

CHAPTER 26

Burroughs and
The Ticket That Exploded

I stopped at a newsstand on Shaftsbury Avenue and bought a copy of *Encounter*. Contemplating on their eros the feet of prose abstracted to a point where no image track occurs.[121]

Burroughs is putting picture image track as an equivalent of the tape recording in the mind of the word. He mixes here, cuts out some of his plot, his cosmic detective story consciousness plot, with some parodies and prose, which I believe are actual cut-ups of *Encounter* prose. *Encounter* magazine being a British Anglo-American literary magazine which was subsidized by the CIA during the early fifties.

 (desperately effete negation of societal values fecundate with orifices perspective and the ambivalent smugness of unavowed totalitarianism.)
 I knew why he was standing there. He didn't have the ready to fill his script. He was waiting for somebody he could touch.
 (foundering in disproportionate exasperation he doesn't even achieve the irrelevant honesty of hysteria . . .[122]

That is one of the phrases that George Steiner or somebody in *Encounter* wrote as a negative review of *Naked Lunch*. "Foundering in exasperation of hysteria." Burroughs is pointing out, as Orwell pointed out, it's just attitudinal abstractions and has absolutely no referents for these words, there's no sight, sound, smell, touch. They are just referring back to other abstractions. One abstraction referring to another abstraction, receding infinite.

> "Need bread for your script, man?"
> He turned and looked at me decided I wasn't the heat and nodded. I passed him a quid. "That should buy six jacks. I'll see you outside."
> He nodded again went in and sat down in the script line.
> (ironically the format is banal to its heart of pulp ambivalently flailing noneffectual tentacles of verbal diarrhea)
> I waited half an hour of word sludge[123]

This is Burroughs's parody of manipulative prose. If you cut it up you realize the essentially empty nature of it. Burroughs was also trying to cut up his own thoughts, feelings, and his own sexual obsessions, which he felt were tied to certain sensory impressions.

Another notion of cut-up is whenever you find a sender, a sender like Nixon, or the CIA, or *Encounter* magazine, your mother, your father, yourself, the great ego self the sender, then the way to deal with the sender is by feedback. So if you wanted to destroy the CIA, you just trace along the word line to find where the human put-down language imagery came from, and then you cut up that negative human language put-down imagery that's being fed to you and you feed it back to the CIA or your mother. "Cut-up and spray back of all minds living." "To see or switchblades are preferred cut the word lines." "No one can con cut-up. Cut your own . . . cut the."

What he does in *Soft Machine, Nova Express,* and *The Ticket That Exploded*, structurally, is to use random cut-up material. He still has his plots, his routines, just like *Naked Lunch*, like the blue movie, or like Dr. Benway, and then he'll take several of these scenes and cut them up together and distill the essence of nostalgia or poesie from each of the scenes, reductively cutting them up to shorter and shorter sections, eliminating more and more until he may have a whole paragraph, which is the cut-up essence of previous chapters.

Burroughs had an excuse. He thought that nova conditions were approaching, he thought that there were only minutes to go. He thought that some radical means of getting inside language itself, getting inside consciousness, and altering consciousness, was urgently necessary on a large scale. He felt that drugs were manipulated by the government and therefore not available, and other methods like Buddhism, psychoanalysis, etc., were slow and archaic.

As a Yankee inventor, like his grandfather, Bill invented the cut-up to look inside language. Take your rational consciousness and spread it out on the table before you and objectively take a razor to it, cut it up, recombine it, thus extending it, opening it up, putting more space into it. Then rearrange it to give it a little bit more air and then feed it back into the soft machine. This will cause feedback short-circuiting, thus perhaps liberating the mind for an instant or a whole novel. I think the practice of cut-up is a very witty, interesting form, probably an ancient form of meditation. In other words, the cut-up brings unconscious intention in a piece of writing to the surface. All of his later writings are extensions of this central idea.

For an obsessive decade, 1958 to 1968, this was his whole purpose, one hundred percent, deconditioning. That comes back to what I said was our original purpose with this course, [that] it was primarily a probe into consciousness. Different decades of progressive development and experiments through literary means of relating to our minds and to subjective consciousness and to the phenomenology of consciousness. That's probably why the Beat shot has lasted, rather than being a transient social phenomenon.

CHAPTER 27

Neal Cassady and *As Ever*

The book *As Ever* is a collection of letters between me and Neal [Cassady].

Dear Neal:

Letters between you and me is like conversation between two equally beat bums, either we are garrulous and complaining or short-writ and enigmatic; but I don't think we make sense. Take this as garrulity. If I thought writing you a 1000 page letter would answer enigmas, either mine or yours, I would sit down with quill and scroll and furiously scribble. A week ago I reread all of my Denver and Texas notebook, long ramblings of subjective worry, and was absolutely amazed at how cracked it sounded; reawoke in me memory and breath of how totally unified my soul was in love rapture; but read it; so long winded and frustrating it seemed I couldn't finish—not boredom, but oppression.

The and and . . . and style of my last letter was like Ezra Pound. And I received a letter from him in same mail as yours, in answer to letter to him asking questions about meter. He wrote A. Ginsberg and address in wavering infantile scrawl all over the envelope front, and covered a whole page of blank paper with the notes:

S. Liz. (—this means St. Elizabeth's Bughouse Wash.) AG

Dear AG

None of you people have least concept of FATIGUE. I have said it all in print, i.e. all answers to yrs.——— Cantos no use to people writing shorts. E.P.[124]

Pretty good answer, I thought, at least he took the trouble. I had written Ezra Pound some long bullshit letter about what kind of prosody or what kind of meter you need for writing and asked what is the new meter, and what are your thoughts about meter? William Carlos Williams talks about meter and so I said to Pound, "What do you think?"

"Don't you people have the least concept of Fatigue, I've said it all in print." It took me about two days to figure out what Pound meant, "I have said it all in print, i.e. all answers to yours." He meant he had already answered all my questions elsewhere. Sometimes when somebody writes me a letter I reprint that. But then he had this afterthought of Bodhisattva generosity. "Cantos no use to people writing shorts." He was saying that the extended variable meters in the *Cantos* and the ideogramic method he was using were not the thing to study if you were writing a short, concentrated poem. Then I had more advice for Cassady.

Seriously: You should attempt then something you think I may take and others take for granted: an outline of your emotions of loss of love, a long confession of your secret feelings; not only the frenzy and perceptions and activity, but the deep single real personal unstated suffering you feel and felt. By take for granted

I mean you never avail yourself of human ears to confess to, you always confess your crimes, but I know little of your feelings as a boy and man—even in Joan letter.[125] Certainly I never understood how much you wanted Luanne. Did she? You have felt more unhappiness than almost anybody, but seldom do you allow it to be shared—as Jack knows; he remembers your crying in the eatery now as the center of his book. God, Neal, I wish I could see you, (in a timeless world in the sunlight)—I suppose you know all this.

Even that fool Bill, in his last letter, told me all about himself and then ends his paragraphs "I hope I'm not boring you with all this." Heaven, heaven, things I've been waiting and wondering about for years.[126]

What I was getting at there was the unstated, that interests me now. We take for granted that other people know what we're thinking about or feeling and we write poems taking for granted something that has never been stated and has never been understood. The poems have a thin surface because the substance of what we were feeling was never laid out to begin with. That is important because people write poetry that nobody understands because they assume that it's understood already. They just write poems where the language is thin because it didn't include the original complaint, so to speak. It didn't include the original heart throb fear, or whatever.

Then a letter to Neal on October 31, 1950, which was a moment that affected everybody of this group, Cassady and Burroughs and myself and Kerouac quite a bit. It's about [the death of] a friend of ours named Bill Cannastra who moved in high artistic circles.

The great question on everybody's soul, was, was it an accident or did he do it on purpose? I met Ann Adams, who was with him, and she gave me a minute account of details. The party was leaving her house after a night of sticking and wandering, and on the way to Claude's [Lucien Carr], Claude and Cannastra had become friendly and got drunk, pawing each other, recently. Subway to Claude's to get money, a touch O'the dawn. When they talked about the Bleecker Tavern (negress Winnie's hangout) Bill lurched out of the window as a joke. He stuck his head and shoulder out, but apparently had misjudged his lurch and found himself half hanging unbalanced out of the window. The others rushed to pull him back, and hung on to him, as the subway roared through the tunnel. His coat ripped, and they couldn't get a grip on him by his shoulders as he was too far out. When he saw what was happening he began screaming to be pulled back. He ducked, trying to avoid the pillars in the tunnel, and hunched his head, but suddenly there was a thud and he was knocked out of the window to the tracks, out of their hands. When the train stopped, she went to the last car where his body was dragged and saw that his head was broken and brains showing out the temple.[127]

That was one of the best minds of my generation destroyed by madness, in a sense. It went into my own poem "Howl." It was one of the first community deaths, or deaths in our community, that affected everybody. We shuddered and had an awareness that it was a mortal place we were in, a reminder of mortality.

Although [Cassady] had been a very energetic hero figure for Kerouac and for myself, he began to go through an early period of disillusionment and blankness around that time. The point I'm trying to make is that his career as a hero was worn out already by 1950. Neal was much mythologized as a hero figure into the mid-sixties, but he himself already felt worn out, worn down, and blanked out by

November 1950. There are a series of statements about that that are really interesting, because they fit in like a jigsaw puzzle to Kerouac's writing about him in *On the Road* and *Visions of Cody*.

Nov. 25, 1950

Dear Allen:

It is not an easy task to write to you, or anyone; in fact I cant's bring myself to write at all. In regard to this vacuum wherein I can find nothing to say to anyone, Diana [Hansen] has the worst of it. Accordingly, if you see her at any time please tell her I just can't write or do anything else and that's the end of it. I have many beautiful instances of my inability to function at hand, and could recite them for you, but need not since I really haven't the strength. I can't overemphasize too strongly how ugly my life has become, simply because of this "do nothingness," and how low I've gotten by realizing emotionally *every* damn moment what a really disgusting fish I am. Honestly it's awful, not only am I unable to do the ordinary things necessary (brush teeth, see doctors, do important RR things, sleep) but also, can't do absolutely imperative things, i.e. my car's broke down, needs easy to fix spark plugs, do you think I'm able to walk two blocks to get them and take ten minutes to fix it? no, no, I've been riding streetcar to work for weeks, etc. etc. things even worse, but suffice to say I just eat every 12 hours, sleep every 20 hours, masturbate every 8 hours and otherwise just sit on the train and stare ahead without a thought in it. One thing I do is think every 5 seconds of the things I have to do, I keep reciting them over and over in my mind?, "fix car, fix feet, fix teeth, fix eyes, fix nose, fix thumbs, fix bronchial tubes, fix asshole, get new RR lantern, get RR pass for trip back here in March for Hairy Jack and Harassed Diana, (if they want it) get started on book, get lined up for RR jobs on way east, get dog (I got thorobred cocker for Cathy) rabies shot, get backyard fixed for Cathy to play in, get this read and that written etc." The net result of all this is my belly is sick all the time, it's loose, I eat and I feel sick after, I smoke and get mad for not stopping, etc. etc. I wish I had a toad stool to crawl under and die.

Then, I remember reading this letter and thinking that it was odd prose.

To attempt to get an exact fix on the ever-mysterious soul is futile. But nowadays one must needs have abstract thinking and it forces the physicist of the inner world to elucidate a fictitious world for oneself by fictions piled on fictions, notions on more notions. He transmutes the non-extended into the extended.[128]

Then there is a whole disquisition on the effects of marijuana on him and on Jack, marijuana making them both blank-minded. This is an early notice of that.

The particular Mexican t [marijuana] that Jack and I have been blasting (I ran out almost a month ago and if you lovely boys would take pity and just send me any small amount available I'd surely swoon) was different than any other t because I've noticed that anyone who uses it has a tendency to think the same strange things as do others who have it. I know t has similar effects on all of us, but this stuff was more so; even Al Hinkle entered completely into the same pattern of kicks once he's blasted.

Hinkle was a Denver friend who was a railroad brakeman. A big, tall, scholarly, quiet, resolutely silent fellow.

In the light of this, and letters Jack has written me, I suspect the brooding alone on Richmond Hill for what it was; a final and most disheartening realization of himself. This is not to say he was not happy, it was that itself which showed him the truth of the matter. Under its (t) influence he was really stoned consistently for long period; and alone. When one is alone on this stuff the sheer ecstasy of utterly realizing each moment makes it more clear to one than ever how impossibly far one is from the others. Not different from them or intolerant; one is more close than ever to people and the world, but, in the end alone for no one can ever follow the complexities that make up the mind that is so t conditioned. One, then, cannot make ones self clear to others; the difficulties of yourself tracing the trail of inner feeling and conviction are so insurmountable that not only in writing, but even in speech and action, one is completely misunderstood—because all that comes out of one is a caricature of what one is thinking & that is so distorted from the actual thought that people pick up on this caricature as your action or thought about the matter at hand, whereas really one *had meant* it for a caricature (realizing inwardly the incapability of even beginning to speak or show action about what one is experiencing) and once beginning this trait is unable to stop and so, actually, becomes artificial. A horrible fate to be artificial, no genuine feeling left; all is bemused thought that means nothing to anyone else but ones self.[129]

Neal goes on and on about the subject. I thought that the little disquisition was pretty archetypal as a description of teahead subjectivity. I also thought that was a funny sentence about, psychologically, "whereas one *had meant* it for a caricature."

One thing that comes out of this is that this guy was interested in his mind and the process of mind and thought forms. Maybe it was in a very crude way, but quite subtle for a self-taught Denver intellect. Cassady was investigating the phenomena of his own thoughts from a very odd angle. And it had literary ramifications in that it turned Kerouac on to listening to his own mind, also, and then to build a prose based on the ramblings of the mind itself.

There are a few comments that he makes about Kerouac which get to be a little bit interesting. Neal begins talking about Kerouac's marriage in the same letter.

As time passes he'll loose the strength to be consistent in this (as he knows more) and will hanker elsewhere even if there is great love and they are welded solid, for the actual task of rising to the game is too difficult, unbeknown to us all, and, unless by that time there are other things, Jack will fall prey to this inherent weakness (no hardon) and fuck big only in imagination. But, that's another problem. So where do we stand? nowhere, yet; I haven't said anything valid about Jack's marriage. Where does one begin? I prefer China since it's furthest away, but, being practical, Ha, how about starting with looking at Jack objectively, Ha, Ha. More shit; I'm dashing it off now—

The intense drives that affect Jack's actions are extremely varied and strong; this is of prime importance and I must continually orient to one and then another of these multitudinous forces to escape oversimplification, and so will seem quite contradictory—as he himself is. Ah! but to properly etch in the exact shades of his personality, so that the degrees of conflict can be approximated and his whole upright self stand firmly, sharp and clear. A delineation of his mind seems in order, but, his emotions are so pronounced! Ach, bah, anyway—But, by god, Allen, what a man he is, just stop and think of it. Certain traits stand out so as to make him a true peasant, as he says, "like a potato" and, again, what wisdom he can flash! He lets people bully him, intellectually & otherwise, he shows always a shy diffidence, a gentle nature; witness, tho, his claws as he rants for pages on end and sometimes, at parties, raises up in anger at wrongs (usually social) he imagines inwardly or witnesses; yet, he'll be the first to wither under any real hint of sweetness on the part of the other person. He has a morbid dread of hassles (he will attempt mightily to escape even the suggestion of one in his marriage) but when it comes down to it won't knuckle under. He has consideration, but a manly selfishness, boyishness, but a certain poise, etc. etc. Damn it, I don't want to, and can't be presumptuous enough to, give you any of this simple trash. You know him a hell-of-a-lot better than I do, longer than I have probably probably love him the more. You see, when I began this I was just struck by the thought of the actual difference between you and Jack. (What if you had married and I was writing Jack your traits?)[130]

He goes on and on with more interesting bullshit. What I chose here were comments by Neal on Jack. This is May 10, 1951.

Great news that Jack's finished *On the Road,* I trust in his writing, but fear for it because the theme of *On the Road* is too trivial for him, as his dissatisfaction shows. He must either forget it or enlarge it into a mighty thing that merely uses what he's written as a Book 1, since what he's done doesn't lend itself to stuffing he should create another and another work (like Proust) and then we'll have the great American Novel. I think he would profit by starting a Book 2 with the recollections of his early life as they were sent to me and then blend that into his prophetic *Dr. Sax.* Of course, I'm sure I don't know what I'm talking about, but I do worry for him and want him happy.[131]

That's actually what Kerouac did. He finished *On the Road* and then went on to write *Visions of Cody,* which was precisely what Neal suggested, enlarging it into a mightier thing, more Proustian. The narrative style was dropped as being too slow. He came back to *Visions of Cody* and continued and concluded that with many different kinds of experiments in spontaneous athletic composition. It includes some chapters which are pure verbal sound and babble and some chapters which are direct transcriptions of taped conversations between him and Neal. Those are the best tape transcriptions I've ever seen for stylistics. He catches coughs, and ahh ums and flubs and muffled comments. It is a real actual exact transcription of the events on the tape, rather than complete sentences. Then in the same letter, Neal is talking about Jack on the road and his own situation.

Tell Jack I become ulcerated old color-blind RR conductor who never writes anything good and dies a painful lingering death from prostate gland trouble (cancer from excessive masturbation) at 45. Unless I get sent to San Quentin for rape of teenager and drown after slipping into slimy cesspool that work gang is unclogging. Of course, I might fall under freight train, but that's too good since Carolyn would get around 40 or 50 thousand settlement from RR (god's truth, maybe more—only reason I keep job instead of driving Greyhound bus with gals to sniff at) one thing sure, I'll just keep withering away emotionally at about same rate as have last

3 years, so unlikely that I can become insane or kill myself because there can be no further explosions except cap-pistol blow offs. Have attained a run-of-the-mill schizophrenia brought on by past dwelling on loss of love and guilt of actions, but it is still a petty watery bluegreen and can't fade into a real greyness until another 10 years of steady Proustian recollection of life. There is hope for some unhealthy blast sooner tho because my frustrations are at a near-record high. I'm afraid I've irrevocably slipped however and in my mediocrity have become precisely what Jack long ago feared was my fate; I am blank and getting more so.[132]

Then there's a long long letter, talking again at great length about [his] writing block and the difficulty of getting anything down on paper. It's a pretty intelligent analysis of anyone's sense of inadequacy, the mind going too fast for a writer to get down. He ends the letter talking about F. Scott Fitzgerald.

What I perhaps mean is that I feel he [Fitzgerald] and I both try with about equal intensity. If I can't come to eventually write as good as he did I fear I'll honestly be pretty much of a failure, ego? No, truth. I realize he's not much and only extolled as American (at least a dozen, including your pal Jack K. are better) and I can see him as a baby compared to Proust or Celine. I halt these digressions so that I may begin the next page clean.[133]

That was Cassady's mind as of 1950. In his attitude toward Neal, subsequent to the blankness described by Cassady in these letters, Kerouac took pity on Cassady and, having written most of *On the Road* and being in the middle of *Visions of Cody,* he thought I was being too pushy in thinking that Neal was supposed to create some giant, dramatic work of art and turn himself into a big artist like Kerouac. So Jack wrote a little poem letting Neal off the hook as far as ambition. This is from Kerouac's *Scattered Poems*.

He's your friend, let him dream;
He's not your brother, he's not yr. father,
He's not St. Michael he's a guy.

He's married, he works, go on sleeping
On the other side of the world,
Go thinking in the great European Night

I'm explaining him to you my way not yours,
Child, Dog—listen: go find your soul,
Go smell the wind, go far.

Life is a pity. Close the book, go on,
Write no more on the wall, on the moon,
At the Dog's, in the sea in the snowing bottom.

Go find God in the nights, the clouds too.
When can it stop this big circle at the skull
oh Neal; there are men, things outside to do.

Great huge tombs of Activity
in the desert of Africa of the heart,
The black angels, the women in bed

with their beautiful arms open for you
in their youth, some tenderness
Beginning in the same shroud.

The big clouds of new continents,
O foot tired in climes so mysterious,
Don't go down the outside for nothing.[134]

"O foot tired in climes so mysterious." I remember that was his comment on Neal's [injuring] his foot in a railroad accident around that time. He prevented a big train crash by jumping on the train just in time to uncouple one car from another so that there wasn't a giant crash. In the jolt that ensued he fell and had his foot crushed between the trains. He was hospitalized and given $32,000 compensation, with which he bought a house for his wife. I think this "O foot tired in climes so mysterious" relates to that.

CHAPTER 28

Kerouac and the "Essentials of Spontaneous Prose"

By hindsight, the writing method that Kerouac used is explained in his essay "Essentials of Spontaneous Prose." It gives a very clear practical set of suggestions for how to relate to both natural flow and balance of form. I think it's one of the great practical writing essays of the century. It's dated 1958, but it describes the method Kerouac used earlier.

Set-up. The object is set before the mind, either in reality, as in sketching (before a landscape or teacup or old face) or is set in the memory wherein it becomes the sketching from memory of a definite image-object.

Procedure. Time being of the essence in the purity of speech, sketching language is undisturbed flow from the mind of personal secret idea-words, *blowing* (as per jazz musician) on subject of image.

Method. No periods separating sentence-structures already arbitrarily riddled by false colons and timid usually needless commas—but the vigorous space dash separating rhetorical breathing (as jazz musician drawing breath between outblown phrases)—"measured pauses which are the essentials of our speech"—"divisions of the *sounds* we hear"—"time and how to note it down." (William Carlos Williams)

Amazingly, here he's quoted the classicist William Carlos Williams.

Scoping. Not "selectivity" of expression but following free deviation (association) of mind into limitless blow-on-subject seas of thought, swimming in sea of English with no discipline other than rhythms of exhalation and expostulated statement, like a fist coming down on a table with each complete utterance, bang! (the space dash)—Blow as deep as you want—write as deeply, fish as far down as you want, satisfy yourself first, then reader cannot fail to receive telepathic shock and meaning-excitement by same laws operating in his own human mind.

[That was] demonstrated in some of his sketches, that slight telepathic shock of recognition of "meaning-excitement by same laws operating in his own human mind."

Lag in Procedure. No pause to think of proper word but the infantile pileup of scatological buildup words till satisfaction is gained, which will turn out to be a great appending rhythm to a thought and be in accordance with Great Law of timing.

Timing. Nothing is muddy that *runs in time* and to laws of *time*—Shakespearian stress of dramatic need to speak now in own unalterable way or forever hold tongue—*no revisions* (except obvious rational mistakes, such as names or *calculated* insertions in act of not writing but *inserting*).

He allows for little, additional, calculated insertions in the act of writing. The center of interest applies more to *Visions of Cody*.

Center of Interest. Begin not from preconceived idea of what to say about image but from jewel center of interest in subject of image at *moment* of writing, and write outwards swimming in sea of language to peripheral release and exhaustion—Do not afterthink except for poetic or P.S. reason. Never afterthink to "improve" or defray impressions, as the best writing is always the most painful personal wrung-out tossed from cradle warm protective mind—tap from yourself the song of yourself, *blow!—now!—your* way is your only way—"good"—or "bad"—always honest, ("ludicrous"), spontaneous, "confessional" interesting because not "crafted." Craft is crafty.

[Kerouac] said that a lot, "Craft is crafty." He was associating with the word "crafty." "Crafting" was the pejorative. That's a funny one. It always struck me, because I was a crafty one.

Structure of Work. Modern bizarre structures (science fiction, etc.) arise from language being dead, "different" themes give illusion of "new" life. Follow roughly outlines in outfanning movement over subject, as river rock, so mindflow over jewel-center need (run your mind over it, *once*) {In other words, prepare it once by running your mind over the subject before you write} arriving at pivot, where what was dim-formed "beginning" becomes sharp-necessitating "ending" and language shortens in race to wire of time-race of work, following laws of Deep Form, to conclusion, last words, last trickle—Night is The End.

I'm not quite sure I understand that. "Follow roughly outlines in outfanning," well that's kind of complicated, it's really giving method. "In outfanning movement over subject," well that's obvious, "as river rock," as river flows over rock, "so mindflow over jewel-center need (run your mind over it, *once*) arriving at pivot," this is where I get a little confused, "where what was dim-formed 'beginning' becomes sharp-necessitating 'ending.'" Run your mind over it once, come to whatever that jewel center of interest is, the point where you get a little epiphany of what it is you wanted to say, and then begin there, "and language shortens in race to wire of time-race of work, following laws of Deep Form, to conclusion, last words, last trickle—Night is The End."

Mental State. If possible write "without consciousness" in semi-trance (as Yeats' later "trance writing") allowing subconscious to admit in own uninhibited interesting necessary and so "modern" language what conscious art would censor, and write excitedly, swiftly, with writing-or-typing-cramps, in accordance (as from center to periphery) with laws of orgasm, Reich's "beclouding of consciousness." Come from within, out—to relaxed and said.[135]

It says "to relaxed and said," but I think he really was relaxed and sad. So that's his method.

CHAPTER 29

Kerouac and *On the Road*

In April 1951 Kerouac wrote *On the Road* in a one-room studio apartment that Jack shared with his new wife, Joan Haverty. She had been a friend of the fellow Bill Cannastra, who had climbed out of the subway window [and was killed]. There was a general shock in our community and very soon afterward Kerouac married her. They settled down and had a little wifey-husband relationship. While he sat down to write, she went out and did some work. Lucien Carr had given him a teletype roll from the UPI and he put that in the typewriter and began an experiment in writing from the center outward, swimming in seasoned language.

Around that time T. S. Eliot published an essay on Joyce and Milton as great blind artists who were able to encompass in the sweep of a single syntactical structure the entire panorama from heaven all the way down to hell. Just as Proust was able to encompass the panorama of all Jewish Hebrew history in Baron de Charlus's hair, so Kerouac was interested in long extended, balanced, symphonic sentences. Kerouac felt that Proust's technique was too halting an approach to both speech, which was his model, and typewriting athletics. He decided to abandon that cadence of the Proustian sentence [because] although it is balanced it is not an extended breath, it's a broken breath. Kerouac was interested in a cadence rising out of an extended exhalation. He mentioned that exhalation in his "Essentials of Spontaneous Prose."

To write *On the Road,* Kerouac stopped writing the prose that he [had been] working on for the opening chapters of *Visions of Cody.* He wanted to do something else and so he took Lucien's teletype roll and began feeding it into the typewriter. Jack was a swift typist, 120 words a minute, an athletic typist like a football player typist. That was a fact that people didn't quite understand, the neural rapidity between his brain and his fingers was amazing. Whatever arrived in his larynx or his mind, subvocally, could be immediately translated into typewritten finger pecks fast enough to complete long, long sentences including all his parenthetical subdivisions of thought form.

The entire manuscript of *On the Road* was originally one single sentence. I read parts of it at the time, when I would come visiting him. It took about three weeks or four weeks. His wife was complaining that he was lazy, hanging around the house, not going out and getting a job, so it was a classic situation. I'm sure he was very difficult to live with, but I don't think his wife appreciated the necessities of his artistic situation.

The completed manuscript was given to Malcolm Cowley, who was the one person who understood it, and he proposed to publish it years later. When it was handed in to Ace Books it was a scandal, because they'd given him an advance and what does he turn in but this vast teletype roll of a single sentence which nobody would ever publish. They thought they were buying some sort of potboiler about hippies or beatniks. It freaked me out too, because I was his business agent and this wasn't what I had sold them. I had sold them an extended novel, with extended sentence prose, and instead Kerouac gave me this scroll to bring in. I got mad at him and wrote him a stupid letter saying, "Are you trying to fuck us up purposely?"

Kerouac was really a solitary genius, innovating and going forward into as yet unrecognized and unmapped areas of composition all by himself, with the courage necessary to do it all by himself. He had no support, not only from "society" but also from his friends, his wife, his mother, or anyone. I was involved in an intimate way, but I was nothing but an anchor drag. I'm quite ashamed of my role. Within a few months I was writing him letters trying to apologize and tell him how much I liked it. I liked it immediately, but on the other hand it was just unsalable, and [as agent] I was thinking in terms of selling it somewhere. That was a traumatic lesson I learned about the conditions of real art. Sometimes things are messy. When you break the shell, shit comes out of the shell and it's sometimes a mess, as it is in real birth.

> But Dean's intelligence was every bit as formal and shining and complete, without the tedious intellectualness. And his "criminality" was not something that sulked and sneered; it was a wild yea-saying over burst of American joy; it was Western, the west wind, an ode from the Plains, something new, long prophesied, long a-coming (he only stole cars for joy rides). Besides, all my New York friends were in the negative, nightmare position of putting down society and giving their tired bookish or political or psychoanalytical reasons, but Dean just raced in society, eager for bread and love; he didn't care one way or the other, "so long's I can get that lil ole gal with that lil sumpin down there tween her legs, boy," and "so long's we can *eat*, son, y'ear me? I'm *hungry*, I'm *starving*, let's *eat right now*!"—and off we'd rush to eat, whereof, as saith Ecclesiastes, "It is your portion under the sun."[136]

He went seventy. I tingled all over; I counted minutes and sub-
tracted miles. Just ahead, over the rolling wheatfields all golden
beneath the distant snows of Estes, I'd be seeing old Denver at last.
I pictured myself in a Denver bar that night, with all the gang, and
in their eyes I would be strange and ragged and like the Prophet
who has walked across the land to bring the dark Word, and the
only Word I had was "Wow!"[137]

My stay in San Francisco was coming to an end. Remi would never
talk to me again. It was horrible because I really loved Remi and
I was one of the very few people in the world who knew what
a genuine and grand fellow he was. It would take years for him
to get over it. How disastrous all this was compared to what I'd
written him from Paterson, planning my red line Route 6 across
America. Here I was at the end of America—no more land—and
now there was nowhere to go but back. I determined at least to
make my trip a circular one: I decided then and there to go to
Hollywood and back through Texas to see my bayou gang; then
the rest be damned.[138]

This is kind of interesting because this was whiskey and he died
of alcohol. So this is an early account of drinking.

She was slow and hung-up about everything she did; it took her
a long time to eat; she chewed slowly and stared into space, and
smoked a cigarette, and kept talking, and I was like a haggard
ghost, suspicioning every move she made, thinking she was stalling
for time. This was all a fit of sickness. I was sweating as we went
down the street hand in hand. The first hotel we hit had a room,
and before I knew it I was locking the door behind me and she was

sitting on the bed taking off her shoes. I kissed her meekly. Better she'd never know. To relax our nerves I knew we needed whisky, especially me. I ran out and fiddled all over twelve blocks, hurrying till I found a pint of whisky for sale at a newsstand. I ran back, all energy. Terry was in the bathroom, fixing her face. I poured one big drink in a water glass, and we had slugs. Oh, it was sweet and delicious and worth my whole lugubrious voyage.[139]

One thing that occurs throughout his prose is a mellow-cellos about old October moons. Thomas Wolfe made much of October and Kerouac made a lot of October. He died in October, so there's a kind of Octoberal, I think it was from Shakespeare, an old October barrenness everywhere. That's where he got his October from.

I had a book with me I stole from a Hollywood stall, *"Le Grand Meaulnes"* by Alain-Fournier, but I preferred reading the American landscape as we went along. Every bump, rise, and stretch in it mystified my longing. In inky night we crossed New Mexico; at gray dawn it was Dalhart, Texas; in the bleak Sunday afternoon we rode through one Oklahoma flat-town after another; at nightfall it was Kansas. The bus roared on. I was going home in October. Everybody goes home in October.[140]

There are long, long serenades about October from book to book.

Suddenly I found myself on Times Square. I had traveled eight thousand miles around the American continent and I was back on Times Square; and right in the middle of a rush hour, too, seeing with my innocent road-eyes the absolute madness and fantastic hoorair of New York with its millions and millions hustling forever for a buck among themselves, the mad dream—grabbing, taking, giving, sighing, dying, just so they could be buried in those awful cemetery cities beyond Long Island City.[141]

When I got home I ate everything in the icebox. My aunt got up and looked at me. "Poor little Salvatore," she said in Italian. "You're thin, you're thin. Where have you been all this time?" I had on two shirts and two sweaters; my canvas bag had torn cottonfield pants and the tattered remnants of my huarache shoes in it. My aunt and I decided to buy a new electric refrigerator with the money I had sent her from California; it was to be the first one in the family. She went to bed, and late at night I couldn't sleep and just smoked in bed. My half-finished manuscript was on the desk. It was October, home, and work again. The first cold winds rattled the windowpane, and I had made it just in time.[142]

The shrouded stranger of the night was a common fantasy we had and out of this particular image came my own poem "The Shrouded Stranger" and Kerouac's *Doctor Sax*.

Just about that time a strange thing began to haunt me. It was this: I had forgotten something. There was a decision that I was about to make before Dean showed up, and now it was driven clear out of my mind but still hung on the tip of my mind's tongue. I kept snapping my fingers, trying to remember it. I even mentioned it. And I couldn't even tell if it was a real decision or just a thought I had forgotten. It haunted and flabbergasted me, made me sad. It had to do somewhat with the Shrouded Traveler. Carlo Marx and I once sat down together, knee to knee, in two chairs, facing, and I told him a dream I had about a strange Arabian figure that was pursuing me across the desert; that I tried to avoid; that finally overtook me just before I reached the Protective City. "Who is this?" said Carlo. We pondered it. I proposed it was myself, wearing a shroud. That wasn't it. Something, someone, some spirit was pursuing all of us across the desert of life and was bound to catch us before we reached heaven. Naturally, now that I look back on it, this is only death: death will overtake us before heaven. The one thing that we yearn for in our living days, that makes us sigh and groan and undergo sweet nauseas of all kinds, is the remembrance of some lost bliss that was probably experienced in the womb and can only be reproduced (though we hate to admit it) in death. But who wants to die? In the rush of events I kept thinking about this in the back of my mind. I told it to Dean and he instantly recognized it as the mere simple longing for pure death; and because we're all of us never in life again, he, rightly, would have nothing to do with it, and I agreed with him then.[143]

I left everybody and went home to rest. My aunt said I was wasting my time hanging around with Dean and his gang. I knew that was wrong, too. Life is life, and kind is kind.[144]

That's pretty good. "Life is life, and kind is kind." It's a pun, like kindness is kindness, but also it takes one kind to recognize another kind, relatives are relatives, that is to say, friends are friends, types are types. That comes from a wordplay by Lucien Carr, who on an early trip down into Greenwich Village had written on the urinal of the Minetta Tavern, "Humankind-ness," and under that, "Human-kindness," take your choice. Life is life and kind is kind.

Burroughs:

Bull had a sentimental streak about the old days in America, especially 1910, when you could get morphine in a drugstore without prescription and Chinese smoked opium in their evening windows and the country was wild and brawling and free, with abundance and any kind of freedom for everyone. His chief hate was Washington bureaucracy; second to that, liberals; then cops. He spent all his time talking and teaching others. Jane sat at his feet; so did I; so did Dean; and so had Carlo Marx. We'd all learned from him. He was a gray, nondescript-looking fellow you wouldn't notice on the street, unless you looked closer and saw his mad, bony skull with its strange youthfulness—a Kansas minister with exotic, phenomenal fires and mysteries. He had studied medicine in Vienna; had studied anthropology, read everything; and now he was settling to his life's work, which was the study of things themselves in the streets of life and the night.[145]

Burroughs prophetic, on science. They went out to the racetrack playing the horses.

In the car as we drove back to his old house he [Bull] said, "Mankind will someday realize that we are actually in contact with the dead and with the other world, whatever it is; right now we could predict, if we only exerted enough mental will, what is going to happen within the next hundred years and be able to take steps to avoid all kinds of catastrophes. When a man dies he undergoes a mutation in his brain that we know nothing about now but which will be very clear someday if scientists get on the ball. The bastards right now are only interested in seeing if they can blow up the world."

We told Jane about it. She sniffed. "It sounds silly to me."[146]

"The bastards right now are only interested in seeing if they can blow up the world." That's quite literally correct in terms of where the money goes. Burroughs's contention always was that science was a great answerer. He can dig science except he thinks that all the experimental research is going into destructive science rather than something interesting and curious and worth a grown man's attention.

Meanwhile Dean took a carton of cigarettes from the gas station and we were stocked for the voyage—gas, oil, cigarettes, and food. Crooks don't know. He pointed the car straight down the road.[147]

"Crooks don't know." I don't know quite what that meant but I always dug that insertion.

Either crooks don't know what karma they're building, or else the gas station owners are all crooks and they don't know who they've stolen from. It's a weird line. It is a funny kind of intelligence that he has of one swift thought that passes by. Crooks don't know. It's almost like an apothem, or an axiom. He's got another one in here, "The earth is an Indian thing," which is a really beautiful phrase.

Kerouac's characters are modeled on real people, but Kerouac is a novelist and a fiction maker, so the anecdotes are embellished and exaggerated for dramatic charm. What he did was fictionalize people, or fictionalize reality, so that there's not a one-to-one correlation. The quotations are invented by Kerouac, paraphrasing or imitating the rhythms or diction of the people talking, sometimes a little crudely and sometimes very, very wittily. They're stereotypes of the way Burroughs talks or the way I talk or the way Cassady talked. They aren't quotes for real, although occasionally, since he kept small swiftly writ notebooks, some of the conversation might be identical with actual words that came out of people's mouths. For the most part, while he was typing, he had to make up speeches that sounded like the people or as he remembered it sounding. He took from real characters but he's fictionalizing them.

Biographers tend to assume that the incidents and speeches are one-to-one reality and construct biographies out of his novels. They're all awry, the facts are not accurate, because he's invented scenes and invented confrontations and exciting conversations. In this case [*On the Road*] the editing of the single-sentence teletype roll down to paragraphs, pages, sections, chapters of the published book involved the condensation of six cross-country trips into two for dramatic purposes.

[My character] Carlo Marx is taken from Jack's fictionalization, so it isn't identical. I have to keep relating to the problem of people asking, "Are you Carlo Marx?" Well I'm not. Carlo Marx is a fictionalization. As far as I'm concerned, it's Jack's somewhat goofy, charming, tender invention, but not me. However, it was a picture that I thought was rather cute at the time and still do. Sometimes a bit vicious, I thought. However, it was his thing and it never bugged me, I sort of liked it. I thought it was fiction after all, and he had a right to use his imagination to express himself. One or two people got really mad, though.

"I know," I said, and I looked back east and sighed. We had no money. Dean hadn't mentioned money. "Where are we going to stay?" We wandered around, carrying our bundles of rags in the narrow romantic streets. Everybody looked like a broken-down movie extra, a withered starlet; disenchanted stunt-men, midget auto-racers, poignant California characters with their end-of-the-continent sadness, handsome, decadent, Casanovaish men, puffy-eyed motel blondes, hustlers, pimps, whores, masseurs, bellhops—a lemon lot, and how's a man going to make a living with a gang like that?[148]

It's pretty good. I would say "I write poetry" and he would say "I write poetry too, but I have a longer line," and it really is as good as anything I can write. "Disenchanted stunt-men," a fantastic idea. Amazing combination, "end-of-continent sadness," well that's just mood music, but "withered starlet," that's very good. That's amazingly intense for prose, amazingly vivid and inventive as language. The concept is great, "disenchanted stunt-men." The book is studded with these throwaway insightful, incisive phrasings. That's his real genius, I think, because there's some kind of extraordinary intelligence both of language and of ear. Jack Kerouac is not given credit for the sophistication of his insight into characters and stereotypes and archetypes of society. A line like this about stunt men or withered starlets, it's not merely sophisticated, not merely society wise, but world wise. "A lemon lot, and how's a man going to make a living with a gang like that?" That's basic bourgeois attitude, a middle-class attitude, a lemon lot. It has humor and he's imitating, parodying, and paraphrasing a middle-class macho all-right-nik comment here.

The point I'm trying to make is that, whatever Kerouac's supposed reputation as an oddball or a curious genius of beatnik prose, his attitudes encompassed the attitudes of middle America at their wittiest. Kerouac's attitudinal rhetoric, side remarks like "a lemon lot, and how's a man going to make a living with a gang like that?," is so recognizably macho and at the same time understandable, simpatico, basically commonsense, down to earth, redneck aspected, is again a measure of his worldly sophistication. He's considered a naive, or a primitive, but Kerouac had a better grasp on American manners and political manners than most writers, although some American novelists do have that kind of scope, like Dos Passos, Fitzgerald, and Hemingway. That quality of rueful wisdom and intelligence isn't very often commented on in Kerouac. That's the thing I find the most interesting despite the fact that I might have gone into a snit or put him down.

Suffering and mutability, transitoriness, mortal poignancy or swiftness of mortal life are the most characteristic motifs of Kerouac. There's a basic grounding in sanity with all this excitement and offset joy and puffs of grass. This is grounded in an unadulterated appreciation of pain. That's about as good as you can get for an American exemplar of transitoriness, "withered starlets."

I looked out the window at the winking neons and said to myself, "Where is Dean and why isn't he concerned about our welfare?" I lost faith in him that year. I stayed in San Francisco a week and had the beatest time of my life. Marylou and I walked around for miles, looking for food-money. We even visited some drunken seamen in a flophouse on Mission Street that she knew; they offered us whisky.[149]

I walked around, picking butts from the street. I passed a fish-n-chips joint on Market Street, and suddenly the woman in there gave me a terrified look as I passed; she was the proprietress, she apparently thought I was coming in there with a gun to hold up the joint. I walked on a few feet. It suddenly occurred to me this was my mother of about two hundred years ago in England, and that I was her footpad son, returning from gaol to haunt her honest labors in the hashery. I stopped, frozen with ecstasy on the sidewalk. I looked down Market Street. I didn't know whether it was that or Canal Street in New Orleans: it led to water, ambiguous, universal water, just as 42nd Street, New York, leads to water, and you never know where you are.[150]

This is quite smart about 42nd Street, because when you look deep into 42nd Street you realize there's water at both ends of the street, but when you're in the middle of 42nd Street you think you're in the middle of the continent with all the neon blinking and the tall buildings.

I was delirious. I wanted to go back and leer at my strange Dickensian mother in the hash joint. I tingled all over from head to foot. It seemed I had a whole host of memories leading back to 1750 in England and that I was in San Francisco now only in another life and in another body. [. . .] And for just a moment I had reached the point of ecstasy that I always wanted to reach, which was the complete step across chronological time into timeless shadows, and wonderment in the bleakness of the mortal realm, and the sensation of death kicking at my heels to move on, with a phantom dogging its own heels, and myself hurrying to a plank where all the angels dove off and flew into the holy void of uncreated emptiness, the potent and inconceivable radiancies shining in bright Mind Essence, innumerable lotus-lands falling open in the magic moth swarm of heaven. I could hear an indescribable seething roar which wasn't in my ear but everywhere and had nothing to do with sounds. I realized that I had died and been reborn numberless times but just didn't remember especially because the transitions from life to death and back to life are so ghostly easy, a magical action for naught, like falling asleep and waking up again a million times, the utter casualness and deep ignorance of it. I realized it was only because of the stability of the intrinsic Mind that these ripples of birth and death took place, like the action of wind on a sheet of pure, serene, mirror-like water. I felt sweet, swinging bliss, like a big shot of heroin in the mainline vein; like a gulp of wine late in the afternoon and it makes you shudder; my feet tingled. I thought I was going to die the very next moment. But I didn't die, and walked four miles and picked up ten long butts and took them back to Marylou's hotel room and poured their tobacco in my old pipe and lit up. I was too young to know what had happened. In the window I smelled all the food of San Francisco.[151]

That's an amazing passage, that "moth swarm of heaven." This was the heart of Kerouac at that point in time and I think it's the jewel center of interest in Kerouac. It is one of the earliest complete statements of his sense of "everything belongs to me because I am poor," or total loss, earth loss. It's the recognition of mortality as the main theme and the emotional poignancy of that flowerness of the moment. It relates to his vision of himself in relation to his mother, returning to his mother's hash joint. It seemed to have been a constant theme in his mind, or thesis, the idea of him having been hanged in London for murdering one of his old girlfriends, maybe he was Jack the Ripper or something.

"Mind essence" is straight out of Dwight Goddard's *Buddhist Bible,* the classic Buddhist translation of that time. My question was whether he inserted it into *On the Road* when he was preparing a final manuscript or whether it was originally written in there? The "intrinsic mind" is probably a phrase that he's taken from Goddard, "ripples of birth and death, like the action of wind on a sheet of serene, mirror-like water." That sounds like some kind of paraphrase of a Zen commentary he might have gotten out of D. T. Suzuki quoted in Goddard. We didn't know Alan Watts at the time.

It amazed me when I read the manuscript that he knew so much. That kind of insight seemed frightening to me, frankly, because it meant that the whole of my own existence was insubstantial and I thought I was getting to be pretty substantial. Kerouac was already writing this immensely compassionate, sad, empty prose about existence turning into golden ash. My first reaction was that he was being negative and mean, coming on in favor of death or something. But he was waxing poetic and rhapsodic over the immensity of death and the immensity of life and their interpenetration.

It's this insight into pain and transitoriness and emptiness which is dominant in *On the Road* and of the subsequent writings, which later becomes the vanity of Kerouac, as seen in *Vanity of Duluoz,* or *Vanity of Kerouac.* It is the recognition of the emptiness of his ambitions, the emptiness of his graspings to be a solid, substantial novelist with fireplace and desk in the library, a house in the country and a picture window on a Connecticut lawn. The emptiness of his fantasy of that kind of karma for himself or for his friends.

I didn't know anybody in America writing who had that grasp on the great goof of existence, except Burroughs and Herbert Huncke, not that my acquaintance with letters was vast at the time. Later Norman Mailer came to get some glimpse of the apocalyptic nature of our times and the insubstantiality of time itself. Thomas Wolfe, of course, was a big inspiration. He wanted to get it back and go home. He never gave it up. Kerouac gave up utterly, I think, beginning with 1950 or so. He'd already written one monumental, well-received, middle-class

bildungsroman novel, *The Town and the City*. He was already a celebrated young novelist with a great deal of promise and the editors in
New York were all in love with him. He was handsome and he was
young, so he could have had a nice career as a novelist, but instead he
decided to write directly out of his brains rather than fill out a form
like he was supposed to, to be reviewed in the *New York Times*.

There is a tradition, particularly in Herman Melville in *The
Confidence-Man* and his later works. There's the phantom tradition in
Melville, the phantom nature of the universe, including the Great White
Whale. You get little shudders of it in Tolstoy, when Prince Bolkonsky
is lying wounded on the battlefield and Napoleon comes by and he
looks up past Napoleon's horse's ass into blue sky and has a vision. And
you get some psychological fetterings of that kind in Dostoyevsky.

It seemed to me that the older traditional American middle-class
novelists like Sinclair Lewis and Theodore Dreiser somewhat, still
had either a hope for progress or a despair over progress, but the
idea was still progress in a sense. [John] Dos Passos and [James T.]
Farrell were still basically rooted in the world and dealing with the
world as if it were real, permanent, in a sense Marxist. Most American
writing was sociological or psychological. It was my impression that
very few people had a grasp of the phantom, or samsaric, or elusory
nature of existence. They didn't have any idea of alternative modes
of consciousness, to put it vulgarly. My impression was that there
wasn't anybody that had a visionary view piercing through mortal
phenomena to something uncanny that everybody knew and had
not revealed publically. It wasn't spoken of as an ordinary part of
our minds, but it was really a part of our lives.

If there were religious experiences in novels, say in Evelyn Waugh,
it was generally something erratic or extraneous or an intrusion of
a deus ex machina. It was an odd and perhaps alien intrusion that

was genuine but not part of this world. There were some Catholic novelists that had an idea of a vision of Christ. T. S. Eliot in *The Cocktail Party* made reference to one of the characters offstage who had a vision of Christ. He goes to Africa to become a saint and gets eaten by ants. It was always done in garish terms like that.

In terms of the popular culture, Kerouac was preternaturally brilliant and penetrant. I think that's why the whole Beat Generation, beginning in the mid-fifties, had so much power. Not that Kerouac was that smart, or Burroughs, but that what they were looking at was very basic and common sense. American cultural mentality, media consciousness, Hollywood, radio, TV, the new magazines that intellectuals nourished themselves on were so shallow in their spiritual ambition that any basic statement, even if couched in bohemian terms, was a revelation.

I had a visionary experience in 1948, or what seemed to me a visionary experience. It probably was just an experience of what everybody is experiencing all the time, which is just being in this space, but I had been so tied up in a superstructure of mental constructions as a result of my Columbia college education that a moment's relaxation of that whole set of references and preoccupations and a few moments opening my mind to see the space around me seemed to me to be supernatural. I thought I had seen God, when I was just seeing what everybody sees all the time. That drove me into a bughouse because I kept thinking I was seeing something special, that I had been gifted with seeing something special, not realizing that I was just seeing what any ordinary drunken Indian sees every five minutes. One touch of nature and you think you're Santayana and William James all put together, rather than just realizing you're seeing what the ice carrier gets all the time. The intellectual cadres in the forties and early fifties were locked up in a vast and systematized set of rationalizations, like Blake's figure of Urizen bound down in the chains of his own rationalizations and the nets of his own mind, that the glimpse of original nature of the mind and of the world that Kerouac presented, or the glimpses of political humor that Burroughs presented, or even the glimpses of frankness that I presented in the mid-fifties broke through as prophetic statements, because everybody else was so dopey. Literally everybody else.

There is such a disjunction between the consciousness cultivated in grammar school [and the real world] that a breakthrough from one to the other is a major miracle. I guess we all remember how we thought when we were in high school. With me there was a certain point when the bottom fell out of my mind, when everything that I had thought was true turned out to be not true. It was conditioning that [had] sustained my adolescent mentally. When I lost my mental cherry, I realized that everything was different from what I thought it was. There wasn't a black and white, right and wrong, like I thought. The moral laws that I thought were taken for granted didn't have anything to do with anything once you knew somebody who [had] killed somebody. Life was completely different than a newspaper or storybook idea.

In the fifties there was a deep public mind-set among the middle class. That's why it's miraculous for Kerouac to come on (not merely radical leftist, because he wasn't radical leftist at all, but cutting left and right), getting to the basis of mind itself as his preoccupation. He was not even interested in who was right and wrong, not even interested in whether the generals in America were good or bad, or whether automobiles were good or bad. He was interested in what was the nature, the phenomenon, of mind. Whether it was grief and sorrow and death and loss, what was the reason for the feeling of phantomness and emptiness everywhere? Not a sociological reason, but an understanding based on experience of the taste of mortality.

It seemed to me then that there was a universal public consciousness that everybody shared that was completely papier-mâché.

At that time most novels that were reviewed in *Time* magazine were taken up with current events or plots having to do with getting ahead in the business world, the man in the gray flannel suit. A little bit of bitterness about it, bittersweet about success, maybe, but nothing reduced the whole thing to idiot's dust and ashes, which it was.

Something interesting comes up now.

> The last night Dean went mad and found Marylou somewhere downtown and we got in the car and drove all over Richmond across the bay, hitting Negro jazz shacks in the oil flats. Marylou went to sit down and a colored guy pulled the chair out from under her. The gals approached her in the john with propositions. I was approached too. Dean was sweating around. It was the end; I wanted to get out.
>
> At dawn I got my New York bus and said good-by to Dean and Marylou. They wanted some of my sandwiches. I told them no. It was a sullen moment. We were all thinking we'd never see one another again and we didn't care.[152]

On the next page there's a very famous passage, which was much discussed in the late fifties when it came out.

> At lilac evening I walked with every muscle aching among the lights of 27th and Welton in the Denver colored section, wishing I were a Negro, feeling that the best the white world had offered was not enough ecstasy for me, not enough life, joy, kicks, darkness, music, not enough night. I stopped at a little shack where a man sold hot red chili in paper containers; I bought some and ate it, strolling in the

dark mysterious streets. I wished I were a Denver Mexican, or even a poor overworked Jap, anything but what I was so drearily, a "white man" disillusioned. All my life I'd had white ambitions; that was why I'd abandoned a good woman like Terry in the San Joaquin Valley. I passed the dark porches of Mexican and Negro homes; soft voices were there, occasionally the dusky knee of some mysterious sensual gal; and dark faces of the men behind rose arbors. Little children sat like sages in ancient rocking chairs. A gang of colored women came by, and one of the young ones detached herself from mother-like elders and came to me fast—"Hello Joe!"—and suddenly saw it wasn't Joe, and ran back, blushing. I wished I were Joe. I was only myself, Sal Paradise, sad, strolling in this violet dark, this unbearably sweet night, wishing I could exchange worlds with the happy, true-hearted, ecstatic Negroes of America. The raggedy neighborhoods reminded me of Dean and Marylou, who knew these streets so well from childhood. How I wished I could find them.[153]

Then later on the [next] page:

Near me sat an old Negro who apparently watched the games every night. Next to him was an old white bum; then a Mexican family, then some girls, some boys—all humanity, the lot. Oh, the sadness of the lights that night! The young pitcher looked just like Dean. A pretty blonde in the seats looked just like Marylou. It was the Denver Night; all I did was die.

Down in Denver, down in Denver
All I did was die

Across the street Negro families sat on their front steps, talking and looking up at the starry night through the trees and just relaxing in the softness and sometimes watching the game. Many cars passed in the street meanwhile, and stopped at the corner when the light turned red. There was excitement and the air was filled with the vibration of really joyous life that knows nothing of disappointment and "white sorrows" and all that. The old Negro man had a can of beer in his coat pocket, which he proceeded to open; and the old white man enviously eyed the can and groped in his pocket to see if *he* could buy a can too. How I died! I walked away from there.[154]

It's an odd passage, very lyrical. Norman Podhoretz said that this was some idealistic, romantic notion. Well, of course it's idealistic and romantic, and it's presented in precisely that way, but on the other hand it contains a germ of a truth, that blacks in America at that time had a more down-home existence than whites did. With all the suffering it involved, still they had more of a basic sense of reality and joy of common existence than whites. It's not universal, it's not one to one, but there was the basic cultural strength in the black community that it could produce the greatest art for America, namely jazz. Jazz was a kind of speech that went round the world and influenced every country. The only art form, the only cultural push, that came out of America that transformed the political structure of the world through the Beatles and the Rolling Stones and rock 'n' roll and the youth culture.

It was a basic truth that Kerouac was [talking about]. It was ambiguously put, but a lot of critics howled like stuck pigs when they read that. [They] thought it was something terribly irresponsible to say, just a simple appreciation of black culture that is charming and which everybody knows about. Kerouac was accused of being a false nigger and a dope and an idiot and a sentimentalist because he had appreciated it with a good heart. Ishmael Reed dug this passage,

Reed being one of the bitterest and most critical black writers. Reed grew up on the book and thought [the passage] did represent some affirmative statement about their quality of life.

Podhoretz said that "blacks ain't happy, how dare you say they're happy." But Kerouac didn't mean happy, like economically happy. He meant that there was some integrity in connection with their suffering, an integrity of awareness of it that was different from the white world that was more fake and plastic.

Either way you take it, Kerouac doesn't have to be right or wrong ideologically. Kerouac was saying, "I'm a white kid come from a sterile, middle-class, industrial background and I'm having an experience of another culture." Which he does again, later in the book, when he gets to Mexico and experiences another culture. I remember the first time I went to Mexico and I suddenly realized that the world was not the United States of America, that the bigger part of the world simply wasn't like this. The idea that America was the way the world was supposed to be was completely nuts. Jack was just having this little breakthrough, a little cross-cultural appreciation, put lyrically. It wasn't a sociological survey of the suffering of blacks versus whites, it was just an appreciation of their suffering. Kerouac's amazement was that there's another world of art, rhythm, language outside of the regulation world he learned at Horace Mann. Kerouac had an open heart, he was trying to make sense, and his vision of blacks is openhearted, I think. He said, "Not enough life, joy, kicks, darkness, music, not enough night."

There are a couple more passages of heavenly whispers, or prophetic characters in the desert. There's a whole panorama that goes on in a still moment.

Out of the tenement next to Camille's house filed eleven Greek men and women who instantly lined themselves up on the sunny pavement while another backed up across the narrow street and smiled at them over a camera. We gaped at these ancient people who were having a wedding party for one of their daughters, probably the thousandth in an unbroken dark generation of smiling in the sun. They were well dressed, and they were strange. Dean and I might have been in Cyprus for all of that. Gulls flew overhead in the sparkling air.

"Well," said Dean in a very shy and sweet voice, "shall we go?"

"Yes," I said, "let's go to Italy." And so we picked up our bags, he the trunk with his one good arm and I the rest, and staggered to the cable-car stop; in a moment rolled down the hill with our legs dangling to the sidewalk from the jiggling shelf, two broken-down heroes of the Western night.[155]

That scene reminded me of the main thing that Kerouac got out of Fyodor Dostoyevsky and the Russian novels we all read. This sole confrontation, as in *The Idiot,* was the key—just like our own experiences when we met each other and confronted and inquired inquisitively after each other's soul. In Dostoyevsky the characters are constantly rushing up to each other, as in *The Possessed,* "Nikolai, Nikolai, how can we forget you?" says character Nitkin, when Nikolai wants to quit the revolution. There are moments of intimacy between men and women and between men and men, soul to soul. I don't find that represented in American writing much, except in Kerouac and a couple little moments between Ishmael and Queequeg, in *Moby-Dick,* that love between men. A frankly uttered thing like in Whitman with heartthrobs and thrills between men. Not necessarily sexual, even chaste, but nonetheless the thrill of recognition and thrill of feeling in the heart, which is an ache between men. It is not well known and not much written about except in Whitman, but I think it is probably universal.

It's a staple of the American character, but it isn't very often pre-sented. Whitman thought it was the salvation of the nation and that unless the nation were made up of comrades democracy couldn't work. A bunch of macho competitors all hating each other, or indifferent to each other, or scared of each other emotionally, would leave no possibility of a cooperative, democratic, functioning political system. Only with basic friendliness would it be possible for a nation to create a political world that was livable. That was one of the breakthroughs that Kerouac presented. Of course you get it a little bit in movies, with *Rebel Without a Cause* and Marlon Brando's *Wild Ones*. The softness inside the hero, the difficult hero with a soft tender center.

I remember Kerouac telling me that there was a point where he and Neal were taking a piss together, without any erotic interest in each other, and Neal looked up and acknowledged, "I love you, Jack" and Jack did the same to him. It was the epiphanous moment in *Visions of Cody,* when they declared their love for each other openly in an odd moment and told each other. What always struck me was that the thing I wanted most was just that, exchanging love with another man. I interpreted it as a sexual or genital thing, but I've experienced it over the years as just heart feeling.

At this point in the book the girls have all turned on the hero Dean Moriarty, and denounced him as a jerk and a creep and a lousy lay and irresponsible and insensitive.

Just as flat as that. It was the saddest night. I felt as if I was with strange brothers and sisters in a pitiful dream. Then a complete silence fell over everybody; where once Dean would have talked his way out, he now fell silent himself, but standing in front of every-body, ragged and broken and idiotic, right under the lightbulbs, his bony mad face covered with sweat and throbbing veins, saying,

"Yes, yes, yes," as though tremendous revelations were pouring into him all the time now, and I am convinced they were, and the others suspected as much and were frightened. He was BEAT—the root, the soul of Beatific. What was he knowing? He tried all in his power to tell me what he was knowing, and they envied that about me, my position at his side, defending him and drinking him in as they once tried to do. Then they looked at me. What was I, a stranger, doing on the West Coast this fair night? I recoiled from the thought.[156]

Later on a similar blankness and insensitivity that all the women objected to was due to speed [amphetamines], which desensitized Cassady. At this point, however, there was no particular physiological chill in his brain or in his body. As indicated in the book, the main character was trying to satisfy everybody sexually and set afire everybody's imaginations, and act as everybody's Bodhisattva, but it was too hard a juggling act to keep everybody happy.

One idea that occurred to Jack was that jazz was a clarion call to a spiritual awakening. It was a fellaheen language, so it spoke for the most oppressed. The rejected and condemned became agents of the divine. Kerouac saw new jazz as a clarion of a new consciousness. It wasn't only bebop, it was the whole notion of American blues and black music. It came in a slightly different way than he expected with the Beatles and the Rolling Stones and Bob Dylan adapting old black blues, Skip James and Robert Johnson. African body rhythms penetrating through the mechano-civilized world, setting up a vibration in the human body that made people dance together again.

Mission Street that last day in Frisco was a great riot of construction work, children playing, whooping Negroes coming home from work, dust, excitement, the great buzzing and vibrating hum of what is really America's most excited city—and overhead the pure blue sky and the joy of the foggy sea that always rolls in at night to make everybody hungry for food and further excitement.[157]

The first stop would have to be Sacramento, which wasn't even the faintest beginning of the trip to Denver. Dean and I sat alone in the back seat and left it up to them and talked. "Now, man, that alto man last night had IT—he held it once he found it; I've never seen a guy who could hold so long." I wanted to know what "IT" meant. "Ah well"—Dean laughed—"now you're asking me impon-de-rables—ahem! Here's a guy and everybody's there, right? Up to him to put down what's on everybody's mind. He starts the first chorus, then lines up his ideas, people, yeah, yeah, but get it, and then he rises to his fate and has to blow equal to it. All of a sudden somewhere in the middle of the chorus he gets it—everybody looks up and knows; they listen; he picks it up and carries. Time stops. He's filling empty space with the substance of our lives, confessions of his bellybottom strain, remembrance of ideas, rehashes of old blowing. He has to blow across bridges and come back and do it with such infinite feeling soul-exploratory for the tune of the moment that everybody knows it's not the tune that counts but IT—" Dean could go no further; he was sweating telling about it.[158]

That's a pretty accurate description of inspiration, which is to say breath. I would now define it by hindsight as unobstructed breath, as a physiological state of unobstructed breathing, which is known as inspiration, spiritus, breath. It was that particular breakthrough to unobstructed inspiration and expiration of breath that was the key to most of *On the Road*. Kerouac was discovering it in black music and somewhat in black speech and black society. He didn't find it as evident in white society and that's why he had at least that little glimpse or vision of black America as being the salvation of the United States, as having the soul, or as having the ultimate spirit of the United States. Strictly fellaheen in the sense that it was just taking place in little tiny jazz clubs in San Francisco or Detroit or Cleveland or New York. It wasn't official, people were doing it by themselves, out of their own sense of joy.

What he's admiring in the musicians is their individual caricature and then every once and a while some heroic kid will come with a breath of extreme sweetness and gentleness and delicacy. Kerouac's original interest was in the spiritual personality of the musicians and their American archetypal gestures. What kind of men they were, what kind of sensibility they had. Nobody had looked on jazz musicians with that kind of insight, except other jazz musicians.

> We were both exhausted and dirty. In the john of a restaurant I was at a urinal blocking Dean's way to the sink and I stepped out before I was finished and resumed at another urinal, and said to Dean, "Dig this trick."
>
> "Yes, man," he said, washing his hands at the sink, "it's a very good trick but awful on your kidneys and because you're getting a little older now every time you do this eventually years of misery in your old age, awful kidney miseries for the days when you sit in parks."
>
> It made me mad. "Who's old? I'm not much older than you are!"
>
> "I wasn't saying that, man!"
>
> "Ah," I said, "you're always making cracks about my age. I'm no old fag like that fag, you don't have to warn me about *my* kidneys." We went back to the booth and just as the waitress set down the hot-roast-beef sandwiches—and ordinarily Dean would have

leaped to wolf the food at once—I said to cap my anger, "And I don't want to hear any more of it." And suddenly Dean's eyes grew tearful and he got up and left his food steaming there and walked out of the restaurant. I wondered if he was just wandering off forever. I didn't care,—I was so mad—I had flipped momentarily and turned it down on Dean. But the sight of his uneaten food made me sadder than anything in years. I shouldn't have said that . . . he likes to eat so much . . . He's never left his food like this . . . What the hell. That's showing him, anyway.

Dean stood outside the restaurant for exactly five minutes and then came back and sat down. "Well," I said, "what were you doing out there, knotting up your fists? Cursing me, thinking up new gags about my kidneys?"

Dean mutely shook his head. "No, man, no, man, you're all completely wrong. If you want to know, well—"

"Go ahead, tell me." I said all this and never looked up from my food. I felt like a beast.

"I was crying," said Dean.[159]

That's their relationship. There's an enormous tenderness in Dean, which is unusual in American literature with heroes. It's implicit in Whitman but it isn't in most novels. I think that's why this book made a breakthrough.

"Well," they said, "we never knew we'd get to Chicago so fast." As we passed drowsy Illinois towns where the people are so conscious of Chicago gangs that pass like this in limousines every day, we were a strange sight: all of us unshaven, the driver bare-chested, two bums, myself in the back seat, holding on to a strap and my head leaned back on the cushion looking at the countryside with an imperious eye—just like a new California gang come to contest the spoils of Chicago, a band of desperados escaped from the prisons of the Utah moon.[160]

I always liked that phrase. "A band of desperados escaped from the prisons of the Utah moon." Utah moon, because Utah looks like the moon, the lunar landscape, maybe. Kerouac makes this little suggestion, when you're finished making your statement, add a little extra word, "from the prisons of the Utah moon." A little extra note in the cadenza. One association added on to another, just for the sheer pleasure of reflecting the intelligence of the mind. I remember that as one of the glorious sentences in his book.

These are Cassady's instructions to Kerouac on prose and on storytelling.

We all decided to tell our stories, but one by one, and Stan was first. "We've got a long way to go," preambled Dean, "and so you must take every indulgence and deal with every single detail you can bring to mind—and still it won't all be told. Easy, easy," he cautioned Stan, who began telling his story, "you've got to relax too." Stan swung into his life story as we shot across the dark. He started with his experiences in France but to round out ever-growing difficulties he came back and started at the beginning with his boyhood in Denver. He and Dean compared times they'd seen each other zooming around on bicycles. "One time you've forgotten, I know—Arapahoe Garage? Recall? I bounced a ball at you on the corner and you knocked it back to me with your fist and it went in the sewer. Grammar days. Now recall?" Stan was nervous and feverish. He wanted to tell Dean everything. Dean was now arbiter, old man, judge, listener, approver, nodder. "Yes,

yes, go on please." We passed Walsenburg; suddenly we passed Trinidad, where Chad King was somewhere off the road in front of a campfire with perhaps a handful of anthropologists and as of yore he too was telling his life story and never dreamed we were passing at that exact moment on the highway, headed for Mexico, telling our own stories. O sad American night![161]

That business of telling all the details of a whole life story was characteristic. Kerouac did that in his art and that was his whole thing, to be the recording angel, or the great rememberer. He wanted to tell the entire detailed story of his lifetime. We thought our own personal histories were forever forgotten, lost and unimportant. Then as we began telling each other what we thought when we were young and the progress of our soul's consciousness insights, we found that we all had the same sort of divine ambition. We all had discovered how big the universe was, discovered death, had our first sexual tickle, got scared at the movies. We began to discover that our own lives were mythological in the sense that everybody's life was mythological. We all had a tender poignant memory of our old blankets and dolls and kiddie carts and supermarkets and childhood curbstones and marble games and picket fences and storm fences behind telephone buildings. We all had these archetypal recollections and it seemed that if one talked with anybody else, they also had their own archetypal recollections, but they had no way of realizing that those archetypal recollections were the very angelic bricks of their own lives, the foundation of their lives. Their early childhood thrills and symbols were the basis of all adult judgment and opinions and trips to the moon. It was a whole hidden memory life that was never expounded or exposed or shared or traded. That was the significance of this passage and what Cassady was especially interested in. Everyone he met had his own history all the way back, rather than the history he read in the books about World War I, Bismarck, and the Greeks and Romans. It was the real tangible history of our own history, which was almost as hidden and mysterious as the history of the Egyptians, because when finally somebody began telling the complete story of his life they would discover that they had forgotten many giant pyramids and huge sphinxes that stood in the department stores of Lowell and Paterson, and strange characters that had prophetic meaning from River Street or Merrimack banks, shrouded strangers and old bag ladies that were prophetic of later understandings and insights. This little passage of telling histories, life stories, is a memento of that, but the whole book is that also.

> I was so exhausted by now I slept all the way through Dilley and Encinal to Laredo and didn't wake up till they were parking the car in front of a lunchroom at two o'clock in the morning. "Ah," sighed Dean, "the end of Texas, the end of America, we don't know no more."[162]

That theme goes all through the book, the end of America, going to the extreme coasts, restoring the country physically and coming to the end, then having to face a blank wall, like the redbrick wall on Saturday night where nothing's happening despite all the excitement of everybody wanting to get into ecstasy, coming to a blank wall at the end of America. It has been noted by many commentators that this era was the end of the exploration of America. The last gasp of the automobile cowboys before the gasoline shortage, before gasoline itself became suspect. Magic land, end of the road. Neal's advice is:

> "Now, Sal, we're leaving everything behind us and entering a new and unknown phase of things. All the years and troubles!

and kicks—and now *this*! so that we can safely think of nothing else and just go on ahead with our faces stuck out like this you see, and *understand* the world as, really and genuinely speaking, other Americans haven't done before us—they were here, weren't they? The Mexican war. Cutting across here with cannon."

"This road," I told him, "is also the route of old American outlaws who used to skip over the border and go down to old Monterrey, so if you'll look out on that graying desert and picture the ghost of an old Tombstone hellcat making lonely exile gallop into the unknown, you'll see further . . ."

"It's the world," said Dean. "My God!" he cried, slapping the wheel. "It's the world! We can go right on to South America if the road goes. Think of it! Son-of-a-*bitch*! Gawd-*damm*!"[163]

It was the first time they'd ever been out of the United States, that bespeaks the provincialism of American mind at that time. Like the assumption that what we had in New York or Denver was some self-enclosed universe and all of a sudden these guys found themselves going into a completely strange other nation and realized that the American standard was not the only standard. That was also part of the breakthrough of the Beat Generation. It was a surprise to find out that it was different everywhere in the world *except* here and that this was not the entire universe of consciousness or discourse or manners or plumbing.

Now, the fellaheen. Of course, a naive view, but not too naive for those days.

The city of Gregoria was ahead. The boys were sleeping, and I was alone in my eternity at the wheel, and the road ran straight as an arrow. Not like driving across Carolina, or Texas, or Arizona, or

Illinois; but like driving across the world and into the places where we would finally learn ourselves among the Fellahin Indians of the world, the essential strain of the basic primitive, wailing humanity that stretches in a belt around the equatorial belly of the world from Malaya (the long fingernail of China) to India the great sub-continent to Arabia to Morocco to the selfsame deserts and jungles of Mexico and over the waves to Polynesia to mystic Siam of the Yellow Robe and on around, on around, so that you hear the same mournful wail by the rotted walls of Cadiz, Spain, that you hear 12,000 miles around in the depths of Benares the Capital of the World. These people were unmistakably Indians and were not at all like the Pedros and Panchos of silly civilized American lore—they had high cheekbones, and slanted eyes, and soft ways; they were not fools, they were not clowns; they were great, grave Indians and they were the source of mankind and the fathers of it. The waves are Chinese, but the earth is an Indian thing. As essential as rocks in the desert are they in the desert of "history." And they knew this when we passed, ostensibly self-important moneybag Americans on a lark in their land; they knew who was the father and who was the son of antique life on earth, and made no comment. For when destruction comes to the world of "history" and the Apocalypse of the Fellahin returns once more as so many times before, people will still stare with the same eyes from the caves of Mexico as well as from the caves of Bali, where it all began and where Adam was suckled and taught to know. These were my growing thoughts as I drove the car into the hot, sunbaked town of Gregoria.[164]

That's pretty sublime, I thought. That's also influenced by his readings in Spengler's *Decline of the West*. He's basically taking off from Spengler's prose in this particular passage. They discover that what was bohemian in America was just ordinary lifestyle in Mexico, eating off a newspaper or eating a cow's head.

> This was the great and final wild uninhibited Fellahin-childlike city that we knew we would find at the end of the road.[165]

Culturally that's probably the point. Most critics have assumed that there is no point to the book or that there is nothing at the end of the road but blankness. But they get to the end of the American road and discover that there's a world outside of America, and a whole vast fellaheen, non–*Time* magazine, nonmechanical, non–petrochemical existence, that escapes the purview of the *New York Times* and the *Washington Post* and the universities and the calculations of academics and mathematicians and politicians and artists. And then the conclusion.

> So in America when the sun goes down and I sit on the old broken-down river pier watching the long, long skies over New Jersey and sense all that raw land that rolls in one unbelievable huge bulge over to the West Coast, and all that road going, all the people dreaming in the immensity of it, and in Iowa I know by now the children must be crying in the land where they let the children cry, and tonight the stars'll be out, and don't you know that God is Pooh Bear? the evening star must be drooping and shedding her sparkler dims on the prairie, which is just before the coming of complete night that blesses the earth, darkens all rivers, cups the peaks and folds the final shore in, and nobody, nobody knows what's going to happen to anybody besides the forlorn rags of growing old, I think of Dean Moriarty, I even think of Old Dean Moriarty the father we never found, I think of Dean Moriarty.[166]

CHAPTER 30

Kerouac and
The Subterraneans

So Jack had written *The Town and the City* by 1950 and then he'd written the first part of *Visions of Cody*, "In the pool halls of Denver long ago in the red sun . . ." Then he wrote *On the Road* before returning to *Visions of Cody*, all the sketches. His next work was *The Subterraneans*. In 1953 Burroughs arrived in New York after having been absent since the late forties. [He'd lived in] Texas, New Orleans, Mexico, and South America by then. He stayed with me for a couple of months on East 7th Street where we put together all of his letters of the previous three or four years for *The Yage Letters*. A lot of his early work was in the form of letters, written mostly to me. They were just straightforward letters, which he wrote half to be informative and half just to be a writer.

Burroughs fell in love with me around that time. Probably because of all the people that he'd known since 1945 I was the one that was most in contact with him. I was still insistent on him writing, so he came up to put together *The Yage Letters*. Kerouac was in Long Island so he came in visiting. Corso was in New York so he was in and out of the apartment. There was a young lady around, who had been my girlfriend for a while. She had been hanging around the San Remo tavern and living in a place called Paradise Alley at 11th Street and Avenue A. Mardou Fox of *The Subterraneans* was a very good typist, so Bill and I hired her to type up *The Yage Letters*. Jack began having an affair with her. So that's the background of *The Subterraneans*.

Kerouac's method for writing was to take some amphetamine, Benzedrine generally, and just sit down and stay there at the typewriter, exhausting his mind completely, everything in his mind, everything he could think of relating to the subject. Not at random, it would have to be a subject that he was obsessed with, that he'd thought about and maybe at some point had realized, "Ahh I could write a whole novel about this." He sat down and did it like an athlete, like an athletic event.

That period of *Maggie Cassidy* and *The Subterraneans* and *Doctor Sax* is, in a sense, Jack's most energetic, dense prose period. He's gone through the obsessional romantic material of Neal Cassady in a total experimental explosive form in *Visions of Cody*. He's already written thousands of pages of mad prose. "Adios, King" is the last line of his farewell to his youthful hero. He's already disillusioned, he's already looking out to the grave.

Then he goes back to the madness of the present moment in *The Subterraneans*. At this point he's mature with his ax and he also looks back at his high school girl friend [in] *Maggie Cassidy*. That's a book about actual life in high school, a humble subject, but some of his prettiest prose. He's still young, he's thirty-one years old. He's in his prime, not affected unnaturally by the disillusionment of chemical alcohol. Though that's not well known as his prime material, it really is, I think. He's in his prime as a novelist and he's just writing for his own soul at this point.

He realizes he's had some success with his heroic young novel *The Town and the City,* had nice reviews, and then a total flop failure with *On the Road,* which nobody would publish. Even worse, even I hated *Visions of Cody.* Jack's in there writing all by himself, for himself, for his own ear or for some universal consciousness, just for pure art. *Springtime Mary / Maggie Cassidy* is a rare thing, one of the few large pieces of prose since Herman Melville written in isolation and solitude by somebody accomplished. Kerouac was writing in eternity, for eternity. He wasn't writing for publication, not even for friends, because we were an unreliable ear too.

CHAPTER 31

Jack Kerouac and Fame

Then in 1956, [Kerouac] began to write an account of the scene and called it *Desolation Angels*. It was going to be a big novel but he only finished part one of it. He returned to it five years later, after his books were published, after *On the Road* was published, after he was famous, after there was a Beat Generation. In the middle of that, just at the crest of the Beat Generation, he wrote a novel describing from the inside the mass hallucination of publicity and how all that affected him and his family and his friends. That was *Desolation Angels,* his fourteenth book.

In addition to all that, *Mexico City Blues* is worth reading. Michael McClure and I and Gary Snyder think it's one of the great seminal books of poetry of midcentury because it's the loosest and most open free form of all poetry written at a time when people were experimenting with open form. Kerouac had such a good ear and he'd written so much already that in writing these little ditties there was always some electrical connection in the rhythm. He was such an experienced writer that tossing them off was high fun. His model on that was none other than Herman Melville because it was after the disappointment of Melville's career as a writer that he turned to writing little poems for his own soul.

Kerouac, like Melville, was also a total failure, he couldn't get anything published. By 1955 Jack had written all the books that are now classics, but no publisher understood them. Then he started [writing] little poems, because we were all poets actually. We were babbling about poetry all the time and Kerouac said, "I'm an epic poem writer. What's the difference between what I write and what you write? You keep calling it poetry as if it was something special. I write poems a thousand feet long, page after page of poems. I'll show you poetry." So he wrote this little book of poems, just to show his poetry skills.

Finally *On the Road* was published, but instead of following up by publishing everything chronologically, like they should have, Malcolm Cowley said, "Well we have all this furor about the Beat Generation, Jack, and we should do something about that. The public is confused, they don't know what this is all about, your writing is very confusing in a sense, we can't publish *Visions of Cody* because it's too dirty and nobody understands it anyway. Why don't you write a book in nice simple sentences?" After he'd gone through all of this and he'd finally written *Old Angel Midnight* with all this heavenly gibberish, they're asking him to write a book with simple sentences. For him it's child's play. So he said, "Well, I think I will," and he did. He wrote this exquisite little novel, *Dharma Bums,* presenting the notion of beatniks and knapsack revolutionaries and long-haired kids and marijuana and parties and mountain climbing and tin cook pots for mountains, and muesli, and granola. Everything that everybody wants to know about it. Beautiful, crystal clear prose, but sweeter than Hemingway as far as directness of description. And it also has little cadenzas of nonsensical composition.

After *Dharma Bums* he wrote a play, which was called *The Beat Generation in Three Acts.* Robert Frank and some other people made the first act into a scenario for the movie *Pull My Daisy.* Jack narrated that spontaneously and it was later published as a book. Yet another brilliant little composition.

Then he drove back to New York from San Francisco with Lew Welch and Albert Saijo, another Jap poet, and wound up at my apartment in New York. They kept a little notebook called *Trip Trap,* full of haikus and nonsensical musings on the road. It was actually chaotic at the time, but is kind of a charming journal now, very brief.

Then Kerouac put together the *Lonesome Traveler* book, which is early and late writings. Very early writings from the fifties, the brakeman on the railroad, and then little essays. Then he put together all his poems for City Lights and called it *Pomes All Sizes.* The second part of *Desolation Angels,* an accounting of the years of fame, is kind of interesting. It is a fascinating subject, because everything else was written in solitude. Here he's writing about the big world and radio and TV and Madison Avenue and how his friends all interacted with that and going to Tangier and going to Paris.

The next work written in October 1961 is a monumental work. Crash of fame and alcoholism, *Big Sur.* It is one of the most amazing pieces of writing that I've ever heard of, because he was totally sick with the DTs, but still he had the presence of mind and the physical stamina to face all that depression and compose a giant work, a huge book. It is very closely written and brilliantly written, full of invention and full of poetry, full of shudders and nightmares too. Prior authors who were considered great celebrities, like F. Scott Fitzgerald or Hemingway, were never able to get aside from themselves sufficiently to compose their own requiems, so to speak. Fitzgerald started a book called *The Crack-Up,* and I don't think he was ever able to finish it, about the same subject. Hemingway never was able to completely write about himself cracking up, but Kerouac did it several times. The complete story of his own physical and emotional degeneration, *Big Sur,* after the disillusioned second half of *Desolation Angels*. That's twenty-three books in a period of eleven years, an incredible amount really, as well as endless journals, poems, and notebooks.

Then a big hiatus, 1961 to 1965, during which time he was typing up all his prior work, actually working editing journals, poems, novels, and preparing one by one all these for publication. And all that brings us back to *Vanity of Duluoz*.

CHAPTER 32

Kerouac, Sketching, and Method

I want to pick up again on Kerouac's idea of sketching and look at it one more time with his 1952 letter to me describing his method. It's a crucial moment for him when he's discovered something and is simultaneously commenting on it to his friends. It's like a frame, a great moment to tune in. I think this was his big breakthrough period, during the time of *Visions of Cody,* particularly when he arrived at sketching.

> . . . Sketching (Ed White casually mentioned it in 124th [Street] Chinese restaurant near Columbia, "Why don't you just sketch in the streets like a painter but with words?") which I did . . . everything activates in front of you in myriad profusion, you just have to purify your mind and let it pour the words (which effortless angels of the vision fly when you stand in front of reality) and write with 100% personal honesty both psychic and social etc. and slap it all down shameless, willy-nilly, rapidly until sometimes I got so inspired I lost consciousness I was writing. Traditional source: Yeats' trance writing, of course. It's the *only way to write.* I haven't sketched in a long time now and have to start again because you

get better with practice. Sometimes it is embarrassing to write in the street or anywhere outside but it's absolute . . . it never fails, it's the thing itself natch.

Do you understand sketching?—same as poetry you write— also never overdo it, you should normally get pooped in fifteen minutes' straight scribbling—by that time I have a chapter and I feel a little crazy for having written it . . . I read it and it seems like the confessions of an insane person . . . then next day it reads like great prose, oh well. And just like you say the best things we write are always the most suspected . . . I think the greatest line in *On the Road* (tho you'll disagree) is (apart of course from description of the Mississippi River "Lester is just like the river, the river starts in near Butte Montana in frozen snow caps (Three Forks) and meanders on down across states and entire territorial areas of dun bleak land with hawthorn crackling in the sleet, picks up rivers at Bismarck, Omaha and St. Louis just north, another at Kay-ro, another in Arkansas, Tennessee, comes deluging on New Orleans with muddy news from the land and a roar of subterranean excitement that is like the vibration of the entire land sucked on its gut in mad midnight, fevered, hot, the big mudhole rank clawpole old frogular pawed-soul titanic Mississippi from the North full of wires, cold wood and horn.")

How do you think I arrived at last four five words if not in trance?

But here's that (best) line "The charging restless mute unvoiced road keening in a seizure of tarpaulin power . . ." This is obviously something I *had* to say in spite of myself . . . tarpaulin, too, don't be frightened, is obviously the key . . . man that's a road. It will take fifty years for people to realize that that's a road. In fact I distinctly remember hovering over the word "tarpaulin" (even thought of writing tarpolon or anything) but something told me that "tarpaulin" was what I'd thought, "Tarpaulin" was what it is . . . Do you understand Blake? Dickinson? and Shakespeare when he wants to mouth the general sound of doom, "peaked, like John a Dreams" . . . simply does what he hears . . . "greasy Joan doth keel the pot; (and birds sit brooding in the snow . . .").[167]

So that's the specific explanation there. Ed White the architect suggesting sketching. In *Jack's Book,* White said, "'I think I was actually using a sketch pad then and just suggesting he could do the same thing with notes. I think he thought about it. I don't think he said much about it, but then he began carrying his little notebooks around, filling them up. He printed faster than most of us can write. He would show up with his notebook sometimes in the evening, after he'd been downtown all day—at the library, in my apartment, or wherever we happened to be at the time; and he'd read parts aloud he'd been writing. We'd usually end up drinking beer and going out and listening to music." These little notebooks provided raw materials of two kinds: diaristic details, like a reporter's notes, about events at hand and an endless retracing in memory of all the events of his life, reaching back to his earliest childhood memories in Lowell."[168] He applied that exhaustive sketching to total mind's eye, interior dream recollection.

It's amazing, I used to know very clearly what came first in the sequence of Kerouac's books, but at the time I never toted it up in terms of thinking of teaching it or trying to expound it. I just knew it was of some historic importance, you know one thing came after another, what were the different stages. It is interesting to pick up on these different stages, because if you do, then you understand it much better. The method of composition, how you can get there to do what he was doing, because most of my writing in the fifties, including "Howl," "Sunflower Sutra," "Transcription of Organ Music," and all that, are primarily just imitations at his direction of this form of sketching, and the prose poems that he has are as good as anybody's poems. They aren't broken up into little lines, but they could be if you wanted to and made to look like William Carlos Williams or something. Basically they are prose poems.

Jack's prose considerations were Melville at the time and there's a little hint of that.

> Roaming those subways I see a Negro cat wearing an ordinary gray felt hat but a deep blue, or purplish shirt with white shiny pearl-type buttons—a gray sharkskin suit jacket over it—but brown pants, black shoes, deep blue ordinary one-strip socks and gabardine topper short and beat, with edgebottoms rain-raveled—carrying brown paper bag—his face (he's sleeping) is big powerful fighter's sullen thicklipped *(thick Afric lip)* but strangely pudgy sweet face—dark brownskin—his big hands hang, his fingernails are pink (not white) and are soiled from a laboring job—Looks like Joe Louis only a Joe Louis who has known nothing but the freezing cold Harlem winter mornings when old blackbums infinitely beater than old Cody Pomeray of wino Denver go by with wool caps pulled over their ears with no prospects for the future whatever except below zero filthy snows—[169]

"Thick Afric lip" is from Melville's poem "A Night Piece," a description of the cannons that were bombarding Vicksburg in the Civil War. And the kind of prose he's writing here derives from Melville's *Moby-Dick* and *Pierre* for the subtleness and the playfulness of the thought. The author having enough leisure to talk to himself and to talk to you the reader, instead of just telling the story, also stops and gossips with you on the way. As you can see here, Kerouac is endlessly gossiping with himself and his reader about the phrasing he's using, or about the vision he's having, or about the face he's seeing. Little thoughts that go off into a shudder at the end because they're so horrible, like this "wool caps pulled over their ears with no prospects for the future whatever except below zero filthy snows." While reading [aloud], he had a very funny habit of reading to the end of an exhalation or breath, and ending with a shudder of laughter, at the extremity of the thought and outrageous exquisiteness of the language he arrived at, like "tarpaulin power." The next thing was sketches of people and faces.

The poor lonely old ladies of Lowell who come out the five-and-ten with their umbrellas open for the rain but look so scared and in genuine distress not the distress of secretly smiling maids in the rain who have good legs to hop around, the old ladies have piano legs and have to waddle to their where-to—and talking about their daughters anyway in the middle of their distress.

People going by. The big cowlick Irishman with camel's hair belted coat who lumbers along, his lips loosened in some sullen thought and as though it wasn't raining in his huge dry soul—

The fat old lady incredible-burdened not only with umbrellas and rain cape but underneath bulging pregnantly with hidden protected packages that stick so far out she has trouble avoiding bumping people on sidewalk and when she gets in the bus it will create a major problem for the poor people who are now, in their own parts of the city headed for the bus, unsuspecting of this—

The sharp little rich Jewish lady in a fur coat who lofts an umbrella that catches the eye it's so expensive and designed (red

on brown) so beautifully, cutting along with that surefooted bandy
legged gazotsky waddle that distinguishes her from other ladies,
the great high civilization peasant woman of swank apartments
with a hairy husband Aaron who deals in high finance with the
gravity and hirsute slowness of an ape, she's headed home with
a package and the rain like other things does not distress her—

The Irish gentleman all bundled tightly in a dark greenslick
raincoat, collar up, tight at his raveled chin, hat, no umbrella,
a little anxious as he proceeds somewhat slowly to his objective
and lost in thought of his job or wife or by God anything including feelings of homosexual deterioration or that Communists are
secretly controlling his life at this very moment by thought-waves
from a machine projecting from a submarine five miles offshore,
maybe a teletype operator at U.P., thinking this as he goes down
Sixth Avenue the name of which was changed to Avenue of the
Americas some years ago to his complete disgust, going along surrounded by this entire night of dark rain in this moment of time
that he occupies with a white scared sidelook at something on the
bottom of the sidewalk (which isn't me) —[170]

There are a lot of other sketches of people here. There's an interesting moment where he connects everything. This is a kind of new
consciousness for him, it's the birth of his masculine and grown-
up matured consciousness, kicked out of the womb into the world
and seeing the world as a vast breathing animate place, fresh to be
described, because nobody ever described the phenomenal world
around his sensorium in exactly the same way. It was as if Kerouac
had entered into a state of consciousness where he was one big eye-
ball or ear. That's maybe a little too exaggerated. What I mean is he's
entered into a state where for the first time he's looking on the planet

as novelists had not before looked. You get it in some of Rimbaud's prose poetry and I suppose it's in Shakespeare but there's a certain uncanny vibration in Kerouac's sketching descriptions, which may be either amphetamine or some twentieth-century vibe from having been kicked out of old familiar earth and entering into a social planet that includes the atom bomb and ants and orchestras, Buchenwalds, pieces of the Buddha material, frozen and sliced microscopically. The sense of all of mankind as a giant empty anthill scurrying in a mechanic future that has been cut off from the cozy old hometown wooden parlor living room radio steaming pudding kitchen with momma, of the past. There's no longer any home, it's a strange open universe where there's a possibility of being lost in infinitely large scale where thousands of people could go over a cliff and nobody would notice. Yet it's balanced because he's got this desire for icy joy, and shiverings of joy.

Now, an interesting thing, one of the most amazing, I thought, in terms of psychological acuity or penetration or empathy, was the description of a girl sitting in a cafeteria eating in solitude. Kerouac entering into her solitude and trying to feel what she was feeling inside, trying to psych out or guess what the meaning of some of her gestures and attitudes and body language was.

> Now exactly in his place without knowing who was there before, the poor lost history of it, sits a pretty brunette with violet eyes and a flowing purple drapecoat—takes it off like stripteaster, hangs it on hook (back to it) and starts eating with pathetic delicate hunger her hot plate—deep in thought while she chews—wearing cute little white collar draped over black material and three pendants, pearls; lovely mouth; she just blew her nose daintily with

a napkin; has private personal sad manners, at least externally by which she makes her own formal existence known to herself as well as polite social cafeteria watchers she's imagining, otherwise why the act though it is genuine. She took a bite off the fork and THEN and how she'd *blow!* she licked the side of it in a slight furtive movement of pleasure, her eyes darting up to see if anybody noticed this—as her hunger is appeased she grows less interested in outward manners, eats more rapidly, has sadder more personal bemusements with herself over the general rim and consciousness of her cunt which is in her lap as she sits—

[. . .] With her head down inexpressible purity shows in her face, like a young Princess Margaret Rose, and beauty, slant-eyed young girl beauty with freshness of the cheeks and upward-sending rosy-glow lips—she's reading a library book! and sighing!—a freshness that comes from her lips being chastely compressed and is aura'd from the tendernesses of her neck just beneath the ear from the fragile white breakable susceptible cool brow which will never know wild sweats, just cool beads of joy—as she reads she fondles the creases that run from her nose to her mouth each side with doubly applied fingertips and is really digging her own face and beauty as much as I—turns the bookpages with small finger, so long, ridiculously far out—the book is a Modern Library!—therefore she's probably no dumb little book-of-the-monther typist but maybe a hip young intellectual girl from Brooklyn waiting for Terry Gibbs to pick her up and take her to Birdland. She'd melt for me in two minutes, I can tell by looking at her. Big horrible middleaged Jewish couple sitting now with her—like invading Ammonites. Now she goes—beautifully, with simplicity. It no longer makes me cry and die and tear myself to see her go because everything goes away from me like that now—girls, visions, anything, just in the same way and forever and I accept lostness forever.

Everything belongs to me because I am poor.[171]

That's a great sentence to end it with, "Everything belongs to me because I am poor." I guess that was one of the scenes at the time, one of the key classic sentences in this book, like in *On the Road*, "The earth is an Indian thing" was one of the classic lines.

CHAPTER 33

Corso and
The Vestal Lady on Brattle

About 1950 or 1951 I ran into Gregory Corso at the Pony Stable bar, which was a dyke bar in Greenwich Village. He had just come out of jail for irrelevant juvenile delinquency problems. He was a loner wandering by himself in the Village. He was a young kid with very dark hair, it looked like a little cap of hair, bright eyes, very handsome, intelligent, lively face, a little streak of dark Italian Mafia in it, cherubic looking. Gregory was born on the corner of Bleecker and Macdougal directly across from the San Remo bar, which was the bohemian meeting place. Dylan Thomas had passed by there, and Maxwell Bodenheim had passed by there, and probably Upton Sinclair had passed by there too. [Gregory] knew the whole Italian Village as an insider and was familiar in the neighborhood, but I had no idea who he was. I was out on my own wandering around with no particular aim, probably trying to get laid or meet somebody, looking for Gregory Corso for all I know.

When we met, I don't know how we got into conversation, but he brought out a sheaf of poems. I had already been involved with Kerouac and Burroughs as artists, so there was some sense in my head that I had a dowsing wand for poetic beauty. When I saw Corso's poetry, I was immediately struck by the fact that it was immortal in some funny way. The poems I saw don't exist [anymore] and the only one that I remember is a poem that began, "The stone world came to me and said 'Flesh gives you one hour's leave.'" I interpreted the stone world as a world of eternity, the world I'd seen in my own Blake visions or the world of supreme reality, but I was reading into it some kind of mystical signal, which probably wasn't there. The language was so strong and so original and also so sublime that I didn't realize what it meant.

He was saying that the world of ancient beauty had come to him and given him a year, or an hour, or a lifetime to accomplish the same beauty. I thought he meant eternity and he meant classical Greece and classical Rome, the statues of Aphrodite or Apollo or the Parthenon frieze. He was looking back to his own classical background. In prison he'd read a lot about Greek and Roman literature and then he went back even further and read a lot of things like *Gilgamesh,* and the first epics and the pre-Greek histories, Babylonian and Sumerian, going back to Ur. That always has been his specialty so he thought he should go back to the first "daddies," the first histories. The poem was strong enough that I was immediately taken.

It was rare that somebody took their own poems seriously enough to carry them around and pull them out. The fact that they made sense on top of it and had some kind of mortal shudder in them was more indicative, so I immediately took him seriously. I hadn't seen anybody that wrote a classic poetry somewhat in vernacular.

One of his earliest poems, "Sea Chanty," is in *The Vestal Lady on Brattle.* It is a little book published by some rich young Harvard kids in 1955. Gregory had been hanging around there.

Sea Chanty

My mother hates the sea
My sea especially
I warned her not to
it was all I could do
Two years later
the sea ate her

I immediately interpreted that as mass unconscious, my mother hates the world of eternal mass unconscious, my exhibition of it especially, and I warned her not to go, two years later mass unconscious lapped her up. Then the next part of it is even weirder.

Upon the shore I found a strange
yet beautiful food
I asked the sea if I could eat it
and the sea said that I could
— Oh, sea, what fish is this
so tender and so sweet?
— Thy mother's feet[172]

Well, that's really weird for a young kid. To be eating his mother's feet and to be getting his mother's feet back from the sea. It starts nursery rhymish, something that might be just childishness or sublime, but it has such a strange twist of mind, daring in a way, because most people wouldn't want to imagine eating their mother's feet, much less think that it was funny or pretty. Almost inharmonious discordant beauty, which was his genius, a genius of discord, which has been raised to monumental proportions. In the actual music of the language and the imagery, it's the introduction of a stoppage or a break or a discord or a contradictory hit, line by line, as finding a strange and beautiful food and then finally defining it as his mother's feet. It's obviously fantasy and yet at the end the fantasy turns around and the image is something that's horribly realistic. It would take a poet to find his mother's feet as strange and beautiful food.

Corso's aesthetic was contradiction, discord of idea, and also music, sound of the line. Which means that he would have to be writing realistic to begin with, and taking the ideas from his own mind or his own experience rather than from an ideal of beauty, such as I had or Kerouac had. Some beautiful ideal of Melvillean Wolfe full-tongued vowelic harmony. Gregory wanted sudden disharmony as his beauty.

Song

Oh, dear! Oh, me! Oh, my!
I married the pig's daughter!
I married the pig's daughter!

Why? Why? Why?

I met her in the evening
in the moon in the sky!
She kissed me in the evening
and wed me in her sty!
Oh, dear! Oh, me! Oh, my!
I married the pig's daughter!
I married the pig's daughter!

Why? Why? Why?

Because I felt I had oughta!
Because I was the one that taught her
how to love and how to die!
And tomorrow there'll be no sorrow
no, there'll be no sorrow
when I take her to the slaughter!
When I take her to the slaughter!

Why? Why? Why?[173]

A very strange song done in the form of a nursery rhyme and yet the most horrible nursery rhyme conceivable. I don't see how anybody could have thought of that. Except he did. I think those are a young man's poems, but a really brilliant kid to be saying instead of "I married the angel's daughter," "I married the pig's daughter." Very few people would think of that. Who'd put themselves down so, put themselves in that clownish role? "I married the pig's daughter, and I'm going to lead her to the slaughter." Again the disharmony, which he's working with rather than being brought down by. The unexpected surprising upside-down twist change or discord are his aesthetics. There's very little obvious self-pity there. It's more like a horrible comedy.

You Came Last Season

You came and made penny candy with your thumbs
I stole you and ate you
And my feet crushed your wrappers
      in a thousand streets
You hurt my teeth
You put pimples on my face

You were never anything for health
You were never too vitamin
You dirtied hands
And since you were stickier than glue
You never washed away
You stained something awful.[174]

His method already begins to come in. "You were never anything too vitamin." A kind of weird phrasing. It's condensed, the line is tailored down, cut down. The generalization that there were no vitamins in candy is reduced almost to the archetype, single use of the word, "you were never anything too vitamin." He's made a noun out of the adjective. What he's done is taken the adjective, cut off the end, and left it as a noun, "you were never vitamin." And if you notice in a lot of his poetry, he's condensing like that, syntactically condensing. This is one of the earliest shots where he does that.

It's interesting to note his particular genius of condensation and abstraction of an idea, isolating the idea to a single word, making a noun out of an adjective or a verb out of a noun and cutting out all the articles and prefixes and suffixes. "You were never too vitaminy" becomes "you were never too vitamin." You find that tailoring and condensation of the language developing more and more into his later poetry until he becomes a real master of that and the shrewdest, sharpest master of those scissors that I know in modern poetics. Gregory called it tailoring, he cuts and snips and shapes it, sewing up, putting cuffs on his poems, putting a vest on it, making it fit the size.

I had a girlfriend who lived next door to the New School for Social Research on 12th Street and Corso had a furnished room across the street facing her apartment. He watched her undress every night for months before we met. The night we met Corso started describing the girl and the situation and the street and the place and I realized this was my [girlfriend]. I was trying to make Gregory, and so I said, "You want me to introduce you? I have magical powers." So we went up and visited her. She immediately took a shine to Gregory and so they had a little affair.

Gregory was somewhat of a madcap then. He didn't drink much, had no particular bad habits, just a little provocative line here and there. I remember he came wanting money one day with a suitcase full of crème de menthe, Pernod, and other undrinkable liquors, which had fallen into his hands somehow from some car theft. Burroughs and I were putting him down as a troublemaking kid quite a bit, mocking him. He was writing [in an] early juvenilesque style, like "my mother hates the sea," in this weird Emily Dickinson way. Then around 1953 Burroughs left for Tangier, I left for Mexico and San Francisco. Gregory with a girlfriend, Hope Savage, went up to Cambridge, where he settled down for a year.

Hope Savage was a tremendous influence on Corso. She was the daughter of the mayor of some mid-southern town where she had been a rebel in her early teens and had been sent to a private bughouse and given shock treatments. She came away a total idealist. Gregory recalling that she wrote "revolution is the solution" way back in 1954 or 1955, on the walls in New York and Cambridge. This was the first time anybody in my group of peers had come on with the word "revolution" as something that you put on city walls. She was Gregory's ideal mind, the first revolutionary he ever heard of. She and Gregory went up to Cambridge and sat together reading all through Spenser's *Faerie Queene* aloud, Milton's *Paradise Lost,* much of Blake, and a lot of Shakespeare. Gregory spent two years in Cambridge hanging around with the high-class ashfoot legions of young diplomatic adolescents that go to Harvard. At that time, Cambridge was also a center of poetic ferment, because Frank O'Hara, John Ashbery, Kenneth Koch, Bunny Lang, and many other poets were there. Gregory was one of the poetic heroes of that scene. Hope had some money and so they lived very elegantly in a large high-ceilinged room with velvet furniture, couches, chairs, big curtains, giant windows overlooking the street, fireplace, big poppa armchairs, smoking jackets, velvet clothes.

From that period Gregory's earliest work, *The Vestal Lady on Brattle,* poems written Cambridge Mass, 1954–55, was published by some of the rich young Harvard boys. I want to run through some of those, giving little pictures of him. First of all recollections of Greenwich Village.

Greenwich Village Suicide

Arms outstretched
hands flat against the windowsides
She looks down
Thinks of Bartok, Van Gogh
and New Yorker cartoons
She falls

They take her away with a Daily News on her face
And a storekeeper throws hot water on the sidewalk[175]

Well, that's a bit curious for a young kid to write in the sense that it's realistic, not influenced by William Carlos Williams, but just some kind of naked harsh observation. Still there's a romantic sympathy, she thinks of Bartók, van Gogh, and *New Yorker* cartoons. It's almost a *New Yorker* cartoon itself, the stereotyping of the suicidal girl, but it's also a shrewd appreciation of a little girl, full of funny noble ideals that ends with the *Daily News* on her face and hot water on the sidewalk. And a poem I thought at the time was his best poem, an early classic, which proved his human genius called:

In the Morgue

I remember seeing their pictures in the papers;
Naked, they seemed stronger,
The bullet in my stomach proved that I was dead.
I watched the embalmer unscrew the glass top.
He examined me and smiled at my minute-dead-life
Then he went back to the two bodies across from me
And continued to unscrew.

When you're dead you can't talk
Yet you feel like you could.
It was funny watching those two gangsters across from me
    trying to talk.
They widened their thin lips and showed grey-blue teeth;

The embalmer, still smiling, came back to me.
He picked me up and like a mother would a child,
Rested me upright in a rocking chair.
He gave a push and I rocked.
Being dead didn't mean much.
I still felt pain where the bullet went through.

God! seeing the two gangsters from this angle was really
    strange!
They certainly didn't look like they looked in the papers.
Here they were young and clean shaven and well-shaped.[176]

That was Gregory's private insight into the world of gangsters, the difference between *Daily News* and reality, strange musings on death, curious imagination about what it would be like to be dead, amazing appreciation of the pale bodies of gangsters naked on a morgue table, a little bit sexy even. I saw through that and said [it was] really universal mind. It has a funny kind of compassion, a funny kind of detachment. Pretty straightforward about it, actually. For a young kid it's amazingly smart. That was the end of it. "I remember seeing their pictures in the papers." You know, the diction, the cadence is absolutely Greenwich Village born. The pronunciation, as Gregory would pronounce it, indistinguishable from ordinary speech, and yet completely clear ideas, and a little discordant too, although the discord gives birth to a little vibration of beauty. Here they were young and clean shaven and well shaped. I appreciated his Whitmanic appreciation of their well-shaped bodies. There is a masturbatory, strange, and juvenile element in his early work.

Then there's a picture of himself, "In the Tunnel Bone of Cambridge," a little fragment. He's displaying his rough trade, gangster, or jailboy background to the Cambridge aesthetes.

In the Tunnel Bone of Cambridge

1

In spite of voices —
Cambridge and all its regions
Its horned churches with fawns' feet
Its white-haired young
            and ashfoot legions —
I decided to spend the night

But that hipster-tone of my vision agent
Decided to reconcile his sound with the sea
      leaving me flat
North of the Charles
          So now I'm stuck here —
          a subterranean
          lashed to a pinnacle

    2

I don't know the better things that people know
All I know is the deserter condemned me to black —
He said: Gregory, here's two boxes of night
      one tube of moon
And twenty capsules of starlight, go an' have a ball —
He left and the creep took
      all my Gerry Mulligan records with him

And it ends:

Far into the tunnel-bone I put my ear to the ear
      of the minister—and I could hear
      the steel say to the steam
      and the steam to the roar: a black ahead
A black ahead a black and nothing more.[177]

That was his prophecy for himself. He had a lot of funny imaginings, like little archetypal cartoony, fantasy, daydream short movies that made use of images that were culturally common in anybody's head. He dealt with them in a very lively, complete, intelligent way, making use of them for poems. There's one here,

"In the Early Morning," in the City Lights *Gasoline and The Vestal Lady on Brattle.*

In the Early Morning

In the early morning
          beside the runaway hand-in-pocket
          whistling youth
I see the hopping drooling Desirer
His black legs . . . the corncob pipe and cane
The long greasy coat, and the bloodstained
    fingernails
He is waiting
          flat against the trees[178]

It's some kind of old bogeyman, out of Fritz Lang maybe, out of the movie *M* or *Metropolis*, or some early Carl Dreyer, Danish cinema dealing with vampires, Dreyer's *Vampyr* perhaps, if you know that film from the 1932, "corncob pipe and cane, who owned greasy coat with bloodstained fingernails." It's just a little sketch, but pretty.

Another major poem that he wrote at that time was a "Requiem for Charlie Parker," a curious, early appreciation for Parker. A lot of poems to Charlie Parker or to Jimmy Dean or even to Kerouac these days have a kind of overblown, romantic rhetoric. They exaggerate everything and make it gushy or creepy or overaggressively angry. Here's something that's very straight and flat, like a masque play for several voices. I'm also pointing out that it's a really young poem, hence the twisty, upside-down toylike imagery that a kid plays with.

Requiem for "Bird" Parker, Musician

this prophecy came by mail:
in the last murder of birds
a nowhere bird shall remain
and it shall not wail
and the nowhere bird shall be a slow bird
a long long bird

somewhere there is a room
in a room
in which an old horn
            lies in a corner
like a handful of rice
wondering about BIRD

"An old horn lies in the corner like a handful of rice." I couldn't
imagine anybody else thinking something like that.

   first voice

hey, man, BIRD is dead
they got his horn locked up somewhere
put his horn in a corner somewhere
like where's the horn, man, where?

   second voice

screw the horn
like where's BIRD?

   third voice

gone
BIRD was goner than sound

broke the barrier with a horn's coo
BIRD was higher than moon
BIRD hovered on a roof top, too
like a weirdy monk he dropped
horn in hand, high above all
lookin' down on them people
with half-shut weirdy eyes
saying to himself: "yeah, yeah"
like nothin' meant nothin' at all

   fourth voice

in early nightdrunk
solo in his pent house stand
BIRD held a black flower in his black hand
he blew his horn to the sky
made the sky fantastic! and midway
the man-tired use of things
BIRD piped a varied ephemera
a strained rhythmical rat

That's Gregory's own, his disharmonics, "a strained rhythmical rat."

like the stars didn't know what to do
then came a nowhere bird

   third voice

yeah, a nowhere bird —
while BIRD was blowin'
another bird came

an unreal bird
a nowhere bird with big draggy wings
BIRD paid it no mind; just kept on blowin'
and the cornball bird came on comin'

first voice

right, like that's what I heard
the draggy bird landed in front of BIRD
looked BIRD straight in the eye
BIRD said: "cool it"
and kept on blowin'

second voice

seems like BIRD put the square bird down

first voice

only for a while, man
the nowhere bird began to foam from the mouth
making all kinds of discords
"man, like make it elsewhere," BIRD implored
but the nowhere bird paced back and forth
like an old cornball with a nowhere scheme

I like that, "an old cornball with a nowhere scheme." You can see that this is all written in some kind of early fifties hip talk, maybe one of the first poems written making use of that newborn language. This is the first introduction of Beat or hippie vernacular into poetry that I know of. [Along with] Kerouac's roughly contemporaneous *Mexico City Blues,* this may be some of the earliest use of that language, which later became very widespread in poetry and imitated badly.

third voice

yeah, by that time BIRD realized the fake
had come to goof
BIRD was about to split, when all of a sudden
the nowhere bird sunk its beady head
into the barrel of BIRD's horn
bugged, BIRD blew a long crazy note

first voice

it was his last, man, his last
the draggy bird ran death into BIRD's throat
and the whole building rumbled
when BIRD let go his horn
and the sky got blacker . . . blacker
and the nowhere bird wrapped its muddy wings round BIRD
brought BIRD down
all the way down

fourth voice

BIRD is dead
BIRD is dead

first and second and third voices

yeah, yeah

fourth voice

wail for BIRD
for BIRD is dead

first and second and third voices

yeah, yeah[179]

That's where it ends, a pretty strange masque for four voices. Really pretty because it's not overstated at all. The imagination is very pretty, big bird sinking its beady head into bird's horn. Bird opposed by the bird of death. Using that kind of fugitive language for playfulness with funny modern concepts, it's nicely done. Imaginative with real poetic images in it and at the same time flat culturally, not overambitious, poetically just right. It's down home in a way, "yeah, yeah" being the chorus for many voices. Just the idea of people saying "yeah, yeah" as choruses in itself is odd and original and imaginative for a young kid.

He developed that language through the fifties. In 1955, Corso went out to San Francisco and met everybody. He brought some new poems and wrote a lot of poems while developing a style more and more extravagantly. At the beginning of his book *Gasoline*, there's a fantastic long line style, "Ode to Coit Tower," which ends on the most fantastical Shakespearean line in hippie poetry.

> I saw your blackjacketed saints your Zen potsmokers
> 　　　　Athenians and cocksmen
> Though the West Wind seemed to harbor there not one
> 　　　　pure Shelleyean dream of let's say hay-
> 　　　　　　　like universe
> 　　　　　　　　　golden heap on a wall of fire
> 　　sprinting toward the gauzy eradication of
> 　　　　　Swindleresque Ink[180]

I read that and it blew my mind. I thought, that doesn't make any sense at all, except actually it makes a great deal of sense, if you figure it out. What he's saying is "I came to San Francisco, but I'm a Shelleyan and I don't believe all this Zen, pot smoking bullshit, because

I didn't see any pure Shelleyan dream in it." So what's swindleresque ink? Disappearing ink. The universe disappearing into itself, a golden universe, the concept of conceptualization erasing itself. Kerouac's golden ash anyway. "Swindleresque ink" is a perfect characterization of Gregory's own poetry, where he presents an idea which disappears on itself when you look at it carefully.

Or disharmony contradiction, where one image will contradict another image. It doesn't seem to make sense, but it does make sense, because he's playing with words and suggesting something curious. Corso was thinking of some great Shelleyan outburst of pure swindleresque ink language, that is poetics, pure poesie. I thought that was a big touch of genius.

Gregory's interest was in disharmony. Discord was his method. That is, taking things, turning them inside out, making words contradict each other, or making the image or metaphor clash in a logical way. There is a poem called "This Was My Meal," or this was my matter, or this was my poetics, or this was my method, this is my way, this is my actuality, this is my beauty.

This Was My Meal

In the peas I saw upside down letters of MONK

Thelonious Monk. Now, how does he do that? Well, he'd look at the peas and say "I saw upside down," looking at peas he sees something upside down, which is ridiculous to begin with. What? Letters. Of what? Monk?

And beside it, in the Eyestares of Wine
I saw Olive & Blackhair
I decided sunset to dine

I cut through the cowbrain and saw Christmas
& my birthday run hand in hand in the snow
I cut deeper
    and Christmas bled to the edge of the plate

I turned to my father
    and he ate my birthday
I drank my milk and saw trees outrun themselves
    valleys outdo themselves
      and no mountain stood a chance of not walking

Dessert came in the spindly hands of stepmother
I wanted to drop fire-engines from my mouth!
But in ran the moonlight and grabbed the prunes.[181]

It's total contradiction but okay. "I wanted to drop fire-engines from my mouth!" In other words, he wanted to make the big sound, wanted to make big metaphor, big fire engines out of his mouth. Incredible idea of how to say poetical power. Really direct, totally direct, in the sense of what's the most powerful screamy red majestical noise maker you can imagine? A fire engine! Okay, now "I wanted to drop fire-engines out of my mouth." You may not understand that he means he wants to achieve great rhetoric, which is what that line means, but it is so strange in itself that even if you don't understand what it means it penetrates the mind immediately with some kind of unconscious excitement in the language, excitement of having jumped over a chasm of nonassociation into a real clear logical association, so that it does mean something.

But what contradicted him? "In ran the moonlight," beauty, "and grabbed the prunes." In ran beauty and grabbed reality. How can moonlight grab the prunes? What was the moonlight doing running in there anyway? It's obviously playful, obviously an imaginary world of contradictions.

He was interested in taking the actuals of his own thoughts, like moonlight, prunes, fire engines, Christmas, father, mother, peas, and then turning it upside down so that it contradicts itself. And by these discords, or self-contradictions, making a funny kind of harmony or beauty.

CHAPTER 34

Corso and
Gasoline and Other Poems

Peter, I, and Gregory were living in Amsterdam in October 1957. He was preparing this book [*Gasoline*] for City Lights and so he asked me to write an introduction. I asked him to write something about his method, because he had once given me a long lecture on his method, which completely knocked me out. It was a description of his mind process while writing and I'd never heard anybody talk so precise in such a funny direction as he did. Gregory's method was that if he wanted to write a romantic poem about a young girl, then he would follow her in his mind's eye to the courtyard and climb up her balcony to the fire escape like Romeo and Juliet, but once he got on the fire escape he would extend the image somewhere else. Not into some corny regular idea, he would find something that would contradict it. If there was laundry hanging from the fire escape, then there would have to be corpses, laundered human skins, and that would lead to [asking] how'd that get there? Well, maybe there was a fight on the moon or whatever occurred to him. And if there was a fight on the moon there had to be a spaceship. In other words, following mind associations and making a metaphor, but rather than completing it logically, completing the metaphor by making it contradict itself constantly, twisting it around and turning it upside down. He called that automaticism. Taking those automatic associations and making them contradict.

I asked him to write a little essay that I could enclose within his preface, explaining his precise method of association. And he said, "With me automaticism is an intract moment in which the mind accelerates a constant hour of mind-foolery, mind genius, mind madness, when Bird Parker or Miles Davis blow a standard piece of music, they break off into other ownself little understood sounds, well that's my way with poetry. X, Y, and Z, call it automatic, I call it a standard flow because the offset words are standard, that is intentionally distractive, or diversed into my own sound. Of course many will say that a poem written on that order is unpolished. That's just what I want them to be. Because I have made them truly my own which is inevitably something new, like all good spontaneous jazz, newness is acceptable and expected by hip people who listen."

One excellent example is an odd poem, very Shelleyan, which he has down here as characterization, "Don't Shoot the Warthog," the warthog as being the muse. He chose the most ugly beast imaginable for his muse. He identifies with that strange ugly muse. "My goodness" is his comment on that one. Which is another way of putting his aesthetic out front.

Don't Shoot the Warthog
A child came to me
swinging an ocean on a stick.

Well, see, he's doing that again, a child swinging an ocean on a stick. Kind of a weird idea. Why not?

He told me his sister was dead,
I pulled down his pants
and gave him a kick.

What he's trying to do is contradict each line. Each line contradicted a little bit.

I drove him down the streets
down the night of my generation
I screamed his name, his cursed name,
down the streets of my generation
and children lept in joy to the name
and running came.
Mothers and fathers bent their heads to hear;
I screamed the name.

The child trembled, fell,
and staggered up again,
I screamed his name!
And a fury of mothers and fathers
sank their teeth into his brain.
I called to the angels of my generation
on the rooftops, in the alleyways,
beneath the garbage and the stones,
I screamed the name! and they came
and gnawed the child's bones.
*I screamed the name: Beauty
Beauty   Beauty   Beauty*[182]

A funny combination. So his conception of beauty is as a warthog, discord. His method of writing was to go to the opposite, to be

contrary, as with all of his life, to create beautiful objects out of the unexpected contradictory imagery. Beauty as the unexpected, like a fire engine dropped out of your mouth. Beauty as ugly, beauty as discord, beauty as contradiction, beauty as surprise, beauty as unreality, beauty as anything except the expected. So beauty as the ugly old self. Beauty as a dumb kid in the Lower East Side.

"The Last Warmth of Arnold." Arnold is a form of Corso or some Lower East Side jerk. Gregory identifies himself with the warthog, with the ugly, with the rejected, with the prisoner, with the criminal, with the worst, with what would be put down, with what would be rejected, with the rejected and canceled passage. He puts the romance into the loser, to Arnold as the loser. It's a self-portrait.

The Last Warmth of Arnold

Arnold, warm with God,
hides beneath the porch
remembering the time of escape, imprisoned in Vermont,
shoveling snow. Arnold was from somewhere else,
where it was warm; where he wore suede shoes
and played ping-pong.
Arnold knew the Koran.
And he knew to sing:
   Young Julien Sorel
   Knew his Latin well
   And was wise as he
   Was beautiful
   Until his head fell.

You know Julian Sorel, the hero of *The Red and the Black* [by] Stendhal?

In the empty atmosphere
Arnold kept a tiplet pigeon, a bag of chicken corn.
He thought of Eleanor, her hands;
watched her sit sad in school
He got Carmine to lure her into the warm atmosphere;
he wanted to kiss her, live with her forever;
break her head with bargains.

Who is Arnold? Well,
I first saw him wear a black cap
covered with old Wilkie buttons. He was 13.
And afraid. But with a smile. And he was always
willing to walk you home, to meet your mother,
to tell her about Hester Street Park
about the cold bums there;
about the cold old Jewish ladies who sat,
hands folded, sad, keeping their faces
away from the old Jewish Home.
Arnold grew up with a knowledge of bookies
and chicken pluckers

And Arnold knew to sing:
   Dead now my 15th year
   F.D.R., whose smiling face
   Made evil the buck-toothed Imperialist,
   The moustached Aryan,
   The jut-jawed Caesar—
   Dead now, and I weep . . .
   For once I did hate that man
   and no reason
   but innocent hate
   —my cap decked with old Wilkie buttons.

[Wendell] Willkie ran against Roosevelt in 1940.

Arnold was kicked in the balls
by an Italian girl who got mad
because there was a big coal strike on
and it forced the Educational Alliance to close its doors.
Arnold, weak and dying, stole pennies from the library,
but he also read about Paderewski.
He used to walk along South Street
wondering about the various kinds of glue.
And it was about airplane glue he was thinking
when he fell and died beneath the Brooklyn Bridge.[183]

That was Kerouac's favorite line in Corso's earlier work. "He used to walk along South Street wondering about the various kinds of glue." That's a very funny line, it's so totally literal. Totally unliterary, unpretty line, but also realistic. It's nonsensical, but that's exactly what people do wonder about. Like somebody walking down South Street would be wondering about various kinds of glue, why not? Hot glue, paste glue, thinking about glue, people do think about glue. It's so completely surrealist and at the same time totally realistic that it's mind-blowing. Corso's genius is in isolating these literalities which are simultaneously surrealist.

"Arnold was kicked in the balls by an Italian girl who got mad because there's a big coal strike on and the Educational Alliance was closed again." I think that was the original form of the line. That was my favorite line because it was so mysterious, meaningless, and at the same time completely coherent and completely nonsensical. Apparently it's just a little piece of real life history, he'd made a date for this youth club, the Educational Alliance, and planned to have a little rendezvous. And then there was a coal strike, it was closed, and the girl got mad and kicked him. That's just a piece of history so absurd that when you reduce it to its abstract notation, warthog reality, [it becomes] beauty. Very funny actually.

There's another element in Corso that begins to emerge, his ability to take archetypal situations or feelings or emotions and humorously parade them forth extending them out with his imagination until it becomes a recognizably familiar poeticism, as in a poem called "Hello," to be read in a kind of weak voice.

Hello

It is disastrous to be a wounded deer.
I'm the most wounded, wolves stalk,
and I have my failures, too.
My flesh is caught on the Inevitable Hook!
As a child I saw many things I did not want to be.
Am I the person I did not want to be?
That talks-to-himself person?
That neighbors-make-fun-of person?
Am I he who, on museum steps, sleeps on his side?
Do I wear the cloth of a man who has failed?
Am I the looney man?
In the great serenade of things,
am I the most cancelled passage?[184]

Each one of those is a thought that everyone has had about himself at one time or other, or a fear of himself of being the man to wear the cloth of the man who's failed, who sleeps on his side on the museum steps, a Bowery bum. And a kind of humor, willing to start a poem with the idea of "hello." I don't think any other poet has that much obvious mindfulness of the quirks of everyday goofiness. And along with the everyday goofiness is a recognition of everyday miracles, which become amazing contradictory realities, like "Last night I drove a car." It is one of a series of very realistic poems that might have come out of William Carlos Williams's ordinary mind rhetoric.

Last Night I Drove a Car

Last night I drove a car
   not knowing how to drive
   not owning a car
I drove and knocked down
   people I loved
   . . . went 120 through one town.

I stopped at Hedgeville
   and slept in the back seat
   . . . excited about my new life.[185]

It's a marijuana thought. I remember we were smoking a lot of marijuana when he wrote that and I remember hearing it read high on grass for the first time. Just the idea "I stopped at Hedgeville . . . excited about my new life" is the kind of feeling that you would have a dream about and he's notated it very succinctly.

My own favorites in this book are three or four very brief poems. Corso's attitude toward people, women, and his own loves is very realistic for that age, "On the Walls of a Dull Furnished Room."

On the Walls of a Dull Furnished Room

I hang old photos of my childhood girls—
with breaking heart I sit, elbow on table,
Chin on hand, studying
> the proud eyes of Helen,
> the weak mouth of Jane,
> the golden hair of Susan.[186]

That's another of those archetypal self-images of the poet looking at his old girlfriends. That weak mouth of Jane set between the proud eyes of Helen and the golden hair of Susan, most people wouldn't think of that. It is unexpected, and real, realistic.

Then "Italian Extravaganza," which is a takeoff on a poem by William Carlos Williams, "The Dead Baby." "Sweep under the bed, the baby is dead" it begins, which was Gregory's particular connection with Williams's imagery. "Italian Extravaganza," remembering that he was born above a funeral home on Bleecker and Macdougal.

Italian Extravaganza

Mrs. Lombardi's month-old son is dead.
I saw it in Rizzo's funeral parlor,
A small purplish wrinkled head.

They've just finished having high mass for it;
They're coming out now
. . . wow, such a small coffin!
And ten black cadillacs to haul it in.[187]

It's like a haiku. All totally realistic and naturalistic in style. Then the same detail of naturalism, realistic detail, applied in a surrealist way in "Birthplace Revisited." Remembering that Gregory's been out of New York, been to jail, been to Paris, been to San Francisco, been poet, been fucked by poets, and making it with poets, and making it with weak Jane mouths and golden hair Susans in Cambridges and now returning to Greenwich Village.

Birthplace Revisited

I stand in the dark light in the dark street
and look up at my window, I was born there.
The lights are on; other people are moving about.
I am with raincoat; cigarette in mouth,
hat over eye, hand on gat.

Gat, gun. You know, from Hollywood, from Edward G. Robinson. "Watch out, he's got a gat!"

I cross the street and enter the building.

In a sense he's coming on in the role of a torpedo, a hit man, revisiting his birthplace. It's an Italian neighborhood and there were mafiosi around him. He actually did know all the local hoods and bosses.

The garbage cans haven't stopped smelling.
I walk up the first flight; Dirty Ears
aims a knife at me . . .
I pump him full of lost watches.[188]

There his mind leaps, "I pump him full of lost watches." That's a genius touch. He's remembering Dirty Ears, an old childhood enemy, attacking him in that same smelly garbage can stairway, but now he's going back and realizing the patheticness of Dirty Ears after two or three decades, so he's pumping him with lost time. The time's transshifted, and Corso's alive and Dirty Ears may be in jail or dead or who knows? But by recollection, insight, memory, nostalgia, compassion, and poetic imagination, he's summoned up Dirty Ears. He's no longer afraid because he can pump him full of poetry, lost watches. In other words, Gregory has his weapon, his imagination, which is above and beyond Dirty Ears's knife. When that was first written, I didn't understand what that meant, and when this book first came out everybody said, "What does he mean by lost watches, or fried shoes, or those funny combinations?" It's so perfect a metaphor for lost time, time gone by.

Then "The Last Gangster," which is the best of these surrealistical-imaged time transshifting tiny poems.

The Last Gangster

Waiting by the window
my feet enwrapped with the dead bootleggers of Chicago
I am the last gangster, safe, at last,
waiting by a bullet-proof window.

I look down the street and know
the two torpedoes from St. Louis.
I've watched them grow old
. . . guns rusting in their arthritic hands.[189]

It's like the "lost watches," such a very precise realistic image using naturalistic forms to make a magical ellipse of time. Corso's method of writing involved an element of discord, or disharmony, or contradiction from image to image or from word to word. The next composition in his mind contradicted the previous composition. One phrase following another phrase that would completely disrupt the thinking process of the reader and disrupt the poet's composition process and create some kind of a weird mind warp or gap or temporary apocalypse inside the brain.

An example was when interviewed in the late 1950s by *Time* magazine and asked, "What is poetry?" Corso said, "Fried shoes!" At the time that was considered to be a weird statement, but it was just a very logical sensible example of an image that he considered poetic, fried shoes, or pipe butter, radiator soup, penguin dust.

CHAPTER 35

Corso and
The Happy Birthday of Death

From 1956 on Corso began a whole series of poems with single-word titles. [Each] took a very simple idea like marriage, or bomb, or death, or clown, or hair, or police, or army, or food and wrought all the changes possible that could be applied to each central theme word, still making use of that notion of contradiction. This included a poem called "Discord," which explains his poetic method.

> **Discord**
>
> Oh I would like to break my teeth
> by means of expressing a radiator!
>> I say I must dent that which gives heat!
>> Dent! regardless the tradition of my mouth.

It's a direct expression of his method again, as before he laid out his aesthetic in "I wanted to drop fire-engines out of my mouth." Here he would like to "break my teeth by means of expressing a radiator!," whatever that means. The title is "Discord," which is his method, not to make beauty out of some corny logical harmony but to make beauty out of a contradiction, like fried shoes.

I would like to drive a car
      but I must *drive* it!
Look—there must be a firing squad, yes,
      buy why a wolf?
I mean if I pass by with a rainball ball
      should I pass by with a jackinthebox instead?
      Confused I'd best leave wonder and candy and school
and go find amid ruin the peremptory corsair.

    Sober
Wier Moors furs tails deer paws
  risked and fevered thinking
    owls in flashlight.[190]

What does all that mean? To begin with he's theorizing the terms of his speech, like dropping a fire engine out of his mouth. A kind of literal joke-surprise, "break my teeth by means of expressing a radiator." So a surrealist mixture of word combinations. As he opens his mouth he expresses a radiator or a fire engine drops out. It's like a surrealist thing where you take one object and put it juxtaposed inside of another, like a mouth, where they don't belong, but they make sense, they actually make sense. "By means of expressing it" is a funny way of putting it. It's sort of Italian American double talk. Then he takes on a kind of rhetorical, traditional tone. "I say I must dent," that would make sense in some traditional context. But then what does he say? "Dent that which gives heat," which within itself is an odd idea, to dent that which gives heat. It's abstract, funny syntax. "Regardless the tradition of my mouth." Not regardless *of* the tradition of my mouth, but "regardless the tradition of my mouth." He tailored the line down. That's his word, "tailoring." He cut out possessive articles, cut out as many commas as possible, cut out any-thing extra, and just kept to the nub or most exact, pointed, sharp, fast, funny way of saying the idea he has in mind. His poems are made up of ideas in a way that other people's poems aren't.

It's an idea to have a theory of poetry which would be discordant, it's an idea to have an example of that discordance be the sound of a fire engine, the loudness of a fire engine coming out of the mouth. It's an idea that is expressed by saying, "I drop a fire-engine out of my mouth," or an idea to express heated language by means of a radia-tor, breaking his teeth on a radiator. Only a true artist would offer to break his teeth on a radiator.

I think discord came out of his own head, his own early intuition into poetry. His idea is one idea following another by association visually but contradicting and going off in different directions, just for the playfulness or the weirdness of it. It ends up with an abstract painting of words that exemplify the essence of the essential point he's making. The point he's making is that through discord and contradic-tion he can arrive at literal beauty. It's a flat, straightforward picture. These little sparks of discord, like flint against iron, are theorized as little glimpses of poetic wisdom.

Then there's another exercise that he did, which is pretty well known, on the subject of pure invention. The point where he passes from some kind of logical sense into totally nonlogical sense is a middle point, before he gets completely crazy. "Look there must be a firing squad, yes." Well, whoever said there must be a firing squad? Because there must be a firing squad, sure, life has a firing squad, okay, so look, there must be a firing squad, yes, but why a wolf? Well, he's substituted one scare for another, the wolf for the firing squad. And why is it a wolf? Well, if you can accept that there should be a firing squad on earth, then how come he's asking why there should be a wolf? It doesn't make sense, he's just kidding you. And he continues kidding you. "I mean if I pass by with a rainball ball, should I pass by with a jack in the box instead?" Or if I invent a rainball ball, if I invent the conception, is there something so illogical about that that you prefer I come along with a jack-in-the-box instead? He's talking about his poetic method and being very courteous, having a conversation with you about how he's going about it. Finally says, "Confused"? If you're going to deny his methods, he'd best leave all the early childlike apprehensions like wonder and candy and school and go find amid ruin, what? The "peremptory corsair," some immediately demanding pirate. Finally it ends with a little collage of exquisite essence of weir, which he also caps by "owls in flashlight," little flashes of wisdom. It makes some funny kind of sense. It's a progression from the beginning of the idea of discord, it's a progression in images, a continuing, it's a sequence of ideas following from the first one, almost logical.

In *Happy Birthday of Death* is a relatively well-known poem called "Poets Hitchhiking on the Highway." The actual situation was me and Gregory hitchhiking down around Big Sur in 1956, going to visit Henry Miller and not being able to get a ride. We were stuck on the highway, and conversing, talking about discord, talking about his method of composition. I finally got the idea that he was just fooling around, using contradiction as the method, basically trying to tease the reader's mind. It has some function if you need a practical function for that kind of beauty.

Poets Hitchhiking on the Highway

Of course I tried to tell him
but he cranked his head
    without an excuse.

I told him the sky chases
   the sun
And he smiled and said:
   "What's the use."
I was feeling like a demon
   again
So I said: "But the ocean chases
   the fish."
This time he laughed
   and said: "Suppose the
      strawberry were
         pushed into a mountain."
After that I knew the
   war was on —
So we fought:
He said: "The apple-cart like a
        broomstick-angel
      snaps & splinters
        old dutch shoes."
I said: "Lightning will strike the old oak
     and free the fumes!"
He said: "Mad street with no name."
I said: "Bald killer! Bald killer! Bald killer!"
He said, getting real mad,
     "Firestoves! Gas! Couch!"
I said, only smiling,
     "I know God would turn back his head
     if I sat quietly and thought."
We ended by melting away,
   hating the air![191]

What's weird about it is that the ultimate poetic moment comes when there are no more opposite combinations, just the words "couch," "stoves," "gas," "firestoves," "gas," "couch." The hottest point is just the simple words "firestoves," "gas," "couch." He's substituted incredibly odd and unexpected or discordant combinations of words, like "apple-cart," "broomstick-angel," or conceptions like "ocean chases the fish," he substitutes these opposites or inside-out ideas or weird "fried shoes" combinations of language. We were hitchhiking and we had to pass the time, so we made up phrases to astound each other. In the course of trying to astound each other by the twists and turns of unlikely juxtapositions of words making strange, startling images, it went from ideas, which were upside-down ideas, like "the sky chases the sun" and "the ocean chases the fish," from koan-like idea inversions to weird juxtapositions like "apple-cart," "broomstick-angel," to almost ordinary mind noticings. I remember saying, "mad street, no name." We didn't know where we were, a mad street with no name. He came up with "bald killer." They seemed at the moment, in the hysteria of Salingeresque high school kids putting each other on, to be funnier and funnier. But finally the ultimate in funniness was when the words appeared in the air with no relevance at all but were totally ordinary facts like "gas" or "couch." So the highest poetry in that were just the ordinary words. Of course it took a little preparation but that's his basic method.

We'd arrived at a point where contradiction was so obvious that reality itself was sufficient to be self-contradicting. Or reality itself was funnier even than contradiction. That gas, couch, just to say a single word like "gas" or "couch" was funnier than to say "pipe-couch," "water-gas." It was easy to do, but the couch sitting down in the middle of the road like that in our brains, just reality itself, a simple real word like "couch" was, in this context, total solidification of poetry.

CHAPTER 36

Corso and "Bomb"

I think "Bomb" is one of Gregory's greatest poems. "Marriage" is famous because it's in all the anthologies, it's obvious and it's a good poem, but there are other poems just as good, just as funny, just as powerful, and just as suggestive in method of that series. They become more and more refined until you get to "Clown" and finally "Death."

Originally published by City Lights as a broadside, "Bomb" was printed in the form of a mushroom cloud. He begins Wagnerian, addressing the bomb: "Budger of history." It's already Gregory being funny. The bomb budges history, a very interesting phrase.

Budger of history   Brake of time   You Bomb
Toy of universe   Grandest of all snatched-sky   I cannot hate you
Do I hate the mischievous thunderbolt the jawbone of an ass
The bumpy club of One Million B.C.   the mace the flail the axe
Catapult Da Vinci   tomahawk Cochise   flintlock Kidd
dagger Rathbone
Ah and the sad desperate gun of Verlaine   Pushkin   Dillinger   Bogart
And hath not St. Michael a burning sword   St. George a lance
David a sling

Bomb   you are as cruel as man makes you   and you're no crueller
than cancer
All man hates you   they'd rather die by car-crash
lightning   drowning
Falling off a roof   electric-chair   heart-attack   old age
old age   O Bomb
They'd rather die by anything but you   Death's finger is free-lance
Not up to man whether you boom or not   Death has long
since distributed its
categorical blue

It's a very funny approach, reminding everybody that they're going to die anyway, so why are they getting all creepily scared about the bomb? The hysteria of the bomb is really hysteria at the universe itself, the bomb was just an excuse for further spitefulness and hysteria. Which is true, everybody's gonna die anyway. "Death has long since distributed its categorical blue." That's the ultimate nature of things, a great blue empty.

Gregory is an idea man and the opening of this poem, gorgeous as it is and full of humor, is a very clear, simple idea that bomb is no crueler than cancer, so he can not hate it. And you can't hate people for the bomb either. It's not up to man whether the bomb booms or not.

There's a long extravaganza imagining a bomb falling on New York and all the havoc and comedy that would wreak. It's seen almost as a Marx Brothers comedy, like at the end of *Duck Soup*. Then a series of discord contradictions, how the bomb will disrupt "The top of the Empire State arrowed in a broccoli field in Sicily," or "Penguins plunged against the Sphinx." A series of images like that. Then a little historical roundup in which the visiting team of the present and the home team of the past are put together in a final amphitheater of life and death, all booing and cheering to the end. Then an address to the bomb in very pretty language invoking an explosion of the bomb in very rosy terms.

> Stick angels on your jubilee feet
> wheels of rainlight on your bunky seat
> You are due and behold you are due
> and the heavens are with you

Then a long section of apocalyptic rhetoric done in humorous style about the horrible effects of the bomb.

> From thy nimbled matted spastic eye
> exhaust deluges of celestial ghouls
> From thy appellational womb
> spew birth-gusts of great worms
> Rip open your belly Bomb
> from your belly outflock vulturic salutations
> Battle forth your spangled hyena finger stumps
> along the brink of Paradise

Mouthfuls of language there. Then after this climactic explosion of language a quiet legato section where he examines what he is doing.

> That I lean forward on a desk of science
> an astrologer dabbling in dragon prose
> half-smart about wars   bombs   especially bombs
> That I am unable to hate what is necessary to love
> That I can't exist in a world that consents
> a child in a park

So what's so weird about a bomb? It's the same trick he [always] pulls. Simple, ordinary, odd as wearing shoes, it is as astounding as a child in the park, a man dying in an electric chair. Those are as astounding as the vast drama of the poetic bomb.

> That I say I am a poet and therefore love all man
> knowing my words to be the acquainted prophecy of all men
> and my unwords no less an acquaintanceship

The ambitiousness and brashness of the language is just the common heart of everybody. A common chord that everybody actually feels, a common fantasy of wanting to be above the bomb, or wanting to be more beautiful than the bomb, or wanting the imagination to surpass the bomb. And then he says "and my unwords," the things he doesn't say, "no less an acquaintanceship."

> That I am manifold
> a man pursuing the big lies of gold

He's admitting it. His rhetoric is always these great big lies of gold. "Or a poet roaming in bright ashes," which is what this poem has been doing. "Or that which I imagine myself to be." And now he goes out again on discordant, imaginary constructions. He imagines himself to be "A shark-toothed sleep a man-eater of dreams." Then he says,

> I need not then be all-smart about bombs
> Happily so   for if I felt bombs were caterpillars
> I'd doubt not they'd become butterflies

Then he puts them all in hell and makes fun of the bombs. Finally he gets right at it and gets into the bomb with his mind, begins mind fucking the bomb itself.

> I am standing before your fantastic lily door
> I bring you Midgardian roses   Arcadian musk
> Reputed cosmetics from the girls of heaven
> Welcome me   fear not thy opened door
> nor thy cold host's grey memory
>
> [...]
>
> Yet   not enough to say a bomb will fall
> or even contend celestial fire goes out
> Know that the earth will madonna the Bomb
> that in the hearts of men to come more bombs will be born
> magisterial bombs wrapped in ermine   all beautiful
> and they'll sit plunk on earth's grumpy empires
> fierce with moustaches of gold[192]

All that rhetoric boils down [to the fact that] the bomb comes out of men's hearts. That if men created the bomb, they're going to get what they deserve. And it's not the first time and it may not be the last time. Even more monstrous projections of the imagination will be created that we'll have to deal with and if we can't deal with them, then we'll get what we created. If we're going to hate it, we're gonna have to hate ourselves and our own imagination for being capable of creating universal death. It's not enough to get resentful that the whole universe is gonna go out, the celestial fire is gonna go out, we're going to kill God with the bomb. Since we created the whole shebang anyway, the imagination which created the bomb is bigger than the bomb. The poetic imagination is beyond the bomb, because the bomb is only a piece of noisy poetry after all. It is of man's mind and man's creation is poetry. Everything is poetry in the sense that we've imagined it, we've figured it out and we do it. So the bomb is just a noisy epic.

Gregory's asserting his imagination. Specifically this poem is more expansive than the bomb, more explosive in the imagination than the bomb. It's the first poem that I know of that faced the bomb with imagination and was unafraid of the bomb. And probably the first poem that did any good in "fighting" the bomb, because it freed minds from the fear-thrall of the bomb. The thinking that the bomb was some great god independent of us.

Corso is the most inspired and intelligent and excellent of all the poets. He's the poet's poet, the perfect poet in a way. Traditional classic *poète maudit,* that is to say, poet whom society puts down because of his bad behavior. He's an offensive poet, an outrageous poet, a drunken poet, a strung-out poet, an insulting poet, a bedbug poet, a tragic poet, but he survived instead of dying young. Survived to haunt everybody. And he sees himself as kind of a holy fool or tragic clown.

"How Happy I Used to Be" may be a little difficult to understand, but I remember him writing it and I enjoyed the process of him writing it, because we were all high on grass and every time he had a new line it was really interesting. So the idea is Gregory the orphan.

How Happy I Used to Be

How happy I used to be
imagining myself so many things—
 Alexander Hamilton lying in the snow
 shoe buckles rusting in the snow
 pistol shot crushing his brow.

Behind a trail of visiting kings
I cried:
    Will Venice and Genoa
    give welcome as did Verona?
    I have no immediate chateau
    for the Duke of Genoa
    no African bull for the Doge of Venice
    but for the Pope!
    I have the hideout of the Turk.
    Informer? No—I'm in it
    for the excitement;
    between Afghanistan and Trinidad
    intrigue and opera are electrified
    everywhere is electricity!
The mad spinning ballerina
sees me in the audience and falls into a faint,
    I smile I smile I smile —
Or yesterday when I heard a sad song
I stopped to hear and wept
for when had I last imagined myself a king
a kind king with ambassadors and flowers and wise teachers —
What has happened to me now that
everything has been fulfilled?
Will I again walk up Lexington Avenue
or down it
feeling warm to Richard the Third
and the executioner
whose black hood is oppressive to wear?
Am I not music walking behind Ben Franklin
music in his two loaves of bread

and Massachusetts half-penny?
I knew 1768 when all was patched eyes and wooden legs
How happy I was fingering pieces of eight, doubloons —
Children, have you not heard of my meeting
with Israel Hans, Israel Hans—[193]

He starts with kind of grammar school mythology, imagining himself in different roles out of history. "Alexander Hamilton lying in the snow." Hamilton was killed in a duel with Aaron Burr, so Alexander Hamilton lying in the snow. Either Gregory read it or he figured out that it was a winter snowy scene.[194] Immediately his first thought was to take the abstract historical event but put in the snow and have shoe buckles rusting in the snow. You'd have to be high on grass to imagine shoe buckles rusting in the snow, rather than just leaving it. He detailed it, particularized it, humanized it, put a little shoe buckle into it.

"Behind a trail of visiting kings I cried: Will Venice and Genoa give welcome as did Verona?" So now he's imagining himself a Renaissance artist or prince. "I have no immediate chateau for the Duke of Genoa," everybody giving out presents. He's imagining himself through history, giving out castles to Genoese dukes. "No African bull for the Doge of Venice," a present of an African bull. "But for the Pope! I have the hideout of the Turk." He's a spy actually, so what he has is secret information on where the Turks are hiding out with their armies. "Informer? No—I'm in it for the excitement; between Afghanistan and Trinidad intrigue and opera are electrified everywhere is electricity!" That's a very high funny idea. The Renaissance and former poet, diplomat, spy, in it for the excitement, traveling "between Afghanistan and Trinidad," that's pure sound. Intrigue and opera.

Then all of a sudden a hypnotic movie image, "the mad spinning ballerina sees me in the audience and falls into a faint." I don't know where that came from, maybe from some old movie like *Dead of Night*, where there's a phantom face that haunts the hero.

"For when had I last imagined myself a king." I thought it was a great line when I first heard it. He's boasting about the power of imagination, boasting his poetic imagination. His genius here is not only being smart about history, because he's smart about history, but also imaginatively interested [in the details]. There's a very famous image of the hooded executioner with the ax, but Corso knows that the hood is oppressive to wear, it's all sweaty inside the hood of the executioner. How many people have actually empathized inside the executioner's head and tried to figure out what it would feel like [to be] in that role. "When did I last imagine myself a king?" Beyond imagination there's a quality of extent of Mahayana bodhisattvic compassionate empathy, of extending awareness out into strange interesting places. Everybody in grammar school knows about the executioner, but nobody thinks [about how he] feels. Everybody hears about Alexander Hamilton's duel, but nobody connects it with some living reality like the shoe buckle in the snow, which is a very brilliant idea. Make the duel and the death real, a shoe buckle in the snow. The humor and intelligence and jump of the mind [are] amazing.

> Am I not music walking behind Ben Franklin
> music in his two loaves of bread
> and Massachusetts half-penny?

This is all 1930s grammar school mythology, Ben Franklin walking into Philadelphia with two loaves of bread and a half-penny. It's some kind of subliminal American archetype that he must have read or seen a little drawing of in the *Reader's Digest* in 1935.

> I knew 1768 when all was patched eyes and wooden legs
> How happy I was fingering pieces of eight, doubloons —
> Children, have you not heard of my meeting
> with Israel Hans, Israel Hans —

He thought of children. It's the poet talking to another generation, saying haven't you heard of the great deeds that I did? I'm that old that I've met Israel Hans. "Who's Israel Hans?" I kept thinking, "Who's Israel Hans?" because it's somehow interesting. Israel Hans apparently was some figure of the American Revolution. Oddly enough, Corso was quite learned in old, funny history.[195]

There's an element, a motif underneath it, that is Gregory as an orphan. Somebody completely dispossessed and disinherited and yet completely genius, a voracious reader, displaying his trinkets and toys of the mind, displaying his empathy. Maybe because he was in prison and had to develop a more powerful imagination. He's an orphan prisoner saying, "Children, have you not heard of my meeting with Israel Hans?" The time George Washington and I played cards? The time I lent money to Thomas Paine? And the repeat of Israel Hans is heartbreaking. I always liked that poem, it's such an odd thing, but it is a great display of imagination. He wrote it in Amsterdam in 1958 when we were all living together in a furnished room meeting Dutch poets. I guess Israel Hans had originally been Dutch, I think that was the connection, he was some sort of Dutch, Jewish American revolutionary. That's how Gregory knew about it.

CHAPTER 37

Corso and "Power"

One of the earliest of Corso's one-word subject poems was "Power," which is one of the most brilliant and I think one of the great poems of the century. [His publisher Lawrence] Ferlinghetti didn't like it, he got scared of it. He thought it was a fascist poem because it was about power. Actually it was like an empty hand of power. Here he takes on another big subject and begins to play cadenzas on power. The opening is very strange, too, and was done [at the] same time as the Israel Hans poem.

> Power
> We are the imitation of Power
> Every man is to be doubted
> There is no mouth no eye no nose no ear no hand enough
> The senses are insufficient
> You need Power to dispel light
> Not the closing of an eye

"You need Power to dispel light." I don't know what that means anymore. Probably to give out light, not the closing of the light, as if you're blind. This is ambiguous, what he's getting at to begin with. I don't know whether he means dispense or dispel. I think he's intentionally trying to get you confused.

> Since I observe memory and dream
> and not the images of the moment
> I am become more vivid

Since he makes use of imagination, memory, dream, the mind, intellectual beauty, rather than just the materialistic literality, "I am become more vivid" rather than less vivid, he says, so he's making paradoxical statements. He's dealing here in paradox.

> And need not open the eye to see

He's at it again. Actually he doesn't open up his eyes to see.

> With me light is always light
> How powerful I am to imagine darkness!

He's playing with ideas. He's thought it in a very funny way that makes metaphors out of ideas. He's manipulating ideas around, maybe because the ideas are attached to words and you can turn the words inside out, so you can confuse the reader. There's a kind of con game going on where he's trying to confuse the reader by saying something absolutely dumb-simple, which if you follow along logically will lead you upside down, constantly. The idea is to finally get to saying something upside down which will be absolutely right side up and true. What I like about this poem is that finally he arrives at a point where by saying everything upside down it's absolutely correct and undermines the state and the universe and everybody's bullshit. It undermines power, to begin with. What does he mean by power? He's going to define power, but in sixteen different ways and then finally settle on one that's so tricky it pulls the rug out from under power, out from under aggressive power.

Since I depend on heroes for opinion and acceptance

And depends on Kerouac or me or Burroughs. There's almost a little sleight of hand in the language here. You never can tell if it means something or if he's just suggesting that it might mean something, and it doesn't. Like "how powerful I am to imagine darkness." There's always a little trickery, but when you begin examining it, at the bottom of the trick is always another little trick. So his trickery, precision, paradoxical inventiveness with language, like "I pump him full of lost watches," a trick ending. It's like a magic trick, you pull a rabbit out of the hat, or "guns rusting in their arthritic hands," or the "hopping drooling desire awaiting flat against the trees with bloodstained fingernails."

I live by proper truth and error

The heroes, well if you depend on heroes, you can't go wrong.

SHAZAM!

The superhero, Batman or something?

O but how sad is Ted Williams gypped and chiseled
All alone in center field
Let me be your wise Buck Rogers!

Since I contradict the real with the unreal
Nothing is so unjust as impossibility

That follows logically from everything else. The discord idea was contradicting the real with the unreal, pipe butter, pipe is real, butter is real, pipe butter is contradicting the real with the unreal. His method in poetry is to take something that seems real, pipe, butter, all that, and then by combining them weird, fried shoes, pipe butter, to make something unreal out of it. To put two reals together to make something unreal, but beautiful, pretty. To make another reality in a sense, like fried shoes. It's certainly real as a phrase. Fried shoes, it's real, you could read it on the page. And at the same time it does give a real crinkle in your brain, some little shiver, or some weird little piss of beauty. It indicates how language works, that you can create imaginary things with language. You can make up pretty little things like that, but they're unreal in certain respects.

Gregory is saying that since his method of poetry is to contradict the real with something imagined, to contradict the real with the unreal (and by the unreal he means imagination), he hereby declares that nothing is so unjust as impossibility. Since the imagination is superior to appearance, nothing is so unjust as to limit yourself to only what you can see in front of you and eliminate the imaginative possibility. Impossibility is unjust because he likes to make impossible combinations, so therefore he is saying that impossibility is unjust to him as a poet. As a poet he demands justice, which is that he be allowed to play with the impossible, which is very human.

He's expressing that same tendency. The point I'm trying to make is, how witty that line is, "Since I contradict the real with the unreal, nothing is so unjust as impossibility." It's a very childish piece of insistency. Whereas all the other poets want to grow up and be mature and write books like *In Dreams Begin Responsibilities*. Or they want to be grounded, or they want to be wise and truthful, like Robert Frost. They want to be disillusioned and have everything accurate and real, or they want to be grounded with their minds clamped down on objects, like William Carlos Williams, or they want to preach "no ideas but in things." They want everything to be right. But Gregory says he doesn't want everything to be right. He wants to be a poet of the impossible. His first statement of power.

The logical end of this kind of poetry is to make all of ordinary reality appear to us as strange, fresh, new, and weird, new-minted, new-born, as it is all the time without our noticing it. He's deconditioning us to our ideas, he's cutting up our ideas, cutting up logic. He's throwing the brain into chaos, he's throwing mind into chaos, he's dealing with chaos in order to do the classical thing that poetry does, which is to show us the beauty or wonder or strangeness of the actual world.

And with a heart of wooing mathematics soar to passion a planet

O but there are times SHAZAM is not enough
There is a brutality in the rabbit
That leads the way to Paradise

He's just saying the realistic cynic element, not a Kewpie doll, Walt Disney rabbit, but a real rabbit, that has teeth, that kind of understanding can lead to Paradise or Heaven. However a fourth contradiction comes. "There is a brutality in the rabbit." It's quite consistent within itself. There's the element of ordinary fuck-up evil death, aggression, the element of teeth in the rabbit proposes a psychological realism that is the only paradise we have, and that doesn't include a sugar candy god.

There is a cruelness in the fawn
Its tiger-elegance gnawing clover to the bone

The fawn cruelness is eating the grass, the clover. The faun's cruelness, from the point of view of the clover. The faun is some kind of tiger
elegance. But there's the disharmony again, the "tiger-elegance gnawing
clover to the bone." Now he finally gets into the middle of his subject.

I am a creature of Power
With me there is no ferocity
I am fair   careful   wise and laughable
I storm a career of love for myself
I am powerful humancy in search of compassion
My Power craves love   Beware my Power!

Know my Power
I resemble fifty miles of Power
I cut my fingernails with a red Power
In buses I stand on huge volumes of Spanish Power
The girl I love is like a goat splashing golden cream Power
Throughout the Spring I carried no Power

But my mission is outrageous!
I am here to tell you various failures of God
The unreasonableness of God
There is something unfair about this
It is not God that has made Power unbearable   it is Love

Here he's going to contradict everything and denounce love.

Love of Influence   Industry   Firearms   Protection
Man protected by man from man   this is Love

Good has no meaning and Sympathy no message   this is Love
THINK signs will never give way to DREAM signs   this is Love
We are ready to fight with howitzers!   this is Love
This has never been my Love
Thank God my Power

That's just a simple, straightforward attack on middle-class sentimentality, which leads to patriotism, aggression, or self-contradiction,
implicit in that. He takes the idea and carries it from one logical
extension to another, taking it further and further from where it
began, but going through all the possible changes on the word or the
idea or the conception. This depends on the actual mind to provide
the contradictions, because everybody can think of all these.

Who am I that sing of Power
Am I the stiff arm of Nicaragua
Do I wear green and red in Chrysler squads
Do I hate my people
What about the taxes
Do they forgive me their taxes
Am I to be shot at the racetrack—do they plot now
My monument of sculptured horses is white beneath the moon!

Am I Don Pancho Magnifico Pulque no longer a Power?

He's just empathizing as he did under the hood of the executioner,
now he's empathizing into the psyche of the dictator.

No I do not sing of dictatorial Power
The hail of dictatorship is symbolic of awful Power
In my room I have gathered enough gasoline and evidence
To allow dictators inexhaustible Power

He's saying, "In my room I've got enough poetry and intellectual evidence to be an inexhaustible source of power." This is more like the American Indian use of the word "power," which is to say spiritual presence or imaginative presence, ultimately self-confidence, undauntedness, majestic posture, unobstructed humor, and royal elegance of language, as well as complete confidence in the kingdom that he owns and rules, which is the kingdom of the imagination. Most people don't own their own imaginations and are afraid of the imaginations of others. It's a literal thing, that this power poem cracks the code of military dictatorship power, because it takes up the word "power" and examines what is power. You find his definition of "power" accords with the ancient definitions, of Taoists, or Indians, or Whitman, and does not accord with the mechanical power of the modern hyperindustrialized, hypertechnocratic state.

> I *Ave* no particular Power but that of Life
> Nor yet condemn fully any form of Power but that of Death
> The inauguration of Death is an absurd Power
> Life is the supreme Power
> Whoever hurts Life is a penny candy in the confectionary of
>   Power
> Whoever complains about Life is a dazzling monster in the zoo
>   of Power

Anybody neurotic complaining "you're a dazzling monster," just another monster, just another dazzling creature.

> The lovers of Life are deserved of Power's trophy
> They need not jump Power's olympics nor prove pilgrimage
> Each man is a happy spy of Power in the realm of Weakness

That's pretty good too. We're all weak, but we all realize that we're weakened and that's what our power is. Basic Shambhala [Buddhist] teaching is that this comes from realizing that you're weak and vulnerable. People who don't realize that they're weak and vulnerable are going to die or they're a bunch of nuts that go around kicking dead dogs. The people who realize they're weak are a little more tender toward what they see in front of them, they know it's all as vulnerable as they are.

Power
What is Power
A hat is Power

Now he's going to get to it. What is power? "A hat is Power." That's the best line in twentieth-century poetry. This is like "gas" or "couch," "a hat is Power." It's almost the same thinking process to finally [get to] where he's saying that poetry is the realization of the magnificence of the actual, even just a word like "gas" or "couch."

The world is Power
Being afraid is Power
What is poetry when there is no Power
Poetry is powerless when there is no Power
Standing on a street corner waiting for no one is Power

And this is the greatest line I think: "Standing on a street corner waiting for no one is Power." There's no intent if there is no intentionality. If there's no preconception, the mind is open, therefore supreme power of awareness and imagination possible. Supreme power of possibility, because you're not limited.

The angel is not as powerful as looking and then not looking
Will Power make me mean and unforgettable?

This is funny as a monologue because from line to line he's taking the word "power" and bringing every possible subtle change
you could imagine. This poem is really smart. That's the great thing
about it. It's smart in the way that most people are dumb and don't
understand their own smartness, because they don't believe their
own minds. This is an amazing declaration. I would say it is Gregory
Corso's first major adult poem, his empowerment of himself, and his
empowerment of poetry.

Strangely enough at this time, Ferlinghetti thought that this was
a pro-power, pro-fascist poem. Ferlinghetti thought it was something
to do with Hitler, not realizing that it was inside out. If you get that
powerful, will you become like other people that he likes, or will he
be like Jimmy Dean or Marlon Brando, mean and unforgettable?

Power is underpowered

How did he arrive at that? "Power is underpowered." This is the
key. It's absolutely logical in the course of this and yet it's the same
discord, the same contradiction. The same thing as poetry, really.
Poetry is not poetry. You try and write poetry and you get all hung
up in self-conscious ambition, and you just write your ego. The actual
definition is right there.

Power is what is happening
Power is without body or spirit
Power is sadly fundamental
Power is attained by Weakness

Walt Whitman also said that. "Not till the sun rejects you, do I reject you. Vivas to those who have failed, vivas to the losers, vivas to those whose ships have gone down in the sea and those who lost the battle."

Diesels do not explain Power
In Power there is no destruction
Power is not to be dropped by a plane
A thirst for Power is drinking sand
I want no song Power
I want no dream Power
I want no driven-car Power
I want I want I want Power!

Power is without compensation
Angels of Power come down with cups of vengeance
They are demanding compensation

The angels from heaven, like a heaven and a hell, with cups of vengeance they want compensation, they're not as powerful as looking and then not looking, of being wounded and then letting go. Being insulted and letting go.

People! where is your Power
The angels of Power are coming down with their cups!

I am the ambassador of Power
I walk through tunnels of fear
With portfolios of Power under my arm
Look at me
The appearance of Power is there

I have come to survey your store of Power—where is it
Is it in your heart your purse
Is it beneath your kitchen sink
Beautiful people I remember your Power
I have not forgotten you in the snows of Bavaria
Skiing down on the sleeping villages with flares and carbines
I have not forgotten you rubbing your greasy hands on aircraft
Signing your obscene names on blockbusters
No! I have not forgotten the bazooka you decked with palm
Fastened on the shoulder of a black man
Aimed at a tankful of Aryans

An image of the black soldiers during World War II after the war in North Africa. Tobruk and whatnot. A bazooka decked with palm fronds or palm leaves as disguise, as camouflage, on the shoulder of a black man aimed at a tankful of Aryans.

Nor have I forgotten the grenade
The fear and emergency it spread
Throughout your brother's trench
You are Power beautiful people

And that brings it to the climax. Well, we might as well go on with this, this is what we're into. Then there's a little halt, a break before he goes on to consider all this, going back to childhood life.

In a playground where I write this poem feeling shot in the back
Wanting to change the old meaning of Power

This is a reaction to our situation in 1958 in Europe, reading *Time* magazine, which was announcing this as the American century, announcing this as the century of unlimited American power, military power. We were just beginning to send CIA liaison people into Laos. The French had been beaten in Indochina and were still fighting in Algeria. They'd lost their colony five years earlier in Indochina and America was replacing all this colonialism with its own world guns. There was lots of talk about the man of distinction and responsibility and power.

> Wanting to give it new meaning my meaning
> I drop my unusual head dumb to the true joy of being good

Then he looks back to all the power guys of his youth in the Mafia when he was growing up in Greenwich Village. All the dumb Italians that were beating everybody up and telling him he was a freaky poet and [that] they had good jobs. He's looking at it from the perspective of having become a big international celebrity poet genius, and realizing the pathos of all those left behind, who either get drafted to go to some imaginary war or wind up lesser men in the factories of the universe.

> And I wonder myself now powerless
> Staggering back to the feeble boys of my youth
> Are they now lesser men in the factories of universe
> Are they there compressing the air
> Pumping their bully profanities through long leafy tubes
> I see them perched high on the shelves of God
> Outpecking this offered hemisphere like a crumb —

O God! what uttered curse ushers me to them
Like a prisoner of war . . .
Be those ominous creaks of eternity their sad march?

How powerless I am in playgrounds
Swings like witches woosh about me
Sliding ponds like dinosaur tongues down to my unusual feet
To have me walk in the street would be *both* unusual

Another of those weird mind-blowing ideas from smoking grass.
Grammatically an impossible statement, except it sounds logical here.
Ferlinghetti didn't want to print this in *Gasoline* because he thought
it had something to do with fascist power, so Gregory quit writing
the poem in 1956. He completed it in Amsterdam two years later.
The opening line of the 1958 continuation is:

Power is still with me! Who got me hung on Power?

So what is he going to do with it now? Of course he's grown as
a poet and he's gotten much more imaginative and funny, far out.

Am I stuffed in the grizzly maw of Power's hopped-up wheel
Will I always be like this   head in   legs out
Like one of Ulysses' men in the mouth of Polyphemus

[Reference to the] myth in the *Odyssey* about Polyphemus the
one-eyed Titan, a Cyclops. He was the guy in the cave who had cap-
tured all of Odysseus's men and Odysseus blinded Polyphemus and
got his men out by making them cling to the bellies of sheep while
Polyphemus felt the sheeps' backs. It's from a painting by Goya, a

really mean image. There is one of Polyphemus eating Odysseus's men and the feet are coming out of his mouth.

Am I the Power drag? Me the Power head?
Just what Power am I for anyway!

Here Gregory has the chance to demonstrate his poetic power by a series of word combinations that are mind-blowing by themselves.

The seized bee in a blaze of honey Power —
The spider in the center of its polar veil
With a fly-from-another-world Power —

That's from the movie *The Fly*, I guess.

Good noon nap on adoration lap with all cozy cruelty Power—
Towering melt like an avalanche of glass never ending chirring
    Power—

Stooped and hushed Chronicleleer of Spenserian gauderies
Is surely maybe my Power—
Whenever I play the fiery lyre with cold-fingered minstrelry
A luscious Power gives me a heavened consequence good as
    sunlight—

This is pretty good. He's playing the fiery lyre now. The cold-fingered minstrel, the deliberate, cold, calculating combination of words. Words that are both unusual. Now he's going to do a climactic credenza of pure improvisation of powerful contradictory impossible poetical diamond-like images. Really odd phrasing, a

heavened consequence. A heavenly consequence becomes a heavened consequence.

> Awful blank acreage once made pastoral by myths
> Now abandoned to mankind's honest yet hopeless
> Anthemion-elixir is in need of my Power —

One of the interesting things about Corso is all those odd Greek
names, the name for Mercury's sandals [talaria] and things like
anthemion.[196] I forgot what anthemion is, it's a Greek god that
did something awful, like fuck up the city for some money. He's
in need of my power. He's very good at Greek mythology. "Awful
blank acreage once made pastoral by myths," New York City, or
he might be talking about the Plaka.[197] Boiled down, it is that the
modern civilization chewing up the earth is in need of his power.
Also "blank acreage," that's the parking lots. At one time the poets
celebrated the pastoral quality of the field, which is now turned
into a parking lot.

> But the Power I have I built with my own help!
> That bad wolf approach in dim-divine disguise Power
> All mine! All illumination sheep Power!
> That woodsy savant fetch-eyed scarce perspective from
> Balm-volumed epics that prouds shy fantasy my Power!

You can try to sit down and figure out every one of these lines.
This one, "that woodsy savant," is a wise hermit in the woods, or
a witch or a warlock. "Fetch-eyed," usually used for a woman in a
pastoral painting where she's saying "come along with me." I don't
know why he's using "scarce perspective" except that he's talking

about painting her probably. "Balm-volumed epics," volumes which are like balm in Gilead, [which is] a line of Poe. "Is there balm in Gilead?" That is a question that the gallant knight asks in one of Poe's mysterious little poems. Is there any honey in heaven? Volumes of epics are in themselves balm for Gregory.

> That hand-grenade humor dropped down the hatch
> Of an armoured suit my proposed bit come doomsday Power!

That's actually quite a good definition of his method. "That hand-grenade humor dropped down the hatch of an armoured suit." That's very funny, straight out of comics, like a Disney cartoon or *Tom and Jerry*.

> O joy to my human sparkle Power!
> Joy to its march down the street!
> Ha! The envy of diamonds in the windows!
> The child of Power is laughter!

Having stated and demonstrated his power, the last statement is a mellow, violin cadenza of eternity. Coda.

> October you fat month of gloom and poetry
> It's no longer your melodious graveyard air
> Your night-yanked cypresses
> Your lovely dead moon
> It is October of me! My Power!
> Alive with a joy a sparkle a laugh
> That drops my woe and all woe to the floor
> Like a shot spy[198]

That last line, "like a shot spy," is real sharp, witty, absolutely sparkling. It echoes the very beginning of the poem, "I am the ambassador of power." Constant improvisation, a constant discordant or exuberant human sparkle, line by line. Every line some funny twist, either of syntax or language or shortcut or cartoon archetype image like the "hand-grenade humor dropped down the hatch of an armoured suit."

It's beautiful. Every one of these images is reminiscent of something. If you pay attention to the twists and turns of his mind as he completed these little puzzles, you can do it with words, and you can also do it with ideas. He's great as a poet of ideas, like archetypal ideas, setting them out in a remarkable way that hadn't been said before but had been thought.

"Power is underpowered," meaning anybody that thirsts for power is drinking sand. Anybody that wants power can't have it, in the sense that they're a prey to their desire. So there's no power there. It's like somebody trying too hard to get laid, they can't make it because they're so anxious, that the actual lovemaking is displaced by self-conscious anxiety and ambition. There's no power when there's ambitious and greedy grasping.

CHAPTER 38

Corso and
Herald of the Autochthonic Spirit

A more recent poem [is] called "The Whole Mess . . . Almost," which is one of the supreme poems of the half century in terms of its thought and what it's got to say.

> **The Whole Mess . . . Almost**
> I ran up six flights of stairs
> to my small furnished room
> opened the window
> and began throwing out
> those things most important in life

That's a great opening for a poem. He's proposing the poem to give you an itemization of what's truly important, but he has to set it dramatically in a poem in a witty way that isn't corny. Here's what the most important things are, [stated] in this totally simple way. It gives his whole situation, he lives in a furnished room up six flights. He states his nature, his relation to property, to morals, to ethics, to life itself, and then he begins throwing out those things most important in life.

First to go, Truth, squealing like a fink:
"Don't! I'll tell awful things about you!"
"Oh yeah? Well, I've nothing to hide . . . OUT!"

Among all poets he's the most *maudit,* French for the damned
poet, or the poet who's got a bad reputation. The two greatest lyric
poets of France, Villon and Rimbaud, are both considered *poètes
maudits.* I say van Gogh would be a painter *maudit.*

Then went God, glowering & whimpering in amazement:
"It's not my fault! I'm not the cause of it all!" "OUT!"
Then Love, cooing bribes: "You'll never know impotency!
All the girls on *Vogue* covers, all yours!"
I pushed her fat ass out and screamed:
"You always end up a bummer!"
I picked up Faith Hope Charity
all three clinging together:
"Without us you'll surely die!"
"With you I'm going nuts! Goodbye!"

Then Beauty . . . ah, Beauty—
As I led her to the window
I told her: "You I loved best in life
. . . but you're a killer; Beauty kills!"
Not really meaning to drop her
I immediately ran downstairs
getting there just in time to catch her

With words Gregory has accomplished what they do in cartoons.
It's amazing, the trickery of that, and the simplicity, because he's got

mouthfuls of gibberish in "Power," intelligent gibberish or sensitive combination, but he can also not really mean to drop her. It is the creation of a kind of miracle simile. I don't know another poet who does that. Just totally straight, clear, simple, almost monosyllabic words.

> "You saved me!" she cried
> I put her down and told her: "Move on."

So what else has he got to eliminate? It's the distillation of a lot of the wisdom put into street-smart language. He's dealt with truth, god, love, hate, hope, beauty, so it's actually very interesting. He's taken what he would call the biggies, the big themes, and dealt with them in one or two lines each. Appreciation, but nonattachment, not getting addicted.

> Went back up those six flights
> went to the money
> there was no money to throw out.
> The only thing left in the room was Death

Now he's going to tackle death.

> hiding beneath the kitchen sink:
> "I'm not real!" It cried
> "I'm just a rumor spread by life . . ."

One of Gregory's favorite cocktail party tricks was to go up to someone and say, "I'm never going to die!" Of course you're going to die, but he'd say, "I'm never going to die, because I'll never know it, I'm not going to be there, so I'm not going to die." Very literal people wouldn't understand the level he was talking at. "Of course you're going to die, everybody dies." And Gregory would keep baiting them. "I'm not going to be there, I don't even know about death, don't tell me about death, I don't know anything about it." So this is a little boiled-down version of his routine.

> Laughing I threw it out, kitchen sink and all
> and suddenly realized Humor
> was all that was left—
> All I could do with Humor was to say:
> "Out the window with the window!"[199]

That's a brilliant touch. Out the frame of reference with the frame of reference. Out the conception with the conception. That's like the supreme Zen, one hand clapping, out the window with the window. So the image eliminates itself finally. Conception eliminates conceptualization. The mind erases itself.

CHAPTER 39

Ginsberg's Early Writings

In 1948 Jack Kerouac's first book, *The Town and the City,* was published. I read the manuscript and I was amazed that any of us had actually accomplished a work of art. It was the first time anybody that I knew had done anything that looked like a professional novel. It hadn't occurred to me that we would grow up and do things that were as real as what you read about in the *New York Times.* I was so amazed that I wrote a sonnet after reading Kerouac's manuscript. It refers to the general social scene that we were living in then.

[from Two Sonnets]

I dwelled in Hell on earth to write this rhyme,
I live in stillness now, in living flame;
I witness Heaven in unholy time,
I room in the renowned city, am
Unknown. The fame I dwell in is not mine,
I would not have it. Angels in the air
Serenade my senses in delight.
Intelligence of poets, saints and fair
Characters converse with me all night.

But all the streets are burning everywhere.
The city is burning these multitudes that climb
Her buildings. Their inferno is the same
I scaled as a stupendous blazing stair.
They vanish as I look into the light.

I'm unknown, I dwell in a famous megalopolis, but none of it is mine. I wouldn't have it in those terms, because right now I have a better deal. Angels in air serenade my senses in delight, which is to say Symphony Sid on the radio, playing early bebop, and intelligence of poets, saints, and fair characters conversed with me all night. Quite literally I was hanging around with Neal Cassady and Kerouac and going downtown to Times Square and talking with Herbert Huncke all night long at Bickford's. "But all the streets are burning everywhere." I took that from T. S. Eliot's *Four Quartets*, where he's on a dead patrol in the middle of the night in the fog during an air raid in London. Their inferno is the same. There was a thing called "The Fire Sermon" in T. S. Eliot, "burning burning burning burning | To Carthage then I came | where a cauldron of unholy love boiled about my ears." I was just saying the city is burning, however, the fire for me was like a visionary experience. All the mortals were vanishing as I look into the great rows of paradise. "They vanish as I look into the light." I got inspired by the fact that Kerouac's work seemed to be immortal, so I began comparing his immortality to the mortality of the city itself. And so I wrote a little mock sonnet.

[from Two Sonnets]

Woe unto thee Manhattan
Woe unto thee, Manhattan, woe to thee,
Woe unto all the cities of the world.

Repent, Chicagos, O repent; ah, me!
Los Angeles, now thou art gone so wild,
I think thou art still mighty, yet shall be,
As the earth shook, and San Francisco fell,
An angel in an agony of flame.
City of horrors, New York so much like Hell,
How soon thou shalt be city-without-name,
A tomb of souls, and a poor broken knell.
Fire and fire on London, Moscow shall die,
And Paris her livid atomies be rolled
Together into the Woe of the blazing bell—
All cities then shall toll for their great fame.[200]

It was like a little atomic bomb sonnet. These sonnets are more or less the kind of poetry I was writing at the time, mainly influenced by Sir Thomas Wyatt, John Donne, Andrew Marvell, and metaphysical poetry, which was the vogue at the time. The following poem is a parody of Marvell's "The Garden" and was dedicated to Neal Cassady, but I changed the sex of the reference.

A Lover's Garden

How vainly lovers marvel, all
To make a body, mind, and soul,
Who, winning one white night of grace,
Will weep and rage a year of days,
Or muse forever on a kiss,
If won by a more sad mistress—
Are all these lovers, then, undone
By him and me, who love alone?

O, have the virtues of the mind
Been all for this one love designed?
As seconds on the clock do move,
Each marks another thought of love;
Thought follows thought, and we devise
Each minute to antithesize,
Till, as the hour chimes its tune,
Dialectic, we commune.

The argument our minds create
We do, abed, substantiate;
Nor we disdain, in our delight,
To flatter the old Stagirite[201]:
For in one speedy moment, we
Endure the whole Eternity,
And in our darkened shapes have found
The greater world that we surround.

In this community, the soul
Doth make its act impersonal,
As, locked in a mechanic bliss,
It shudders into nothingness—
Three characters of each may die
To dramatize that Unity.
Timed, placed, and acting thus, the while,
We sit and sing, and sing and smile.

What life is this? What pleasure mine!
Such as no image can insign:
Nor sweet music, understood,
Soft at night, in solitude

At a window, will enwreathe
Such stillness on my brow: I breathe,
And walk on earth, and act my will,
And cry Peace! Peace! and all is still.

Though here, it seems, I must remain,
My thoughtless world, whereon men strain
Through lives of motion without sense,
Farewell! in this benevolence—
That all men may, as I, arrange
A love as simple, sweet, and strange
As few men know; nor can I tell,
But only imitate farewell.[202]

Those of you who have read a little bit of classic English poetry will know Marvell's "The Garden" and I did a little paraphrase of Donne and a little bit of paraphrase of "Come Live with Me and Be My Love." Then I had an actual visionary experience, so I tried to encase the insight of that in the same kind of rhymed hermetic esoteric metaphysical poetry. I wrote a couple enigmatic poems that aren't necessarily understandable, in fact they're probably incomprehensible at this point, but that is what I was doing. Basically this shows where I came from and what I got out of. "The Eye Altering Alters All," a little epigram from Blake.

The Eye Altering Alters All

Many seek and never see,
anyone can tell them why.
O they weep and O they cry
and never take until they try

unless they try it in their sleep
and never some until they die.
I ask many, they ask me.
This is a great mystery.[203]

This was serious because if I were looking at it now I would say that this has a kind of extraordinary rhetorical power, although it's very confused. I would have to say this is a work of some kind of strange genius that didn't surface.

Vision 1948

Dread spirit in me that I ever try
   With written words to move,
Hear thou my plea, at last reply
   To my impotent pen:
Should I endure, and never prove
   Yourself and me in love,
Tell me, spirit, tell me, O what then?

And if not love, why, then, another passion
   For me to pass in image:
Shadow, shadow, and blind vision.
   Dumb roar of the white trance,
Ecstatic shadow out of rage,
   Power out of passage.
Dance, dance, spirit, spirit, dance!

Is it my fancy that the world is still,
   So gentle in her dream?
Outside, great Harlems of the will
   Move under black sleep:

Yet in spiritual scream,
    The saxophones the same
As me in madness call thee from the deep.

I shudder with intelligence and I
    Wake in the deep light
And hear a vast machinery
    Descending without sound,
Intolerable to me, too bright,
    And shaken in the sight
The eye goes blind before the world goes round.[204]

Anybody who's dropped a little acid might make some hermetic message out of it, like an experience of some sort of break in the nature modality of regular thought forms and glimpse of something slightly larger. But since the poetry was a remanipulation of old images and old symbols that were traditional and classical there was no offering of direct perception of whatever it was that was seen and so there is no way to interpret or decipher what the writer has observed. It's just a rehash of words like "light" and "power" and "passage" and "glee." I was reading a lot of Blake, so next I wrote a little song, the first song I ever wrote, when I was having an affair with Neal Cassady. He had decided that it was all over and I went through this visionary experience, a withdrawal symptom, and then felt that in a sense I had suffered a spiritual death.

A Western Ballad

When I died, love, when I died
my heart was broken in your care;
I never suffered love so fair

as now I suffer and abide
when I died, love, when I died.

When I died, love, when I died
I wearied in an endless maze
that men have walked for centuries,
as endless as the gate was wide
when I died, love, when I died.

When I died, love, when I died
there was a war in the upper air:
all that happens, happens there;
there was an angel at my side
when I died, love, when I died.[205]

That form of poetry didn't seem to deliver any direct clarity, however. Kerouac has a character in *The Town and the City,* which had
been modeled on me, Leon Levinsky. I didn't like his caricature, so
I made up for it by writing a poem dedicated to the character called
"Sweet Levinsky."

Sweet Levinsky

Sweet Levinsky in the night
Sweet Levinsky in the light
do you giggle out of spite,
or are you laughing in delight
sweet Levinsky, sweet Levinsky?

Sweet Levinsky, do you tremble
when the cock crows, and dissemble
as you amble to the gambol?

Why so humble when you stumble
sweet Levinsky, sweet Levinsky?

Sweet Levinsky, why so tearful,
sweet Levinsky don't be fearful,
sweet Levinsky here's your earful
of the angels chirping cheerfully
Levinsky, sweet Levinsky,
sweet Levinsky, sweet Levinsky.[206]

There was an interest in bop as well as that lyric and so a little mad song, since we were reading Christopher Smart, who wrote his long poem *Jubilate Agno*. So Kerouac and I collaborated on a lyric, called "Pull My Daisy," and we used that as a title ten years later for a song by David Amram for a film, half an hour film, made by Robert Frank. "Pull my daisy, tip my cup, all my doors are open." I had started a lyric, "Pull my daisy, tip my cup, cut my thoughts for coconuts," meaning that my thoughts had become so palpable, or supposedly some kind of esoteric visionary reference, you know like "Pluck my flower," you know everything's flowered, or "Cut my thoughts for coconuts." Thoughts that are so solid they could be cut like coconuts. However, Kerouac came in with another formula, a different form for the stanza, "Pull my daisy, tip my cup, all my doors are open," and so we worked with that.

Pull My Daisy

Pull my daisy
tip my cup
all my doors are open
Cut my thoughts
for coconuts
all my eggs are broken

Jack my Arden
gate my shades
woe my road is spoken
Silk my garden
rose my days
now my prayers awaken

Bone my shadow
dove my dream
start my halo bleeding
Milk my mind &
make me cream
drink me when you're ready
Hop my heart on
harp my height
seraphs hold me steady
Hip my angel
hype my light
lay it on the needy

Heat the raindrop
sow the eye
bust my dust again
Woe the worm
work the wise
dig my spade the same
Stop the hoax
What's the hex
where's the wake
how's the hicks
take my golden beam

Rob my locker
lick my rocks
leap my cock in school
Rack my lacks
lark my looks
jump right up my hole
Whore my door
beat my door
eat my snake of fool
Craze my hair
bare my poor
asshole shorn of wool

say my oops
ope my shell
bite my naked nut
Roll my bones
ring my bell
call my worm to sup
Pope my parts
pop my pot
raise my daisy up
Poke my pap
pit my plum
let my gap be shut[207]

We were composing it and we went downtown to see Neal Cassady, who was working in a parking lot, and we were doing the phrase "woe the worm, work the wise, dig my spade the same, stop the hoax," and I think Kerouac said, "stop the hoax," I said, "what's the hex," then Kerouac said, "where's the wake?" And Cassady looked at us and said, "How's the hicks?"

The most solid rhyme metaphysical-sounding poem was written next. It's called "Stanzas: Written at Night in Radio City" and that is probably the most successful of these archaic, outdated-style verses. Still it has somewhat of a hippie message in it. I was working as a copy boy for Associated Press and had lots of time at night to write little verses. Simultaneously with that was another kind of poem, totally different in method, called "After All, What Else Is There to Say?"

After All, What Else Is There to Say?

When I sit before a paper
    writing my mind turns
in a kind of feminine
    madness of chatter;
but to think to see, outside,
in a tenement the walls
    of the universe itself
I wait: wait till the sky
    appears as it is,
wait for a moment when
    the poem itself
is my way of speaking out, not
    declaiming of celebrating, yet,
but telling the truth.[208]

The point there is that I was having a kind of schizophrenic poetic method. Then a monk poem that connects them both, called "Metaphysics," which is a Zen-style statement.

Metaphysics

This is the one and only
firmament; therefore
it is the absolute world.
There is no other world.
The circle is complete.
I am living in Eternity.
The ways of this world
are the ways of Heaven.[209]

Then the next move was [a collaboration] with Lucien Carr who
worked for United Press. He had originally introduced me to Kerouac
and introduced Kerouac and myself to Burroughs. He had a kind of
Shakespearean modern voice himself but never did write. I had gotten out of a mental hospital and was working in a ribbon factory in
Paterson and I got fired and went to see him and told him my story.
He said, "I'll show you how to write a poem about that." So he dictated
the following poem, which I took down quite literally and rearranged
it into lines. This should give you some sense of the voice that you'll
hear Kerouac imitating also if you read *Old Angel Midnight*.

How Come He Got Canned at the Ribbon Factory

Chorus of Working Girls
There was this character come in
to pick up all the broken threads
and tie them back into the loom.

He thought that what he didn't know
would do as well as well did, tying
threads together with real small knots.

So there he was shivering in his shoes,
showing his wish to be a god of all the knots
we tended after suffering to learn them up.

But years ago we were employed by Mr. Smith
to tie these knots which it took us all
of six months to perfect. However he showed

no sign of progress learning how after five
weeks of frigid circumstances of his own
making which we made sure he didn't break
out of by freezing up on him. Obviously
he wasn't a real man anyway but a goop.[210]

In another situation Lucien Carr dictated the following text,
which I rearranged into lines because it seemed so sharp. We were
talking about how to write a modern poem and he applied his news-
papery style to it.

The Archetype Poem

Joe Blow has decided
he will no longer
   be a fairy.
He involves himself
in various snatches
   and then hits
a nut named Mary.

He gets in bed with her
   and performs
as what in his mind

would be his usual
  okay job,
which should be solid
  as a rock
  but isn't.

What goes wrong here?
  he says
to himself. I want
  to take her
but she doesn't want
  to take me.

I thought I was
  giving her * * *
and she was giving
  me a man's
position in the world.

Now suddenly she lays
  down the law.
I'm very tired, she says,
  please go.

Is this it? he thinks.
  I didn't want it
to come to that but
I've got to get out
  of this situation.
  So the question
resolves itself: do
  you settle for her

or go? I wouldn't
    give you a nickel,
you aren't much of a doll
    anyway. And he

picks up his pride
and puts on his pants
    —glad enough
to have pants to wear—
    and goes.

Why is it that versions
    of this lack
of communication are
    universal?[211]

However, what was necessary to add to this naturalistic style was
some magical montage taken from the nature of the mind.

CHAPTER 40

Ginsberg and
William Carlos Williams

All along there was William Carlos Williams in Paterson, New Jersey. Around the time I met him he was writing ⌊his long poem⌋ *Paterson*. I had written a couple of letters to him in the late 1940s. Williams was interested in creating his own measure. As his editor John C. Thirlwall says in "Ten Years of a New Rhythm" in *Pictures from Brueghel,* "This measure he was not to find until *Paterson,* developing the 'variable foot' which produced *versos sueltos,* 'loose verses,' as he called them. There was a danger that even with the 'variable foot,' the triadic stanza might become monotonous as free verse had become monotonous." Williams was arranging his lines into triadic stepping-stones down along the page. It was measure that rescued Williams first by rhythmical variations, as the blank verse of Shakespeare and Milton was rescued by rhythmical variations of iambic pentameter. "The iamb is not the normal measure of American speech," Williams told me in 1953. "The foot has to be expanded or contracted in terms of actual speech. The key to modern poetry is measure, which must reflect the flux of modern life. For man and poet must keep pace with his world." He was looking for a variable foot, so to speak, after Einstein, a relative measure, or variable measure. "Relative measure" is another phrase he used. Williams was also investigating the nature of his own speech and the nature of his own mind, just like Kerouac.

I ran into Williams in 1948 and didn't quite understand what he was doing until I heard him read in the Museum of Modern Art. I wrote him a couple of letters and Williams liked them. It was like the voice of Paterson speaking back to him from the streets. He had written a huge epic called *Paterson* and all of a sudden here was a poetic kid from Paterson writing him back, so it knocked him out. Williams got this letter and then wrote back saying, "I'm going to put this in my book, do you mind?" And I said, "Gee, I'm going to be immortal," because I thought he was immortal.

Dear Doctor,

In spite of the gray secrecy of time and my own self-shuddering doubts in these useful rainy days, I'd like to make my presence in Paterson known to you and I hope you will welcome this from me, an unknown poet, to you, an unknown old poet who live in the same rusty county of the world. Not only do I inscribe this missive somewhat in the style of those courteous sages of yore who recognized one another across the generations as brotherly children of the muses (whose names they well know) but also as fellow citizenly Chinamen of the same province, whose gastanks, junkyards, fens of the alley, millways, funeral parlors, river-visions—aye! the falls itself—are images white-woven in their very beards.

I went to see you once briefly two years ago (when I was 21), to interview you for a local newspaper. I wrote the story in fine and simple style, but it was hacked and changed and came out the next week as a labored joke at your expense which I assume you did not get to see. You invited me politely to return, but I did not, as I had nothing to talk about except images of cloudy light, and was not able to speak to you in your own or my own concrete terms. Which failing still hangs with me to a lesser extent, yet I feel ready to approach you once more.

As to my history: I went to Columbia on and off since 1943, working and traveling around the country and aboard ships when I was not in school, studying English. I won a few poetry prizes there and edited the *Columbia Review*. I liked Van Doren most there. I worked later on the Associated Press as a copyboy, and spent most of the last year in a mental hospital; and now I am back in Paterson which is home for the first time in seven years. What I'll do there I don't know yet—my first move was to try and get a job on one of the newspapers here and in Passaic, but that hasn't been successful yet.

My literary liking is Melville in *Pierre* and *The Confidence Man,* and in my own generation, one Jack Kerouac whose first book came out this year.

I do not know if you will like my poetry or not—that is, how far your own inventive persistence excludes less independent or youthful attempts to perfect, renew, transfigure, and make contemporarily real an old style of lyric machinery, which I use to record the struggle with imagination of the clouds, with which I have been concerned. I enclose a few samples of my best writing. All that I have done has a program, consciously or not, running on from phase to phase, from the beginnings of emotional breakdown, to momentary raindrops from the clouds become corporeal, to a renewal of human objectivity which I take to be ultimately identical with no ideas but in things. But this last development I have yet to turn into poetic reality. I envision for myself some kind of new speech—different at least from what I have been writing down—in that it has to be clear statement of fact about misery (and not misery itself), and splendor if there is any out of the subjective wanderings through Paterson. This place is as I say my natural habitat by memory, and I am not following in your traces to be poetic: though I know you will be pleased to realize that at least one actual citizen of your community has inherited your experience in his struggle to love and know his own world-city, through your work, which is an accomplishment you almost cannot have hoped to achieve. It is misery I see (like a tide out of my own fantasy) but mainly the splendor which I carry within me and which all free men do. But harking back to a few sentences pervious, I may need a new measure myself, but though I have a flair for your style I seldom dig exactly what you are doing with cadences, line length, sometimes syntax, etc., and cannot handle your work as a solid object—which properties I assume you rightly claim. I don't understand the measure. I haven't worked with it much either, though, which must make the difference. But I would like to talk with you concretely on this.

I enclose these poems. The first shows you where I was years ago. The second, a kind of dense lyric I instinctively try to imitate—after Crane, Robinson, Tate, and old Englishmen. Then, "The Shroudy Stranger" less interesting as a poem (or less sincere) but it connects observations of things with an old dream of the void—I have real dreams about a classic hooded figure. But this dream has become identified with my own abyss—and with the abyss of old Smokies under the Erie R.R. tracks on Straight Street—so the shroudy stranger speaking from the inside of the old wracked bum of Paterson or anywhere in America. This is only a half made poem (using a few

lines and a situation I had in a dream). I contemplated a long
work on the shroudy stranger, his wanderings. Next an earlier
poem, Radio City, a long lyric written in sickness. Then a mad
song (to be sung by Groucho Marx to a Bop background).
Then an old style ballad-type ghost dream poem. Then, an ode
to the setting sun of abstract ideas, written before leaving the
hospital, and last an Ode to Judgment, which I just wrote, but
which is unfinished. What will come of all this I do not know
yet.

I know this letter finds you in good health, as I saw you speak
at the museum in N.Y. this week. I ran backstage to accost you,
but changed my mind, after waving at you, and ran off again.

Respectfully yours,
A.G.[212]

Then I sent him those poems and he wrote me back, no, they
wouldn't do. Then I went to my journals and took concrete direct
prose statements from my journals and sent that to him, like "Marijuana Notation."

Marijuana Notation

How sick I am!
    that thought
always comes to me
    with horror.
Is it this strange
    for everybody?
But such fugitive feelings
have always been
    my métier.

Baudelaire—yet he had
great joyful moments
   staring into space,
looking into the
   middle distance,
contemplating his image
   in Eternity.
They were his moments
   of identity.
It is solitude that
produces these thoughts.

It is December
almost, they are singing
   Christmas carols
in front of the department
stores down the block on
   Fourteenth Street.[213]

It takes an interior rumination and then suddenly [there's] a switch and the attention goes to the external world from the interior illumination and bullshit. As with marijuana or just plain ordinary mind, suddenly waking up out of interior rumination and putting attention into the external world. Finally I came back to myself or located myself in space and time with a specific image and it was that jump from the interior to the observation of external ground or detail or fact that really struck me. I was high on grass and so it was triply awesome or doubly awesome, the realization that the mind could be spaced out and then come back and focus. That was also an aspect of the notion of a gap or jump from one phase of consciousness to another, one unconscious daydreaming to a real place, a focus on the external phenomenal world.

That is one of the poems I still read a great deal when I give readings, trying to expound where I came from and what I'm doing, and that's very much under the influence of William Carlos Williams's clamp the mind down on objects or get to actuality. At least that's the basis of my poetry. So I put together a bunch of poems for Williams like these. The whole point is that from the subjective babble, meandering, thinking, and daydreaming you've got reality all of a sudden, shifting and becoming aware of the actuality outside, just like Williams was writing about actualities. That he dug immediately.

A couple other little things that I sent him were:

A Meaningless Institution

I was given my bedding, and a bunk
in an enormous ward,
surrounded by hundreds of weeping,
decaying men and women.

I sat on my bunk, three tiers up
next to the ceiling,
looking down the gray aisles.
Old, crippled, dumb people were

bent over sewing. A heavy girl
in a dirty dress
stared at me. I waited
for an official guide to come

and give me instructions.
After awhile, I wandered
off down empty corridors
in search of a toilet.[214]

Instead of getting hung up on metaphysical visionary Rimbaud derangement of the senses, I started looking, like Williams,
to ordinary-mind observations for visionary perception. To look at
ordinary fact rather than supernatural fact. Then "The Trembling of
the Veil," the trembling of the veil of consciousness. The title is taken
from an essay by William Butler Yeats in the 1890s on the trembling
of the veil of civilization. So "trembling of the veil" means coming
on with some big revelation.

The Trembling of the Veil

Today out of the window
the trees seemed like live
organisms on the moon.

Each bough extended upward
covered at the north end
with leaves, like a green

hairy protuberance. I saw
the scarlet-and-pink shoot-tips
of budding leaves wave

delicately in the sunlight,
blown by the breeze,
all the arms of the trees

bending and straining downward
at once when the wind
pushed them.[215]

I was working under the influence of William Carlos Williams's example, who said "direct contact with external phenomenal world is the only way you can, in describing what your perception is of objective reality outside of you, it's the only way you can make a coordinate point where others can see, compare their perceptions with your perceptions." If you describe accurately what you see outside of yourself, you will transmit your mind that way rather than try to do it by means of symbolic or rehash of esoteric symbols, but direct contact with the external world will give you a coordinate to work with other people's perceptions. You present what you perceive through your senses and others will be able to compare their own sense experience with yours, and thus you present your mind. Then I began writing in a more up-to-date modern style, at the same time mixed up with writing rhymed lyrics and straightforward modern poems modeled on Williams. It was just a little animistic description of nature, but taken from fact rather than making a big trip. He immediately wrote back saying, "How many more of these do you have? I shall see that you get a book." He was amazed that somebody understood the quick shift of perception that he was into.

The Bricklayer's Lunch Hour

Two bricklayers are setting the walls
of a cellar in a new dug out patch
of dirt behind an old house of wood
with brown gables grown over with ivy

on a shady street in Denver. It is noon
and one of them wanders off. The young
subordinate bricklayer sits idly for
a few minutes after eating a sandwich
and throwing away the paper bag. He
has on dungarees and is bare above
the waist; he has yellow hair and wears
a smudged but still bright red cap
on his head. He sits idly on top
of the wall on a ladder that is leaned
up between his spread thighs, his head
bent down, gazing uninterestedly at
the paper bag on the grass. He draws
his hand across his breast, and then
slowly rubs his knuckles across the
side of his chin, and rocks to and fro
on the wall. A small cat walks to him
along the top of the wall. He picks
it up, takes off his cap, and puts it
over the kitten's body for a moment.
Meanwhile it is darkening as if to rain
and the wind on top of the trees in the
street comes through almost harshly.[216]

So I'm looking out the window, direct observation, with a kind of erotic projection as you may notice. I was looking at what was going on outside and trying to sketch it, as a painter makes a little sketch. The description of the bricklayer is a bit awash with erotic feeling and the interest in what he did with the little kitty. Then, all of a sudden, this glimpse of the panorama of the space in the sky beyond. It's a jump of attentiveness of the mind from a small thing to awareness of a giant panorama, just like there was a jump in the marijuana notation from thinking about how sick I am to suddenly realizing "It is December almost, they're singing Christmas carols in front of the department stores down the block." Clamping the mind back down on objects, getting back to reality. That was what Williams noticed and dug in the poems that I sent him.

"A Poem on America" was another one. We were all reading Dostoyevsky's *Raw Youth,* his penultimate novel, in which there's a character, Versilov, and so I wrote, "America is like Russia. Acis and Galatea sit by the lake." That was a painting described in the novel.

A Poem on America

America is like Russia.
Acis and Galatea sit by the lake.
We have the proletariat too.

Acis and Galatea sit by the lake.
Versilov wore a hair shirt
and dreamed of classical pictures.

The alleys, the dye works,
Mill Street in the smoke,
melancholy of the bars,
the sadness of long highways,
negroes climbing around
the rusted iron by the river,
the bathing pool hidden
behind the silk factory
fed by its drainage pipes;
all the pictures we carry in our mind

images of the thirties,
depression and class consciousness
transfigured above politics
filled with fire
with the appearance of God.[217]

Well, I don't know about the end. The alleys, the dye works, Mill Street in the smoke, the sadness of long highways. Kerouac loved it and then Williams immediately recognized that and liked it. It was just simple realistic stuff.

CHAPTER 41

Ginsberg and "The Green Automobile"

That was still not energetic enough, it was still like a setting sun in a sense, the notions are still lacklove, haunted, defeat. What was necessary was some kind of a discovery of my own imagination. And that comes out in a poem called "The Green Automobile," which is 1953. Basically it is a reaction to—if I could do what I want, then what would I do? Green is a gay color of Roman togas, or Roman galavant. The poem is prophetic because there's a miraculous college of the body mentioned, which likely enough is an inkling of the Buddhist school Naropa Institute's Jack Kerouac School of Disembodied Poetics.

The Green Automobile

If I had a Green Automobile
    I'd go find my old companion
    in his house on the Western ocean.
        Ha! Ha! Ha! Ha! Ha!

I'd honk my horn at his manly gate,
    inside his wife and three
    children sprawl naked
        on the living room floor.

He'd come running out
    to my car full of heroic beer
    and jump screaming at the wheel
        for he is the greater driver.

We'd pilgrimage to the highest mount
    of our earlier Rocky Mountain visions
    laughing in each other's arms,
        delight surpassing the highest Rockies,

and after old agony, drunk with new years,
    bounding toward the snowy horizon
    blasting the dashboard with original bop
        hot rod on the mountain

we'd batter up the cloudy highway
    where angels of anxiety
    careen through the trees
        and scream out of the engine.

We'd burn all night on the jackpine peak
    seen from Denver in the summer dark,
    forestlike unnatural radiance
        illuminating the mountaintop:

childhood youthtime age & eternity
    would open like sweet trees
    in the nights of another spring
        and dumbfound us with love,

for we can see together
    the beauty of souls
    hidden like diamonds
        in the clock of the world,

like Chinese magicians can
     confound the immortals
     with our intellectuality
          hidden in the mist,

in the Green Automobile
     which I have invented
     imagined and visioned
          on the roads of the world

more real than the engine
     on a track in the desert
     purer than Greyhound and
          swifter than physical jetplane.

Denver! Denver! we'll return
     roaring across the City & County Building lawn
     which catches the pure emerald flame
          streaming in the wake of our auto.

This time we'll buy up the city!
     I cashed a great check in my skull bank
     to found a miraculous college of the body
          up on the bus terminal roof.

But first we'll drive the stations of downtown,
     poolhall flophouse jazzjoint jail
     whorehouse down Folsom
          to the darkest alleys of Larimer

paying respects to Denver's father
     lost on the railroad tracks,
     stupor of wine and silence
          hallowing the slum of his decades,

salute him and his saintly suitcase
    of dark muscatel, drink
    and smash the sweet bottles
        on Diesels in allegiance.

Then we go driving drunk on boulevards
    where armies march and still parade
    staggering under the invisible
        banner of Reality—

hurtling through the street
    in the auto of our fate
    we share an archangelic cigarette
        and tell each other's fortunes:

fames of supernatural illumination,
    bleak rainy gaps of time,
    great art learned in desolation
        and we beat apart after six decades . . .

and on an asphalt crossroad,
    deal with each other in princely
    gentleness once more, recalling
        famous dead talks of other cities.

The windshield's full of tears,
    rain wets our naked breasts,
    we kneel together in the shade
        amid the traffic of night in paradise

and now renew the solitary vow
    we made each other take
    in Texas, once:
        I can't inscribe here. . . .

• • • • • •

• • • • • •

How many Saturday nights will be
    made drunken by this legend?
    How will young Denver come to mourn
        her forgotten sexual angel?

How many boys will strike the black piano
    in imitation of the excess of a native saint?
    Or girls fall wanton under his spectre in the high
        schools of melancholy night?

While all the time in Eternity
    in the wan light of this poem's radio
    we'll sit behind forgotten shades
        hearkening the lost jazz of all Saturdays.

Neal, we'll be real heroes now
    in a war between our cocks and time:
    let's be the angels of the world's desire
        and take the world to bed with us before we die.

Sleeping alone, or with companion,
    girl or fairy sheep or dream,
    I'll fail of lacklove, you, satiety:
        all men fall, our fathers fell before,

but resurrecting that lost flesh
    is but a moment's work of mind:
    an ageless monument to love
        in the imagination:

memorial built out of our own bodies
    consumed by the invisible poem—
    We'll shudder in Denver and endure
        though blood and wrinkles blind our eyes.

So this Green Automobile:
    I give you in flight
    a present, a present
        from my imagination.

We will go riding
    over the Rockies,
    we'll go on riding
        all night long until dawn,

then back to your railroad, the SP
    your house and your children
    and broken leg destiny
        you'll ride down the plains

in the morning: and back
    to my visions, my office
    and eastern apartment
        I'll return to New York.[218]

There are many allusions here. I was reading a lot of William Butler Yeats, [in "Lapis Lazuli"] with his Chinamen, "their ancient, glittering eyes, are gay," so that line about "like Chinese magicians can | confound the immortals | with our intellectuality | hidden in the mist." And from "The Delphic Oracle Upon Plotinus," "Behold that great Plotinus swim | Buffeted by such seas; | Bland Rhadamanthus beckons him, [AG has left out a line here: "But the Golden Race looks dim,"] | Salt blood blocks his eyes." From Yeats was "We'll shudder into Denver and endure | though blood and wrinkles blind our eyes." That's a little paraphrase of Yeats's "Delphic Oracle Upon Plotinus."

The arrangement of the line was interesting because after fifty years of experimentation Williams has come to this approximation of a measure for his speech. [Robert] Creeley noticed it, I noticed, [Robert] Duncan noticed. It was a big deal. Williams was proposing this as the American line or the American measure. In 1953 I began experimenting with it, consciously, in a poem called "Sakyamuni Coming Out from the Mountain."

Sakyamuni Coming Out from the Mountain

He drags his bare feet
        out of a cave
                under a tree,
eyebrows
        grown long with weeping
                and hooknosed woe,
in ragged soft robes
        wearing a fine beard,
                unhappy hands
clasped to his naked breast—
        humility is beatness
                humility is beatness—
faltering
        into the bushes by a stream,
                all things inanimate
but his intelligence—
        stands upright there
                tho trembling:

Arhat
    who sought Heaven
        under a mountain of stone,
sat thinking
    till he realized
        the land of blessedness exists
in the imagination—
    the flash come:
        empty mirror—
how painful to be born again
    wearing a fine beard,
        reentering the world
a bitter wreck of a sage:
    earth before him his only path.
        We can see his soul,
he knows nothing
    like a god:
        shaken
meek wretch—
    humility is beatness
        before the absolute World.[219]

That was also written in triadic and I read it with that slight pause between phrases. I decided I'd better leave New York, so headed out toward Mexico on my way to San Francisco to join Neal Cassady in San Francisco in 1953–54. On the way I stopped off in Cuba where I wrote a minor poem, sketches of Havana called "Havana 1953." It was my 1953 imitation of Kerouac's sketches put into Williams's relative measured triadic line.

Havana 1953

I

The night café—4 A.M.
     Cuba Libre 20c:
          white tiled squares,
triangular neon lights,
     long wooden bar on one side,
          a great delicatessen booth
on the other facing the street.
     In the center
          among the great city midnight drinkers,
by Aldama Palace
     on Gómez corner,
          white men and women
with standing drums,
     mariachis, voices, guitars—
          drumming on tables,
knives on bottles,
     banging on the floor
          and on each other,
with wooden clacks,
     whistling, howling,
          fat women in strapless silk.
Cop talking to the fat-nosed girl
     in a flashy black dress.
          In walks a weird Cézanne
vision of the nowhere hip Cuban:
     tall, thin, check gray suit,
          gray felt shoes,

blaring gambler's hat,
  Cab Calloway pimp's mustachio
    —it comes down to a point in the center—
rushing up generations late talking Cuban,
  pointing a gold-ringed finger
    up toward the yellowed ceiling,
other cigarette hand pointing
  stiff-armed down at his side,
    effeminate:—he sees the cop—
they rush together—they're embracing
  like long lost brothers—
    fatnose forgotten.
Delicate chords
  from the negro guitarino
    —singers at El Rancho Grande,
drunken burlesque
  screams of agony,
    VIVA JALISCO!
I eat a catfish sandwich
  with onions and red sauce
    20¢.[220]

Once in Mexico I lived in the rain forest of Chiapas for several months, working on a cacao plantation, still kind of lacklove. I wrote another little song, the second song I wrote.

Green Valentine Blues

I went in the forest to look for a sign
Fortune to tell and thought to refine;
My green valentine, my green valentine,
What do I know of my green valentine?

I found a strange wild leaf on a vine
Shaped like a heart and as green as was mine,
My green valentine, my green valentine,
How did I use my green valentine?

Bodies I've known and visions I've seen,
Leaves that I gathered as I gather this green
Valentine, valentine, valentine, valentine;
Thus did I use my green valentine.

Madhouse and jailhouses where I shined
Empty apartment beds where I pined,
O desolate rooms! My green valentine,
Where is the heart in which you were outlined?

Souls and nights and dollars and wine,
Old love and remembrance—I resign
All cities, all jazz, all echoes of Time,
But what shall I do with my green valentine?

Much have I seen, and much am I blind,
But none other than I has a leaf of this kind.
Where shall I send you, to what knowing mind,
My green valentine, my green valentine?

Yesterday's love, tomorrow's more fine?
All tonight's sadness in your design.
What does this mean, my green valentine?
Regret, O regret, my green valentine.[221]

While I was in Chichén Itzá and Palenque, cities of the old Maya empire on the Yucatán peninsula, I thought that [it] would be interesting to treat them as if they were the great ruins of Greece that Shelley and Keats wrote about. Why couldn't the Americans use those Central American ruins for the same nostalgia and classical reference, the same sense of the eternal, time in eternity? I wrote [a long poem, "Siesta in Xbalba"] during the six-month period traveling through Mexico. I was living in the jungle area, rain forest near Chiapas.

Once I arrived in California I moved in with Neal Cassady in San Jose. I'd trained with Williams in the sense that I had some idea of direct concrete pictures, objectivity, I had somewhat mastered that. The earlier poems that I'd been writing up to 1955 were examples of that, like "Song" and "In Back of the Real," which Williams liked quite a bit.

In "Song: the weight of the world is love" I talk about a return to my own body, getting back into my own skin. This is straight out of Williams, the idea of isolation, "Yes, yes, that's what I wanted." It's actual speech, real talk, intense fragments of spoken idiom. Later, Louis Zukofsky noticed this poem. Although he ignored "Howl," ignored everything else of mine, this he dug. I was pleased, because this was the basis of everything I was doing, this kind of hearing and balancing. I was trying to do it with longer lines as well. "Song" is considered by that era of poets to be an excellent example of this kind of poetry, where everything is divided up right and the poems are balanced by the ear. Most of the lines indicate a new breath, each pause is a new breath. You especially find it in Creeley, and Olson, and in Williams, and the words "breath stop" I first heard from Williams. You halt the line at the end of the breath or use the breath as the measure of the verse line. That could mean a long, long line with a long breath, or it could be a short breath. That's the way you divide your line, depending on the way that you breathe it.

In Back of the Real

railroad yard in San Jose
    I wandered desolate
in front of a tank factory
    and sat on a bench
near the switchman's shack.
A flower lay on the hay on
    the asphalt highway
—the dread hay flower
    I thought—It had a
brittle black stem and
    corolla of yellowish dirty
spikes like Jesus' inchlong
    crown, and a soiled
dry center cotton tuft
    like a used shaving brush
that's been lying under
    the garage for a year.

This was just a description of a thistle, the center tuft of a dried
thistle.

Yellow, yellow flower, and
    flower of industry,
tough spiky ugly flower,
    flower nonetheless,
with the form of the great yellow
    Rose in your brain!
This is the flower of the World[222]

"Great yellow rose" is a reference to Dante's rose of paradise, at the end of the thirty-fourth canto of *Paradiso*. What I was interested in was the "brittle black stem and corolla of yellowish dirty spikes like Jesus' inchlong crown." I thought that was the best poetry I had written up to that date. It was the most focused and exact and clear and funny at the same time. Williams dug that, comparing a flower to an old used shaving brush that had been lying around in a garage for a year.

Williams's later work, like "Pictures from Brueghel," experimented with this kind of verse, like a used shaving brush that's been under the garage for a year. Around 1948 to 1950 we were interested in trying to arrange it on the page so that it was measurable free verse with some meter or some measure. "Measure" was his word. He got sick of the looseness of free free verse in a sense that there didn't seem to be any basic principle of regularity in it. As people were using it in that day it was sloppy, undisciplined in the sense of no order within it and no sense of proportion and balance. Unbalanced minds writing unbalanced poetry. He became interested in balancing the phrases on the page, weighing them and balancing them, like a mobile, maybe. Something that would have balance within each line. He tried to divide each lengthy line into three parts, triadic, as in the poem "To Daphne and Virginia." It's relatively abstract, but it's an old man talking.

This is 1954 and I was interested in these poems because I was working in a somewhat similar vein. Williams had made an advance in his prosody and was now beginning to arrange his lines in this peculiar way and I was trying to figure out why he was doing it and whether I could use it. I was imitating that.

To Daphne and Virginia

The smell of the heat is boxwood
    when rousing us
        a movement of the air
stirs our thoughts
    that had no life in them
        to a life, a life in which
two women agonize:
    to live and to breathe is no less.
        Two young women.
The box odor
    is the odor of that of which
        partaking separately,
each to herself
    I partake also
      .   .   separately.[223]

He divided his lines that way. It could be written in prose, however, the mind's attention and the eye's attention would go through it so rapidly it would miss certain subtle divisions of phrase. It's the way he talked. Around that time he was saying that he thought American speech tended toward anapestic, or rising verse, as it is called. There are certain phrasings that you could emphasize when you divide it up. There's some kind of humor about the way it is balanced.

[While living in San Francisco] I had a retrospective dream of the late Joan Burroughs who had been killed in Mexico in 1951 just after I visited and I'd been haunted by her memory, because I knew her well. I wondered about what her attitude would be about her husband who had shot her and so had a dream apparition in which

I had a chance to interrogate Joan about it. This was the last poem I wrote before I wrote "Howl" and is in a sense a survey or summary of what might be called the major characters of the Beat Generation as of that date. The style of the poem is more formal. It was a literal record of a dream I had.

Dream Record: June 8, 1955

A drunken night in my house with a
boy, San Francisco: I lay asleep:
darkness:
     I went back to Mexico City
and saw Joan Burroughs leaning
forward in a garden chair, arms
on her knees. She studied me with
clear eyes and downcast smile, her
face restored to a fine beauty
tequila and salt had made strange
before the bullet in her brow.
We talked of the life since then.
Well, what's Burroughs doing now?
Bill on earth, he's in North Africa.
Oh, and Kerouac? Jack still jumps
with the same beat genius as before,
notebooks filled with Buddha.
I hope he makes it, she laughed.
Is Huncke still in the can? No,
last time I saw him on Times Square.
And how is Kenney? Married, drunk
and golden in the East. You? New

loves in the West—
　　Then I knew
she was a dream: and questioned her
—Joan, what kind of knowledge have
the dead? can you still love
your mortal acquaintances?
What do you remember of us?
　　She
faded in front of me— The next instant
I saw her rain-stained tombstone
rear an illegible epitaph
under the gnarled branch of a small
tree in the wild grass
of an unvisited garden in Mexico.[224]

This was a literal record of a dream. Burroughs had shot his wife in a William Tell accident in Mexico and I had been with Joan until about two days before she died. This is now five years later and suddenly she returned in a dream. I was beginning to investigate my dreams, waking up in my dreams and becoming conscious inside the dream. I was aware enough that I could turn the dream in the direction that I wanted. I realized that she was dead and this was my chance to find out straight [from] the mouth of the dead what they knew and how much they could remember. The answer was this quick cut, jump cut, to a graveyard, "an illegible epitaph under the gnarled branch of a small tree in the wild grass of an unvisited garden in Mexico." I woke up with a kind of shock, like a total satori, because I had asked those questions and I got the answer. It wasn't an answer I expected at all. The answer was an implacable tombstone rather than charming Joan leaning forward explaining.

What I found interesting here, besides the sociology and literary history, was the intense frame [of] the dream to the poem. The key seemed to be, as in dreams, the shift from a vivid living image to a montage. Or a jump cut from the image of the person talking to the question "What do you remember of us?" The next thing just a rain-stained tombstone bearing an illegible epitaph under the gnarled branch of a small tree in the wild grass. What I was trying to do was transcribe that almost cinematically, as swiftly as possible. I was interested in the notion of a gap between thoughts, or the gap between words as creating positive and negative holes between two thoughts through which the mind connected the disparate imagery, like lightning flash flint spark. Your mind can fill in the relationship, or in Yeats's phrase, "out of the murderous innocence of the sea." Your mind fills in the gap between murderous and innocence. Or "O ant climb up Mount Fuji, but slowly, slowly." Your mind fills in the gap between the tiny ant and the vast slope of Fuji.

From that I got an idea about the nature of haiku and the nature of poetry and the nature of metaphor. That still sticks with me and is the basis of the rhetoric in "Howl," which has the same immediate jump cuts. They are condensed so that they jump in between the words themselves rather than just scenes like this. I worked on this poem and sent it to Burroughs who was really startled by it.

I also sent a copy to Kenneth Rexroth with a letter explaining my theory. [I said that] what gives the charge or the visionary aspect of poetry is when you present one clear picture and then without any explanation jump to another completely clear picture. The gap or space in between those pictures is a kind of mind space or gap in time or a gap in consciousness or a gap in vision. As in movies, the poignancy or charge or visionary aspect or satori or sunyata or mental electric comes from setting up one pole of thought form or word or picture and then setting up another pole. Then the mind has to fill in the space between by connecting them. The connection that the mind makes is like an electric charge between the two poles. The thought rises naturally in order to connect the two polarized images, disparate images, perhaps even opposite images, perhaps even contradictory images. One minute it's somebody talking, the next minute it's a tombstone.

The theory of poetics that I got out of it was the effect of poetry that makes your hair stand on end on the back of your neck, or gives you [a] shiver on your spine. This is not only in poetry but in other kinds of aesthetic experience. It's akin to déjà vu or religious experience or "new shiver" as invented by Rimbaud and Baudelaire. It's a new shudder, a new wrinkle, a new tingle in art, but the tingle or shock or impact of a work of art is the mind filling in the space between two images.

Rexroth wrote back and said, "Listen Ginsberg, you went to Columbia University too long. You're too old to be going on with all this formal stuff like that, all these bullshit theories. And the poem itself is very stiff and formalistic and academic, what's the matter with you at your age?" So I thought, "Ah, fuck, I've failed again. I can't write poetry." I really worked on "Dream Record" and had revised it over and over again to get just the precise words. All Rexroth could say was that it was an academic exercise. He was right in a way, but I felt like a complete failure as a poet at this point. I decided that I was a failure, quite literally, and gave up. I changed my life quite a bit. I decided I'd go live with Peter Orlovsky and quit my job in market research and began to pick up my unemployment compensation.

CHAPTER 42

Ginsberg and "Howl"

I was about three weeks into my unemployment compensation, after five years working as an executive in market research, when I sat down at the typewriter and thought I would just write whatever I felt like writing, instead of writing a regular poem. Something looser, like prose or something. The first lines of "Howl" are written in somewhat more extended but the same triadic verse as Williams. That's where all that started, the first line of "Howl." "I saw the best minds of my generation," but that seemed a little too long, so "generations destroyed by madness," "generation madness." Those two will balance out in the middle, one side is the generation and the other side is madness like a pack saddle on a mule. "Generation" is one pack and "madness" is another. I did not make any corrections till I was done typing. Later on I began *x*-ing things out and getting all tangled up and messed the thing up a bit.

One of the first lines I thought of was by William Butler Yeats, "Out of the murderous innocence of the sea" in his poem "Prayer for My Daughter." They both fit, the murderous sea and the innocent sea, but usually not together. When you can put words like "murderous" and "innocence" together the mind has to figure out how such a total contradiction makes sense. Naturally there's going to be a little brain pop. There are a number of such mental jump cuts in Blake, like "a robin red breast in a cage, puts all heaven in a rage."

You have to figure those out because they're sort of opposite things. How could a wounded murdered worm forgive the plow? It's an opposite. So poetry in a way is composed of opposites. You take two opposite things and put them together, set them next to each other without any explanation, and the mind has to have a little explosion to make the connection. The mind has to connect them and create an understanding of what the relationship is. The operation of the mind creating that understanding is the aesthetic charge, filling in the gap.

Another example of that gap is a line in *Hamlet,* when the ghost of his father appears on the wall and says, "In the dread vast and middle of the night." I always thought that was such a funny contra-dictory combination of words. The dread vast and middle. Amazing Shakespeare, tremendously conjurative in the sense it does conjure up the big infinity of the night, but also right in the middle of it. That one concept of poetry is, as Aristotle says of metaphor, the apt relationship of dissimilars. Take two dissimilar things and put them side by side and the mind puts them together and relates them. That's what metaphor is like. You're sweeter than a flower.

I began figuring that the more opposite the words, the more amazing the flash in the mind. The mind will create a flash just like a lightning flash between two poles. If you set up a positive and nega-tive pole in the mind, the wider apart they are the bigger the flash will be. The more contradictory the two poles, the more explosive and inclusive the mental flash to bind them together. That was the basic principle I was operating under when I sat down to write "Howl."

I had already experimented with triadic verse forms somewhat like Williams in "The Green Automobile." The first page of "Howl" was basically an attempt at staying within Williams's triadic line. It extended itself a little too much and the lines are heavier and longer and there was a point, "the Brooklyn Bridge, a lost battalion of platonic conversationalists jumping down the stoops," where there was more than could be contained in the three-line triadic form. Within one single breath of thought there were more extended ideas and more extended improvisations. It reminds me of a line of Kerouac's about that a few years later in 1959. He said [in] *The New American Poetry,*

> Add alluvials to end of your line when all is exhausted but something has to be said for some specified irrational reason, since reason can never win out, because poetry is NOT a science. The rhythm of how you decide to "rush" yr statement determines the rhythm of the poem, whether it is a poem in verse-separated lines, or an endless one-line poem called prose . . . (with its paragraphs). So let there be no equivocation about statement, and if you think this is not hard to do, try it. You'll find that your lies are heavier than your intentions. And your confessions lighter than Heaven.
>   Otherwise, who wants to read? [225]

So that's what I was doing. Alluvials, he was referring to James Joyce's "Anna Livia Plurabelle," the mythological eternal woman, heroine of *Finnegans Wake.* Finnegan is masculine, Anna Livia Plurabelle [means] many rivers, the Liffey River. Anna Liffey River of many beauties is the goddess of Joyce's *Finnegans Wake.* When Kerouac said "alluvial" in that line he was talking about *Finnegans Wake* prose, which is the babble sound, the subconscious continuing babble behind the ear. Extra-alliterative assonants and Jupiter pluvians raining out of your brain. After you've thought you've said what you had to say, but you're still thinking of something, you continue saying it. Like "the Brooklyn Bridge, a lost battalion of platonic conversationalists jumping down the stoops." That's what he means by an alluvial. Add extra phrasing, extra tongue mouthings, extra thoughts, just to finish the thought completely and to exhaust the thought spurt.

Basically what I was doing was just making up stuff for my own amusement. As this went along, I had the idea that it couldn't be published anyway, so I might as well be totally free and say anything I wanted, because it wasn't really in poetry form. It didn't succeed in being neatly put together like the Williams triads, it got too clunky and big and dumpy, and then I began breaking up the lines weirdly, so it didn't have any form, I thought. It was prosaic, it wasn't long enough to be a novel and it wasn't short enough to be a lyric, so I figured it wasn't a poem. In that case I might as well write what I felt like, which was a fortunate mistake, because that way I was able to escape the self-consciousness of writing a poem. That is a constant trap, it is *the* constant trap for me continuously, the constant awareness of setting something down which other people will read. Therefore you don't say what you really think, you say something you want them to think you think. It's just as simple as that.

Saying what you actually think, instead of what you want people to think you think, is a big problem. What would you write if you were up on the moon and you knew nobody would ever see it? The writing would be sublime because there would be no reason not to say everything. So that's the method here.

The line was originally "the best minds of my generation starving, mystical, naked," so that was the secret undertone of that. Then when I looked at it, I realized "mystical" was just like a crybaby complaint. Williams wouldn't approve of that, because what the fuck does that mean anyway? But if I said hysterical, which sounded like mystical, all of sudden it brought it down to earth because obviously these people were hysterical and people would recognize hysterical. It also gives it the point of view of *Time* magazine. In other words, this poem was written for the people who read *Time* magazine as well as for the bohemian left.

There are specific things crossed out on the manuscript of "Howl." Here's an interesting one: "anarchy & Blake-light tragedy." It sounded corny, hallucinating anarchy, how can you hallucinate anarchy? You can hallucinate Arkansas, but how can you hallucinate anarchy? Anarchy is an abstraction, so I've put in something that you could hallucinate. It was much better than Arkansas and Blake, but I was digging the idea of putting opposites together, what could be more opposite from Blake-light tragedy than Arkansas, I thought? If I put "Arkansas" next to "Blake-light tragedy" that would create a little flash of "How could these two things be put together?" The very goofiness makes it interesting, the unexpected. When you read it, it's beautiful that way, better than something smooth and pretty.

Then the phrase "among the postwar cynical scholars." I took out "cynical among postwar scholars" because I thought that was too editorializing and then later changed that to "scholars of war." I was thinking of someone like Norman Podhoretz. "Who burned in the hells of poetry," what does that say? I changed that from poetry to turpentine and paint. It had the same sound, "poetry," "turpentine," and if I was going to describe an artist's loft with paint and turpentine I shouldn't say art or poetry. I should just say turpentine and paints or turpentine and pigment or something. "Who ate fire in paint hotels" or "drank turpentine in Paradise Alleys." That's the same thing, in other words, people who suicided themselves or suffered for art, you know. The idea was the old bohemian image of somebody who's suffering for his art as a painter. The original was "who burned in the hells of poetry and making paintings, whose apartments flared up in the joyous fires of their heavenly brains." That was all very corny, so that's all left out. I replaced it with "who ate fire in paint hotels." "Ate fire" was an opposite, a juxtaposition, how can you eat fire? I thought that was somewhat interesting. And "drank turpentine," meaning that he committed suicide.

Mainly I was amazed at just how many lines remained intact. I kept the really good ones. The beginning is more or less the same. "Bared their brains" and so on. "Got busted in their beards" was corny, so it became "busted in their pubic beards."

The precursors to this were things like Apollinaire's poem "Zone." The parallel texts to this, the things I drew on in addition to the "Zone" poem, were Christopher Smart's "Rejoice in the Lamb," which had the same construction. He used "who who who," or "that that that," "and and and" in that poem. Lorca's ode to a bullfighter "Ode to Walt Whitman" has some great lines in it that have these opposites. "You looked for a naked body like a river. Bull and dream who would join wheel with seaweed," trying to describe a boyfriend as a lover, a toreador lover. He has another line about a bullfighter, "Sleep, fly, rest: even the sea dies!" The idea is similar to the "murderous innocence of the sea."

I had a job mopping Bickford's cafeteria, so "mopped all night in desolate Bickford's" is here. "Listening to the crack of doom on the hydrogen jukebox." That was the inspired line, my favorite phrase in "Howl." So hydrogen jukebox is murderous innocence. It's the same thing, taking two opposite words or two words that would be theoretically unrelated and putting them together to make a connection which comes surrealistically from the unconscious but really makes sense. I was talking about that relationship between the extreme roar of sensation of the jukebox and the prophetic apocalyptic lyrics of the jukebox. In those days you had [songs like] "Open the Door, Richard." Neal Cassady and I interpreted that as "open the door to the future, the apocalypse, the door of Christ." Let me in, I want to get into heaven, open the door to the other universe. Anyway, hydrogen jukebox was the method.

You get a general idea of listening to the crack of doom on the jukebox to begin with, but you want to say "the crack of doom on the jukebox" is a little boring, it isn't enough. It needs something else to balance it out, it needs a punch line. You need something that will electrify the jukebox, so to speak. Or you need something to plug in the jukebox to some kind of supersonic metal idea, so you put an opposite word to jukebox. I could have said, "listening to the crack of doom on the classic jukebox." That wouldn't have been too bad, or capitalist jukebox, or communist jukebox. If you have one abstract word, then put another abstract word next to it which is its opposite and you make a concrete image.

That's a classic method from the surrealists. Hop up your image with some totally opposite zonk. You zonk the image with something so weird that people will ask, "How'd you get to that?" One way of doing it is to put the word "meat" in front of it: in front of the meat jukebox, in front of the meat scholar, in front of the meat lady, in front of meat walls. They'll all sound good, "meat" is an invariable, perfect word.

It was a bold move to say "absolute reality" because it's a caricature of itself. That's why it succeeds. The tricks of this particular trade are to take nonsense and elevate it to an art. It's not really nonsense, it's taking the promptings of your imagination, otherwise known as the unconscious, and yoking the unconscious with the conscious. Take an adjective, an unconscious intuition, and yoke it with a conscious noun or a conscious verb. Make it a surrealist or unconscious or imaginative adjective or adverb and yoke it next to a conscious noun or verb. A regular, ordinary thing like an angel. If you take "Indian" and put it next to "angel" it becomes a visionary Indian angel. Well of course nowadays that's corny, but at this time it was a new invention. The idea of putting an Indian next to an angel, or putting "teenage" before "angel" was new in 1957. The notion of the angel was just coming into American mentality around that time, probably on account of peyote being circulated around then, so a certain angelic light ray entered the absolute brain.

"Howl" uses the longer line, like Whitman or Smart, but stuffed with artifacts and noticings of the phenomenal world in a kind of shorthand. [That's] William Carlos Williams's influence, though you'll find a lot of the detail with Whitman if you go through his catalogues, exquisite observation of detail also. The problem is that it's a little long-winded, syntactically, and so use surrealist methods of conjunctions, or juxtapositions of words like "hydrogen jukebox" in order to keep the long line active all the way through, the long, long verse lines, or inject it with a lot of curious interesting sparkles within the line. There are always crazy poetic juxtapositions within the line, phrasings within the line, like "angry fix," or "Mohammedan angel." The Moloch section, trying to make a rhythmic machine, something similar to Shelley's "Ode to the West Wind" or Hart Crane's "Atlantis," which I point to as specimens in this workbook of "Howl" precursors.

When you get to "Moloch whose fate is a cloud of sexless hydrogen," that combination of "sexless hydrogen" is pretty far out, but it's actually got a lot of thought in it. There's the hydrogen bomb, but there's also the displacement of sexuality, all that energy going to war, a displacement of eros, so sexless hydrogen, and also quite literally hydrogen is pretty, it's the liberation of hydrogen, the splitting of the atoms, splitting rather than the atoms hugging and uniting. A lot of the visual imagery of Moloch is taken from surrealist movies such as Fritz Lang's *Metropolis*, *M* with Peter Lorre, another German film, *The Last Will of Dr. Mabuse* by Fritz Lang, the pre-Hitler German films, where the psychological anarchist attacks the police state.

CHAPTER 43

Ginsberg, "Howl," and Christopher Smart

Christopher Smart provided the method of the line when my idea of William Carlos Williams's triadic lines broke down under the pressure of too much to say and too big a breath for the triadic breakdown of the line.

Smart's poem *Rejoice in the Lamb* was a transition text. Christopher Smart was a friend of Dr. Samuel Johnson. He was a great scholar in Greek and Latin and went to Cambridge where he won all the prizes year after year for about fifteen years steady for poetry composition. In those days it was quite an honor and also would lead to a big position in the city, in the diplomatic service, or in society, but Smart was eccentric and would stop on the streets of London and get down on his knees and pray to God. He was always being kicked around and scuffed by the constables. He was also in debt and drank, hanging around Grubb Street and working as a journalist. At that same time he wrote very tight, rhymed, complicated poems, especially *A Song to David,* which is in almost all anthologies. Smart was also one of the few people who could write a good Sapphic verse with his ear tuned to the length of the vowel rather than the accent.

He was one of the [few] people in the whole English tradition who had a good ear, an ear like Ezra Pound wanted twentieth-century poets to develop. An ear for the weight of the syllable or the length of the syllable, the duration of the syllable.

I wrote a poem back in 1948 that went "Smart went crazy, Smart went crazy." He wound up in Bedlam, Bethlehem, a madhouse where he started writing a poem called *Rejoice in the Lamb*. The myth is that he did it three lines a day. He wrote single lines, like a line out of Whitman or the Bible. The method of composition he used was anaphoric. He returned to the margin with a word like "who," like I did in the text of "Howl"—"who did this, who did that."

I got the idea of the structure from reading a lot of Christopher Smart and just imitating him. There are a lot of academic commentators who have looked at my poetry and have said that "Howl" is modeled on examples from Kenneth Fearing and Kenneth Patchen and Carl Sandburg and Whitman but, though I'd read Whitman, I wasn't that interested in his form. I was interested in Smart's form. And I was very familiar with *Rejoice in the Lamb: Jubilate Agno*. The manuscript was never published in Smart's time because everybody thought he was crazy and that his book was off the wall. Finally in 1920 it was put together and published for the first time and everybody said it was like a great modern surrealist poem in a kind of twentieth-century style. It's constructed in antiphonal form.

Rejoice in the Lamb: Jubilate Agno

Rejoice in God, O ye Tongues; give the glory to the Lord, and
   the Lamb.
Nations, and languages, and every Creature, in which is the breath
   of Life.

Let man and beast appear before him, and magnify his name
together.

Let Noah and his company approach the throne of Grace, and do
homage to the Ark of their Salvation.

Let Abraham present a Ram, and worship the God of his
Redemption.

Let Isaac, the Bridegroom, kneel with his Camels, and bless the
hope of his pilgrimage.

Let Jacob, and his speckled Drove adore the good Shepherd of
Israel.

Let Esau offer a scape Goat for his seed, and rejoice in the blessing
of God his father.

It begins "let, let, let, let, let, let." The entire manuscript was so
messed up that by the time the twentieth century came around they
didn't know which page belonged where. It wasn't until probably
about the 1950s that an Oxford scholar arranged the manuscript in
such a way that the facing pages echoed each other. The "let"s were
echoed with the "for"s. After some of the best lines of the opening, it
will go into the antiphonal form, which is a statement and a response.
The statement is "let" and the response is "for." That's similar to "who
burned in the hells of turpentine . . . who purgatoried their torsos."
The form is exactly the same as "Howl"'s form.

Let Moses, the Man of God, bless with a Lizard, in the sweet
majesty of good-nature, and the magnanimity of meekness.

Let Othniel praise God with the Rhinoceros, who put on his
armour for the reward of beauty in the Lord.

Let Tola bless with the Toad, which is the good creature of God,
tho' his virtue is in the secret, and his mention is not made.

Let David bless with the Bear—The beginning of victory to the Lord—to the Lord the perfection of excellence—Hallelujah from the heart of God, and from the hand of the artist inimitable, and from the echo of the heavenly harp in sweetness magnifical and mighty.

Let Joseph, who from the abundance of his blessing may spare to him, that lacketh, praise with the Crocodile, which is pleasant and pure, when he is interpreted, tho' his look is of terror and offence.

Let Ucal bless with the Chameleon, which feedeth on the Flowers and washeth himself in the dew.

Let Jebus bless with the Camelopard, which is good to carry and to parry and to kneel.

Let Huldah bless with the Silkworm—the ornaments of the Proud are from the bowels of their Betters.

Let Malchiah bless with the Gnat—it is good for man and beast to mend their pace.

Let Mattithiah bless with the Bat, who inhabiteth the desolations of pride and flieth amongst the tombs.

Let Asaph rejoice with the Nightingale—The musician of the Lord! and the watchman of the Lord!

Let Zurishaddai with the Polish Cock rejoice—The Lord restore peace to Europe.
For I meditate the peace of Europe amongst family bickerings and domestic jars.

Let Helon rejoice with the Woodpecker—the Lord encourage the
propagation of trees!
For the merciful man is merciful to his beast, and to the trees that
give them shelter.

Let Amos rejoice with the Coote—prepare to meet thy God,
O Israel.
For he hath turned the shadow of death into the morning, the
Lord is his name.

Let Ephah rejoice with Buprestis, the Lord endue us with temper-
ance and humanity, till every cow have her mate!
For I am come home again, but there is nobody to kill the calf or
to pay the musick.
For I shou'd have avail'd myself of waggery, had not malice been
multitudinous.
For there are still serpents that can speak—God bless my head,
my heart and my heel.

He's using biblical names and then scientific names for animals
and then responding with funny, totally personal, madhouse proph-
ecies. It's good writing, good sounding. Some kind of completely
eccentric individual bedlam humor, conjunctions of classical mythology and Colonel Draper.

For I am a little fellow, which is entitled to the great mess by the
benevolence of God my father.
For I this day made over my inheritance to my mother in consideration of her infirmities.
For I this day make over my inheritance to my mother in consideration of her age.

For I this day made over my inheritance to my mother in consideration of her poverty.

For I bless the thirteenth of August, in which I had the grace to
obey the voice of Christ in my conscience.

For I bless the thirteenth of August, in which I was willing to run
all hazards for the sake of the name of the Lord.

For I bless the thirteenth of August, in which I was willing to be
called a fool for the sake of Christ.

For I lent my flocks and my herds and my lands at once unto the
Lord.

For nature is more various than observation tho' observers be
innumerable.

That's really a knockout. That's really totally cornerless mystery.
Post-Einsteinian. He was very sharp and smart. Smart was smart.

For my seed shall worship the Lord JESUS as numerous and musical as the grasshoppers of Paradise.

The rhetoric of "Howl" comes straight out of "the grasshoppers of Paradise." Remember I was talking about putting opposite
abstractions together? The grasshoppers and paradise. Take paradise,
which is a theory, and you put a grasshopper in it, and you have what
would be in the twentieth century a surrealist combination. This
kind of completely wild language combination is rare. You get it in
Shakespeare, strangely. You get it in good poetry, but it's abundant
here. Hardly anybody writes as well as that. There's a funny kind of
insight in it.

On page two [of "Howl"] my literary references are to Robert Fludd. "Who studied cabbala and Fludd." He was a hermetic

philosopher in England, who had a picture of the universal body in the design of man. Yeats depended a lot on Robert Fludd. He was the great English inspirer and an interesting character, seventeenth century, magician, hermetic alchemist. It was "cabbala and Wilhelm Reich," originally. Gurdjieff, Reich, and orgones, I think. "Because the cosmos instinctively vibrated at their feet in Kansas," but that's the best part of the line and I kept that straight. I changed that to "who studied Plotinus, Poe, St. John of the Cross, telepathy and bop kabala." The reason I changed that was that it ran trippingly on the tongue. It was a beboppy line that way.

Under Burroughs's suggestion, I was reading a lot of cycles of history, realizing just at this time when the American century, the American empire was being proclaimed by the CIA and Henry Luce and his organizations. I was thinking a lot about the decline of the West and the decline of America, the fall of America. There are references to Giambattista Vico too. Joyce's *Finnegans Wake* is founded on Vico's cyclical vision of history. Vico was a big, important reference point for a lot of twentieth-century modernist poets, a renaissance historian and scholar.

While we're at it, Spengler. The Modern Library edition of *The Decline of the West* is abridged, unfortunately.

At this level all civilizations enter upon a stage, which lasts for centuries, of appalling depopulation. The whole pyramid of cultural man vanishes. It crumbles from the summit, first the world-cities, then the provincial forms and finally, the land itself, whose best blood has incontently poured into the towns, merely to bolster them up for awhile. At the last, only the primitive blood remains, alive, but robbed of its strongest and most promising elements. This residue is the fellaheen.

Consequently we find everywhere in these Civilizations that the provincial cities at an early stage, and the giant cities in turn at the end of the evolution, stand empty, harbouring in their stone masses a small population of fellaheen who shelter in them as the men of the Stone Age sheltered in caves and pile-dwellings. Samarra was abandoned by the tenth century; Pataliputra, Asoka's capital, was an immense and completely uninhabited waste of houses when the Chinese traveller Hsüan Tsang visited it about A.D. 635, and many of the great Maya cities must have been in that condition even in Cortez's time. In a long series of Classical writers from Polybius onward we read of old, renowned cities in which the streets have become lines of empty, crumbling shells, where the cattle browse in forum and gymnasium, and the amphitheatre is a sown field, dotted with emergent statues and hermae. Rome had in the fifth century of our era the population of a village, but its Imperial palaces were still habitable.

This, then, is the conclusion of the city's history; growing from primitive barter-centre to Culture-city

By "Culture-city" he means the time of greatest energy and vigor, when the original techniques and implements and inspirations and Faustian conceptions had muscle and strength, finally coming into a fruition. Then an imperial phase where the cities' wealth is spent in imperial armies and expenditures on rockets and trophy horses.

and at last to world-city, it sacrifices first the blood and soul of its creators to the needs of its majestic evolution, and then the last flower of that growth to the spirit of Civilization—and so, doomed, moves on to final self-destruction.

As for the fellaheen,

> Life as experienced by primitive and by fellaheen peoples is just
> the zoological up and down, a planless happening without goal or
> cadenced march in time, wherein occurrences are many, but, in the
> last analysis, devoid of significance. The only historical peoples,
> the peoples whose existence is *world-history,* are the nations.[226]

Kerouac was picking up on the fellaheen as people outside of history, and therefore free of history, free to be themselves, free to look into each other's eyes, smoke a little grass, listen to jazz, and have a good time. So he abandoned the Hitlerian-Faustian ambitiousness of Spengler and said, "The earth is an Indian thing." The fellaheen were the Indians that would inherit the earth when the big world-cities had passed over with their mortars and tractors and petrochemical agriculture and had finally ruined their oasis, ruined the land, crumbled the land, and eroded the fertile land, drained and poisoned all the rivers, as happened in Egypt and in Mesopotamia, cut down all the forests as happened in China and India in the eleventh century. It happened to the Americas in the nineteenth century and ruined and made barren the actual habitable land as civilization declined. Wasting all their blood and money and raw materials on conquest and imperial wars just like the Romans. Extending their empire outward cost them more to maintain than they ever got out of it.

"Who painted their pictures on fish paper." In 1950 a lot of painters in New York were poor and were using fish-wrapping paper to paint their pictures on the Lower East Side. One nice line on page four is "returning to the magnetic reality of the wards." That's not bad. This gives an idea of how "Howl" was modified and changed.

CHAPTER 44

Ginsberg and Cézanne

Kerouac shamed me into doing spontaneous writing by about 1953. I didn't really get it on until I wrote "Howl," though, that was the first time I accepted his message and worked on it. "Howl," "Sunflower Sutra," that whole period was a breakthrough for me where I finally abandoned any prior idea I had of writing poetry and just wrote. I decided that I wasn't going to write poetry, because whatever I wrote was going to be whatever I wrote and it didn't have to have a name [like] poetry or prose or scribbling or anything. Why do you have to know what you're doing all of a sudden? Like saying you're going out to take a walk and you know every step you're going to take in advance. Who needs that?

I learned that from Cézanne, because Cézanne was interested in his method and wasn't interested in other things. He had the idea that he'd like to paint those things that they put up in the museums, but he didn't know how, so he just painted whatever he could paint. He became interested in this special kind of painting and then after a while he realized this was the same way Poussin worked. They put it in the museum after you paint it, but first you've got to paint it.

The method I worked out finally was a compromise, because I don't feel confident like Kerouac just to write a lot, giant pieces, and then put them out. My own method is that I keep a journal and anything that goes into the journal is anything that goes into the journal. Then a couple months or years later I'll go through it and pick out the things that look like poems. Things that have a beginning, a middle, and an end, and are in separate lines rather than paragraphs, and seem to have some kind of poem theme. Those I'll separate out and type up and sometimes present them without any change. Sometimes I don't realize that they are poems until they are typed up. Then I'll read it aloud a lot, maybe for a year or two or three years until I'm ready to send in a manuscript, and in the course of reading it aloud I'll find out what are the weak spots. I'll find there are certain dead areas that I find a drag to read and I might cut them out or improve them. So I depend on the original spurt and cadence and structure and then over years I might make changes on the basis of reading. The poems I like best, the poems that seem to be strongest, are those which don't require changes. And there's quite a few of those.

When I was hanging around with Kerouac in the 1950s, I always felt like a shabby, shoddy, shallow liar all the time. How was I going to live up to his ideal? But then Kerouac said, "I myself have trouble covering up my bullshit lies too." He felt that way too, so it was a question of courage, being a liar and having the courage to go on, and reveal yourself inadvertently, let it go anyway.

CHAPTER 45

Ginsberg and the San Francisco Renaissance

We're now up to the period of the San Francisco Poetry Renaissance. Having prepared the ground with William Carlos Williams's style [of] realistic description, then the next stage was to expand on that, take a combination of "The Green Automobile," making use of the imaginative expansion, the notion of swift mind jumps, to allowing the mind to free play and using a basic realistic theme we arrived at "Howl" and later poems. In "Transcription of Organ Music" it's an attempt to sketch.

In the same mode, "Sather Gate Illumination." Sather Gate is at the University of California in Berkeley. It's the gate that leads down to Telegraph Avenue and it's a plaza where people meet and sit and read and talk and gossip or write poems.

We were back and forth to Europe and on the return a summary poem, July 1958, so I'm skipping two years. "'Back on Times Square, Dreaming of Times Square'" is an old Zen or haiku-ish poem, returning to Kyoto dreaming of Kyoto.

'Back on Times Square, Dreaming of Times Square'

Let some sad trumpeter stand
  on the empty streets at dawn
and blow a silver chorus to the
  buildings of Times Square,
memorial of ten years, at 5 A.M., with
   the thin white moon just
     visible
  above the green & grooking McGraw
   Hill offices
a cop walks by, but he's invisible
  with his music

The Globe Hotel, Garver lay in
  gray beds there and hunched his
  back and cleaned his needles—
where I lay many nights on the nod
  from his leftover bloody cottons
  and dreamed of Blake's voice talking—
  I was lonely,
   Garver's dead in Mexico two years,
  hotel's vanished into a parking lot
And I'm back here—sitting on the streets
again—
The movies took our language, the
  great red signs
A DOUBLE BILL OF GASSERS
  Teen Age Nightmare
  Hooligans of the Moon

But we were never nightmare
hooligans but seekers of
the blond nose for Truth

Some old men are still alive, but
the old Junkies are gone—

We are a legend, invisible but
legendary, as prophesied[227]

So that covers that.

In a more recent poem called "Today" I was very much influenced by Kenneth Koch and Frank O'Hara. The key here is to write different kinds of poetry, so you don't have to be stuck with one kind of poetry. This is the kind of poetry you write when you can't think of anything to write. Suddenly you realize, well, why not the world as it is? Why do I have to wait for a big inspiration or fake it?

CHAPTER 46

John Clellon Holmes

In 1948 I had a visionary experience. I talked about it quite a bit both to Kerouac and to John Clellon Holmes and Holmes made use of it in his book *Go*, published in 1952. It was probably written the same time as *On the Road* although it was published first and used many of the same characters as Kerouac. It was a laborious novel and Holmes has the character of David Stofsky, who was modeled on myself, as well as [characters modeled on] Neal Cassady, Huncke, and Kerouac.

Holmes had an apartment on Lexington Avenue at 56th Street where several novelists and intellectuals hung out between 1946 and 1950. There was Alan Harrington who was a very interesting minor novelist, A. J. Ayres the philosopher, Neal Cassady the automobile driver, Kerouac, myself, all of us mixing together in the apartment. Holmes was a very dignified fellow whose idea was to be a novelist, like a novelist novelist, like Steinbeck or Dos Passos or Dostoyevsky. [He wanted to] write big books about major cultural tendencies. His novel *Go* is one of the best sociological, historical novels dealing with that period of 1947 and 1948. I don't like the novel, in fact I can't stand it, and I don't like my own character in it. It tends to flatten out or make garish and vulgar certain very delicate matters, like visionary experience. Holmes's prose was a little exaggerated and not quite as delicate as I thought Kerouac's was. I was upset when I first saw the book. I tried rereading it recently and I got equally upset. I was supposed to write a preface, being an elder statesman, but I was too ashamed of the prose to do it. So Holmes, whom I love, got mad at me.

Holmes got some of his ideas from Kerouac. By the time *Go* was published, Kerouac had finished four books, so Kerouac got mad at Holmes for stealing his theme, although he had given him the theme. Kerouac was always resentful and sometimes paranoid, thinking that he was a British Shakespeare and that [although] other people were getting their novels and poems published nobody was publishing his books.

Another book at that time was *Who Walk in Darkness* by Chandler Brossard, which was about a junkie in Greenwich Village. I don't think *Go*, *The Horn* [Holmes's second book], and *Who Walk in Darkness* are the same high-quality prose, they don't have the same kind of angelic ambition and panoramic awareness and taste of mortality and Dostoyevskean sense of confrontation of one soul with another that you find in Kerouac. They're minor works, indicative sociologically, and aesthetically interesting occasionally, but they never would have made a generation of literature. Holmes was interested in generational literary notions, like Hemingway, Steinbeck, and all that. He was considered by *Partisan Review* and *New York Times* as the respectable Malcolm Cowley-esque literary critic, responsible spokesman, humane, pipe smoking, somewhat professorial, reliable, and defendable essayist who would explain the strange shenanigans of the new generation.

This is Holmes's version of Stofsky's [Ginsberg's] vision, Holmes's view of this kind of metaphysical shenanigans.

Stofsky sat, propped up like an invalid in his armchair, feverishly reading Blake by the early afternoon light through his windows. An intense silence actually seemed to grip the room as his eyes darted along the page and his mind swam.

"I wander through each charter'd street . . . {quoting Blake's "London"} Marks of weakness, marks of woe."

The pitch of the day before had not let down. He was in the midst of a sort of delirium that seemed to transform everything around him. He had spent the whole day devouring, at one and the same time, Blake and Kierkegaard, although the latter had been slow and he had skipped. But he mulled each poem of Blake's, tracing his finger along every line of print, making a perfect, sharpened point of his mind so as to crack the images open. And then that morning, upon arising with a strange magnified emotion, he had found himself anticipating each metaphor, and the heart of the poetry seemed visible to him through a brilliant and, up until then, blinding glare.

He tossed the book aside, tipping over a glass, and snatched up paper and pencil, and wrote without stopping—an avid and incredulous expression transfixing his features:

"Flower of soul, flower of glare,
Stricken Rose who is so numb:
Is this shrunk impulse, like a star,
A prideful light where I succumb?
I head where dreadful wisdoms are:
Is this the knowledge that is numb?"

He sat there quivering a little, staring at the lines with a feeling of acute surprise, yet not really reading what he had just written.

Moments came like this now: separated from all others, and from his surroundings, as by immense voids of meaning; and yet they seemed to be limp with light of a whiteness and power to illuminate unlike any he had ever experienced. He basked in these blank moments of entranced cognition as though will-less.[228]

Then, the description of the character Stofsky going into the bookstore at Columbia, meandering through the bookstore, bookstore shelves and stacks.

Lines kept on pulsing through his head and, when staring at a page, before his eyes as well:

"The look of love alarms . . .
The weeping child could not be heard . . .
And her thorns were my only delight . . ."

Then, without warning, it happened for the first time. Aware of a sudden flush of warmth, he looked up over the edge of the book he was holding, out into the store and back through its whole length in the direction he had been working, until his gaze reached the door. It seemed a terrible distance. But everything was different, doused in that same all revealing glare of whiteness, and yet also as it normally was. He seemed to have gained a sort of X-ray perception, and he peered through the stacks of books and the browsing students as though the surface of reality was some kind of film-negative. He was at once startled and paralyzed as he had been the night before.
[. . .]
A vision! A vision! The words kept stinging into his consciousness like quickening waves of fever. As he went on, almost running

now, he found himself haunted by the odd uprush of pity and rage that had taken control of him during the moment in the book store. It was love! he cried to himself. A molecular ectoplasm hurtling through everything like a wild, bright light! And they were afraid, afraid, almost as if they all suspected. He had seen it clearly, in an instant of pure clarity: the chemical warm love that swam thickly beneath their dread![229]

There's more to that later, but the thing I remember most from reading it in 1953 was "he had a remote sensation that his eyes were giving off pools of red light that changed to white and then faded palely away." At the time it seemed like terrible hokum to me, although he was describing my experience through his interpretation of what I had described to him. My first reaction when I read it was one of cringing and embarrassment, that it had come out so corny or seemed so drugged and hallucinatory, pitifully creepy, in fact.

The poems Holmes is paraphrasing were written between 1948 and 1950 in a book called *The Gates of Wrath*. His paraphrases are pretty funny, "Flower of soul, flower of glare, Stricken Rose who is so numb."

Rose of spirit, rose of light,
Flower whereof all will tell,
Is this black vision of my sight
The fashion of a prideful spell,
Mystic charm or magic bright,
O Judgment of fire and of fright?

What everlasting force confounded
In its being, like some human

Spirit shrunken in a bounded
Immortality, what Blossom
Gathers us inward, astounded?
Is this the sickness that is Doom?[230]

Mine is just as corny as his, I guess. "See the changing dolls that gaze . . . the changing . . . of dancing glare" is more his own. Probably he got that from "Voice of Rock."

I cannot sleep, I cannot sleep
until a victim is resigned;
a shadow holds me in his keep
and seeks the bones that he must find;
and hoveled in a shroudy heap
dead eyes see, and dead eyes weep,
dead men from the coffin creep,
nightmare of murder in the mind.

Murder has the ghost of shame
that lies abed with me in dirt
and mouths the matter of my fame.
With voice of rock, and rock engirt,
a shadow cries out in my name;
he struggles for my writhing frame;
my death and his were not the same,
what wounds have I that he is hurt?

This is such murder that my own
incorporeal blood is shed,
but shadow changes into bone,
and thoughts are doubled in my head;

for what he knows and I have known
is, like a crystal lost in stone,
hidden in skin and buried down,
blind as the vision of the dead.[231]

Whatever that means now. What I meant then by "voice of rock" was some kind of visionary voice of absolute, ultimate, big basso profundo rocklike prophecy. And "I can't sleep" because this other part of my own nature wants to be heard and will not be heard until I myself personally die. Then the other doppelganger, visionary, prophetic voice of rock takes over. That is a little bit schizophrenic and maybe Holmes was right, maybe that's the way I appear to him. What I thought were visionary experiences were more akin to the naturalistic description that Huncke gave rather than this theatrical version that John Holmes eloquently fictionalized. When I first read it I was absolutely horrified, and said, "Oh, my God, everybody's going to get the wrong idea."

Holmes's version is like some descriptions of acid trips, especially the electrical part. He hadn't had acid and I don't think peyote was on the scene when he wrote that. He'd had a lot of grass, because Neal Cassady had come to New York and we had all started smoking grass. I had turned Neal on to grass and then he picked up on it very strongly back in California. Then he went down to Mexico and brought some back maybe and turned on John Holmes and Kerouac and myself quite often. In those days smoking grass was kind of a breakthrough. I remember getting into trembling fits and giant paranoiac ecstasies, which is one of the first virgin kicks of smoking cannabis. This might have been an extrapolation from his own grass experience or just purely imaginary. We were all looking at *Varieties of Religious Experience* by William James, which was a book commonly read at that time for reference to states of consciousness.

At any rate, you can see from Holmes's book that there was a preoccupation with an altered state of mind or an enlarged or expanded consciousness, a new consciousness. That phrase "new consciousness," or supreme reality or new vision, had been bandied about from Kerouac's mouth to mine and a few other people from 1945 on. You can find that phrase occasionally mocking me in Kerouac poems: "So what, you got gefilte fish for the new consciousness?"

In 1951, 1952, 1953, nobody had published anything except a few rare novels. [Kerouac had published *The Town and the City*] and Burroughs had published *Junkie* under the pseudonym William Lee. The only "artifact" of that era was an essay by John Clellon Holmes in the *New York Times* magazine, saying, "This is the Beat Generation."[232] It was an article that Kerouac didn't like much, incidentally. It was an account of a conversation with Kerouac in Holmes's apartment on Lexington Avenue in 1948 or 1949. Kerouac had very casually said, "Naw, this isn't a lost generation, this is a beat generation." Just meaning nothing special, not intending to make a big slogan. However, it was so apt and appropriate and poetic that Holmes picked up on it in terms of headline, or in terms of a literary generation, stylism, and wrote the article for the *Times*.

Like [Norman] Mailer and [Lawrence] Lipton and almost every other intellectual commentator, Holmes dwelt at great length on violence, on the elements of psychopathic violence. Like juvenile delinquents with knives cutting their grandmothers' throats or drowning little kittens for fun. The kind of alienation that society had better watch out for if it wanted to be healthy. They were saying that society in general had better watch out because these young people were committing *actes gratuits*, gratuitous acts, like murdering old ladies in empty lots. They said that this was some form of social protest and so society had better take note of what the social protest was about.

Kerouac objected to that because he thought that the original perception had been of the lamb of mind, "kind king light of mind," heart to heart, Dostoyevskean confrontation, mellowness. What is now being recognized as the purity of the original Beat group. [Ken] Kesey, for instance, commented that he felt more akin to the old beatniks than the later hippie phase. There does seem to be a revival these days culturally, in the punk movement, of Kerouac of the 1950s style, which is to say nonpolitical. Looking for kicks, or looking for soul, or looking for lost Saturday night personal romance mystery. Some people see this as a return to the silent 1950s, silent 1970s apathy, but other people, myself included, see it as a deepening of insight, and the entry of the void, sunyata, dharma, the entry of emptiness into our skulls, awareness of death as the original beatnik perception, and so a deepening of heart rather than a shallowness of heart.

Holmes's second book, *The Horn,* was taken from an anecdote Kerouac told about a jazz player who used to play with his horn up at the side of his mouth and as time went on, as dope and time weakened the imaginary character in *The Horn,* the horn became vertical. So the idea was Kerouac's to write a novel about a horn player, "the" horn player, the Prez, the Bird. It was quite a good genre piece about jazz and is a minor classic.

CHAPTER 47

Peter Orlovsky

Peter Orlovsky is an old veteran of the spiritual wars in America and a very central figure in Beat Generation cultural and literary development, both as a cultural activist and as an historically important poet. Peter was considered in 1959 by William Carlos Williams to be the most gifted lyric poet of all of the poets that were associated with the Beat Generation. This was documented in the Wagner College literary review[233] when William Carlos Williams wrote a small critique of these writers on the occasion of a very early and historically interesting Beat celebration out at Wagner College organized by a young student, Gerard Malanga, who later became a poet and also an intimate of Andy Warhol and the central figure in Andy Warhol's original movie *Sleep* and one of the people who worked at Warhol's factory. At that early time [there] was a congregation of LeRoi Jones, Ray Bremser, myself, and Peter Orlovsky, out at the college on Staten Island, of all places. I think that was the first venue in New York where everybody came together. We joined with people that were involved with underground film.

By 1954–55 Peter Orlovsky was an integral part of the San Francisco Renaissance group, and as such is memorialized by Kerouac in the book *Dharma Bums* as well as *Desolation Angels*. Peter was present at the historic reading [the Six Gallery] where I first read my poem "Howl," and Gary Snyder, Philip Whalen, Michael McClure, Philip Lamantia, and Kenneth Rexroth attended and read, all of them giving their first poetry readings at a series of historic readings that both Kerouac and Neal Cassady were a part of in the audience. That series inaugurated the new wave of poetry vocalized, before an audience, rather than read just on the page, carrying out Whitman's instructions for a poetry that was out loud and not just for scholars and not just imitating the older literary style.

Orlovsky went on through Europe during the early days of Beat exile and lived for a long time with Gregory Corso and myself in Paris and with William Burroughs in Tangier in 1957 and again in 1961. Then he went on his own through Greece, Cairo, Jordan, Jerusalem, Israel, and then joined with other poets including Gary Snyder and Joanne Kyger on a year-and-a-half, two-year trip to India, which was perhaps the significant cultural India trip that began a whole wave of young kids with long hair going to India and smoking hashish and going up to Nepal. That particular trip is considered by historians to be one of the significant moves, along with Kerouac's *Dharma Bums*, in the introduction of Buddhism to the United States by this cross-fertilization and young guys trekking back and forth. Orlovsky then went back through Persia and the Middle East before returning to New York.

He had a long experience as a mental hospital attendant and an ambulance driver and so was quite competent to take care of people. As I said he then went on to India later and there took care of lepers and beggars in Benares in the burning grounds and marketplaces. Throughout the 1960s he has been one of the stalwart poets of the antiwar movement and a leader in the commune where he was the manager of the Committee on Poetry farm upstate New York. Ray

Bremser, Charlie Plymell, Gregory Corso, Robert Creeley, and many other poets visited and stayed there. And so he's had a long long history and knows a great deal and has a very good memory and has published his book *Clean Asshole Poems and Smiling Vegetable Songs* from City Lights in 1978. In 1980 *Straight Hearts' Delight* was published filled with letters, literary letters, and poems exchanged between myself and him.

CHAPTER 48

Carl Solomon

Carl Solomon is a graduate of Brooklyn College and an extraordinary prose poet and critic. He writes in the style of an American French surrealist dadaist. Carl and I first met almost forty years ago in the hallway of the New York State Psychiatric Institute, where we were both inpatients. I was coming in bewildered as a Columbia graduate, who had gotten caught in the usual undergraduate bust, in other words, dope. I was advertised as the genius college boy who was conducting a network of organized burglaries. My parents had to choose between sending me to jail or having me put away in the booby hatch. Everyone felt that I was a middle-class kid who had just gone wrong and needed a little straightening out. So I wound up in the psychiatric institute on 168th Street.

On my admission day I remember I had to sit waiting to be assigned a room and I ran into a fellow trudging up the hall, coming up from shock, named Carl Solomon. We didn't know each other, so he asked me who I was and I said, "I'm Prince Myshkin" Prince Myshkin is the hero of Dostoyevsky's *The Idiot*. Carl's reply after I said I'm Prince Myshkin was to say that he was Kirillov. Kirillov was the political heavy in *The Possessed*. Carl's orientation is interestingly and intensely political. His "Report from the Asylum: Afterthoughts of a Shock Patient" from *Mishaps Perhaps* was written just after getting out of New York State Psychiatric Institute in the late forties. We were classmates there and spent a lot of time discussing the nature of reality.

While we were in the madhouse under the influence of the dadists and surrealists, we wrote a letter to T. S. Eliot. It is a totally punk letter, but there is an element of truth in it. We never sent the letter because we were basically sane, we saw ourselves as a bunch of humorists occupying the psychiatric institute for purposes of literary experimentation. One text which was influential on us in 1948–49 is the stylistic precursor of that letter to T. S. Eliot. It is the "Dada Manifesto" by Tristan Tzara, the manifesto by Monsieur Antipyrine.

I used Carl in a sense, or abused Carl, by dedicating my poem "Howl: For Carl Solomon" to him. That's been a burden to him because it typecasts him in a way which he is not. The line in "Howl" is "who threw potato salad at CCNY lecturers on Dadaism and subsequently presented themselves on the granite steps of the madhouse with shaven heads and harlequin speech of suicide, demanding instantaneous lobotomy." Well, that was Carl. I used poetic license, in that he attended Brooklyn College, it wasn't CCNY, but the rest is true.

Solomon's books are not very well known. He's the author of two very elegant books of rare prose, *Mishaps Perhaps* and its sequel, *More Mishaps,* both published by City Lights. His education is very sophisticated in both political left splinter group ideology and history, where he has an amazing memory going back to the forties, and also in French letters of the twentieth century, especially in the period of dada and surrealist activity. He has a curious style actually, pretty intelligent. He was the person who turned me on to Antonin Artaud. Carl had the first copy of Genet's *Our Lady of the Flowers,* which was published in English and imported illegally back in 1950.

Carl is an intelligent writer from the point of view of using a certain high-class literary tone derived from French dadaists and surrealist manifestos. He has a French rationalism taken to a paranoiac critical excess. Paranoiac critical method was the phrase that Salvador Dalí used for his own style, a kind of black humor probably. Carl also has a few intelligent remarks about Antonin Artaud whom he saw in Paris. He is a Rimbaud type, that is visionary, but one who stumbled over his nose earlier than Rimbaud and immediately gave up writing, and then went on to write little tiny things about having given up writing. Solomon wrote with disdain for all writers, a kind of mockery of the whole ego ambition game that he saw in my antics or Kerouac's or Burroughs's. In him you get a genuine lunatic's-eye view of the best minds destroyed by madness. A genuine critic of the shallowness of my line from somebody who actually was in the hospital.

Carl has been an intimate of almost all the poets and writers of the Beat Generation up to the present. In the early fifties he worked for his uncle the publisher A. A. Wyn at Ace Books and it was Carl who got them to agree to publish Burroughs's *Junkie*. Even with that we had quite a bit of trouble because Carl had to go through a barrier. His uncle was worried about it because in those days to be taking a realistic side in the matter of drugs was counter to all the philosophy of the Treasury Department G-men and narcs. To cover themselves, Ace published two books in one, *Junkie* and a volume by a narcotics agent, Maurice Helbrant. In addition to that, they interpolated a number of editorial comments, like when Burroughs says it is possible for junkies to stabilize their habits and lead normal lives if they can get a medical supply, they inserted a note saying, "This is not the opinion of recognized medical authorities."

Carl managed to give Kerouac a contract and an advance for *On the Road* on the basis of some very complex prose from *Visions of*

Cody. As an editor, Solomon was actually very innovative and had prescient foresight. When Kerouac turned in *On the Road* on that giant scroll of UP teletype paper, he brought the original manuscript to Carl. It had already been rejected by Robert Giroux, the eminent publisher, who could not recognize the totally innovative prose. Carl was shocked, as we all were, by the form and content of the scroll.

Faced with this explosion of interesting literature and composition from Kerouac, Solomon could do nothing with it. At the same time Burroughs was following up his *Junkie,* not with a nice little John O'Hara–style, Hemingway-style book but with a manuscript so indescribably obscene and awful that it wasn't published for thirty years. He called it simply *Queer*. Carl had to follow *Junkie* with all this new literature, and naturally who wouldn't have a nervous breakdown? This fits in with Carl's essays on Artaud and the problem of identity for the dadaists and the surrealists and those people who wanted to alter reality, the post-Rimbaud visionary seers who wanted to alter reality. Carl had started on that literary track but then found himself without any identity at all.

Carl's conscious decision after being institutionalized with amnesia was, "I have a small mind and I mean to use it." The point there was for him to take some job which was absolutely Zen-like ordinary. So selling ice cream or being a messenger was the most average ordinary basic-reality, physical job you could find and that became his career.

CHAPTER 49

Kerouac's "Belief and Technique for Modern Prose"

[In conclusion] I'd like to point out Kerouac's earliest statement of his method of writing, thirty aphorisms which he applied to his work. He was asked to do a summary on how to write for Don Allen and so he wrote a list of essentials called "Belief and Technique for Modern Prose." They are one-line slogans or one-line exhortations for prose writers. It was subtitled "a list of essentials" and was published in Jack's book *Heaven and Other Poems*.[234] The first is:

1. Scribbled secret notebooks, and wild typewritten pages, for yr own joy

Just write for yourself and your gods, rather than for the market. I think this was written after he finished *Visions of Cody* and all his books had been rejected. *On the Road* had been rejected and *Cody* was rejected, so he wrote more than a dozen novels between 1950 and 1957, when *On the Road* came out. His first book to be published was called *The Town and the City*, a traditional novel about a family, brothers and sisters, and their move from the small town to the big city. Then the breakup of the family and the effect of urbanization on the old-fashioned nuclear family.

2. Submissive to everything, open, listening

I would say that when he sat at his desk he made himself submissive to his own mind. His recollections are focused on a subject. Basically, what he would do was to figure out what was interesting to write about, whether it was *The Subterraneans* or *The Dharma Bums* or a high school romance or the bogeyman hero of adolescence like *Doctor Sax.* Then he'd make an outline of that in his mind or on a piece of paper, the main topics, that he wanted to cover. And then like a jazz player he would improvise on those points. He was submissive to everything, recollecting everything, and then beginning to write. Trying to write the stream of his mind. Not so much stream of consciousness, which in literary terms is very random, but focus on a single subject and all the associations of that.

3. Try never get drunk outside yr own house

This concerns his own very real drinking problem.

4. Be in love with yr life

That's something that most people are not. He's saying take your own life as sacred, that way everything comes out artistic.

5. Something that you feel will find its own form

You don't have to have the form in advance if you know the beginning, middle, and end. If there is something that is occupying you, as say the character of Dean Moriarty occupied Kerouac, or Cody, or Burroughs, or any of the people he knew, you ruminate on that and begin writing without knowing how to finish. The work will find its own form.

6. Be crazy dumbsaint of the mind

Which is to say don't be professorial, you're not going to be like those nice novelists in the *New York Times*. Exhaust the subtleties of your personal mind, just say that's me thinking of my childhood fantasies, my first loves, my first vacation in Africa. Use personal details, be coherent, explain to other people. Everybody has their own secret life, their own humiliations and triumphs, their own adolescent fantasies and crushes. If one person can exhibit his own soul in that way, other people will find it, relate to it. You have it in Whitman, in *Huckleberry Finn*, you have it in Sherwood Anderson. You have it especially in Edgar Allan Poe, "The Tell-Tale Heart" or "The Cask of Amontillado," no one in America has such a lucid mind as Poe. Poe was a big influence on Kerouac.

7. Blow as deep as you want to blow

In some of his best sketches he does that.

8. Write what you want bottomless from bottom of the mind

9. The unspeakable visions of the individual

10. No time for poetry but exactly what is

That's a good one. What you really see, what you really think, from your personal mind.

11. Visionary tics shivering in the chest

I think this one is because he was writing on Benzedrine, amphetamine, so there was some shivering from that.

12. In tranced fixation dreaming upon object before you

Focus on what you see and write it down as Kerouac did in those sketches like the old teacup or the movie theater.

13. Remove literary, grammatical and syntactical inhibition

You can begin a new thought without worrying about finishing the old one.

14. Like Proust be an old teahead of time

This is my favorite, like an old marijuana smoker of time, a sophisticated raconteur of one's own consciousness.

15. Telling the true story of the world in interior monolog

16. The jewel center of interest is the eye within the eye

I guess, the mind's eye, inside.

17. Write in recollection and amazement for yourself

You know, amaze yourself.

18. Work from pithy middle eye out, swimming in language sea

By "pithy middle eye out" Kerouac means the pith of the statement or the vision or the epiphany or the moment of recollection that's the most intense that you begin with. Start with the first vivid recollection that recurs in the mind and then work out from there. Start from that jewel center of interest. Whatever comes up in your mouth, gargle it out. Take the sentences and put in all the details.

19. Accept loss forever

Which was Kerouac's realization that life itself was a kind of golden ash. That we were all phantoms in the sense that everything would be gone in a hundred years, we're just a bunch of phantoms. Everything will be lost including our own thoughts.

20. Believe in the holy contour of life

In the sense that his writing is a kind of prayer or devotion, devotional or sacred activity, recollecting the events, looking through the keyhole of his eyes at eternity.

21. Struggle to sketch the flow that already exists intact in mind

You can't write everything in your mind, only what your pen is fast enough to pick up and what your mind is capable of recollecting in the flood of thoughts. Write whatever rises naturally and in whatever sequence and order thoughts rise, and as quickly and in as few words as possible.

22. Dont think of words when you stop but to see picture better

This is a very, very important point. It is real practical technical advice to writers. If you visualize or revisualize your memory, look at the picture, then words come from that very easily. If you lose track of the picture, the actual, visible, palpable event you're recollecting, then you are groundless in space trying to reassociate an old word line instead having the words relate to some substantive picture that other words can connect with. Usually when you're writing you stop when you lose track of what you're thinking, or you lose track of your subject. This is how you get back on to the subject, you go back to your original picture.

23. Keep track of every day the date emblazoned in yr morning

In other words, be conscious of the drama of every day. Kerouac woke up every day and put the date there, realized it was Thursday, then realized he was alive, and kept track of his day-by-day adventure. He felt you should be in love with your life.

24. No fear or shame in the dignity of yr experience, language
    & knowledge

There is nothing to be ashamed of in your own experiences, or language, or knowledge. If you're gay you can write about that, or if you're arthritic you can write about that. So shitting in your pants is a sacred act, instead of being something to be ashamed of. This is a complete reversal of the usual attitude, that you're basically wrong, or that you're stupid, even when you are mistaken.

25. Write for the world to read and see yr exact pictures of it

He's saying that there is an outer world that's also being satisfied by writing.

26. Bookmovie is the movie in words, the visual American form

If you're recollecting your childhood, try to see it as a book-movie, a movie in words, as a basic American form. Kerouac saw his fictions, his novels, as films, scenes that flash onto the camera eye of the recording angel, Kerouac.

27. In Praise of Character in the Bleak inhuman loneliness

That's like saying we know that there's nothing to be gained in the end but death. Jack was interested in his character's individual consciousness and awareness.

28. Composing wild, undisciplined, pure, coming in from under, crazier the better

29. You're a Genius all the time

In other words, trust your own mind.

30. Writer-Director of Earthly movies Sponsored & Angeled in Heaven

The angel is the one who pays for the movie.

Works Cited Within the Text

Note: Classic works are listed by title and author only without reference to a particular edition.

Allen, Donald M., ed. *The New American Poetry 1945–1960*. New York: Grove Press, 1960.

Aronowitz, Alfred G. "The Beat Generation, Parts 1–12." *New York Post* (March 9–22, 1959).

Blake, William. *Songs of Innocence and Experience*

Burroughs, William S. *Junkie*. New York: Ace Books, 1953.

———. *Junky*. New York: Penguin, 1997.

———. *The Naked Lunch*. Paris: Olympia Press, 1959.

———. *Nova Express*. New York: Grove Press, 1964.

———. *Queer*. New York: Viking, 1985.

———. *The Ticket That Exploded*. New York: Grove Press, 1967.

———, and Allen Ginsberg. *The Yage Letters*. San Francisco: City Lights, 1963.

———, and Brion Gysin. *The Exterminator*. San Francisco: Auerhahn Press, 1960.

———, and Jack Kerouac. *And the Hippos Were Boiled in Their Tanks*. New York: Grove Press, 2008.

Céline, Louis-Ferdinand. *Journey to the End of the Night*

Cocteau, Jean. *Opium*

Corso, Gregory. *Gasoline / Vestal Lady on Brattle.* San Francisco: City Lights, 1976.

———. *The Happy Birthday of Death.* New York: New Directions, 1960.

———. *Mindfield.* New York: Thunder's Mouth Press, 1989.

Dostoyevsky, Fyodor. *The Idiot*

———. *The Possessed*

———. *The Raw Youth*

Fields, Rick. *How the Swans Came to the Lake.* Boulder, CO: Shambhala Press, 1981.

Gifford, Barry, and Lawrence Lee. *Jack's Book.* New York: St. Martin's Press, 1978.

Ginsberg, Allen. *Collected Poems 1947–1997.* New York: HarperCollins, 2006.

———. "A Definition of Beat Generation," *Friction,* vol. 1, no. 2/3 (Winter 1982).

———. *Empty Mirror.* New York: Totem/Corinth, 1961.

———. *The Gates of Wrath.* Bolinas, CA: Grey Fox Press, 1972.

———, and Neal Cassady. *As Ever.* Berkeley, CA: Creative Arts Books, 1977.

———, and Peter Orlovsky. *Straight Hearts' Delight.* San Francisco: Gay Sunshine Press, 1980.

Holmes, John Clellon. *Go.* New York: Scribner's, 1952.

———. *The Horn.* New York: Random House, 1958.

———. "This Is the Beat Generation," *New York Times* magazine (November 16, 1952).

Huncke, Herbert. *The Evening Sun Turned Crimson.* Cherry Valley, New York: Cherry Valley Editions, 1980.

———. *Huncke's Journal.* New York: Poets Press, 1965.

Kafka, Franz. *The Castle*

———. *The Trial*

Kerouac, Jack. *Book of Dreams.* San Francisco: City Lights, 1961.

———. *The Dharma Bums.* New York: Viking, 1958.

———. *Doctor Sax.* New York: Grove Press, 1959.

———. "Essentials of Spontaneous Prose," *Black Mountain Review* (Autumn 1957).

———. *Heaven and Other Poems.* San Francisco: Grey Fox, 1977.

[———.] Jean-Louis. "Jazz of the Beat Generation," *New World Writing* (New York: New American Library, 1955).

———. [Letter], *Unspeakable Visions of the Individual,* no. 8 (1978).

———. *Lonesome Traveler.* New York: McGraw-Hill, 1960.

———. *Maggie Cassidy.* New York: Avon, 1959.

———. *Mexico City Blues.* New York: Grove Press, 1959.

———. *Old Angel Midnight.* UK: Booklegger, 1973.

———. *On the Road.* New York: Viking, 1957.

———. "Origins of the Beat Generation," *Playboy,* vol. 6, no. 6 (June 1959).

———. *Scattered Poems.* San Francisco: City Lights, 1971.

———. *The Sea Is My Brother.* New York: Da Capo Press, 2011.

———. *The Subterraneans.* New York: Grove Press, 1958.

———. *The Town and the City.* New York: Harcourt, Brace, 1950.

———. *Vanity of Duluoz.* New York: Coward-McCann, 1968.

———. *Visions of Cody.* New York: McGraw-Hill, 1972.

———. *Visions of Gerard.* New York: Farrar, Straus, 1963.

Korzybski, Alfred. *Science and Sanity*

Mailer, Norman. *The White Negro.* San Francisco: City Lights, 1960.

Melville, Herman. *Billy Budd, Sailor*

———. *Moby-Dick; or, The Whale*

O'Neil, Paul. "The Only Rebellion Around," *Life,* vol. 47, no. 22 (November 30, 1959).

Orlovsky, Peter. *Clean Asshole Poems and Smiling Vegetable Songs.* San Francisco: City Lights, 1978.

Perse, Saint-John. *Anabasis: A Poem* (translated by T. S. Eliot). New York: Harcourt, Brace, 1949.

Podhoretz, Norman. "The Know-Nothing Bohemians," *Partisan Review,* no. 25 (Spring 1958).

Rimbaud, Arthur. *Illuminations*

———. *A Season in Hell*

Solomon, Carl. *Mishaps, Perhaps.* San Francisco: City Lights, 1966.

———. *More Mishaps.* San Francisco: City Lights, 1968.

Spengler, Oswald. *The Decline of the West*

Williams, William Carlos. *Paterson.* New York: New Directions, 1958.

———. *Paterson, Book 3.* New York: New Directions, 1949.

———. *Pictures from Brueghel and Other Poems.* New York: New Directions, 1962.

———. "Symposium: The Beat Poets," *Wagner Literary Magazine,* no. 1 (Spring 1959).

Yeats, William Butler. *A Vision*

Allen Ginsberg's Reading List for "A Literary History of the Beat Generation"

Allen, Donald, and George F. Butterick, eds. *The Postmoderns: The New American Poetry Revised.*

Baraka, Amiri. *Selected Poetry.*

Burroughs, William S. *The Burroughs File.*

Burroughs, William S. *Junky* [*Junkie*].

Burroughs, William S. *Naked Lunch.*

Burroughs, William S. *Nova Express.*

Burroughs, William S. *Nova Express* (paperback includes a version of "Twilight's Last Gleamings").

Burroughs, William S. *Queer.*

Burroughs, William S. *The Soft Machine.*

Burroughs, William S. *The Ticket That Exploded.*

Burroughs, William S. *The Wild Boys.*

Burroughs, William S., and Ginsberg, Allen. *The Yage Letters.*

Cassady, Neal. *The First Third and Other Writings.*

Corso, Gregory. *The American Express.*

Corso, Gregory. *Elegiac Feelings American.*

Corso, Gregory. *Gasoline.*

Corso, Gregory. *The Happy Birthday of Death.*

Corso, Gregory. *Long Live Man.*

Corso, Gregory. *Mindfield.*

Creeley, Robert. *Collected Poems 1945–1975.*

di Prima, Diane. *Pieces of a Song: Selected Poems.*

Dylan, Bob. *Tarantula.*

Dylan, Bob. *Writings and Drawings.*

Ferlinghetti, Lawrence. *Endless Life: Selected Poems.*

Gifford, Barry, and Lawrence Lee. *Jack's Book.*

Ginsberg, Allen. *Collected Poems, 1947–1980.*

Huncke, Herbert. *The Evening Sun Turned Crimson.*

Huncke, Herbert. *Guilty of Everything.*

Kerouac, Jack. *Big Sur.*

Kerouac, Jack. *Desolation Angels.*

Kerouac, Jack. *The Dharma Bums.*

Kerouac, Jack. *Heaven and Other Poems.*

Kerouac, Jack. *Last Words.*

Kerouac, Jack. *Lonesome Traveler.*

Kerouac, Jack. *Mexico City Blues.*

Kerouac, Jack. *On the Road.*

Kerouac, Jack. *Pic.*

Kerouac, Jack. *Pomes All Sizes.*

Kerouac, Jack. *Scattered Poems.*

Kerouac, Jack. *Scripture of the Golden Eternity.*

Kerouac, Jack. *The Town and the City.*

Kerouac, Jack. *Vanity of Duluoz.*

Kerouac, Jack. *Visions of Cody.*

Kyger, Joanne. *The Japan and India Journals, 1960–64.*

Lamantia, Philip. *Selected Poems, 1943–1966.*

McClure, Michael. *Selected Poems.*

Orlovsky, Peter. *Clean Asshole Poems and Smiling Vegetable Songs.*

Orlovsky, Peter. *Unpublished Letters and Journals* (ed. David Greenberg and Paul Rickert).

Plimpton, George, ed. *Writers at Work,* 3rd Series.

Snyder, Gary. *Myths and Texts.*

Snyder, Gary. *Riprap and Cold Mountain Poems.*

Solomon, Carl. *Emergency Messages: An Autobiographical Miscellany.*

Solomon, Carl. *Mishaps, Perhaps.*

Solomon, Carl. *More Mishaps.*

Welch, Lew. *Ring of Bone: Collected Poems.*

Whalen, Philip. *On Bear's Head.*

Wieners, John. *Cultural Affairs in Boston.*

Wieners, John. *Selected Poems, 1958–1984.*

Articles

Ginsberg, Allen. "A Definition of the Beat Generation."

Kerouac, Jack. "Essentials of Spontaneous Prose."

Kerouac, Jack. "Origins of the Beat Generation."

Acknowledgments

I am deeply grateful to a number of people and institutions who have helped make this book possible. The Allen Ginsberg Trust led by Peter Hale and Bob Rosenthal have once again been exceptional in their help. Without their assistance, these tapes would never have been discovered, preserved, or transcribed.

Allen Ginsberg's agent at the Andrew Wylie Agency, Jeff Posternak, became as devoted to the project as I was and he helped secure the interest of the Grove Press. At Grove Atlantic Morgan Entrekin, Peter Blackstock, Judy Hottensen, Nicole Nyhan, and Julia Berner-Tobin have been perfect editors and advisors and have guided the book through the various stages of publication.

Naropa University with Judy and Charles Lief at the helm are the keepers of the Ginsberg flame and have carefully overseen the preservation and distribution of these and thousands of other tapes of faculty lectures. William Gargan, librarian at Brooklyn College, personally recorded Ginsberg's lectures there and generously made them available to my research for which I am eternally grateful. Stanford University, where Ginsberg's personal archive is maintained, also provided several tapes which helped fill in gaps in the series.

In addition to these, the estates of Jack Kerouac, William S. Burroughs, Gregory Corso, and John Clellon Holmes have been most cooperative in allowing us to quote from the original sources that inspired Ginsberg. James Grauerholz, John Sampas, Raymond Foye, and Sheri Langerman-Baird each deserve singular acknowledgment.

I am grateful to Anne Waldman for providing the excellent foreword to this book. She taught with Ginsberg at Naropa for more than twenty years and knew his classroom manner better than anyone alive. I appreciate her taking the time out of a very hectic schedule to help introduce Ginsberg to a new generation of readers.

And finally I want to express my unbounded gratitude to Judy Matz, who nurtured this and all my work and never once complained as I played, and re-played, and re-re-played hundreds of hours of tapes, in an attempt to capture each and every word. Her patience is never ending, as is my love and appreciation for her.

Notes

1. Holmes, John Clellon. "This Is the Beat Generation," *New York Times* magazine (November 16, 1952).
2. [Kerouac, Jack] Jean-Louis. "Jazz of the Beat Generation," *New World Writing* (New York: New American Library, 1955), pp. 7–16.
3. Huncke, Herbert. *The Evening Sun Turned Crimson* (Cherry Valley, NY: Cherry Valley Editions, 1980).
4. Kerouac, Jack. "Origins of the Beat Generation," *Playboy*, vol. 6, no. 6 (June 1959), pp. 31–32+.
5. O'Neil, Paul. "The Only Rebellion Around," *Life*, vol. 47, no. 22 (November 30, 1959), pp. 114–16+.
6. Aronowitz, Alfred G. "The Beat Generation, Parts 1–12," *New York Post* (March 9–22, 1959).
7. Ginsberg, Allen. "A Definition of Beat Generation," *Friction*, vol. 1, no. 2/3 (Winter 1982), pp. 50–52.
8. Biographies of all the main characters of the Beat Generation are readily available.
9. These lines are from William Butler Yeats's poem "The Second Coming."
10. Kerouac, Jack. "Origins of the Beat Generation," in *On the Road* (New York: Viking Critical Library, 1979), p. 359.
11. Ibid., p. 358.
12. Ibid., pp. 358–59.
13. Ibid., pp. 359–60.
14. Ibid., p. 361.
15. Ibid., p. 362.
16. Ibid., pp. 362–63.

17. The full quote is "To burn always with this hard gemlike flame, to maintain this ecstasy, is success in life," and it is taken from Walter Pater's book *The Renaissance: Studies in Art and Poetry* (1873).

18. Kerouac, "Origins of the Beat Generation," p. 363.

19. Ibid., p. 364.

20. Ibid., pp. 364–65.

21. Podhoretz, Norman. "The Know-Nothing Bohemians," *Partisan Review*, no. 25 (Spring 1958), pp. 305–18.

22. Kerouac, "Origins of the Beat Generation," pp. 366–67.

23. Lipton, Lawrence. *The Holy Barbarians* (New York: Julian Messner, 1959).

24. Holmes, "This Is the Beat Generation."

25. *The Sea Is My Brother* was eventually published by Da Capo Press in 2011.

26. Kerouac, Jack. *Vanity of Duluoz* (New York: Coward-McCann, 1968), p. 125.

27. Jack Kerouac attended Horace Mann prep school in the Bronx from 1939 to 1940.

28. Bickford's was a popular and inexpensive all-night cafeteria once located in New York City at 225 W. 42nd Street.

29. Horn & Hardart was a popular chain of automats in New York City during the 1940s and '50s.

30. The Angler or Angle Bar once stood on the corner of Eighth Avenue and West 43rd Street.

31. The Apollo Theatre was located on West 42nd Street between Seventh and Eighth Avenues, not to be confused with the more famous Apollo Theater on 125th Street in Harlem.

32. Kerouac, Jack. *Lonesome Traveler* (New York: Ballantine Books, 1973), pp. 106–7.

33. Le Pavillion was one of the most elegant French restaurants in New York City.

34. Kerouac, *Lonesome Traveler,* pp. 107–8.

35. During World War II the navy developed the V-12 program to train officers on college campuses including Columbia.

36. These lines are from William Butler Yeats's poem "Among School Children."

37. Dr. Mabuse was the fictional villain in several films made by Fritz Lang.

38. Kerouac, *Vanity of Duluoz*, pp. 41–42.

39. Ibid., p. 34.

40. Ibid., p. 44.

41. Ibid., p. 47.

42. Ibid., pp. 62–63.

43. Ibid., p. 63.

44. Ibid., pp. 86–89.

45. Ibid., p. 95.

46. Ibid.

47. Ibid., p. 105.

48. Ibid., pp. 105–6.

49. Ibid., pp. 106–7.

50. Ibid., p. 109.

51. Ibid., pp. 122–23.

52. Ibid., p. 125.

53. Lucien Carr disliked publicity and avoided interviews, asking his friends to respect his privacy.

54. Kerouac, *Vanity of Duluoz,* pp. 163–64.

55. Ibid., p. 169.

56. Ibid., pp. 176–77.

57. Ibid., p. 184.

58. Ibid., pp. 189–90.

59. Ibid., p. 195.

60. Kerouac, Jack. *The Town and the City* (New York: Harcourt, Brace and Company, 1950), p. 3.

61. Ibid., pp. 10–11.

62. Ibid., pp. 11–12.

63. Ibid., p. 13.

64. Ibid., pp. 13–14.

65. Ibid., pp. 14–15.

66. Ibid., p. 15.

67. Andrei Petrovich Versilov is a character in Fyodor Dostoyevsky's novel *The Raw Youth.*

68. Kerouac, *Vanity of Duluoz,* pp. 205–7.

69. Ibid., p. 7.

70. Ibid., pp. 207–8.

71. Ibid., pp. 211–12.

72. Ibid., pp. 212–13.

73. Ibid., pp. 217–18.

74. Ibid., p. 220.

75. Kerouac, Jack. *Visions of Cody* (New York: McGraw-Hill, 1972), pp. 64–65.

76. Ibid., pp. 47–48.

77. Ibid., p. 48.

78. Ibid., p. 57.

79. Ibid., p. 80.

80. Ibid.

81. Ibid., pp. 81–82.

82. Ibid., pp. 67–70.

83. Ibid., p. 398.

84. Kerouac, *Vanity of Duluoz*, p. 273.

85. Kerouac, *Visions of Cody*, p. 3.

86. Kerouac, *Vanity of Duluoz*, p. 280.

87. This was the original 1938 manuscript version of "Twilight's Last Gleamings." A slightly revised version was published as "Gave Proof Through the Night" in Burroughs's book *Nova Express* (New York: Grove Press, 1964).

88. In the summer of 1944, Lucien Carr stabbed and killed his friend David Kammerer in a park near the Columbia University campus. Carr was charged with manslaughter and sentenced to an upstate reformatory where he spent two years.

89. William Burroughs killed his wife, Joan, in Mexico City on September 6, 1951, during a drunken game of William Tell. He fled the country to avoid a prison sentence.

90. This is a line from Arthur Rimbaud's long prose poem *A Season in Hell*.

91. Burroughs, William S. *Junkie* (New York: Ace Books, 1953), p. 11.

92. Ibid.

93. Ibid., p. 19.

94. Ibid., p. 20.

95. Ibid., p. 22.

96. Ibid.

97. Ibid., p. 23.

98. Ibid., pp. 23–24.

99. Ibid., p. 26.

100. Ibid., p. 31.

101. Ibid., pp. 33–34.

102. Ibid., pp. 39–40.

103. Ibid., p. 54.

104. Ibid., p. 71.

105. Ibid., p. 73.

106. Ibid., pp. 99–100.

107. Ibid., p. 107.

108. Ibid.

109. Ibid., p. 120.

110. Ibid., pp. 124–25.

111. Burroughs, William, and Allen Ginsberg. *The Yage Letters* (San Francisco: City Lights, 1963), pp. 13–14.

112. Ibid., pp. 14–15.

113. Ibid., p. 19.

114. Ibid., p. 42.

115. Ibid., pp. 47–48.

116. Ibid., p. 49.

117. Burroughs, William S. *Queer* (New York: Viking, 1985), pp. xiv–xv.

118. Ibid., p. xvi.

119. Ibid., pp. xvii–xix.

120. Burroughs, William, and Brion Gysin. *The Exterminator* (San Francisco: Auerhahn Press, 1960), p. 5.

121. Burroughs, William S. *The Ticket That Exploded* (New York: Grove Press, 1967), p. 27.

122. Ibid.

123. Ibid., pp. 27–28.

124. Ginsberg, Allen, and Neal Cassady. *As Ever* (Berkeley, CA: Creative Arts, 1977), p. 61.

125. This is a reference to a long letter that Neal Cassady had written to Jack Kerouac, which was referred to as "the Joan letter" because it talked about Neal's relationship with a woman named Joan.

126. Ginsberg and Cassady, *As Ever,* pp. 63–64.

127. Ibid., p. 71.

128. Ibid., pp. 85–86.

129. Ibid., p. 88.

130. Ibid., pp. 90–91.

131. Ibid., p. 108.

132. Ibid., p. 109.

133. Ibid., p. 113.

134. Kerouac, Jack. *Scattered Poems* (San Francisco: City Lights, 1971), pp. 8–9.

135. Kerouac, Jack. "Essentials of Spontaneous Prose," *Black Mountain Review* (Autumn 1957).

136. Kerouac, Jack. *On the Road* (New York: Viking, 1957), p. 10.

137. Ibid., p. 37.

138. Ibid., pp. 77–78.

139. Ibid., p. 83.

140. Ibid., pp. 102–3.

141. Ibid., p. 106.

142. Ibid., p. 107.

143. Ibid., p. 124.

144. Ibid., p. 129.

145. Ibid., pp. 144–45.

146. Ibid., pp. 153–54.

147. Ibid., p. 157.

148. Ibid., p. 170.

149. Ibid., p. 171.

150. Ibid., p. 172.

151. Ibid., pp. 172–73.

152. Ibid., p. 178.

153. Ibid., p. 180.

154. Ibid., p. 181.

155. Ibid., p. 190.

156. Ibid., pp. 194–95.

157. Ibid., p. 205.

158. Ibid., p. 206.

159. Ibid., pp. 212–13.

160. Ibid., p. 236.

161. Ibid., p. 269.

162. Ibid., p. 273.

163. Ibid., pp. 276–77.

164. Ibid., pp. 280–81.

165. Ibid., p. 302.

166. Ibid., pp. 309–10.

167. Kerouac, Jack. [letter, May 18, 1952], *Unspeakable Visions of the Individual,* no. 8 (1978), p. 141.

168. Gifford, Barry, and Lawrence Lee. *Jack's Book* (New York: St. Martin's Press, 1978), pp. 159–60.

169. Kerouac, *Visions of Cody,* pp. 18–19.

170. Ibid., p. 21.

171. Ibid., pp. 31–33.

172. Corso, Gregory. *Mindfield* (New York: Thunder's Mouth Press, 1989), p. 5.

173. Ibid., p. 6.

174. Corso, Gregory. *Gasoline / Vestal Lady on Brattle* (San Francisco: City Lights, 1976), p. 57.

175. Corso, *Mindfield,* p. 3.

176. Ibid., p. 4.

177. Corso, *Gasoline / Vestal Lady on Brattle,* pp. 66–67.

178. Ibid., p. 71.

179. Corso, *Mindfield,* pp. 8–11.

180. Corso, *Gasoline / Vestal Lady on Brattle,* p. 13.

181. Corso, *Mindfield,* p. 39.

182. Ibid., p. 34.

183. Corso, *Gasoline / Vestal Lady on Brattle,* pp. 19–21.

184. Corso, *Mindfield,* p. 37.

185. Ibid., p. 42.

186. Ibid., p. 30.

187. Ibid.

188. Ibid., p. 31.

189. Ibid.

190. Corso, Gregory. *The Happy Birthday of Death* (New York: New Directions, 1960), p. 21

191. Corso, *Mindfield,* p. 60.

192. Ibid., pp. 65–69.

193. Ibid., pp. 48–49.

194. In point of fact the duel between Alexander Hamilton and Aaron Burr took place on July 11, 1804, not winter at all.

195. The editor has been unable to find any reference to Israel Hans in historical documents.

196. Anthemion is a floral design used in ancient Greek and Roman architecture.

197. The Plaka is a neighborhood in Athens located just below the ancient Acropolis.

198. Corso, *Mindfield,* pp. 87–92.

199. Ibid., pp. 199–200.

200. Ginsberg, Allen. *Collected Poems 1947–1997* (New York: HarperCollins, 2006), p. 13.

201. Stagirite; Aristotle was a native of Stagira.

202. Ginsberg, Allen. *The Gates of Wrath* (Bolinas, CA: Grey Fox Press, 1972), pp. 46–47.

203. Ginsberg, *Collected Poems 1947–1997,* p. 15.

204. Ibid., p. 16.

205. Ibid., p. 21.

206. Ibid., p. 27.

207. Ibid., pp. 32–33.

208. Ibid., p. 37.

209. Ibid., p. 41.

210. Ibid., p. 68.

211. Ibid., pp. 69–70.

212. Williams, William Carlos. *Paterson, Book 3* (New York: New Directions, 1949), p. 204.

213. Ginsberg, *Collected Poems 1947–1997,* p. 74.

214. Ibid., p. 23.

215. Ibid., p. 22.

216. Ibid., p. 12.

217. Ibid., p. 72.

218. Ibid., pp. 91–95.

219. Ibid., pp. 98–99.

220. Ibid., pp. 100–101.

221. Ibid., pp. 103–4.

222. Ibid., p. 121.

223. Williams, William Carlos. *Pictures from Brueghel and Other Poems* (New York: New Directions, 1962), p. 75.

224. Ginsberg, *Collected Poems 1947–1997,* pp. 132–33.

225. Allen, Donald M., ed.. *The New American Poetry 1945–1960* (New York: Grove Press, 1960), p. 414.

226. Spengler, Oswald. *The Decline of the West* (New York: Modern Library, 1965), p. 251.

227. Ginsberg, *Collected Poems 1947–1997,* p. 196.

228. Holmes, John Clellon. *Go* (New York: New American Library, 1980), pp. 80–82.

229. Ibid., pp. 82–84.

230. Ginsberg, *Collected Poems 1947–1997,* p. 14.

231. Ibid., p. 18.

232. Holmes. "This Is the Beat Generation."

233. Williams, William Carlos. "Symposium: The Beat Poets," *Wagner Literary Magazine,* no. 1 (Spring 1959), p. 24.

234. Kerouac, Jack. *Heaven and Other Poems* (San Francisco: Grey Fox, 1977)

CREDITS